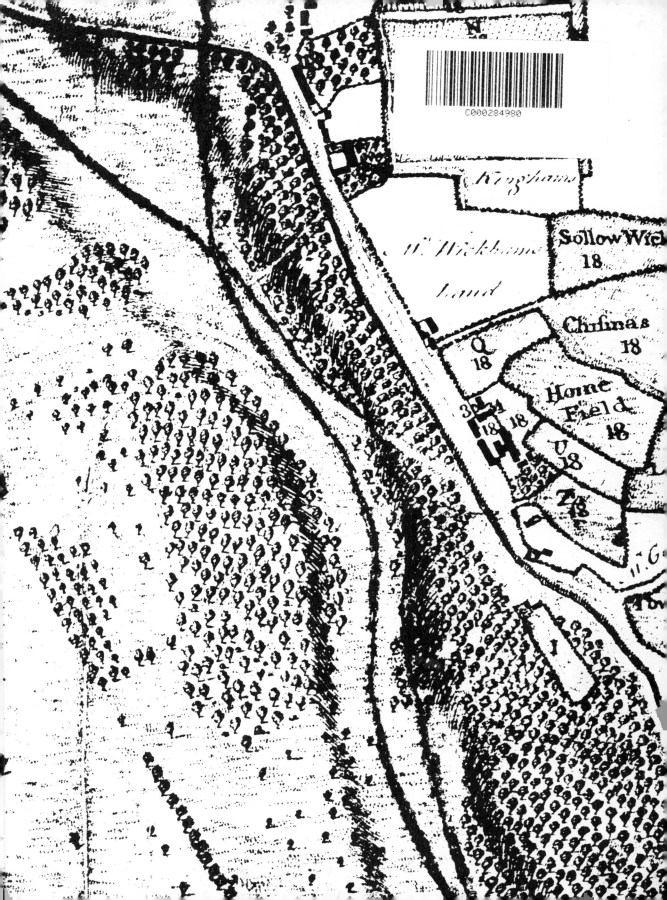

LITTLE GADDESDEN AND ASHRIDGE

LITTLE GADDESDEN and ASHRIDGE

Howard Senar

Phillimore

1983

Published by
PHILLIMORE & CO. LTD.
Shopwyke Hall, Chichester, Sussex

ISBN 0 85033 460 8

Printed in Great Britain by
BIDDLES LTD.
Guildford, Surrey
and bound by
THE NEWDIGATE PRESS LTD.
Dorking, Surrey

CONTENTS

LIST OF PLATES

(*between pages 98 and 99*)

Photographic work by Ernest A. Janes

1. Little Gaddesden parish church, c.1808
2. Ashridge College from the south
3. Thunderdell Lodge
4. Old Park Lodge
5. The Bridgewater Monument
6. Princes Riding towards Ashridge House. The Deer Leap
7. Alderton Drive (a private road)
8. Ringshall Cottages
9. Ringshall Cottages
10. Ringshall Lodge and Deer Leap Garage
11. The Town Houses, Little Gaddesden
12. Benhay, the former Rectory
13. Little Gaddesden cottages, 6-13
14. Wood Ash, a Whitman house
15. Little Gaddesden Post Office and Stores
16. The *Bridgewater Arms*
17. The Rectory, Little Gaddesden, 1981
18. The Alford Cross and the entrance to Ashridge Park
19. The north end of the Green
20. Ringshall Drive
21. Little Gaddesden Church of England School
22. The parish church from the south
23. Bede Court
24. The Chapel and Westmacott Memorial
25. The Chancel, Little Gaddesden parish church
26. The Parish Chest
27. War memorial on the Green
28. The Dutton-Egerton Memorial, Little Gaddesden parish church
29. John O'Gaddesden's House
30. Numbers 31 and 32 The Green
31. The New Houses, Numbers 33 to 37 The Green

LIST OF TEXT FIGURES

PREFACE

In days gone by the story of a parish was engraved deeply in the memories of those whose ancestors had lived there for generations. Today more frequent changes in population result in the loss of much that is worth recording. Newcomers are not least amongst those who enjoy hearing about the place where they have made their home.

This book has been planned to provide information which it is believed to be of interest today as well as to preserve some memories for those who come after. It was intended to be a companion booklet to that recently published about Little Gaddesden church. However the material forthcoming has resulted in a volume more extensive than was anticipated. Repetition in the text occurs to enable articles to be complete in themselves.

The rector of a parish is uniquely placed to become a repository of stories of people and events of years gone by both in his parish church and in his parish. For this compilation it is believed that every resident has had some opportunity of making a contribution. So many have done so that a complete list of acknowledgements would be almost a list of parishioners. All this help is sincerely appreciated.

The author offers this work to Little Gaddesden and Ashridge in the hope that it may play a small part in preserving a respect for the heritage of those privileged to live or work in such a place as this, 600 feet up in the Chiltern Hills.

HOWARD SENAR
Little Gaddesden
1983

ACKNOWLEDGEMENTS

The author is very grateful to all who have assisted in so many ways in the preparation of this book. He is especially indebted to:

Mr W. T. N. Allen, Mr and Mrs E. H. Amer, Mr and Mrs R. J. Baker, Mrs C. Baldwin, Mr C. Baron, Mrs B. Borgeat, Mr W. H. Brooker (Aerofilms Ltd.), Mr G. E. Catchpole, Mrs E. E. Clayton, Mrs D. Cocks, Miss M. Crawford, Mrs A. J. Davis (Aldbury), Mr K. A. M. Dickson, Mr H. Duncan, Mrs A. Duncombe, Mr J. M. Feeney, Mrs C. Francis, Mr Francis Green (Dagnall), Mr H. Halsey, Mr L. C. Hopkins, Mr J. S. Hilton, Mr A. W. Howitt, Mrs V. Hughes, Mr F. E. Jarvis, Mr J. H. Lewis, Mrs V. Mountfort, Mr J. McCracken, Mrs J. Moffatt, Mr and Mrs F. A. Moody, Mr J. Oakins, Mr J. T. Pritchard, Mr E. Roe, The Rural Heritage Society, Mr and Mrs T. G. Sears, Mrs H. Senar, Mrs M. Shepherd, Mrs G. Smalley, Sir William Swallow, Dr L. H. Turner, Mrs D. J. W. Verrin, Mrs J. E. Walker, Mr S. P. Whaley, Colonel A. L. Wilson, Mr J. Wilson (National Trust), Miss P. Wheatley, The Women's Institute, Mr G. Wright.

He would thank Mr Ernest A. Janes for his painstaking co-operation in the photographic work for this book, Mr John Leonhardt for the invaluable diagrams of the parish, and Mr Starr of Hertford County Planning Authority.

He appreciates greatly the interest and continuing study both of Dr S. E. T. Cusdin in the sphere of Monastic Architecture and Mr R. W. Bagshawe in the byeways of Field Archaeology.

Mr Philip Sadler, Principal of Ashridge Management College and members of the College have been invariably helpful.

The staff at the County Record Offices at Hertford and Aylesbury have been indefatigable in their co-operation and patience. In the case of Hertford this help has extended for over twenty years.

Gratitude is expressed to all those too numerous to mention who have supplied information about their own houses and areas, their own societies and organisations.

At a time when Phillimore & Co. have been so much in demand for publishing major works in Local History, the author is very grateful to them for agreeing to publish this book. In particular he would express his gratitude to the Editorial Director, Mr Noel Osborne and to his staff, especially to Miss Jane Phillimore, for the meticulous care they have all given throughout this undertaking.

Part One

1. General Historical Background

'No one before your time knew that Little Gaddesden existed'. These words were spoken by the Swedish naturalist Peter Kalm to William Ellis the 18th-century farmer and author who lived at Church Farm. One could say that as Little Gaddesden was a scattered parish 600 feet up in the Chiltern Hills, there was little reason for anyone to know much about it. Nevertheless for those whose families have lived in Little Gaddesden century after century there have been numerous occasions when great national events and well known people have made their local impact.

Kings and princes, dukes, earls and viscounts, statesmen, soldiers, architects, sculptors, poets, scholars, horticulturalists, industrialists, business managers, as well as bishops, priests and members of religious orders . . . all have been known here. Events of national importance, often connected with such men, have not gone unnoticed in this unnoticed place.

An axehead, said to be of the 6th century B.C. was found in South Field to the north of Little Gaddesden church. Excavations at Wards Combe revealed signs of occupation from the Bronze Age to the 2nd century A.D. during the Roman occupation, covering the period from 300 B.C. to 130 A.D. Roman coins dating from 186-293 A.D. have been found, and in the field to the west of the parish church rough Roman pottery was discovered when digging for a medieval village took place. Other Roman finds have been made along the line of the Golden Valley and Ringshall Drive. A Roman road from the Hemel Hempstead area via Great Gaddesden passed along St Margaret's Lane, and thence after being traced, its exact line is not yet clear, but it is believed to cross Hudnall Lane, continue through the fields, cross Church Road at some point between the Church and Bede Court, and then go on to Ringshall, where a Roman mulling-stone was found, and along to Ivinghoe Beacon. The names of Hadrian, Antoninus Pius, Severus, and even Boudicca may have been heard of in these parts.

One name from that period which has persisted is that of the 3rd-century Roman soldier, Albanus, the first Christian martyr of England.The date of St Alban's execution is said to be 22 June 209, though recent suggestion of a date 50 years later have been made. News of this and of the consequent establishment of a 'shrine of wondrous workmanship' so described in the 8th century by the Venerable Bede, must have travelled along the Roman road. How soon our ancestors here became Christian is not known. What is known is that the kingdom of Mercia was the domain of King Offa, and he was a Christian who established or re-established the monastery of St Albans before his death in about 796 A.D. To that monastery in c. 944 Aethelgiva presented Gadsden, and two years later Godiva of Gadsden gave a towel and a chalice to St Albans. A Saxon Charter had mentioned Gaetesdene in 812 and a Christian seal dated c. 850 was found in Ringshall Drive. Gaetesdene, Gadsden, Gatesden, Gatesdene are variations of the name. 'Gat' means goat; 'Gaete' means kid; and 'den' means valley.

An ancient boundary was probably marked by large stones which followed a straight line from the Golden Valley to Ashridge, through Ashridge House across Thunderdell and thence to Aldbury.

However at this time it was simply called Gaddesden, not Little or Great. When the division was made is not clear though it was certainly by 1065. The Saxon overlord was Edmer, and there were then 600 acres. The legendary name of the war-like Offa now became replaced by that of the Conqueror, William of Normandy. He was as near as Berkhamsted. There Aldred, Archbishop of Canterbury, Edgar, the heir to the Saxon royal family, and the Earls Morcar and Edwin pledged their loyalty, and the Conqueror moved to Westminster for his coronation. The Domesday Survey of 1086 states that (Little) Gatesdene was a bailiwick or outlier of Berchastede. There were five villeins, two borderers, and one serf. There was pasture for 50 pigs and land for two ploughs. The value for tax purposes was £4 and the overlord was Humphrey (Hunfrid) who held it from Robert of Mortain, half-brother to the Conqueror. If there was at this time a priest in Little Gaddesden he would have given evidence before the royal commissioners for the Survey.

The earliest known date when there was a church in Little Gaddesden was 1161. In that year the Archbishop of Canterbury, no less a person than the future St Thomas à Becket, approved the granting of the rectory of Little Gaddesden to the monastery of St James, Northampton. Thus there was a Saxon or Norman church here before the present church was built. In 1209 the Bishop of Lincoln recorded that there was a suitable house for Julian the Cleric adjoining the church. This is the first mention of a house in Little Gaddesden and the first known name of an incumbent.

Owing to family jealousies the land of Robert of Mortain passed back to the crown, and it was held by Henry I. Here again is a royal connection. Henry passed from Dunstable to Berkhamsted through this place. He was riding across the Common at Berkhamsted when his accompanying steward of Berkhamsted Castle had a fall, and a monk (from Ashridge?) rode over him and he was killed. Henry's land later passed to Stephen (1135-1154) and two decades of anarchy followed. Was the former Roman-occupied area to the west of Little Gaddesden church to become one of the 'Motte-and-Bailey' fortifications set up by disaffected barons? This could have been the second stage of its use. A mound (motte) and boundary (bailey) can be seen from the air. From Stephen the manor of Gaddesden passed to his successors until Henry III endowed the new College of the Bonhommes at Ashridge with it. King John's elder son was Henry and his younger son was Richard, Earl of Cornwall. Richard's son Edmund was the founder of the college of Assherugge. The name as thus spelt appears in the Missenden Cartulary of c. 1200. Ash trees were regarded by many people as being sacred. They were also associated with boundaries.

The founding of the College and its first building and dedication took place from 1276 to 1286. A phial of the Precious Blood of Christ was part of the endowment. The phial had been brought back from Germany by Edmund Earl of Cornwall. A portion was given to Ashridge and a portion to Hailes Abbey, Gloucestershire in 1270. It was 'guaranteed as genuine by the Patriarch of Jerusalem, the future Pope Urban IV'. When Edmund died in 1300 his heart was placed in a shrine, and the heart of Thomas de Cantelupe, Bishop of Hereford who was to be canonised in 1320 was placed there also. The College was founded for 20 canons of whom seven or 13 were to be priests. It was to become a place of pilgrimage.

Little Gaddesden was thus initiated into an ownership which was ecclesiastical in its background and control.

Another royal visitor was Edward I who spent Christmas 1290 at Ashridge after his wife Eleanor's death in the previous month. He held a parliament there in January 1291. Whilst the people of Dunstable chafed under the burden of entertaining the royal entourage, the people of Little Gaddesden saw their sovereign and other national figures passing through their village.

One of the problems to be faced then was the shortage of water. The old well at Ashridge probably preceded the establishment of the College, but it was brought into greater use at that time, and it may have been extended and strengthened. The Undercroft beneath the Refectory was also built early in the life of the College, and it was built to last, and to serve. In 1346 Little Gaddesden must have been thrilled to hear of the victory at Crécy when the young Black Prince, owner of Berkhamsted Castle had Richard of Gaddesden as one of his archers.

Another event, and this time one of European proportions was to leave its mark in the parish. The plague struck in the years 1348-49, 1361-2 and 1369. The local tradition is that the parish church stands isolated in the meadows because the houses and cottages around were deserted when the inhabitants died or moved away as a result of the Black Death. For centuries no one would want to build on land where the plagues had taken their toll, nor where the dead had been buried. Bury Grove and Great Bury Grove in old maps may not refer to burial places, but more likely the property of the Bury, the Hertfordshire name of the manor or manor-house, but later generations may have altered the use of the name to fit their reluctance to build there.

It could be that the incumbent of Little Gaddesden and his brother of Great Gaddesden died in the 1361-2 outbreak, for there are changes in incumbency in both places at this time. Hertfordshire suffered badly from the Abbey of St Albans to the Priory at Dunstable, and from Abbots Langley to Ashwell. Buckinghamshire too suffered, and part of the Ashridge lands were in Buckinghamshire. Seventy-seven of the clergy and three heads of religious houses there died. The Wilmslow area suffered very badly. The Rector of Ashridge College died in 1346, but it is not known what caused his death, nor is there evidence of the situation of the College at this time.

One result of the plagues coupled with the bad harvests, was that labour became scarce, and the Peasants' Revolt affected the counties of Hertford and of Buckingham. Lollards were very active. The Rector of Ashridge, like the Abbot of St Albans, was forced to grant a Charter of Liberties to those who besieged the College gates. A Lollard from Little Gaddesden was executed at St Albans. Later the Ashridge prison was to hold men with Lollard opinions, and the last Rector, Thomas Waterhouse, was to be on the panel which resulted in the last burning of a Lollard, at Chesham.

Whether or not the College suffered directly through the troubles, it does appear that it was in need of re-establishment by the last three decades of the 14th century. In 1361 the royal family was at Berkhamsted Castle where Edward the Black Prince passed his honeymoon after marrying the Fair Maid of Kent. The victor of Crécy and Poitiers grew to call Ashridge 'our house'. In the year of his death, 1376, he refounded the College. In his will he made a generous bequest of a great table of gold and silver, together with 25 rubies, 34 sapphires and 15 great pearls and other jewels for the altar. This revival of the College no doubt brought benefits to Little Gaddesden for the establishment was increased to be of 40 canons, of whom 20 were to be in priests' orders. New building in the parish church took place probably at this time.

In the 15th century the half-brother of Henry IV, the Chancellor of England, Cardinal Henry Beaufort, Bishop of Winchester, son of John of Gaunt showed interest in Ashridge by helping with donations which resulted in restoration work to the dormitory, infirmary, sacristy and cloisters. He died in 1447. The monks' barn was built towards the end of the century. Its size suggests a measure of prosperity and increased activity on the local farmlands. During these years echoes of trouble amongst the brethren occur. One Philip Harewell wounded brother Nicholas, from which wound Nicholas expired, after receiving the sacrament and pardoning Philip, who said that it was in self-defence that he had acted.

Visitations of the early 16th century made on behalf of the bishop of Lincoln reflect difficulties. There was little love between the brothers. They were criticised for their eating and drinking habits, their lack of discipline, their implied immorality, their loss of spiritual application and high standards, and their associations beyond the College walls. The local people would not be unaware of this decline.

Henry VIII visited Ashridge for Christmas 1530. The Rector of Little Gaddesden who was resident in his other parish of Oakley in Bedfordshire, had promised several months earlier that the Chancel at Little Gaddesden which was described as 'ruinosus' would be in good condition

Fig. 1 A brass of Henry VIII

for Christmas. In 1535 the value of the Rectory was £11.12s.8d per annum. In 1539 there were four bells in the tower which had a small spire. Had the bells at the College been rung as well as those of the parish church, the hills and valleys must have known the background rhythm of daily prayer.

In 1539 the College was dissolved. There were but 17 Bonhommes left, who were given pensions. The Rector, Thomas Waterhouse, Henry VIII's 'Gentleman Priest' received £100 per year and 50 loads of wood until his death. The others too received pensions which were commensurate with the standard of living when they were first granted. Some who were ordained became incumbents. One William Downham became Rector of Datchworth and a royal chaplain and Bishop of Chester, where he was later described as having been 'an inactive bishop'.

The end of the College could have resulted in tragedy for the local community. The fact that it became a royal residence with accompanying employment meant a new type of life. No doubt to the delight of the people of Little Gaddesden, Ashridge House became a royal nursery. On 12 October 1537 the Queen, Jane Seymour, had given birth to a son, the future Edward VI. She died 12 days later. In October 1538 Sybil Penn (formerly a Hampden) became nurse and foster-mother to the infant prince, and the Ashridge connection with the young Tudors had begun. Sybil Penn remained high in royal favour through the reigns of Henry VIII, Edward VI, Mary, and under Elizabeth. She died in 1562.

To courte she called was, to foster up a king.
Whose helping hand long lingring, sutes, to spedie end did bring
Twoo quenes that scepter bare, gave credyt to this dame,
Full many yeres in cowrt she dwelt without disgrace or blame

In 1543 the future Edward VI and his sisters the future Queens Mary and Elizabeth were all in residence at Ashridge. Edward was a boy of six or seven, Mary was 27 (the famous Holbein portrait of her aged 28 shows what she must have been like when here), and Elizabeth was 10 years old. A meeting of the Privy Council took place at Ashridge in this year. The name Princes Riding may date from this year, and suggests that the avenue in question may be an ancient one. Perhaps Ash Riding is equally old.

When Edward became king he gave Ashridge to Elizabeth. She was in residence in 1553 and had her room above the cloister. She had come a month before Christmas 1552. In February

Mary, now queen, summoned her to London as she believed that Elizabeth was involved in the rebellion of Sir Thomas Wyatt. At the age of 20 the Princess was learning what suspicion and interrogation meant. A letter is extant from Elizabeth to Mary pleading her innocence. Wyatt confirmed this on the scaffold. When Elizabeth went to London she left behind her hair-brushes, high-heeled shoes, and some tiny socks for an infant's feet, probably intended for the child Mary hoped for but never had. These were the work of Elizabeth's own hands. They were to be preserved at Ashridge until 1928.

These events must have had their repercussions in Little Gaddesden. The painting in the Manor House discovered by Mrs Wheatley in the 1890s depicts Elizabeth being arrested before being taken to the tower by the soldiers. It could show how shocked the people here must have been, and later how relieved they were at her release and succession to the throne.

A new era in building began with the replacement of the monastic order. The Dormer family of Wing received some of the Abbey property from St Albans. In 1576 there was rebuilding at the Manor House in Little Gaddesden by Sir Robert Dormer. There was some destruction at Ashridge College, though perhaps not as much as elsewhere. Wainscotting from the College was erected in the dining hall of the house. Aldbury church was to receive one of the monuments and its surrounds and brasses from the College Chapel.

It is not unlikely that the Manor House was the centre of a small hamlet. There were strips behind the present Kingham's Meadow which belonged to the former agricultural system. Hudnall Corner may be the ending of Berry Lane. Richard de Bury may have lived here in 1432.

Ashridge was leased to Richard Combe of Hemel Hempstead in 1556. A name scratched on a pillar in Little Gaddesden church probably reads 'Francis Combes 1569'. The continuing local connection between house and parish church might be indicated by this. The College Chapel at Ashridge was still in existence in 1575, though probably without much of its leaded roof.

In 1604 a new age was heralded by the purchase of Ashridge by Sir Thomas Egerton, Lord Ellesmere, later Viscount Brackley, and Lord Chancellor under James I. He married the widow of Ferdinando the 5th Earl of Derby. They entertained Queen Elizabeth at their Harefield home. Thomas Hackshaw, the curate at Little Gaddesden could have found it daunting to preach to one so distinguished. In 1611 Egerton suffered the bereavement of his grand-daughter Elizabeth within a year of her marriage. Her monument, originally in St Martin's-in-the-Fields, London was brought to Little Gaddesden in 1730. Her death, and that of her father in riots in Dublin must have brought sadness to the new resident, and sympathy from a society which was not aloof from suffering. The establishment of two charities for the poor and for the fatherless children shows the local care needed now that the monastic order was ended.

The Lord Chancellor's son John by an earlier marriage, married his step-mother's daughter by her marriage to Lord Derby. Before her marriage to Derby she had lived at her family home Althorp, Northamptonshire for she was the daughter of Sir John Spencer of Althorp (ancestor of Lady Diana Spencer, the bride of Prince Charles). The marriage of Egerton's son with Frances brought the Egertons into family relationship with one of the most distinguished families in the kingdom, and one with royal connections especially through the mother of Henry VII. This is the background of the Tudor coats of arms and symbols to be seen throughout the present Ashridge House. John became the first Earl of Bridgewater after his father's death in 1617, and he remained at Ashridge until his death in 1649. He determined to lay foundations for a great and noble family. His wife shared this ambition for as her monument in the parish church states, 'she had four sons and eleven daughters. Seven of her daughters she married richly and honorably'.

The locality was entering into a period of greater activity under the Egertons. Ashridge was to be organised with thoroughness and discipline, and the land was to be extended. Todd's great *History of Ashridge* gives the details of the domestic regulations. The estate was to be developed and farm after farm was to be bought. Even in death provision was to be made. A vault beneath the east-end of the parish church, formerly used for the rectors and their families was to be enlarged in 1635 for the benefit of the Egerton family, in spite of the reluctance of the Rector, Barnabas Holloway (Holway).

In the Civil War, the Earl was obviously enough a Royalist for Cromwell's troops to send a detachment to Ashridge and to the church in June 1643. They did much damage, and the local people saw them carry away horses and silver and gold plate, after smashing windows and doors: spectators once again of the local implications of a national scene. What they must have resented most was the breaking and entering of the vault in the chancel where the rector's children and Lord Bridgewater's wife and daughter were laid. The early 17th-century chalice and the flagon dated 1636 survived all the events of this period. Barnabas Holloway had been removed from his Rectory by the sequestration of the Church of England clergy by Cromwell, but his wife remained at the Rectory which had been restored just before the Civil War. A succession of Puritan ministers officiated in the church. Any earlier registers disappeared and no records have survived from this period.

In 1658 the Rev. Thomas Fossan was appointed to the Rectory by Richard Cromwell, the Lord Protector. Fossan was an unsuccessful schoolmaster of Berkhamsted School. He conformed in 1662. With the end of the Commonwealth and the Restoration of the monarchy, the 2nd Earl of Bridgewater became an important national figure. He was concerned with the new Book of Common Prayer of 1662. He became Lord President of Wales and of the Marches. Whether or not he continued the building work of his father is not clear, but he did complain about being involved in expense concerned with the fabric of the parish church. He established a charity for the poor, the income coming from the Dagnall Marshes. In 1682 he appointed Thomas Henshaw to succeed Fossan, and restored the rectorial tithe to the parish. In 1683 the Rectory contained a hall, a little study, a brewhouse, three upper rooms, a school (the first to be mentioned in Little Gaddesden), a stable and two barns.

John the 3rd Earl was a distinguished servant of the realm and was decorated with the Order of the Bath. He established a new Chapel at Ashridge and one of his chaplains who was also Rector of Little Gaddesden, the Rev. George Burghope, preached the first sermon in it in 1699. John's son, Scroop, became the 1st Duke of Bridgewater in 1720. Allied by his first marriage to Elizabeth, daughter of the Great Duke of Marlborough, he married into the family of the Duke of Bedford after her death. The scourge of smallpox shattered his family. He died in 1745 leaving his widow to survive him for a further 32 years before being laid to rest in the family vault beside him. She was Rachel Russell daughter of the 2nd Duke of Bedford. A fourth John succeeded to the Estate but only for a few years, for in 1747 Francis, a boy of eight, became the 3rd Duke. Educated at Eton, he made the Grand Tour of Europe, noting in France the canal work of De Bon Repos, and being introduced to the treasures of Paris, Rome and Florence.

In Little Gaddesden there was little evidence of the presence of the 'Canal Duke' until the turn of the century. For a time he had been involved in horse breeding and racing. He sold his horses at the *Robin Hood* Inn in Little Gaddesden. He used Lancelot (Capability) Brown for work on the Estate in 1759-68. He built some cottages, and one became known as 'Half-Crown Row' because of fines he imposed on workmen who arrived late for work; the fines being used, it was said, to pay for the cost of building. Towards the end of his days he lived at the old gate-house of the College. From there he planned the final destruction of the former monastic buildings together with the Elizabethan and 17th-century work of his predecessors. He began to gather material for a great new mansion on which he would spend some of the fortune which his canal work was bringing in. This was not to happen for on 16 March 1803 he was laid to rest in the family vault at Little Gaddesden. He had requested that his funeral would be quiet without any fuss. The faint stories which came down in parish tradition suggest that it was difficult for the folk on the Estate to understand this man who had done so much for their country.

The 7th Earl, the last to reside in Ashridge was John William, General Egerton, son of the Bishop of Durham. Like the 1st Earl he proceeded to provide a secure foundation for the entire

Fig. 2. Ashridge before the monastic gate house (used by the Canal Duke as his residence) was removed and during the building of the present house.

community using as a focal point the work of the building of Ashridge House and Estate. Careful plans were made for a benevolent dictatorship centred on the great Estate employing at one time 800 men. He was to see James Wyatt begin the building and Jeffry Wyatt complete it. He used some of the ideas suggested by Humphry Repton for the gardens. Everyone was to know his place and to work systematically and thoroughly. New roads were to be built, or old ones restored, milestones were to be erected, a mausoleum was to be constructed at the parish church. He was to be churchwarden there, and to enjoy ringing the bells of Edlesborough tower. He gathered together an able team consisting of R.C. Clarke, George Atty and William Buckingham. He was, according to his monument, 'to improve the morals of the poor'. His death did not mean the end of his authority, for his widow remained, until her death in 1849 26 years later, living by his rules and intentions.

The 8th and last Earl of Bridgewater did not reside at Ashridge. He was a remarkable character; a classical scholar, a prebendary of Durham, Rector of Whitchurch in Shropshire, and an eccentric English nobleman living in Paris who refused to allow land from his property to be taken for part of a triumphal avenue along which Napoleon or later Leopold might travel. In his will he left £8,000 to be divided between eight scholars (one of these was Roget of *Thesaurus* fame) to write theses on 'the wisdom of God's work in Creation'. His monument in the church is by Westmacott, and is created on this theme. He was brought to Little Gaddesden for burial in 1829. His manuscripts are in the British Library. Once again there was a difference of opinion between the rectors of Little Gaddesden and Bridgewater, for David Jenks (the 2nd of this name) was not in favour of the erection of a large monument in Francis Henry's memory in the church. In this the 7th Earl's widow concurred.

The 19th century could be seen through the examination of the lives of three of the ladies of Ashridge House and their impact on the House and the community. From 1803-49 Charlotte Catherine Anne wife, then widow, of the 7th Earl held sway. She was remembered for the creation and the restoration of the pathways and the avenues across the Estate and for her insistence that the rules and regulations of her husband's régime should be observed. She trusted Robert Clarke as the agent and he served her faithfully. She placed a tablet in his memory in Nettleden church. In her will she established a charity to continue the Bridgewater association over the vast Estate.

Her work was followed by that of Lady Marian Alford. She was the daughter of the Marquess of Northampton. Her husband, Viscount Alford, who had succeeded to the Bridgewater Estate died after only two years as owner of Ashridge. She remained in authority during the minority of her elder son, and during his short life which ended in 1867. Adelbert her second son became the 3rd Earl Brownlow, and he was to be at Ashridge until his death in 1921. Lady Marian Alford kept court at Ashridge which became the centre of a vigorous intellectual and social life. Here she entertained prime ministers and poets, artists, architects and sculptors, bishops, deans and higher ecclesiastics.

In her early days at Ashridge there had been the conflict concerning the enclosure of Berkhamsted Common. A similar policy had been adopted earlier in the enclosure of part of the Hudnall area when 200 acres had been enclosed by the 2nd Earl of Bridgewater as recorded in 1682 when commoners surrendered their rights in exchange for allotments of land as private property. The 19th-century Berkhamsted attitude to enclosures was less amenable. The people of Little Gaddesden must have been divided in their reaction to the enclosure of Berkhamsted Common. Those on the Estate might well have been behind William Paxton and the Estate authorities in their desire to prevent local lanes and driveways being churned up by public use of heavy carts; others were concerned about traditional rights. Local excitement at the midnight raid on the fences, after the three mile walk from Tring Station by the labourers hired by Augustus Smith, and the destruction that night of three miles of five foot fences, must have been immense. Later the Little Gaddesden folk watched whilst an iron fence round the park nine miles long was erected, parts of which still exist.

One of the main concerns of Lady Marian was the enrichment of the life of people on the Ashridge Estate, and as so many of these lived in Little Gaddesden much of her work there helped in the creation of the 'first Garden Village' in Hertfordshire. Due to her interest in the care, preservation and extension of property, great efforts were expended in new designs for buildings. G.E. Street was used and his work copied; Godwin too presented his designs. The Church of England School and the parish church were to benefit from these. The result of the association of the 2nd and 3rd Earls Brownlow, and Lady Marian their mother, working with faithful and highly competent staff under J. Wright, was that many older houses were restored, improved, changed externally, painted Brownlow plum colour, and marked with the Alford or Brownlow symbol or shield, sometimes with a date. The houses then were numbered with small white and blue number tiles similar to those seen in Switzerland in the Grisons.

Some of the older cottages at Ringshall and on the Green were extended, and new ones were built in between them. Whether or not there had been a lane behind the cottages on the Green as there was at both ends of the Ringshall cottages is not certain. It would seem, however, that earlier than the present road along the Green there must have been a lane in front of some of the cottages and behind the others, even though a continuous road did not exist until later. In addition to the concern about the houses, the 2nd Earl Brownlow and his mother were responsible for providing each house with piped water by 1858. The importance of this cannot be over estimated in this area.

After their marriage in 1868, Adelaide the wife of Earl Brownlow, and daughter of the 18th Earl of Shrewsbury and Talbot was indefatigable in her kindness to the people on the Estate. The Christian influence of Lady Marian and Lady (Adelaide) Brownlow is shown by both being remembered by the erection of two crosses on the Green, one at the Ashridge Drive entrance and the other outside the Manor House overlooking the avenue down to Ashridge House.

Near the Alford Cross stands the Parish War Memorial (there is another in the parish church). Few could have anticipated the change to take place here in the next 10 years from August 1914. In that month General Kitchener was at afternoon tea at Ashridge when the butler brought in a note for him. Receiving it he stood up, quickly excused himself, and moved to his high command. The House was to become a wartime hospital. Lady Brownlow was to die in 1917, and her husband in 1921. An era was over.

Since the change in local society at the end of the monastic college, the parish had had a feudal-type life, dependent and serving the great house and the families related to its owners. Suddenly this was over. Despite receiving a year's wages and an option on their cottages, there was great insecurity.

No one could envy the Estate Trustees their responsibility for disposing of the extensive property, nor their position when the decision to sell Ashridge was announced in 1925. Little Gaddesden people whose families had worked in the House and on the Estate were not only in fear of the loss of their livelihood, but many of them were to lose many of those incidental and inestimable benefits of that life. Those who worked in the House surrounded by great paintings (some very great paintings), by beautiful treasures of silver and gold which they had handled and cleaned, and by articles of superb craftsmanship; and who had also moved in an environment where men and women of great eminence were daily in residence, were but a few of those whose lives were to be changed. They would enrich their children by their tales, perhaps sometimes romanticised but genuinely appreciative, of the golden days of Ashridge. Though their lives had often been subject to great demands and been far from easy, they were later to regret the passing of that age.

There were great fears nationally as well as locally about the future of the House and of the immediate surroundings. Posterity will admire unstintingly the achievement of one resident, Bridget Talbot, who was determined to prevent the wholesale destruction of the land by uncontrolled private development. She was indomitable in obtaining limitations to be placed on the type of building and extent of areas under the terms of sale when Thomas Place began to sell to individuals the land he had bought.

The National Trust became actively involved in the purchase and preservation of much of the Estate. The founders of the Ashridge Golf Club, men of practical knowledge and foresight, were also committed to this preservation. The two bodies working together brought incalculable blessings to the Estate and to the general public over a wide area.

The inspiration which led Urban Hanlon Broughton to purchase the House as a memorial to the late Prime Minister meant the beginning of a new life once more, not only for Ashridge and Little Gaddesden but for all the surrounding communities. There was to be new employment, new interests, and an attempt to preserve the countryside the residents held dear. Through varying experiences and experiments College and parish moved together.

For 10 years from 1929 Ashridge became a College of Citizenship and many young politicians were trained there. During the war it was adapted once again to become an emergency hospital. University College and Charing Cross Hospitals used the house and the temporary blocks built in front of the main building. Men wounded at Dunkirk and men from the 51st Highland Division were amongst those who came and found local people ministering to their needs. The lanes rumbled to the noise of tanks and equipment and Polish soldiers bivouacked near the Monument. Cockney voices mingled with Hertfordshire ones as children evacuated from London grew up for a time in Little Gaddesden, and many homes were to be enriched by life-long associations begun when the evacuees were housed away from the severity of the London raids.

After the Second World War there was again emphasis on Citizenship. The association with the Conservative Party was officially ended, although local people could not believe this to be true in practice. They watched each stage with interest and valued working at Ashridge. Their commitment during the difficult years, of long hours of unpaid overtime, poor wages, and very hard work should never be underestimated or forgotten. To them the present College and parish owe a great debt.

Finally in 1959 the Ashridge Business Management College was established. With this there came new work, new opportunities and new interests for many people in the Little Gaddesden and Berkhamsted area. The world of business involving new contacts with men and women from all over the world, and new employment under conditions unthought of in years gone by, began to be experienced, and the innate and previously unknown gifts of many people were developed.

An increasing interest in the local community by the College is one of the hopes for growth in future years. The present Rector of Little Gaddesden, like his predecessors for hundreds of years, is Chaplain to the College. The College is generous towards local needs.

The name Ashridge, like the name of Little Gaddesden when Kalm paid his visit in the 18th century, may have been known little beyond its immediate area. Today in both names there is enshrined so much which great national events have brought before the eyes and ears of the inhabitants of this quiet and remote part of the Chiltern Hills.

Perhaps those returning to their homes across the world may go back thankful at having spent a short time where others have the great privilege of living.

PART TWO

1. The Ashridge Estate

Under successive earls and dukes of Bridgewater the Ashridge Estate became very extensive. Today the secretary to the Bridgewater Trust, traditionally the rector of Little Gaddesden, sends cheques to parishes on the the old Estate. These go to places such as Potten End, (for Frithsden), Great Gaddesden, Edlesborough, Totternhoe, Ivinghoe, Ivinghoe Aston, Long Marston, Marsworth, Slapton, Billington, Northall, Pitstone, Studham, Cheddington, and Aldbury. This shows the extent of the Estate in 1849 on the death of Charlotte Catherine Anne, widow of the 7th Earl, the last of the Bridgewaters to reside at Ashridge.

On the death of the 3rd and last Earl Brownlow in 1921 the sale of the Estate began and 11,300 acres were sold. Hearing that the greater part of the remainder of the Estate was to be sold for private development Miss Bridget Talbot with Professor George Trevelyan and Mr J. Craufurd wrote to *The Times* an appeal to save the Estate, and this was signed by Stanley Baldwin, Ramsey MacDonald, Lord Asquith, and Lord Grey. Professor Trevelyan began to raise funds locally and 1,700 acres were acquired by the National Trust.

2. The National Trust and the Ashridge Associates

The National Trust was founded in 1895 by Miss Octavia Hill, Sir Robert Hunter and Canon Rawnsley to preserve the history and beauty of the country. It was incorporated by an Act of Parliament in 1907. It is independent of the state and relies on charitable support. By 1945 there were 8,000 members, and in 1980 there were one million. The Trust protects over 500,000 acres and owns 230 country houses as well as gardens, nature reserves, villages, archaeological sites and many farms. 'Enterprise Neptune' helped in obtaining extensive areas of coastline, so that over 400 miles are now protected. The Earl of Crawford and Balcarres was for many years the distinguished President of the Trust. His father had been one of the main sponsors for the foundation of the National Trust of Scotland. The National Trust has been described as 'The Englishman's most worthwhile club'.

The Trust purchased half of the Estate for £40,000 and of this £20,000 was given by one donor. Additions to the original acquisition were made, including Hill and Coldharbour Farms, and land in the Water End area. By 1934 £70,000 had been expended on the Estate. Ashridge College acquired the 235 acres in the centre of which it now stands. This land is separate from the National Trust property, although there is no defined boundary mark on the ground. At the moment the National Trust owns roughly 4,000 acres of land. There are 1,000 acres of woodland,

1,000 acres of agricultural land and 2,000 acres of wooded commons and heathland. The Trust is responsible for the following commons—

Pitstone Common.

Aldbury Common. Commoners' rights survive here and inhabitants are allowed by right to remove certain sizes of fallen wood for fuel. This is the only one of the commons where this right remains.

Berkhamsted Common. This was the scene of the enclosure battle in 1866 when 120 navvies hired in London travelled to Tring by train. They marched by night to the Common and uprooted the iron railings which were five feet high with broad metal bands between them. Thus the attempt of Lord Brownlow and his advisers to enclose part of the Common was frustrated and three miles of railings were destroyed on 7 March 1866. The rights of the commoners were upheld in a judgement by Lord Romilly, Master of the Rolls, in January 1870.

Lady Marian Alford, mother of Lord Brownlow wrote a booklet in which she sought to show that the action was not as anti-social as her son's accusers believed.

Hudnall Common (excluding Hudnall Common Plantations). This is a detached area, presented to the Trust by the Commons Open Spaces and the Footpath Preservation Society. One half was cultivated during the war. The proximity of the Hudnall Park Environmental Studies Centre is of mutual benefit to the Trust and the students.

Ivinghoe (Ringshall) Common. There is a large area of self-afforested birches here.

The Trust also includes the Frithsden Beeches, Great and Little Frithsden Copses, part of Water End and Little Heath.

The Trust cares for the 'Tree Cathedral' at Studham and Whipsnade. Edmund Blyth began this in memory of Arthur Bailey and John Bennett his fellow soldiers in World War One who were killed. He began the planting in 1939 in the style of a great Cathedral with nave, transepts, lady chapel and outer cloister walk. It has an apsidal east-end. The trees are chosen to represent seasons of the year: cherry for Easter, spruce for Christmas, elm for summer, beech for autumn. There are also Lombardy poplars, oak, rowan, Scots pine, willow, holly, lilac, philadelphus, whitebeam and birch.

The Pitstone Windmill. This is probably the oldest existing post-mill in the United Kingdom and is dated 1627. It was restored by the effort of parishioners from Pitstone and Ivinghoe and their historical society, together with the Little Gaddesden representative, David Wray.

At 811 feet Crawley Wood is the highest point on the Estate, except for the top of the Monument at 829 feet. Ivinghoe and the Beacon are beyond the Little Gaddesden parish boundary. Car parking is not allowed in Ashridge Park beyond the official car parks because of restrictions made in the original purchase.

The Ashridge Estate is a paradise for photographers and for all students of nature. Calendars frequently depict scenes from the Berkhamsted Lodge area or the Golf Club lands. Many 19th-century pictures of Ashridge House frontage show the Ashridge deer, and Baskerville in 1681 spoke of a park for red deer and a park for fallow deer. When Kalm the Swedish naturalist visited Little Gaddesden in 1748 he described some of the deer as being snow-white, but the majority as brownish-grey or fawn. He was told that over 1,000 were kept. The ash was laid for them to gnaw. Sheds were erected throughout the Park for the deer to shelter in bad weather, and arrangements for them to have fodder were made. In the bitter winter of 1963 Miss Helen Cowdell of Little Gaddesden collected about £40 from local inhabitants to provide food for the deer.

The Ashridge herd of red deer was sold in 1920 and taken to Richmond. Their descendants can be seen there today. They were rounded up by deer-hounds, driven into a long funnel whence they were individually handled and placed in crates for transport. The antlers of the stags were sawn off for safety. In 1926 a mixed herd of red and fallow deer roamed the Park. Mr Place who had bought the land thought of putting them in crates and sending them to Northern Ireland. About thirty-five men were to drive the deer (especially the remaining red ones) into a yard at Old Park Lodge. The exercise was not a success. By 1930 only 30-40 red deer remained. They were shot by Mr Appleyard the gamekeeper, a crack shot and were said to have finished up as food for the lions. When the herd was enclosed in 1928 there were 800 deer on the Estate. Just before the Second World War they had been reduced to three hundred and sixty. In 1962-63 there were 170, and 20 less a year later. In 1972 there were 180, in 1971 there were two hundred and seventy-one. In that year the National Trust decided to increase the deer cull from 100 to 120 a year.

At one time Chinese water-deer and Japanese Sika-deer had been reported. Pig-deer are not infrequent. When a white stag was killed by a car on the Ringshall road there was a local outcry against fast driving. 'Sleeping policemen' ramps laid through Ashridge Park have reduced the slaughter of the deer.

Badgers are numerous. They have been seen in the rectory garden and are known in Badger Wood, and in the fields near Cromer Wood. There are foxes, though few hares or rabbits, very few hedgehogs, grey (but not red) squirrels, edible dormice ('glis-glis'), weasels (stoats are very rare), moles, mice, and bats (pipistrelle, long-eared). The black squirrel formerly known in the Monument area was sighted again in 1979 by Deer Leap corner.

Birds of the National Trust and Little Gaddesden Areas.

In 1965 the National Trust list showed 51 breeding species. This included nightingales, lesser redpolls, wood-warblers and all the woodpeckers. Nightingales last bred here in about 1976. The sparrow-hawk seemed to be dying out because of the sprays, but by 1981 their numbers were increasing again. Kestrels breed and buzzards are visitors. Black-headed gulls are common, as also are pigeons, doves, jays, magpies, rooks and crows. Thrushes, missel-thrushes, blackbirds, dunnocks, and robins are all common, and the hawfinch can occasionally be heard.

Amongst the warblers are the chiff-chaff, the garden-warbler, the willow-warbler, the grasshopper-warbler (Ivinghoe beacon) and the wood-warbler (Harding's Rookery). Swallows and swifts and house-martens are regular visitors. For several weeks in 1965 and later, an osprey spent time here. The golden oriole was heard and seen during the 1970s. In addition to the more common birds such as cuckoos and larks, those giving pleasure include the yellow-hammer, the spotted flycatcher, the longtailed tit, the occasional woodcock, the redstart, and the pheasant (the Lady Amherst has been sighted). Redwings and fieldfares make their annual visits, as also do siskins, goldcrests, nuthatches, tree-creepers, and wagtails. Many finches visit the gardens.

Especial observation of the movement of tits has taken place in 1981. A B.B.C. 'Living World' programme in May 1981 presented Mr Chris Mead's tracing of the movement of large numbers in the Chailey Cottage, Witchcraft Bottom, Alderton Drive and Thunderdell areas (The Rural Heritage Society report for 1981 gives details). The proximity of the Tring reservoirs and Ivinghoe Beacon make the area important for ornithologists.

No attempt will be made to give a complete flora of the Ashridge and Little Gaddesden areas. This list is compiled from information given at different times by local residents. Bluebells carpet the woods, especially Pulridge and Hoo Woods in early summer. Primroses grow in some wooded parts, but are not found wild in the hedgerows. Dog-roses grow well. Cowslips, and *Anemone pulsatilla* grow on certain hill-slopes. There are wild daffodils, heather, and green hellebore. *Helleborus niger* grows outside some old cottages.

In a 1930s school notebook (Little Gaddesden) the children noted the following — dog's mercury growing thick in woods and hedgerows; St John's wort; tway-blade (unusual but found in Hoo Wood; wild strawberry; sweet-violets; dog-violets; rosebay willowherb (also called cotton plant and cherry pie); foxgloves; snowdrops (especially in the churchyard); crocuses; celandine; aconites; wood anemones; bladder-campion; ragged robin; deadly nightshade; dead-nettle; red campion; bachelor's button; headache-flower; harebell; tom thumb; honeysuckle; yellow bedstraw; and dog's mercury. Others include meadow crane's-bill; (on the green, 'blue geranium'); milkmaids; lady's smock; cuckoo-pint; old man's beard; giant puff balls; spotted-orchids; knapweeds; valerian; mallows; campanula; and scabious. Six species of orchid are known in the neighbourhood.

THE ASHRIDGE ASSOCIATES

This is the local branch of the National Trust and was founded in 1945. Major T. Hopkins was one of the founder-members, and for many years was the local treasurer. He had been a member of the local committee of the Trust since the acquisition of the Estate in 1926 and continued as such until 1963. In 1957 he donated the money for a small timber pavilion to be built near the Monument as a memorial to the benefactors of the local group. By the end of 1945 the Ashridge Associates had 634 members, almost one hundred of whom were living in Little Gaddesden. The 1,000th member, in the summer of 1971 was Miss Fodd of Rothesay School, Berkhamsted.

The local Association has at least one escorted walk through the Trust property each year. The Head Ranger, Mr John Wilson and the local chairman and committee, together with experts in specialised fields, give talks on the sites. Subjects have been — coppicing projects; bird life; mammals; plant life; general and particular forestry work; machinery; inspections of plantations; clearances; encouragement of animal life; removal of bracken and its replacement by heather; tree-thinning; exploration of the rides and walks; historical matters, especially concerning dating; information about the aged Spanish chestnuts; and older plantations. Concern is expressed about the dangers from too heavy human and motor traffic, and reclamation after damage. As many as 250 take part in these walks. One observation about the Estate has been that 'Open hospitality over six square miles involves a good deal of very expensive control, especially as many visitors feel that the whole property is so much their own that they may do as they please'.

When in the summer of 1962 it was decided to take a toll at the Monument drive, there was great surprise that a total of 2,500 people paid in four days for their cars. By August 1967, 10,000 car-owners had paid for admission. From 6 April to 12 October 1980 on Sundays and Bank Holidays there were 6,457 cars.

The opening of the National Trust Information Centre in 1967 fulfilled a growing need, and its success has been fostered by legacies such as that given by Miss Jean Moore in 1973. The Information Centre and shop were modernised in 1981. A nature trail was first established in 1968, and visits by schools and societies have been greatly encouraged. Publications about the area have been well received and of a high standard. Amongst the members of the committee who contributed greatly to the Association were Richard Cole who was for many years Secretary and Tom Fiske, Treasurer for 11 years. The local Chairman for 29 years was Major Hadden-Paton. At the 75th Anniversary of the Trust HM the Queen Mother presented a long-service medal to Mr Jim Fleckney, woodman on the Estate for 40 years.

The Estate of 4,000 acres with its many woodlands and commons and its beautiful downlands is within 30 miles of London. It must be one of the most beautiful natural parks in the Home Counties.

THE HOPKINS PAVILION

On the left hand side of the Monument stands the Hopkins Pavilion. Its wording—

THIS NATIONAL TRUST PAVILION RECORDS THE GRATITUDE OF THE ASHRIDGE ASSOCIATES
FOR THE NATIONAL TRUST IDEA
FOR THE VISION AND PRACTICAL IDEALISM OF ITS FOUNDERS
AND FOR THE DEVOTION AND GOODWILL WHICH INSPIRED
PAST BENEFACTORS OF THIS ESTATE

On either side of the commemorative tablet are the names of those whose work is especially remembered. Small circular name-plates in the form of medallions have the name encircled with a laurel-wreath. Two medallions are in the centre.

Bridget Elizabeth Talbot	1885-1971
Sydney Renée Courtauld	1873-1962
Arthur Macdonald	1861-1951

Some who gave notable help to this Estate.
They are remembered with gratitude today.

Fred Welch	1877-1956
George Macaulay Trevelyan O.M.	1876-1962
Thomas Henry Curtis Hopkins	1876-1966

THE ASHRIDGE ESTATE *Miss Bridget Talbot*

The account which Miss Bridget Talbot gave to Canon H. Senar when she was in hospital in Cambridge on 31 July 1971 follows. She died the following December 1971.

Miss Talbot heard from her cousin (1925) that Ashridge Park was to be sold for private development, and that the documents were to be signed in one month's time. She left her Yorkshire home, Kiplin Hall, Scorton, Northallerton in heavy rain, and caught the 'Milk Train' to London. She met the Secretary of the National Trust and persuaded him to go round London, as she would do also, and gather signatures for a letter to *The Times* to protest against the sale of Ashridge Estate and to obtain support for its preservation by the Trust. The Secretary was to meet Miss Talbot for luncheon when they would examine the names they had obtained. They would then decide on their action. When they met, Miss Talbot produced her list of supporters. It included Stanley Baldwin, Ramsay MacDonald, Lord Oxford, and Lord Grey of Fallodon. She had called at No. 10 Downing Street where a Cabinet meeting was in progress and she had obtained the co-operation of her cousin Earl Grey. Dr Trevelyan, Miss Courtauld and Mr (later Sir) James Craufurd were prominent in the project.

A note had appeared in *The Times* on 9 October 1925 when Miss Constance Sitwell warned of the possible sale to a syndicate for commercial purposes. She spoke of the unique beauty, grandeur and dignity of the Estate, of the beeches, the lie of the land and the richness of colour. The letter which Miss Talbot had inspired appeared in *The Times* on Tuesday 20 October over the names of the aforementioned gentlemen. They expressed their sympathy with the proposal to acquire Ashridge Park and the adjoining woods and downland for the National Trust and emphasised the urgency of finding the sum required in the space of the three weeks left.

The Estate's destruction was thus prevented.

3. Ashridge Golf Club

The public-spirited efforts of Miss Bridget Talbot in seeking to preserve the Ashridge Estate after the death of the 3rd Earl Brownlow will always be acknowledged with gratitude by the Ashridge Golf Club.

The Club was opened in 1932 after the construction of the course and the Club House. The 6th Earl of Rosebery, K.T., P.C., D.S.O., M.C., was the Club's first president and he held this office until his death at the age of 92 in May 1974. He had brought together a small group including Sir Guy Campbell, Major Hotchkiss and Cecil Hutchinson, who purchased a large section of Ashridge Park for the use of society in general, passing much of the land to the National Trust against a covenant. This covenant ensured the proper formation of the Golf Club and its future as well as providing facilities in Ashridge Park for the general public. Leading golf course architects were engaged, and an 18 hole course was laid out as a 'Clover Leaf' an adventurous pattern at that time.

In 1934 Mr Tom Simpson, regarded as the leading golf architect, modified the course 'with incomparable subtlety to make it a sound test for the good player and a pleasant round for the average player (99% of all golfers)'.

contd. on p. 18

ASHRIDGE FOR THE NATION.

URGENT APPEAL TO THE PUBLIC.

THREE WEEKS FOR DECISION.

TO THE EDITOR OF THE TIMES.

Sir,—We desire to express our strong sympathy with the proposal to acquire as much as possible of Ashridge Park and the adjoining woods and downland to be held by the National Trust for the benefit of the public. We understand that the National Trust has already at its disposal for this purpose a sum of £20,000, contributed by an anonymous donor. Negotiations have been on foot for the purchase with this sum of a stretch of land between Ivinghoe Beacon and Berkhamsted Common. We hope that there will be no doubt that the Trustees will consent to the carrying through of these negotiations to a successful conclusion.

But we wish to express a hope that much more than this may be done. We believe that there are few, if any, parks that combine so many features of desirability for public acquisition as Ashridge. It is within easy reach of London, and has within the last few years come to be visited by a very large number of persons on week-ends and holidays ; it is amongst the most richly timbered of parks, and it has adjoining it stretches of downland, with magnificent views.

For all these reasons we earnestly hope that the Trustees will see their way to give further time for the raising of money. In that case we have little doubt that the generous example set by the anonymous donor will find many imitators, and that, with the support of those who care for the preservation of the kind of woodland scenery in which England stands unrivalled, a very much larger area of this beautiful country than has so far been contemplated may be secured for the permanent enjoyment of the nation.

It is understood that the Trustees stipulate that they should have some idea of the area to be acquired for the public, and the sum that is likely to be raised at the expiration of three weeks from now.

The time, therefore, available for raising the money is very short ; we trust that the general public will realize that the more generous the response to this appeal, the greater will be the area of the property secured for the public benefit.

Contributions should be sent to the Secretary of the National Trust, at 7, Buckingham Palace-gardens, S.W.1. Cheques should be made payable to "The National Trust," and crossed "National Provincial Bank of England."

Yours faithfully,
STANLEY BALDWIN.
J. RAMSAY MACDONALD.
OXFORD AND ASQUITH.
GREY OF FALLODON (Vice-President of the National Trust).
The National Trust, 7, Buckingham Palace-gardens, S.W.1, Oct. 19.

Fig. 3 Letter to *The Times.*

THE ASHRIDGE ESTATE.

I see in your issue of October 5 that there is a possibility of the Ashridge estate being sold to a commercial syndicate ; also that a certain amount of money is available if it is still possible to save for the nation a bit of country which is really unique in its beauty, dignity, and grandeur. The beeches of Ashridge, the whole lie of the land, the peculiar richness of the colour there, make it quite unforgettable to anyone who has seen it, and that such a park, rare even in England and quite unknown in other countries, should disappear if it can be saved, can only be thought of as a disaster. When a house or work of art is sold it still remains intact, although in other hands, but in this case the beauty, which has taken centuries to mature, will probably be destroyed, and one cannot help feeling that a real wrong will have been done to England and to the future if this happens.—Miss CONSTANCE SITWELL, 114, Grosvenor-road, S.W.1.

Fig. 4 Letter to *The Times.*

Player's Name .... Date ....

Marker's Signature .... Competition ....

Signature of Competitor .... Player's Handicap .... Strokes Received ....

Marker's Score	Hole	Names of Holes	Yards	Player's Gross Score	Stroke Index	Par	Won + Lost − Halved 0	Marker's Score	Hole	Names of Holes	Yards	Player's Gross Score	Stroke Index	Par	Won + Lost − Halved 0
	1	Devil's Den	391		11	4			10	Pitstone	355		14	4	
	2	Golden Valley	494		5	5			11	Thunderdell	165		16	3	
	3	The Rookery	165		15	3			12	Deer Leap	405		4	4	
	4	Pooks Hill	410		1	4			13	Queen Elizabeth's Drive	476		12	5	
	5	Witchcraft Bottom	492		9	5			14	Old Park Lodge	431		2	4	
	6	Highwayman's Hide	190		13	3			15	Princes Riding	513		8	5	
	7	Ringshall	400		3	4			16	Willow Pond	167		18	3	
	8	Knob's Crook	179		17	3			17	Hoo	482		6	5	
	9	Cottons	361		7	4			18	Home	432		10	4	
OUT . . .			3082			35		IN			3426			37	

S.S.S. 71   Par 72

Please replace divots, rake bunkers and repair pitch marks

Strokes are to be taken at those Holes opposite which the red figure is equal to or less than the total Handicap Allowance.

1356

OUT . . .	3082		35
TOTAL .	6508		72
HANDICAP			
NET SCORE			
BOGEY RESULT			

PLAY ODDS

Handicap or Handicap Difference	MATCH PLAY		7/8 Stableford Bogey	7-16 Stableford Foursomes Bogey
	3/4 Singles & 4 Balls	3/8 Foursomes		
1	1	0	1	0
2	2	1	2	1
3	2	1	3	1
4	3	2	4	2
5	4	2	4	2
6	5	2	5	3
7	5	3	6	3
8	6	3	7	4
9	7	3	8	4
10	8	4	9	4
11	8	4	10	5
12	9	5	11	5
13	10	5	11	6
14	11	5	12	6
15	11	6	13	7
16	12	6	14	7
17	13	6	15	7
18	14	7	16	8
19	14	7	17	8
20	15	8	18	9
21	16	8	18	9
22	17	8	19	10
23	17	9	20	10
24	18	9	21	11
25	19	9	22	11
26	20	10	23	11
27	20	10	24	12
28	21	11	25	12
29	22	11	25	13
30	23	11	26	13

YELLOW MARKERS indicate Society Tees.
WHITE MARKERS indicate Competition Tees.
FROST GREENS DURING WINTER are Ground under Repair when not in use.

Print/Abbey Press, Abingdon, Oxon. Tel. (0235) 20343   1356

LOCAL RULES

1. The following places are out of Bounds:—
    When playing the 8th hole — over fences and over the service road at back of 8th green but not over through road.
    When playing the 9th hole — over the road on the left.
    Over all fences adjoining the course and field to right of 1st, 2nd and 17th fairways marked by white posts.

2. Hoof marks or wheel marks (cart ruts) may be treated as ground under repair. Rule 32 applies.

3. Stones in bunkers are movable obstructions. Rule 31-1 applies.

4. Fallen or felled timber is deemed to be an immovable obstruction. Rule 31-2 applies.

5. All roads and paths are integral parts of the course with the exception of the road behind the 14th green where Def. 20 and Rule 31-2 applies.

6. All pop-up sprinkler heads are immovable obstructions and relief from interference by them may be obtained under Rule 31-2. In addition, if such an obstruction, on or within two club-lengths of the putting green of the hole being played, intervene between the ball and the hole, the player may obtain relief, without penalty, as follows: —
    (a) If the ball lie on the putting green, it may be lifted and placed, not nearer the hole, at the nearest point at which intervention by the obstruction is avoided.
    (b) If the ball lie off the putting green (but not in a hazard) and is within two club-lengths of the intervening obstruction it may be lifted, cleaned and dropped as in clause (a) above.

The Rules of the R. & A. Golf Club of St. Andrews will be taken as the Rules of the Club with the above exceptions.

N.B. The pond at the 16th is a "water hazard" whether it has water in it or not.

Fig. 5. Golf score card (front and verso).

Henry Cotton, the greatest English golfer of this century, was the professional at Ashridge from 1937-46. Born in 1908, son of a Methodist preacher, and of agricultural parents, he became a professional golfer in 1923. In 1934 he won the 'Open' at Royal St George, Kent, and in 1937 he won the 'Open' at Carnoustie. In 1937 his assistant W. Laidlaw was seventh and his second assistant F. Robertson was seventeenth. It was a unique performance for one club to have three players in the first twenty. In 1948 he won the 'Open' at Muirfield (284), while the king was present. Cotton had been a member of the winning Ryder Cup team in 1929. Jack Nicklaus said of Cotton — 'He is the greatest ever, always in control of himself'. During the war he did very great work for charity, playing 130 games for philanthropic causes.

During the war the Club suffered, being burned down by the 'Fire-raiser' who did extensive damage in the Little Gaddesden area. This caused severe financial problems for the Club. The difficulties were overcome by steady work under the chairmanship of Lord Chesham and with the help of members, especially of the Artisan Section (see page 177), restoration took place.

After the war it was decided to encourage the mid-week use of the course by temporary members, and the number of these golfers built up to over 4,000 per annum from all parts of the British Isles. The high standard of the cuisine contributed in no small way to the retention of their support. The club has over 600 annual members and a regular staff of about fifteen.

Local golfers are well catered for by the Club which in addition to the Private Members Club has the excellent Artisan Section, whose members give much voluntary service in the maintenance of the course and premises.

The secretary's residence is Old Park Lodge. This house was built in 1619 as the home of the 'verderer', the royal solicitor responsible for the royal parks. The central tower gave the verderer uninterrupted views across the grazing.

Since the 1930s trees have grown around the Park, especially silver birch, and the course now appears to have been hewn out of the forest. The view from the second tee and the approach to the ninth green are amongst the more beautiful of any course.

PRESIDENTS

1932-1973	The 6th Earl of Rosebery, K.T., P.C., D.S.O., M.C.
1973-1977	Dr H.D. White
1977-1979	Spencer H. Block
1980-(date)	Clifford Baron

ASHRIDGE GOLF CLUB CAPTAINS

1932/3	F. Turner	1960	M.H. Thackray
1934/5	Major-General Sir Reginald Hoskins	1961	G.T. Harris
		1962	Dr D.O. Walker
1936/7	Lord Chesham	1963	E.G. Pank
1938-45	Air Vice Marshal Sir N.D.K. MacEwan	1964	E. Johnson
		1965	D.C.L. Grigsby
1946	Lt. Colonel R.H. Haslam	1966	G.F. Osborne
1947-51	W.H. Greer	1967	T.J.A. Green
1952	Dr H.D. White	1968	F.J. Goodall
1953/4	S.A. Block	1969	R.G.H. Bertram
1955	Dr W.A. Barnes	1970	R.J. Simpson
1956	M.M. Johnson	1971	Dr C.D. Garratt
1957	S.H. Smith	1972	D.Barker Q.C.
1958	A.E.W. Henderson	1973	S. Broughton
1959	Clifford Baron	1974	Dr R.S. Hynd

1975	G.E. Moore	1979	G.G. Newton
1976	Sir William Swallow	1980	D.G. Welton
1977	S.P. Whaley	1981	R. Blackmore
1978	Air Commodore A.C. Deere	1982	P. Mann

LADY CAPTAINS ASHRIDGE GOLF CLUB

1935-39	The Countess of Rosebery	1965/6	Mrs D.P. Glasgow
1946-48	Mrs H.D. Aylwin	1966/7	Mrs E.G. Williams
1948-50	Mrs F.A. Meyer	1967/8	Mrs D.C. Bulloch
1950/1	Mrs G.V. Miles	1968/9	Mrs W.F. Slator
1951/2	Mrs S. Forbes	1969/70	Mrs B.A. Holloway
1952/3	Mrs F.C. Arnold	1970/1	Mrs C. Baron
1953/4	Mrs J.C. Yewdall	1971/2	Mrs W.W. Stabb
	Mrs H. Paul-Huhne	1972/3	Mrs D. Buick
1954/5	Mrs C.A.G. Hewson	1973/4	Miss E. Boyd
1955/6	Mrs F.A. Meyer	1974/5	Miss D. Rait-Kerr
1956-58	Mrs I.H.B. Macdonald	1975/6	Mrs J.S. Rayner
1958/9	Mrs J.C. Yewdall	1976/7	Mrs P. Kirwan
1959/60	Mrs E. Bennett	1977/8	Mrs E.S. Aylwin
1960/1	Mrs H.D. Aylwin	1978/9	Mrs S.P. Whaley
1961/2	Miss D. Eaton Griffith	1979/80	Mrs S. Fraser-Beck
1962/3	Mrs C. Baron	1980/1	Mrs J. Sandell
1963/4	Mrs A.B. Weir	1981/2	Mrs Y. Rawlins
1964/5	Mrs A. Champion		

4.   Ashridge College

The Little Gaddesden approach to Ashridge and to Berkhamsted begins with an unpretentious white gate leading from the Alford Cross. After about twenty-five yards Ringshall Drive lies to the right, and Ashridge Drive winds to the left through the trees. A pathway to Golf Club Road marks the site where in the 1930s a new road was planned. The Drive crosses the Golden Valley with the golf course on the right. The Rookery is on the left. From this point a road was planned in the 1930s which would have encircled Ashridge House. (This road beginning here, would have followed the Golden Valley, and then turned in a great arc to meet the Ashridge Drive again beyond the College and near Berkhamsted Lodge.) A spur from the drive on the left was an old way down to the Golden Valley and also up to Little Gaddesden. At the spur-point the drive turns sharply to the right up a gentle slope. In the 1940s the buildings on the right were constructed into an emergency hospital. Later they became the Ashridge branch of the Public Record Office until 1980.

Directly ahead stands the formidable structure of Ashridge College, massive and majestic. Its extensive facade of 1,000 feet is the longest of any stately home in England. In the early morning, its silhouette against a blue sky is evocative of an ancient university on a grand scale. At night, graciously illuminated, its tower and spire seem celestial.

The Drive passes the College and winds through Harding's Rookery, passing the turn which would lead to Thunderdell Lodge, and another turn to the Woodyard and to Coldharbour Farm, down a much-photographed avenue of beeches to Berkhamsted Lodge. On the left General de Gaulle resided quietly during the occupation of France, and cellars were reinforced for his safety.

Along the top of the ridge was also a pilgrim's way to Ashridge from Hemel Hempstead. A great chestnut tree of unknown antiquity and made from five saplings planted together was said to be connected with the pilgrims who were to be sheltered from the sun on their journey to the shrine.

Fig. 6. Line drawing of Ashridge College.

The Drive passes down through the Frithsden beeches and then turns right, down to Berkhamsted Castle which had been the home of Edward the Black Prince, who had refounded the College in the 14th century.

The Drive back to Ashridge is a route which pilgrims, visitors and others have worn down over the centuries when this was the main way permitted to the public.

From Ashridge House, Princes Riding stretches through a great avenue of trees to the Bridgewater Monument.

ASHRIDGE HOUSE. ASHRIDGE MANAGEMENT COLLEGE

In the Missenden Cartulary of about 1200 Ashridge appears as Assherugge. There are various later spellings including Asshrigge, Asshrudge, and in 1283-93, Esserugge (also in the patent rolls of 1286). Hrycg meaning a 'ridge' is not uncommon in Hertfordshire and Buckinghamshire. Ashridge does not appear in the Domesday Book.

The present edifice stands on the site of the earlier monastic house. It is in the centre of the great Ashridge Forest and the College owns the 235 acres in which it stands within the Forest. The National Trust owns the surrounding area apart from the Ashridge golf course.

In the closing years of his life the 3rd Duke of Bridgewater, the 'Canal Duke', took up residence at the White Lodge, the former monastic gate house. The central archway had been blocked to make an extra room. From the gatehouse the courtyard of the ancient College stretched across to the north front of the house. Seven lancet windows of the former Refectory were flanked by two projecting wings. The Duke planned a great new mansion; invited James Wyatt to be architect and gathered material together. The remains of the former College were brought to the ground. He died before the foundation stone was laid.

In the same year, 1803, the 7th Earl, the 'Canal Duke's' successor stood before the White Lodge, and in the words of a contemporary, saw the devastation as though an earthquake had taken place. From where he stood he might imagine the mansion which James Wyatt was to build for him, beginning in 1808. Directly in front of the former White Lodge, or perhaps a few yards to the west, would be the new entrance to Ashridge House.

The Grand Entrance. James Wyatt died in a coach accident on the Marlborough Downs in 1813, and his nephew, the future Sir Jeffry Wyatville, was to complete the work. He was responsible for the Grand Entrance. A porte-cochère was planned so that the family and guests could enter the House under cover.

High above the entrance was to be the coat of arms of the 7th Earl impaling those of his wife. Later this would be replaced by the Brownlow coat of arms. On either side of the principal doors were the sculptured heads of Queen Elizabeth I and King Edward VI.

On 14 October 1814, the Earl entered his new home. Like all who walk that way, he saw before him the medieval-style baronial entrance hall. Ahead is the minstrel-type gallery of two storeys. Behind and over the porch is the great north window containing the shields of the Bridgewater and Brownlow families, and above them that of Edmund, Earl of Cornwall. Turning again to face the south gallery, beneath the first storey is the frieze with many shields. Around the east and west walls too are other shields. To the 7th Earl they conveyed a message he wished to pass on to others. To some it would seem that ancestor worship had almost gone beyond control; others who noted the 7th Earl's endeavour to build sound foundations for both house and land considered him a man with a deep sense of responsibility towards his great position.

There were four strands in his ancestry. The first was that he was a loyal Englishman with a devotion to the Tudors. Sir Thomas Egerton, the founder of the family had been Lord Keeper to Queen Elizabeth I, and Lord Chancellor under her successor. Likewise John William chose the anniversary of the coronation of George III for the day of his official entrance into his new home.

Sir Thomas however had done more for his family. He married as his third wife, Alice the widow of Ferdinando the 5th Earl of Derby, daughter of one of the direct ancestors of Lady Diana Spencer. Egerton's son John by an earlier marriage married Frances, Alice's daughter by Lord Derby. The Bridgewaters and the Stanleys were thus united. To the 7th Earl this meant that his family was allied with one of the greatest and oldest families amongst the English aristocracy. The House of Stanley had seen the creation in 1485 of the 1st earldom of Derby, only the Talbots being senior to them, and formerly the Kents (1465).

More than this, Ferdinando, Earl of Derby was said to have had a claim to the throne of England. This was through the marriage of the daughter of Eleanor, grand-daughter of Henry VII, to Henry the 4th Earl of Derby, and thus the ancestor of the Bridgewaters. Indeed it was rumoured that traitors sought to persuade Ferdinando to rise against Elizabeth. He vigorously refused, and the result was said to be that his terrible death by poisoning was the work of the disillusioned traitors.

The coat of arms of Henry VII is therefore in the centre of the south wall opposite the main entrance. It is flanked by the shields of the Houses of York and Lancaster.

The second strand is marked so that along the east wall (to the left of the main entrance as one enters) are shields of the Stanley family. Amongst them is the shield of the Lord of Man, showing the three legs of the Isle of Man. During the lifetime of the 5th Earl of Derby, the earls of the House of Stanley were Lords of Man, and the wife of Sir Thomas Egerton was one of the three heiresses of that Lordship.

The third strand on the west wall, to the right as one enters, are shields of the 7th Earl's family on his maternal side. These were of the Grey and De Grey family, the earls and dukes of Kent. Their earldom went back to 1465 but was extinct by John William's day. Nevertheless this was his mother's ancestry.

The fourth strand was ecclesiatical. His father was the Bishop of Durham and his grandfather Bishop of Hereford. Another ancestor had been Archbishop of York. The Hereford connection is of interest for the shrine of Thomas de Cantelupe in Hereford Cathedral was the shrine of a former Bonhomme whose heart had been kept in the shrine at Ashridge.

These four strands played their part in the heraldry and indeed the building of the House and Chapel.

On the corbels in the ceiling are the shields of the earls of Bridgewater and the bishops of Hereford and Durham. Above them all as they looked down on their forebears below, and almost at the apex of the south wall, is the coat of arms of the College of the Bonhommes — the lamb and flag upon the altar.

So John William, 7th Earl of Bridgewater, was to build a mansion in which his ancestors, especially those of the Tudor period, could be recalled. Tudor portcullises, roses, crowns and coronets, fan vaulting, and work done by men renowned for their contributions to Windsor and Westminster would inspire future generations.

The Ashridge Entrance Hall with its reception desk and porter's desk, today fulfils the functions that the occupants of the monastic gatehouse used to perform. They bring us up-to-date however in recognising that romantic notions of the past should be kept in their place.

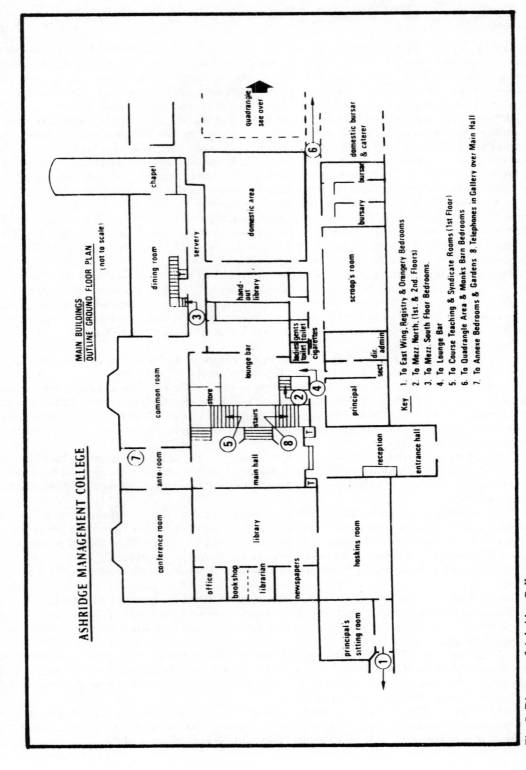

Fig. 7 Diagram of Ashridge College.

Over the mantelpiece is the sculptured head of Andrew Bonar Law, former prime minister. In his honour Urban Hanlon Broughton in 1928 established the modern College of Ashridge. Until 1939 it was a College of Citizenship. During the Second World War it was an emergency hospital. From 1947-58 it was again a College of Citizenship. Its political affiliation with the Conservative Party was ended in 1954 when the original trust deed was amended.

In 1959 the Ashridge Management College was established. Its first 20 years were remarkable for the steady increase in its influence and reputation, and for the number of managers attending courses of various length, covering all aspects of management. Managers from abroad form a growing percentage of course members. Staff members conduct courses in many parts of the world and are regularly seconded to firms requiring expert advice in particular situations. Research work conducted by the College has included projects on behalf of government, industrial and commercial sponsors.

Passing from the Entrance Hall one enters *The Great Hall*. This lies beneath the central tower which is 100 feet high. The weather vane has an interior dial to show the direction of the wind outside. In the 19th and 20th centuries national figures attended balls and banquets in this Hall. Local people recall the 60 feet high Christmas trees laden with presents for estate workers and staff, and the carols sung here, as they are still at the College Christmas Party.

On the main staircase are statues by Sir Richard Westmacott. At the first stage is one of King Edward VI who spent time at Ashridge when he was a young prince. At the level above is a statue of Edmund, Earl of Cornwall founder in 1276-83 of the College of Bonhommes. Here too are statues of his parents, Richard, Earl of Cornwall and Sanchia of Provence.

St Benedict of Nursia (480-550) Founder of Western Monasticism is represented. Richard of Watford, first Rector of Ashridge and one of his brothers is here. St Thomas de Cantelupe, the one canonised member of the community, is also depicted.

Edward the Black Prince who refounded the monastery in 1376 is recalled not only by his statue, but also on the east wall facing the staircase. A replica of his sword has been placed there, the original of which hangs above his tomb in Canterbury Cathedral. He was remembered for his affection for 'our house at Ashridge', and for his will in which he left a table encrusted with precious stones and with gold and silver to the College Chapel. He was remembered for his victories at Crécy and Poitiers. At Crécy he had Richard of Gaddesden as of one his archers. Did the jewellery come from his plunderings in France?

The staircase today leads to the studies of the academic staff, to the offices of their secretaries, to syndicate rooms and lecture rooms, to rooms equipped for internal television and visual aid demonstrations, computer terminals and the offices of the financial and accountancy staffs, together with the centre for illustrative printing, and the word-processing office.

According to one theory the Great Hall here was built (see page 45) within the area of the monastic cloisters. Just as the work of that College radiated from the cloisters, so today radiating from this centre are the different specialised areas of college work.

The College Library. Just as the chapter house was on the east side of the cloisters, so the Library is entered from the door in the east wall. Here one of the foremost business management libraries in the United Kingdom is growing. It contains a comprehensive periodical room, a small bookshop, an enquiry centre, catalogues and the library administrative office. Elsewhere in the building are book-stacks and past periodicals. Cabinet documents from the time that Viscount Watkinson P.C., C.H., was a member of the government have been presented after the appropriate clearances, by a president of the governing body. These could form the nucleus of a very important collection and a specialised section of the Library. The College 'Prestel' centre is here also.

This Library is the descendant of one of the great private libraries of former days. The Egerton and Ellesmere Manuscripts in the British Library came from Ashridge. Of the manuscripts of the former College of the Bonhommes only about a dozen are now known to exist. Todd gives the size of the Library of the College as 33 feet by 23 feet. It could therefore have held many manuscripts. Amongst these is one known and used by Todd and partly included in his 'History of the College'. It contains the Kalendar, Martyrology and Consuetudines (customs) of the College. The Kalendar gives 22 October as the Dedication Festival.

When the Black Prince re-endowed the College in the 14th century, and spent time there, he probably brought manuscripts and other treasures which he had obtained in his wars in France, and especially from around Poitiers which he devastated. The Martyrology may have had its origin in Poitiers, and Miss Eleanor Searle suggests that this was likely and that it had a 9th century origin (*The Calendar and Martyrology of the College of the Boni Homines*).

On the death of the 3rd Earl Brownlow the Huntington Library of California acquired the Kalendar and Martyrology and has encouraged careful study of the manuscripts. The importance of the position of Librarian at Ashridge in the 19th century was shown by the appointment of the Rev H.J. Todd, Librarian here, to be Librarian to the Archbishop of Canterbury at Lambeth Palace. He was the historian of Ashridge.

Pictures of Ashridge, mainly of the 18th century, grace the Library walls. The most important document of historical concern is the conveyance of Ashridge to Richard Combes of Hemel Hempstead by Queen Elizabeth I, whose actual signature is on the document.

The ceiling is the work of Matthew Digby Wyatt (1860). It is similar to his work in the Ante-room and in the Saloon it reaches its zenith.

The door from the Hall into the Library has, on the Library side rows of imitation books, providing a 'secret' entrance, and continuing the book shelves. The subjects inscribed on the spines are amusingly chosen:
'Secret History of Cabinets', 'Ashe's Dictionary', 'Beeche's Voyages', 'Carpenters Works', 'Reports of Various Boards', 'Life of Marcus Plancus', 'Locke on the Understanding', 'Uses of Lignum Vitae', 'Essays on Plane Dealing', 'Bois Secret'.

The Hoskins Room. This room adjoins the Library. The ceiling and the exquisite plaster-work on the walls and the three columns were done by Matthew Digby Wyatt in about 1860. The designs deserve careful study. Intertwined above two bookcases are monograms of Lady Marian Alford. The delicate tracery, including Adam and Eve in the Garden of Eden, resembles other work by Digby Wyatt. In 1852-54 he was responsible for Paddington Station, London. Intricate craftsmanship may still be seen there, not only in the remarkable roof and columnar supports, but also in wall decorations, such as the station-master's oriel window.

The Italian fireplace has the figure of an unknown woman in the style of Della Robbia and is dated 1858. It was carved in Milan by G. Pandiani, and it may have been at one time in a cemetery there. The poetic inscription is from sonnet number 248 of the 'Canzoniere of Francesco di Petracco (Petrarch) 1304-74. It was written in honour of Laura the woman he loved, who died of the plague on 6 April 1348. Lovers of all ages have found inspiration in Petrarch's sonnets and his ideal in Laura. He was the inaugurator of the Renaissance in Italy, and used the pure Tuscan idiom in poems such as this one. 'Chi vuol veder quantunque puo natura e il ciel tra noi venga a mirar costei', 'Who desires to know what nature and heaven can do amongst us should come to admire this lady'.

Lord Fairhaven presented the stately coffer on the reopening of Ashridge College on 3 January 1947 after it had been a hospital during the Second World War.

Adjoining the fireplace is the picture by Sir Frank W. Salisbury entitled 'The heart of the Empire'. He took the title from the opening words of the service in St Paul's Cathedral on the occasion of the Silver Jubilee of King George V, 1935. The King said to the Archbishop of Canterbury that he was surprised at the manifestation of national feeling, adding 'After all I am just an ordinary sort of fellow'. Each member of the royal family gave Salisbury private sittings in order that their pictures should be accurate. The future Edward VIII did not want to be portrayed in uniform nor to have the right side of his face showing, but he relented. Lloyd George told

Salisbury that the best portraits were those of the Prime Minister (Ramsay Macdonald) and Sir John Simon. Salisbury noted that this was a perceptive observation as these two were the only ones who had sat twice for their portrait. At the time in the service here portrayed the Archbishop of Canterbury was in the sanctuary, but as the picture would have been incomplete without him, Salisbury painted his head on to the figure of the Bishop of London. Lloyd George said that Winston Churchill had not been included and 'as he will go down in history for his writing, if for nothing else' he was added in the front row. King George V, for whom Salisbury requested the honour of painting the picture, never saw the complete work.

The room takes its name from the portrait of Major-General Sir Reginald Hoskins, the first Principal of the College. It is the work of Oswald Birley. Sir Reginald was buried in Little Gaddesden churchyard in 1942. In Brownlow days this was the billiards room.

Receptions and small dinner parties are held in this room at the conclusion of College courses.
The Principal's Sitting-room. The Principal's Sitting-room also serves for small receptions, for official guests, for syndicate meetings and for interviews by the chaplain and others. It was Dr Macrae's study, when he was Principal.

This was the first of the family rooms in the east wing. Designated for the lady's maid under Charlotte Catherine Anne, Countess of Bridgewater, it later became the boudoir of Adelaide Countess Brownlow. Her husband, the 3rd Earl Brownlow was interested in carving and he designed this room and the private staircase with its decorated rails which led from one corner of the room to the corridor above. He also designed the angle monograms and the ceiling of the bow-window. This has the Brownlow coat of arms surrounded by Bridgewater and Brownlow mottoes inscribed very precisely in the plaster work. This was his own work. The mottoes were—
NIHIL HUMANI ALIENUM   SIC DONEC   ESSE QUAM VIDERI
OPERA ILLIUS MEA SUNT   TECUM SALUS (See the Gazetteer, p. 127)

In the cabinet is a Baron Brownlow plate. On the walls are hunting scenes, a pair of Arundel prints and 18th-century pictures of Ashridge. The original fireplace was covered with panelling in the 1970s. This room overlooks the Italian Garden.
The Principal's Study. A connecting door joins the two rooms. This room was formerly a family bedroom. The fireplace is of interest. The white tiles have pale-green petals thickly embossed. On both sides at the top is a soldier standing with weapon drawn above a fallen enemy. Several of these tiles have found their way into Little Gaddesden homes. Sir Matthew Digby Wyatt (1820-77) who was responsible for much interior decorating at Ashridge in 1860, designed tiles for the famous Maw and Company of Jackfield, Shropshire. These may be his work. The carved chimney-piece was the work of the Little Gaddesden Carving Class and was to commemorate Queen Victoria's Jubilee. The date is carved, 1887, together with the initials ASC intertwined. The A could stand for Adelbert or Adelaide and the C for Cust. The plan states that the chimney-piece was 'to be fixed in Queen Elizabeth's dressing room in Ashridge Mansion'. Opposite to this room, across the corridor is the Principal's Secretary's office, formerly a syndicate room. This was the first of the suite of rooms occupied by Lord Bridgewater and later by Lord Brownlow, incorporating a study, bedroom and bathroom. The present Registry was the former study of Lord Bridgewater and the private sitting-room of Lord Brownlow. The wall cabinets in the Registry used to be in the present Conference Room opposite. That room with its splendid view of the gardens was Lady Bridgewater's room, then a sitting-room in Brownlow days. It became the Principal's Dining-room, and then the Senior Common Room until 1981.

The stairs from this corridor from a door adjoining the syndicate room lead to the upper corridor with its staff-rooms, all having magnificent views of the lawns and gardens. The stairs leading downwards towards the former cellars now go to reconditioned rooms adapted to library stacks, auxiliary studies and storage rooms.
The Orangery. The whole of this block 130 feet long was designed by Sir Jeffry Wyatville after the main house had been completed. It was intended as private apartments for the family. Over the

north door is a stained glass window portraying St Barbara. The remainder of the Orangery is used for staff and student rooms.

Various reasons have been given for the angle at which the Orangery was built. One such conjecture is — if the College Chapel was on the north side of the Cloisters (see page 45) the east end of the Chapel and the College cemetery which adjoined it would have been in the area now between the Orangery, the Italian Garden and the Yew trees. There could have been reluctance to build on the site of the former sanctuary and cemetery.

The Public Rooms Of The College. The public rooms each have their own magnificence. They are all along the south facing front of the building.

The Conference room or *The Drawing-room*. Used by the College for many years as a conference room this was the principal drawing-room (saloon) of the House in which the Alfords and Brownlows, following the Bridgewaters, entertained their distinguished visitors. Lady Marian Alford, daughter of the Marquess of Northampton, and whose mother was said to be one of the most intelligent peeresses in the realm, entertained with scintillating conversation the many guests whose names represent the leaders of politics, the arts, the armed services and the church. Her daughter-in-law, Lady Brownlow, entertained royalty in this room. It was a women's ward during World War Two, and 3,000 babies were born in Ashridge during that period.

The ceiling is a copy of Guido Reni's *Aurora* in the Palazzo Rospigliosi in Rome. This famous fresco, full of grace and dignity, is the work of the artist who was Gran Maestro of the School of Bologna. Born in 1575 he went to Rome in 1602 and remained there for 20 years. He died in 1642 one of the most admired artists of the 17th century. The Rospigliosi Palace was built on the Via Nationale in 1603, the year after Reni's arrival in Rome, for Cardinal Scipio Borghesi.

The fireplaces are modelled on those in the Doge's Palace at Venice. The mantelpieces are carved in the style of Vincenzo Scamozzi (1552-1616) of Vicenza whose drawings were used in the Ducal Palace at Venice for Tiziano Aspetti to engrave for the Hall of the Ante-College. Scamozzi was responsible for the richly ornamented door opening into the 'College' room of the Palace. His three statues there are inspired by Michelangelo. Thus the Conference Room fireplaces are in a distinguished succession. The four figures supporting the fireplaces were carved from life. Two of the figures were from Ringshall and two from Little Gaddesden, all being chosen as the finest men on the estate. They were Garrett and Fountain from Ringshall, and Stephen Temple and Cains the blacksmith from Little Gaddesden. Local tradition has it that three of the figures were meant to represent men from the colonies, and the other to represent an Englishman. The Englishman (third from the right) was Fountain. His superiority was said to be shown by the fact that he was able to support the mantelpiece at his end with only one arm.

The Brownlow coat of arms can be seen in the firebacks, and 'EB' for Earl Brownlow may be seen in the ceiling angles. Elsewhere in the House the intertwined 'AA' stands for Adelbert and Adelaide, the 3rd Earl Brownlow and his Lady. Such inscriptions denote Brownlow additions to the House.

The wallpaper used for this room, before the present paper, was specially prepared for the visit of the Shah of Persia. It was said to contain gold-leaf and to have cost £200-£300 per roll.

The marble pillars at the entrance door to the Ante-room are magnificent. Matthew Digby Wyatt's work of 1860 endures.

The Ante-room.

This room is favoured by students and staff as a quiet room for relaxation. The portrait by Oswald Birley, of the founder of the College bears the inscription—

URBAN HANLON BROUGHTON
THE DONOR OF ASHRIDGE 1929
BORN APRIL 12th 1857
MEMBER OF PARLIAMENT FOR PRESTON 1915-1918
DIED JANUARY 30th 1929
GIVEN BY HIS WIDOW June 8th 1937

To the right are french windows. From the Ante-room across the terrace there are steps to the croquet lawn much used by students after luncheon on summer days.

On the left may be seen an oak said to have been planted by Queen Victoria in 1823. The view ahead is of a magnificent avenue of Wellingtonias. The *Sesquoidendron giganteum* was introduced to this country as recently as 1853. By 1930 it was the loftiest tree in almost every county. The nearest to Ashridge with a known date is that in Wrest Park, Bedfordshire, planted in 1856. By 1977 it had reached a height of 37 metres. They are believed to have originated in California. Beneath these trees at Ashridge is the avenue of rhododendrons, the joy of management course members and visitors in the month of June. The azaleas in the adjoining beds provide a gloriously colourful display when in full bloom.

At the end of the avenue, said to be one of the longest in England, is a circle of incense cedars which centre on a marble bible. This had a special association for Lady Brownlow, for she kept it as a grove held dear in memory of her sister, the Countess of Pembroke.

The Ante-room is a pivot of the College as it was in the past.

THE FORMER MONASTIC BUILDINGS

Beneath the Ante-room, and extending to the Brown Lounge and the Conference Room is the Undercroft of the College of the Bonhommes. Above the Undercroft was the Frater or Refectory. In a normal lay-out of a religious house the frater would be on one side of the cloisters and the chapel on the opposite one. The chapel would be aligned east-west, with the altar at the (ecclesiastical) east.

The Cloisters were 40 feet square with passageways 11 feet wide. There was a pond in the centre of the cloister garth. The Dormitory was on the east side, and the steps led down the night stairs into the Chapel. The Chapter House was below the Dormitory, and with the Library and the Sacristy it was on the east side of the Cloisters. The cellarer's block was on the west side of the Cloisters. There was probably a parlour on that side also. There was an Infirmarium east of the main blocks and adjoining the College cemetery.

The question still to be finally investigated is whether the Chapel was on the north or south side of the cloisters.

Todd quotes earlier authorities in saying that the visitor crossed from the entrance lodge to the main building in which was the Hall with its gallery, the Screens, and the pantry, and with a passage between the Hall and the Screens. One then could go into the Cloisters which were decorated with New Testament frescoes. The Chapel 'ranged' with the Cloisters. This could make it appear that the Chapel was on the south side of the Cloisters, and thus to be on the site of the croquet lawn area.

On the other hand if the Chapel were on the north side of the Cloisters (a siting which was more common) the Cloisters would have been on the site of the present Great Hall, and the Chapel would have been across the Entrance Hall, from west to east.

The original Wyatt drawings give a measurement of 68 feet from the present terrace to a building to the south 72 feet long, but with the east end bearing the word chapel and the west end having the words laundry and wash house. This does not give proof that this chapel was the original monastic chapel. It could well have been the later chapel of 1699 of the 3rd Earl of Bridgewater.

Whichever of the alternatives is correct, the Library, Dormitory and Chapter House would have been on the east side of the Cloisters.

The vastness of the Wyatt House would make the College of the Bonhommes look very small. H.J. Todd (see page 45) quotes measurements. The Chapel had its chancel which was 81 feet long by 32 feet wide; the nave was 51 feet by 32 feet. The tower was 30 feet square. Two chapels are recorded, St Mary's and St John's and both were 51 feet by 21 feet. The north and south aisles were 26 feet by 32 feet.

The Undercroft was 81 feet by 25 feet; the Chapter House and Library were both 33 feet by 23 feet; the Dormitory was 108 feet by 34 feet; the Refectory was 72 feet by 25 feet; and the White Lodge was 62 feet long.

It would have been necessary for the Shrine to have a processional area around it. The normal situation as at St Albans was that the shrine would be to the east of the high altar, and then the Lady Chapel to be to the east of that. This would mean that the Chapel would have extended a further 51 feet to the east. St John's Chapel could have been alongside the chancel.

The Brown Lounge. This is the main common room of the College, and day-by-day it is the meeting place for staff, course members, visiting lecturers and other guests. It is used for receptions and here at the beginning of their courses, members meet the staff and their wives for the first time.

The Brown Lounge was the original dining-room of the House. The panelling is said to be of Austrian walnut, and some was formerly in the Tuileries in Paris. The ceiling is inspired by that of the Casa d'Oro in Venice, a favourite haunt of the Brownlow family. It depicts the fruits of the earth. Much of it had to be replaced after a fire. Sansovino designed the original in the Casa d'Oro as one of the most sumptuous of the Venetian monuments of the 16th century. It gives theatrical effect to the power of the republic of Venice. Beneath the ceiling the Doge and his visitors passed on the way to the official ceremonies in the Great Hall. The original ceiling was decorated by Scarpagnino who was Master of Works under the Doges Andre Gritti (1523-38) and Francesco Veniero (1554-56). Made in gold and plaster it is semi-circular over the staircase, whilst the Ashridge ceiling is flat. Thus Scarpagnino's work is recalled here.

The portrait over the fireplace is of Scroop the 1st Duke of Bridgewater. In 1701 he became the 4th Earl, his two older brothers having been burned to death in a fire at Bridgewater House, London. Their valet slept when the curtains caught fire. They were buried in Little Gaddesden church. Scroop married firstly Elizabeth, daughter of John, Duke of Marlborough, in 1702, the year he became duke. She was only 15, and daughter of the lovely Sarah Jennings, formerly of St Albans. Elizabeth died of smallpox in 1713, as did her son four years later while at Eton College. Scroop then married the eldest daughter of Wriothesley, 2nd Duke of Bedford, the year after Scroop was said to have made a million pounds by selling before the South Sea Bubble burst. Anne, his daughter by Elizabeth fell in love with Wriothesley the 3rd Duke of Bedford. Scroop was not persona grata with the young couple who fled from Ashridge to Woburn at 5 a.m. on the morning after their marriage on 22 April 1725. Wriothesley died in 1732, and within eight months Anne had married the Earl of Jersey.

Scroop died on 11 January 1743/4 and was buried in Little Gaddesden church, wrapped in linen, beside all the other members of his family. He was the father of the 'Canal Duke'.

From this room the guests at the House would move to the terraces in the summer after their evening meal was over. One great occasion was in 1889 when the Shah of Persia paid his visit. After the banquet all the guests assembled on the terraces looking out on the lawns. The trees were illuminated with fairy lights and the College battlements were specially lit up. The people of Little Gaddesden and the estate workers were assembled on the lawns. Many members of noble families were quickly recognised by the watching folk.

During World War Two the Brown Lounge was the men's ward of the Ashridge Hospital.

The Dining Hall. The College caters for students in different areas, according to their needs. Light meals are served in the bar which stands between the north and south facades of the College. On the north front is the Scroop Room while on the south front stands the main Dining Hall. it is the scene of many special dinners including those of the Ashridge Association, and the Christmas banquet for the staff, as well as the end-of-course dinners.

This room was originally the Conservatory of the College, leading to the Chapel. Clough Williams-Ellis was architect for the development whereby the south wall was built, enclosing the former Conservatory, to create the present Dining Hall.

At the point where the Brown Lounge and the Dining-room meet, a local story tells that Queen Mary was once seated. When asked about what she would like, she said that she favoured red currants with cream (the currants from the Ashridge gardens) more than anything else.

The domestic offices lie between the north and south of the College.

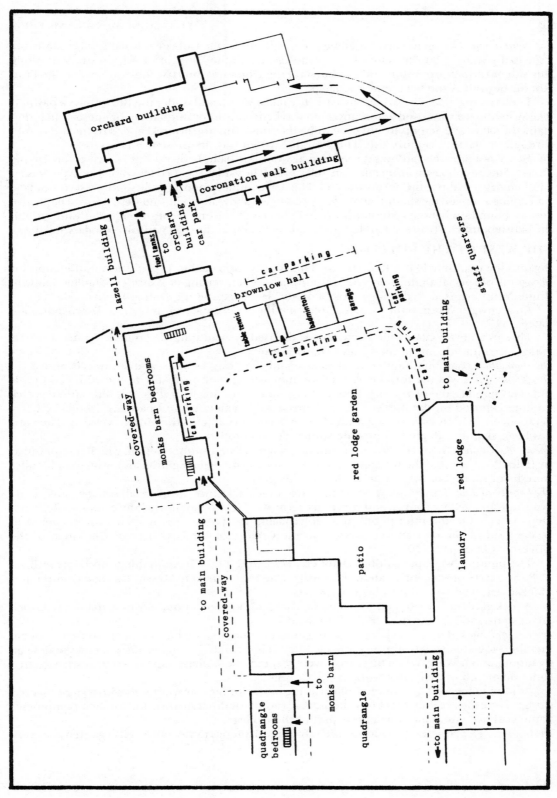

Fig. 8 Ashridge College : plan of west side.

The North Front. The main corridor along the north side of the College housed until recently the Principal's Study (now the Senior Common Room) and the Director of Administration. Along this side is the Scroop Room and the Bursary, the Domestic Bursary, the Surgery and the Print Room. Beyond is the telephone exchange.

The Principal's *former study* was an early breakfast room, and under the Brownlows a parlour. The switchboard room and adjoining room was bedroom accommodation for guests who found stairs difficult. The Scroop Room used to be the still-room, the housekeeper's room and a store throughout its 19th-century use. The Steward's room was the present Bursary.

The Yard For a time the yard was turned into a swimming bath. Earlier it was known as the 'Drying Green'. Square cobbles of former days are still visible. The yard is enclosed by a monastic-type cloister. The laundry remains at the north-west end. The staff common room is at the south-west end and the staff dining-room on the south side. Students' rooms are above the south and west rooms. The ancient county boundary between Hertfordshire and Buckinghamshire went through the yard, as also the parish boundary between Berkhamsted and Nettleden (as the ecclesiastical boundary still does).

THE WEST OF THE COLLEGE

Beyond the quadrangle lies Red House. This is now furnished to provide accommodation for occasions of special significance and importance. When staying at Ashridge, Stanley Baldwin, Prime Minister, used Red Lodge. His bedroom later became the Dining-room.

An archway leads into the former stables and the ancillary accommodation. Downspouts are dated 1817.

This area now contains the Brownlow Hall, used for badminton and table tennis. There is garage accommodation in the former coach house.

The Coronation Walk buildings contain lecture and syndicate facilities and study bedrooms.

The Monks' Barn was the former barn of the monastery, built probably in the 15th century. It indicates stability and prosperity. This timber-framed building with close studding and red brick infilling exposed on the north side, was considerably extended and partially rebuilt by Jeffry Wyatville in 1816. A covered way with cloister-like pillars adjoins the Monks' Garden. The barn has been skilfully adapted to provide student accommodation.

The Monks' Garden. In the centre is the fountain designed by Humphry Repton which was modified by Jeffry Wyatville and the Bridgewaters. The coats of arms of the Egerton and Brownlow families were incorporated in the design of the box hedges.

The Lazell Building. This building contains a large modern lecture theatre, staff study rooms, many syndicate and lecture rooms, and computer terminals. It also has housed the extensive Research Department. On the inscription on a tablet facing the entrance is written— 'It is named in recognition of the outstanding services to the College of Mr H.G. Lazell, Chairman of the Governors from 1963-70'.

The building was opened on 6 October 1972 by the Right Honourable John Davis M.B.E., M.P., Secretary of State for Trade and Industry. The architects were Messrs. Carden, Godfrey and MacFadyen, who were the College architects.

A rock garden, lawn and pond, set in the background of older outhouses in mature red brick are an outstanding design by Malcolm Lingard.

The Orchard Block. This is the latest building and it contains study bedrooms to house 64 course members together with common room facilities. It is separated from the main part of the College by Liquidambar Walk. When these trees were planted, the College staff placed beneath each tree some memento of their own work in the College.

Adjoining the west area of the College is the bothy for the transport staff with a large covered garage. Here too are the workshops and storage rooms for the craftsmen and for their equipment. Some staff accommodation is in this part of the College.

The Gardens. The 90 acres provide innumerable opportunities to view an English garden at its very best, with extensive lawns, well-trimmed hedges, shrubberies, flower-beds, rose-beds, rockeries, elegant walks, avenues and stately trees.

The variety of the College gardens with the Ice House, the grotto, the tunnel, the moat, the conservatory, together with the private corners and hidden nooks provide an ever interesting and imaginative source of wonder and surprise. The collection of Hertfordshire pudding-stone is said to be the largest collection known.

'Capability' Brown made his contribution to Ashridge in the 18th century as Humphry Repton did in the 19th century. The Paxton family of Chatsworth and Crystal Palace fame had their relatives at Ashridge at the end of the 19th century. Humphrey Talbot was deeply concerned after the death of the 3rd Earl Brownlow that the gardens should not be neglected. Nevertheless after the sale of the Estate and the upset of the war years it has been a great achievement to preserve the beauty of the gardens. Malcolm Lingard's contribution towards this end should be mentioned; his work takes its place alongside that of the other distinguished landscape artists who have worked at Ashridge.

The Sunken Rose Garden. This garden which used to be a skating pond is on the site of the former fish-pond of the monastic College. The inscription on the south wall reads:

> This Garden is Dedicated to the Memory of HUGH BEAVER Knight Commander of the British Empire Doctor of Laws Chairman of the Governors of Ashridge Management College 1959-1963.

The main College drain would probably have passed along the south side of the frater and reredorter, and then across in a south-easterly direction towards the pond.

The gardens are to the south of the College. The Italian Garden to the east was created about 1900. Its fountain is a feature of this area which also contains old yew trees which·may descend from the ones of monastic days. The earlier boundary to the east was marked by Lime Avenue. The boundary to the west has the Liquidambar walk. In that area is the Repton-designed Monk's Garden and Rosarie. There is also the limestone Rock Garden adjoining the Lazell Building, designed in 1973 by Malcolm Lingard. The Fernery was designed about the time of World War One. Other features are the grotto and tunnel, the conservatory and garden and small rock gardens. The moat forms the boundary between the gardens and the great avenue of Wellingtonias, with rhododendrons at their base. The avenue on the west side has the arboretum. To the east is the rose garden, and in the former fish pond, the sunken rose garden. The Bible Circle is of incense cedars.

RECTORS OF ASHRIDGE

1. 1276 Ricardus de Watford
2. 1298 Willielmus de Harwold
3. 1335 Ricardus de Sarret
4. 1346 Gilbertus de Bowelles
5. 1353 Willielmus (In 1368 Simon de Wederowe de Tring, one of the Ashridge Brethren was a scribe of consummate skill, working in the Scriptorium)
6. 1373 Radulfus de Aston. In 1376 the Black Prince refounded the College.
7. 1396 Johannes de Trenge
8. Johannes
9. Abel
10. 1428 Robertus
11. 1435 Johannes Awedelee (occurs 1452)
12. Johannes Whytton
13. Radulfus
14. Johannes de Berkhamsted. resigned 1521
15. 1521 Johannes Malden

16. 1529 Thomas Waterhouse, the last rector.
     1539 The Dissolution.
The House was in royal hands until finally it was purchased by Sir Thomas Egerton, Baron
Ellesmere in 1604.
1604-1849 The Earls and Dukes of Bridgewater
1849-53 The Alford Family
1853-1921 The Earls Brownlow
1929 Ashridge College

THE PRINCIPALS OF THE COLLEGE
1929 Major General Sir Reginald Hoskins K.C.B., C.M.G., D.S.O.
1937 E.J. Patterson M.A.
1946 General Sir Bernard Paget G.C.B., D.S.O., M.C.
1949 Admiral Sir Denis Boyd K.C.B., C.B.E., D.S.C.
1958 Major-General E.N.K. Estcourt O.B.E., D.S.O.
1963 Christopher Macrae C.B.E., D. Phil., C.B.I.M.
1969 Philip Sadler C.B.I.M.

ASHRIDGE COURSES
Ashridge Business Management College is now one of the largest institutions of its kind in the
world. In the early 1980s over four thousand managers a year participated in courses, and came
from over nine hundred organisations in industry, commerce, the service industries and the
public sector. Fourteen per cent of course members were from overseas. The Principal, Philip
Sadler expressed his three main aims as being—
1. To provide development programmes for experienced managers. To design special
programmes for particular organisations and industries.
2. To assess present and future needs in management development in co-operation with
organisations served by the College.
3. To conduct research in order to improve the practice of management, and make the results
widely known.
Members of staff conduct courses in different parts of the world. There are also courses specially
designed for client organisations, together with a range of services for management including
training-need analysis and methods of applied research.
    The general plan is to provide courses for each different stage in a manager's career.
GENERAL MANAGEMENT COURSES — The Introduction to Management Course is a week
long course for those who have recently become managers.
    The Younger Managers Course is for people with at least two years experience in
management. Detailed attention is given to developing personal skills. This is a three week
course.
    The Management Development Programme is for middle managers and deals with finance,
marketing, management science, industrial relations, man-management, and the inter-
relationship between these functions.
    The Senior Management Programme is concerned with strategic management, and concentrates
on the environment in which the senior manager has to operate. The course lasts 3 weeks.
    Managing the Retail Process. This course caters for the development needs of district
managers in the retail industry. The course lasts one week.
    The Corporate Strategy for Directors Course. An intensive programme for board level
executives to think through issues of corporate planning in company with their peers.
ORGANISATIONAL BEHAVIOUR COURSES
    Managing people   Counselling & Appraisal skills for Managers
    Interpersonal skills   7 Day Leadership Development Programme

INDUSTRIAL RELATIONS & PERSONNEL MANAGEMENT COURSES

Industrial Relations — Negotiating skills

Personnel Management — Employee Relations skills

MARKETING AND SALES MANAGEMENT COURSES

Introduction to Marketing — Field Sales Management

Marketing Management — Sales Management

International Marketing — Brand Managers Development Programme

Microcomputers and Marketing — Strategic Public Relations

FINANCE AND MANAGEMENT ACCOUNTING COURSES

Financial Knowledge for Managers — Modern Management Accounting

Financial Knowledge for Managers (Follow up) — Financial Knowledge for Directors

Additional courses added in 1982/3 included—

"Performance through People"

"Effective Teamwork skills"

"Using Microcomputers in Decision Making".

Video-films for in-company training are now being produced.

Tailor-made and Special Services. Ashridge College not only runs courses but also provides specialised services which include organisation analysis, training needs analysis, business policy seminars, career development and counselling services, financial modelling, refresher courses and conference facilities. Management research results in contributions to technical journals, and the production of reports, booklets and books. Services are always being added and developed.

More frequently, specially tailored courses for the requirements of specific organisations or groups are being designed. The courses are constantly being re-adapted and developed to include new management techniques. They range from one day to four weeks, with some courses being separated in stages between the first sessions and the later ones.

Ashridge College Association. This is for course members who wish to continue their association with the College. There are monthly dinners throughout winter when distinguished speakers are invited. Visits of a social and educational nature are arranged, and there is a summer barbecue for members and their families.

The Constitution. The College is an independent educational trust which is exercised under the Ashridge (Bonar Law Memorial) Trust. The trustees are the College Governors. The Chairman is Sir John Hedley Greenborough K.B.E. The Governors are appointed from business and public life and include the heads of nationalised industries, senior civil servants, and executives of major British and multi-national companies, and universities.

Academic Staff. There are over forty academic staff together with visiting lecturers. Staff members take on consultancy work, and have sabbatical leave and further development opportunities.

College Chapel. College Services are held each Wednesday morning during term before lectures. Occasional offices for members of the College staff and their families take place throughout the year. The Chapel is always open, and the chaplain available. Organ recitals take place from time to time, and there are visits such as that by the International Organ Festival from St Albans Cathedral.

BRITISH TRANSPORT STAFF COLLEGE

The Staff College at Woking has been transferred to Ashridge and it is planned to establish an international centre for Transport Management Development to include research as well as courses. Transport Management Courses for Senior Managers and for General Management are now held lasting nine weeks and four weeks respectively.

The Ashridge Wartime Hospital

During World War Two Ashridge housed patients from London's University College and Charing Cross Hospitals. There were 16 wards each containing 40 beds. In the House there was a men's ward in the Brown Lounge and a women's ward in the former Drawing-room. The main hospital which included an operating theatre was built in 1940 to the north of the House and occupied the later Public Record Office area. Five hundred men from Dunkirk were sent here. In total there were 20,000 patients, 12,820 operations performed and 3,000 babies born in the House.

The 51st Highland Division and the 11th Hussars were stationed at Ashridge.

The Emergency Training College

From 1946-51 the former hospital buildings became a Teachers' Training College where men were first trained. After 1947 women were also admitted. During this period 270 teachers graduated and the teaching staff numbered twenty-one.

The Public Record Office

The P.R.O. took over the buildings in 1951 and in September of that year the first documents arrived. Many students used the facilities for research provided for them by a very helpful staff. The records were moved to the new P.R.O. at Kew in 1978-79.

Ashridge Park Estate

During the time when the Ashridge Estate was being sold there were plans for new roads to be made. One of these would have resulted in Ashridge College being surrounded by roads and many houses. The road planned was to start from the Rookery, north-east of the College, at the point where the drive from the College opens up to the Golden Valley and the golf course. The road would have gone along the Golden Valley side of the College, and then in a great arc to emerge near the footpath by Berkhamsted Lodge. A spur from this road was projected to go possibly along the top of the ridge above Berkhamsted Lodge and running parallel with the road to Berkhamsted for about seven hundred yards until it turned sharply in a north-easterly direction through Webb's Copse, and then south-east above Nettleden Lodge towards Lady's Mile.

There was building land available on both sides of this spur and also on the Ashridge perimeter to the south-east of the proposed circular road as well as on the lane from Thunderdell Lodge. What is now Golf Club Road was projected to run down to Little Gaddesden-Ashridge College Drive. The Plots for sale were all of considerable size. The affairs were conducted from the Little Gaddesden Estate Office which was at 18, Little Gaddesden.

The measure of the achievement of Miss Bridget Talbot and her fellow workers in preventing this is realised when the plans above are examined.

5.   *The Ashridge College Chapels*

The original College of the Bonhommes was founded in honour of the Sacred Blood of Christ, in the years 1277-83. It was dedicated in 1286, by the Bishop of Lincoln, Oliver Sutton, in whose diocese the College was situated. The College Chapel was the centre of this establishment being the first of the two houses in England of the order of the Bonhommes; the other was founded at Edington in Wiltshire as a daughter-house of Ashridge. The number of brothers was small, and the maximum provided for at the foundation was 20 of whom seven or 13 were to be priests, although it is unlikely that that number was in fact reached at that time. The order was to be organised, and the worship of the Chapel conducted, according to the Augustinian rule. The statutes show that the normal daily pattern of worship was to be observed: matins and lauds (midnight); prime (6 a.m.); terce (9 a.m.); sext (noon); nones (3 p.m.); vespers (6 p.m.); and compline (9 p.m.). The Eucharist was celebrated according to the calendar, and founders and benefactors of the College were to be regularly remembered both at the altar and after the daily chapter meeting in the Chapter-House to the east of the cloister. The Sarum Missal was used, and the chant was plainsong. Special regulations were made for the clothing and tonsure of those admitted to the College. The name 'College' was the style, and the master of the College was styled 'The Rector'. The robes were probably grey (griseus in one document) although it appears that sky-blue or blue-grey may have been remembered locally as the colour.

At the centre of the life of the Chapel was the Shrine. This contained a phial of the Precious Blood of Christ which had been presented at the foundation by Edmund, Earl of Cornwall in memory of his father, Richard. The Shrine would have been a substantial structure. At Hailes Abbey, a Cistercian house to which a similar phial had been presented by Edmund's father in 1270, the shrine base, which still exists, was 10 feet long and 8½ feet wide. At Hailes, as at St Albans, Durham and other great churches, the shrine would have been set beyond the high altar at the east end, and standing so that processions could move easily around.

There is no evidence of an elaborate Normandy-'Chevet' of chapels around the shrine. Nearby, the hearts of Edmund, Earl of Cornwall and St Thomas de Cantelupe were placed, the former in 1300, the latter early in the Chapel's life. These were at first on the north side of the sanctuary, and were no doubt buried. However when Bishop Thomas was canonised in 1320 his relics were translated into a golden shrine above ground in which the phial of the Precious Blood was kept.

Thomas de Cantelupe was Lord High Chancellor of England and twice Chancellor of the University of Oxford. He was fearless and a priest of ascetic discipline. He was ranged on the side of Simon de Montfort and opposed the appointment of foreigners to important posts in church and state. After the battle of Evesham he left the country but Edward I brought him back in 1275 to be Bishop of Hereford, the first of the Bonhommes to become a bishop. He died in 1282 and was greatly mourned. When he was canonised in 1320 his shrine in Hereford Cathedral was placed in the north transept. It became a place of pilgrimage, and King Edward I was present at the dedication of the shrine. The tower of Hereford Cathedral was mostly paid for by offerings at his shrine.

Ashridge having this association with the sainted Bishop as well as with the phial of the Sacred Blood, was favourably placed to become a centre for royal visits and for pilgrims, and provision must have been made for visitors and processions.

The length of the chancel even at the end of the monastic days, was given as 80 feet. It was not therefore a church of great size. The stalls for the brothers would not have required much space. Assuming that the number of canons was 20, there would need to be stalls on either side of the chancel for eight, and the stalls for the rector, precentor and senior dignitaries would require no more than four stalls on each side facing the altar. Some provision for visiting clerics and perhaps royal guests would need to be made, but these would be modest. This is borne out by the size of the ancillary accommodation. The Sacristy (sextrye) was 33 feet by 22 feet and the Plate House was 18 feet by 11 feet. The Chapter-House was 33 feet by 23 feet, and the Library was about the same size. The cloisters were almost forty-two feet square and the cloister walk was about ten feet wide. This was at the end of the life of the College, and one would expect its earlier dimensions to have been smaller than this.

By the beginning of the 15th century, rebuilding work was required and Richard Peteworth, one of the 'domesticks' of the Bishop of Winchester, Cardinal Henry Beaufort, gave £100 to rebuild the choir. There was urgent need to rebuild the Cloisters, the Dormitory, the Infirmary and the Sacristy. The Bishop also gave to the College the patronage of the parish of Ivinghoe which had been in the gift of the bishops of Winchester through the centuries.

The cloisters were lofty for their width after rebuilding. The bosses in the arches bore coats of arms, including those of the founder, Edmund, and of the Bonhommes. Describing the cloisters, which were still in existence in the 18th century, the writer of an article quoted by Todd says that there were 40 compartments with paintings of the life of Christ in water-colour. Whether or not they were connected in any way with the St Albans Abbey schools of wall painters is not known.

Unfortunately the amount of earlier work incorporated in the new cloisters may never be discovered.

Returning to the 14th century, the College seconded two of the brothers to go to Edington where William Edyndone (William of Edington) founded a house of the Bonhommes ('an order which is not known' said the historian William of Walsingham). Edington, Bishop of Winchester, died in 1366, having been bishop since 1346.

The jewelled altar endowed by the Black Prince in his will together with the phial of the Sacred Blood and the Shrine of St Thomas de Cantelupe would have necessitated constant surveillance by the brethren. An increase in the size of the establishment such as the Black Prince desired would have required extra building work, and perhaps the Chapel of the Blessed Virgin Mary was built or extended during the 14th or early 15th centuries. The Chapel of St John may also have been built at this time.

The maintenance of the College and its Chapel was provided for in the normal medieval manner, by giving the endowments of parish churches to the religious house, the house then being responsible for providing a priest for the parish and its worship. Thus Ashridge College was endowed with the livings of Pitstone, Ivinghoe, Hemel Hempstead, Ambrosden, and Chesterton. Little Gaddesden had already in the 12th century been appropriated to the monastery of St James, Northampton.

Burials of people of distinction brought in revenue, and remembrance of the departed, as well as the offerings of pilgrims and visitors, provided income. One distinguished benefactor was Henry de Burghersh, Bishop of Lincoln 1320-40. He directed mass to be celebrated for his parents and relatives at the altar of St Mary Magdalene and the Virgin Katherine in the conventual church near which the body of one of his relatives had been buried. Anthony Bec and Thomas Hatfield, both prince-bishops of Durham, were associated with the College respectively at the time of its first foundation in 1283 and its re-foundation in 1376. Hatfield was a benefactor of the College and of a chantry there.

Sir John Verney, son of the Lord Mayor of London, who had been knighted by Edward IV in 1471 and who had married a Lancastrian heiress Margaret Whittingham of Pendley Manor, Tring, Hertfordshire, was buried in Ashridge Chapel. He was a Yorkist. The Verneys were granted the Whittingham estates. Sir John's son was also buried there as was his grandson, Ralph. The outstanding brasses of Sir Ralph and Elizabeth his wife now in the Aldbury or Leeds Chapel at Aldbury Church, used to be in Ashridge Chapel. Another brass shows the children of Sir Ralph and his wife — nine sons and three daughters — which was also at Ashridge. They were removed to Aldbury in 1575 when Henry, Lord Cheney became owner of Ashridge. Sir Edmund Verney, who had inherited the Pendley estate, established a family chapel at Aldbury called the Pendley or Harcourt Chapel, and he took his family monuments there.

Visitations by the officers of the bishops of Lincoln in the late 15th and early 16th centuries show that there had been a deterioration from the ideals of monastic life amongst the brothers at Ashridge. Their worship was adversely criticised as well as their behaviour towards one another and towards the superiors in the community. Even the ringing of the bells for the daily office and for other services had become a burden.

At the dissolution of the House the bells were soon to be silenced. Six of them were sold in March 1555 for £82, to John a Marlowe. Anything that was saleable in the way of lead and glass was duly sold. Local people were not slow to help themselves. Any plate and vestments of value became crown property. Whether anything remained of the Black Prince's bequest and what happened to it is a matter for conjecture. In some places, anticipating the Dissolution, possessions of value had disappeared before the royal visitors had arrived. The Aldbury Screen was removed from the Chapel, and a screen in Little Gaddesden Manor House also originated at Ashridge.

Fig. 9 A brass of Sir Ralph Verney.

Fig. 10 A brass of Lady Elizabeth Verney.

Fig. 11 A brass of the children of Ralph and Elizabeth Verney.

Worship however continued. The younger members of the royal family were all trained in the daily habits of their religion. The Princess Elizabeth worshipped in the Chapel. How soon the main Chapel became unusable for worship is not clear, but it is recorded that it was not preserved after the 16th century although the Chapel was still there in 1575. With no lead on the roof, and without glass in the windows deterioration soon set in. The 1st Earl of Bridgewater in his instructions provided for the ringing of the Chapel bell for worship. It could be that part of the original Chapel was used for daily services.

In June 1643 Cromwell's troops attacked Ashridge and caused much damage, stealing whatever they could. The pillage of ecclesiastical buildings was typical of the procedure of the Roundheads and they broke into the Bridgewater vault at Little Gaddesden church at the same time.

During the 17th century there was a College Chapel in use.

In 1699 a new Chapel is mentioned. The Rev. George Burghope, one in a long line of Ashridge chaplains, preached the first sermon there. No doubt the Book of Common Prayer of 1662 was used, for the 2nd Earl who had died in 1682 had been responsible for foundation work for its preparation. During the 17th, 18th and 19th centuries, daily worship took place in the Chapel and this is not surprising when the religious affiliations of the owners and their families is examined.

A century later, in 1801 when Wyatt was preparing plans for the new Ashridge House he marked a Chapel 68 feet to the south of the present south terrace doorway, presumably beyond the steps on the croquet lawn and towards the present yew trees. This Chapel was at the end of a suite of buildings 72 feet in length. The west end of this building is marked 'Laundry' and 'Wash house'. Todd, who gave measurements for the College buildings including the Chapel, says that although the Chapel was not in existence at the time, he had seen a picture many years previously in which the Chapel dominated the buildings of the College.

The tower with its base of 30 feet square housed the six bells, and whilst this is not a large size, the tower would have been substantial enough to have been a landmark.

It has been said that Ashridge Chapel was James Wyatt's last and probably his greatest work. He did not align the Chapel east and west but placed it north and south with the 'east end' at the north. Thus the altar is at the south end of the Chapel. The liturgical descriptions will be used in the following comments. When James Wyatt died in a coach accident in 1814 his nephew Jeffry, who was knighted in 1828 and was later buried at Windsor (St George's Chapel), concluded the work. He was responsible for the alabaster altar and the east wall decorations. The choir stalls, the organ casing, the Screen between the Chapel and the Ante-Chapel and the Bridgewater Stalls are all his work set beneath his uncle's fan-vaulted ceiling.

He used Edward Wyatt (1757-1833) at Ashridge. He was one of the most talented of all English woodcarvers, and his work is sometimes mistaken for that of Grinling Gibbons. In 1798 he was appointed Gilder and Carver at the royal palaces. He worked at Windsor under James Wyatt, 1800-11. He restored Westminster Hall in 1818 and Carlton House for the Prince Regent. In 1797 he had designed and gilded the four 'Over-doors' for the Throne Room at Windsor to represent the Orders of the Garter, the Bath, St Patrick, and the Thistle. He was paid in 1815 for his work at Ashridge. This included the magnificent Bridgewater Stalls, said to be amongst the earliest examples of the Gothic Revival in England.

The crocketed canopies above the Bridgewater Stall on the north side of the Chapel (to the left, facing the altar) have been made with meticulous attention to detail. Underneath the canopy, and above the seat, in the ceiling of the stall, are the letters I H S central in the decoration. The doors to the stall have rosettes in the designs. This stall was used daily by the 7th Earl of Bridgewater and the successive owners of the House. The stall on the south side is similar to this one. Lady Bridgewater used this stall. Lady Brownlow used a stall adjacent to the reading desk on her husband's side of the Chapel. After her death the green silk-hanging which is behind her stall was embroidered in her memory. She was the youngest daughter of the 18th Earl of Shrewsbury and Talbot. She died on 16 March 1917 aged 72 and was buried in the Brownlow vault at Belton Church, Lincolnshire.

The domestic staff of the House sat in the front rows of the stalls with senior members behind them. At one time the men sat on one side and the women on the other. Lord Brownlow's dog sat beside his master's stall each day for service.

Edward Wyatt's decorative work above the stalls on both sides depicts the fruits of the earth and God's creation. There are shrubs and fruits and leaves, and several beasts. The capitals on the uprights have carved, lifelike heads which could represent men and women of the period of the Chapel's construction.

Behind the front stalls is a series of shields. Beginning from the great west stall of the Countess of Bridgewater near the screen they represent—
1. Bridgewater lion with the pheons
2. Tudor portcullis
3. Bardolph
4. Tudor portcullis
5. Cantelupe
6. Tudor portcullis
7. Paulet

Passageway
8. Tudor portcullis
9. Algar
10. Tudor portcullis
11. Cavendish
12. Tudor portcullis
13. Scotland

Pulpit
Partly concealed in the foliage. The Earls of Bridgewater.

On the north side of the Chapel
From the Earl of Bridgewater's Stall—
1. Haynes (Lady Bridgewater's family)
2. Tudor portcullis
3. The Legs of Man (Stanley, Earls of Derby)
4. Tudor portcullis
5. McMurrough
6. Tudor portcullis
7. Longchamp

Passageway
8. Tudor portcullis
9. Lupus
10. Tudor portcullis
11. Brune or Portland
12. Tudor portcullis
13. The College of the Bonhommes

Partly concealed in the foliage of the reading desk. Haynes.
On the north side of the Chapel the stall adjoining the reading desk near the altar was used by

Lady Brownlow. Exquisitely worked in silks and placed against the stallback is the inscription —

GIVE GLORY TO GOD
REMEMBRANCE
TO HER
WHO KNELT DAILY
NEAR THIS PLACE
ADELAIDE
WIFE OF ADELBERT EARL BROWNLOW
BORN 1844 MARRIED 1868 DIED 1917

Above the inscription two doves have been inserted in the wood-carving of the stall.

The Altar Ornaments. The silvered crucifix is jewelled, and at the foot is the inscription —

TO THE GLORY OF GOD AND IN MEMORY OF URBAN HANLON BROUGHTON
BORN APRIL 12th 1857 DIED JANUARY 30th 1929
THESE ALTAR PIECES WERE GIVEN BY HIS WIDOW TO THE CHAPEL OF ASHRIDGE
NOVEMBER 1929

There are two candlesticks and two vases. On either side of the alabaster altar are two seats below which are small shields. On the north side is that of Bridgewater and on the south side that of Haynes (representing the 7th Earl and the Countess of Bridgewater).

A comprehensive series of the coats of arms of the ancestors of the 7th Earl of Bridgewater is to be seen along the friezes of the Entrance Hall. There are 44 on the east wall and 44 on the west wall. The east wall shows the Stanley (Earls of Derby), and the west wall the Grey families (Earls and Dukes of Kent). On the south wall opposite the entrance to the left of the royal arms of Henry VII there are six shields depicting the York ancestry, and on the right there are four depicting the Lancaster ancestry. To the left and right of these shields are those of families with whom the Bridgewaters had married or been related. It is from these shields that those in the Chapel have been selected.

The Organ at the west end was built by William Hill for Thomas Elliot and is dated 1818. It has been changed little since then, with the exception of the swell reed and the pedal-board. It is a splendid organ in the style of the late 18th century, ideal for its purposes both then and now. Organ recitals are given regularly and the B.B.C. broadcast one on 1 April 1981. Mr R. Kibby was the organist for over fifty years. The services each Wednesday morning for staff and course members are accompanied by the organ; a member of the College staff Mr A. Johnson being one of the two organists.

The clock is inscribed 'John Thwaites of Clerkenwell, London'.

There are two bells dated 1813 (the heavier) and 1814. There does not appear to be a name or symbol of the bell-founder. Thomas Briant of Hertford was working in this area at that time, and he was employed by the Earl of Bridgewater to cast the Little Gaddesden bells in 1821.

The Spire. The original spire was removed in 1922 because it had become dangerous. A new fibreglass spire was placed in position by helicopter in 1969, and dedicated at the Christmas Carol Service that year. The height of the spire above the ground is 142 feet.

The Stained Glass. The windows of the College are now of glass presented to the College by Lady Fairhaven. This replaces the stained glass which was sold at Sotheby's for £27,000 during the great sale of Ashridge property in 1928. That glass is now in the Victoria and Albert Museum. Mrs Kibby recalled that the stained glass had been removed from the windows for safety during the First World War, and had not been replaced by the time of the 1928 sale.

This glass had been acquired from a stationer in Norwich who obtained stained glass from a dealer in Hamburg and sold it to willing purchasers. There is some of it in churches in the diocese of Norwich. It came probably from the abbeys of Steinfeld and Mariawald in the Rhineland and was the work of the Master of St Severin and Gerhard Remisch.

On the south wall of the Ante-chapel in a cabinet are transparencies made from the original glass. That glass took many years to put in position here, and there was no clear order in its arrangement. However in the cabinet are nine panels from the 120 original ones, and they are here arranged according to a christian order of events—

1. Christ in Glory with His Mother on the left and St John on the right.
2. War in Heaven. St Michael destroys the dragon.
3. The Garden of Eden.
4. The Nativity.
5. The Transfiguration.
6. Palm Sunday. The entrance into Jerusalem.
7. Maundy Thursday. The Last Supper
8. Good Friday. The Crucifixion
9. Easter. The Resurrection.

These are chosen from different series and show the work of each of the artists.

The Medieval Rose Brass. At the foot of the steps to the altar is a replica of a unique 'Rose Brass'. This is its traditional title. The original had been on this site for over half a century. It belonged to the parish church of Edlesborough on the Hemel Hempstead to Leighton Buzzard road. It was removed from there perhaps after the great fire which occurred due to a lightning strike in 1828. It was next found in Pitstone church where the Earl of Bridgewater was patron. Eventually it was brought to this Chapel and was at Ashridge in 1861.

When Ashridge was sold the parishioners of Edlesborough were pleased to receive back this brass, together with another which had been at Ashridge since 1823; that of John de Swynstede Prebendary of Lincoln and Rector of Edlesborough from 1351 who died in 1395. The indent for this splendid brass is beneath the carpet before the altar rails.

There was another 'Rose brass' in St Peter's church, St Albans before 1800, but it was removed, it was said, to Oxford. No trace of it now remains. That brass was said to be 10 inches in diameter, and was fixed at the foot below the figure of a priest on a slab in the chancel.

The inscription of the Edelsborough-Ashridge Brass is—

QUOD EXPENDI HABUI
QUOD DONAVI HABEO
QUOD NEGAVI PUNIO
QUOD SERVAVI PERDIDI

In the St Peter's brass there were two inscriptions; the one as above on the Ashridge brass, *and* a medieval translation—

LO AL THAT 'ERE I SPENT SOMETYM HAD I
AL THAT I GAU TO GOOD INTENT THAT NOW HAU I
THAT WHICH I NETHER GAU NOR LENT NOW ABY I
THAT I KEPT TILL I WENT THAT LOST I

Aby is archaic and means 'to pay as a penalty'.

In the centre of both brasses is the word 'Ecce' meaning 'behold'.

The brass is of the 15th century; the replica was made in 1978. The first sermon in this Chapel was preached by the Rev. Henry John Todd, who was Chaplain to the 7th Earl of Bridgewater, on All Saints Day, 1 November 1817. Todd was later to become Archdeacon of Craven in 1832 and Librarian to the Archbishop of Canterbury at Lambeth Palace.

The Chapel lies now within the parish of Nettleden with Potten End, although one-half of the House is in the parish of Berkhamsted. Formerly the House and Chapel were in the parish of Pitstone (the buildings being to the east of the present Chapel). Traditionally the rectors of Little Gaddesden have been chaplains to the Bridgewaters, Brownlows and their successors in the College.

Services are held for course members and staff and for the families of staff members.

The dedication of the Chapel under its 20th-century ownership can be seen in the memorial tablet on the north wall above the entrance from the Dining hall; and the association with the

Fairhaven family can be seen on the memorial tablet facing this one. Above the main entrance and beneath a figure of Christ in the arms of His Mother is inscribed—

IN HONOUR OF CHRIST CRUCIFIED
AND IN DEAR MEMORY OF URBAN HANLON BROUGHTON
BORN 12th JULY 1859 DIED 30th JANUARY 1929
THIS CHAPEL AND COLLEGE OF ASHRIDGE WERE GIVEN TO PERPETUATE THE WORK AND WORTH OF HIS TRUE FRIEND ANDREW BONAR LAW
SOMETIME PRIME MINISTER
BEFORE THE OPENING OF THIS COLLEGE THE BENEFACTOR HAD ALSO PASSED TO HIS REST.
BENEATH THE ALTAR LIE HIS ASHES
THE WINDOWS AND FURNITURE OF THE ALTAR WERE OFFERED
BY HIS WIDOW AND SONS DECEMBER MCMXXIX
On the wall opposite—
IN HONOUR OF CHRIST CRUCIFIED AND IN DEAR MEMORY OF
CARA LEYLAND BARONESS FAIRHAVEN
BORN NOV. XXIV MDCCCLXVII DIED MARCH XVII MCMXXXIX
WIDOW OF URBAN HANLON BROUGHTON
WHOSE ASHES LIE BENEATH THE ALTAR
SO DUST TO DUST BUT IN HOPE OF A JOYFUL RESURRECTION
HUSBAND AND WIFE SLEEP THE GREAT SLEEP TOGETHER
FROM HER UNFORGETTING SONS DECEMBER MCMXXXIX
On a small tablet beside this one is inscribed—
THE ASHES OF URBAN HANLON BROUGHTON AND CARA LEYLAND BARONESS FAIRHAVEN THAT LAY BENEATH THE ALTAR WERE REMOVED AT THE WISH OF THEIR ELDER SON LORD FAIRHAVEN OF LODE AND ANGLESEA ABBEY TO LODE CHURCH CAMBRIDGESHIRE

1968

The Chapel Doors. The entrance to the Chapel from the domestic service area has a pair of 15th-century doors carved in oak. They come from the days of the Bonhommes and are a reminder of traditional craftsmanship.

In the passageway opposite to the chapel entrance on the wall is a representation of an angel and a saint, which could be an Annunciation plaque. It has been said to have been connected with Lady Brownlow.

The College Well. Beneath the Chapel is the ancient well dating back at least to monastic days. It is 224 feet deep. For the first 28 feet from the top it is brick-lined with flint. Below is solid chalk. There is an arched recess at a depth of about one hundred and forty feet. The well was thoroughly cleaned and investigated by skin-divers in 1970. In Tudor times dogs were used to raise the water pails—

'Itm. the xviij daye Aug. 1530 to Edmonde the foteman for so muche by hym gyven in rewarde at assherige to one that made the dogges to draw water iiijs.viijd.'

Henry VIII was at Ashridge at this time.

The Canal Duke and his successors used a lifting gear which may owe its origin to the Duke's canal engineering background. Donkeys were used and the arrangements for their stabling are to be seen, together with the square sets. Before establishing the College here, and throughout its history, supplying water must have been a very difficult problem and important consideration. John Skelton in 1523 had noted the absence of any brook.

The Coult Museum

Adjoining the well is the Coult Museum. Col. Douglas Coult was firstly Librarian at Ashridge from 1962, and later became College Bursar. He gathered the pictures and artefacts which are exhibited in the stable-like area adjoining the Well House. He wrote *A Prospect of Ashridge,* a book fascinating to all who know the College. It is characterised by his painstaking care in the investigation of sources. He died within a few months of the completion of his great work.

The Undercroft. This was used both by Bridgewaters and Brownlows for wine storage. It was originally the monastic undercroft and lay beneath the Frater or Refectory. It is of the late 13th century. Constructed of Totternhoe stone, the quarry of which for many years belonged to the College and later to the Bridgewaters, it was left as a base for the Wyatt building. It lies beneath the Drawing-room, the Ante-room, and the Brown Lounge. Its length is 67 feet, and it has six arches. It has been earlier suggested that it was 81 feet long. The kitchen would probably have been at the west end, and thus in the direction of the College well, and the reredorter would have been at the east end.

The Undercroft now lies at the south side of a series of passages which almost form a square. The Tudor door is on the north side of the Undercroft, and this would be the normal side where the monastic chapel was on the north of the cloisters. Another entrance further to the west has been blocked. To the west of the Undercroft is the present wine-cellar most of which was built in the early 19th century. The south wall of this cellar is a continuation of the south wall of the Undercroft.

Some infilling has taken place between the west of the Undercroft and the east wall of the cellar. A stone slab on the ground of the cellar between two arches has a square of 15 inches filled in. If this had been the place of a former drain, and if it could be taken up it could give the site of the main drain of the College and thus a clue to the exact location of the reredorter.

To the east of the Undercroft is a small cellar which shows evidence of substantial masonry of the earlier building. Going north from this cellar the passageway continues and on both sides there are remains of earlier stonework. On the east side archways have been filled in with solid masonry, and blocked. Investigation beyond these infillings might produce evidence of the earlier Chapter-House and east cloister area.

The north passageway of the square dates from the Wyatville era. One alcove has an interesting circular construction in brick, as though for a chimney or vent.

The whole of this area shows traces of the earlier building and the use of earlier material, especially in the exterior of the Undercroft. It could all be connected with the cloister and its walk.

Jonah. A statue of Jonah and the whale stands in the river at Turvey in Bedfordshire. It is said to be made of Portland stone and to have once occupied the centre of the cloisters attached to 'Ashridge house of Augustinian friars'. The statue was placed in its present position by Mr John Higgins of Turvey Abbey in 1844, and had been obtained at the destruction of the cloisters at Ashridge c. 1801.

ASHRIDGE PRISON

The rectors of Ashridge as early as 1287 claimed the rights of gallows, tumbrel and pillory. In July 1290 William Rose was imprisoned for the death of William Everard whom he slew by accident. On 15 June 1381 Ashridge was attacked by Wat Tyler's mob, and the Rector was forced to grant privileges, and a Charter of Liberties was extracted from him.

The College continued to deal harshly with Lollards. A Lollard from Little Gaddesden was executed at St Albans. Robert Bartlet a wealthy farmer, and a Lollard, was kept prisoner for seven years at Ashridge. He was not only branded on his right cheek, but was confined in the bishop's prison for 14 weeks (probably at Woburn) where 'He was so cruelly treated with cold, hunger and irons that after coming out of the said prison, he was so lame in his back that he could never go upright as long as he lived'. In the persecution of 1506-7 his sons were summoned to the visitation of the Bishop of Lincoln at Amersham.

The last English Lollard to be burned was Harding at Chesham. The Vicar-General who examined Harding was assisted by Thomas Waterhouse, the last Rector of Ashridge. On 14 April

1515 Attwater, Bishop of Lincoln sitting at Missenden, imposed penance on Thomas Hardynge and his wife Alice for heresy. Every Corpus Christi Day they were to walk barefoot to Ashridge bearing a taper of wax.

Elizabeth Eme was held in prison for two nights and her husband Robert Eme for one night *c.* 1540.

Gravestones of the Brethren. Until the sale of the House on the death of the 3rd Earl Brownlow there were tables in the Entrance Hall made of oak in which polished Purbeck marble slabs had been framed. These were formerly gravestones of the brethren.

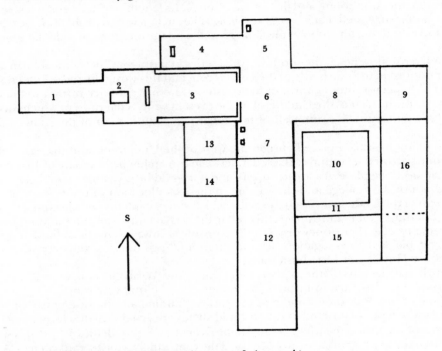

Fig. 12 Original monastic chapel : diagram 1 (facing south)

KEY (for diagrams 1 and 2)
1. The Lady Chapel
2. The Shrine
3. The Monastic Choir, with stalls
4. St John's Chapel
5. The North Transept
6. The central space. Tower above
7. The South Transept
8. The Nave
9. The West Entrance. Porch
10. The Cloisters. Pond in the centre

11. The Cloister Walk. Washing facilities to south
12. The Dormitory
13. The Sacristy
14. The Chapter House. The Library possibly above or adjoining (same measurements)
15. The Refectory (Frater) with Undercroft beneath. The Undercroft is the only part now remaining in this area from the original building
16. The Western range. Later 'Maynes Hall'
17. The Lodge

The course of the main drain and thus of the reredorter is not known. It would normally be adjacent to the frater and dormer. For the College well, see page 42.

NOTES.
DIAGRAM ONE.

1. A rough guide to the site with reference to the present Ashridge House. The Frater (No. 15), above the Undercroft, would stand on the site of the present Brown Lounge, Ante-room and Lecture Room (Saloon). The croquet lawn is the area between the Refectory and the Lodge. The present Great Staircase and Entrance Hall is on or near the site of the earlier Cloisters. The measurements are significantly similar — the Hall is 38 feet square while the Cloisters measured 41 feet square (9-11 feet Cloister Walk in addition)

DIAGRAM TWO

1. This is best understood by seeing it from the present Main Entrance and Hall (near 17). The Ante-room, flanked by the Conference Room (Saloon) and Brown Lounge, is above the Undercroft (No. 15), the only remaining part of the original building in this area. Wyatt noted that 68 feet from the (present) French windows in the Ante-room (facing south) there was a building 72 feet long by 29 feet wide. At the east end he placed 'The Lord's Chapel'. This could have been a part of the original conventual chapel. The measurements of the Cloisters make this possible.

2. The present croquet lawn and terrace would be on the site of the Cloisters. (Cont. over)

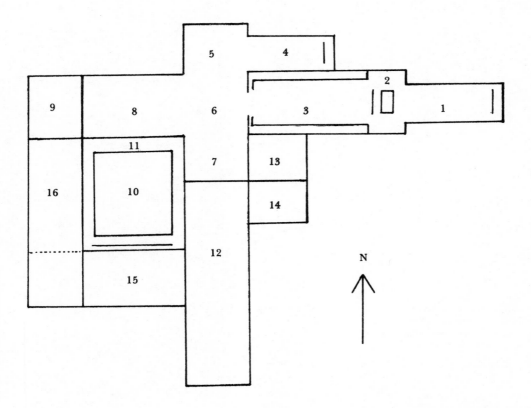

Fig. 13 Original monastic chapel : diagram 2 (facing north)

3. This lay-out seems to be not unreasonable when reading the description of the remains of the House during the 18th century. Pictures of the Frater with seven lancet windows and a door leading into the Screens and thence to the Cloisters, and to the Chapel 'ranging with the cloisters' are given.

This arrangement, whereby the chapel is built on the south side of the cloisters, is less common than building it on the north side.

IN BOTH DIAGRAMS
1. There is no provision made here for a processional route in a north or south choir aisle. No such measurements were given in H.J. Todd.
2. The Shrine is placed to the east of the high altar, and the size is suggested as being not dissimilar from the one at Hailes which was 10 feet long by 8½ feet wide.
3. Side chapels are known to have existed and these could have been on the east side of the transepts.
4. Tombs of those buried near the Shrine would have been in that vicinity. The Verney Memorials may have been there too, with the Verney Brasses.

PART THREE
Little Gaddesden

6. *The Old Dairy to Ringshall*

The Old Dairy to Ringshall including the Bridgewater Monument, Old Park Lodge, and Golf Club Road and Alderton Drive. This area of magnificent trees lies on the B 4506, the Berkhamsted to Dunstable road.

The Old Dairy. In 1543 (34 Hen. VIII) Robert Eme stated that he had been granted a lease of the 'Dayry' House by Thomas Waterhouse, the last Rector of Ashridge, dated 7 November 1536, the agreement bearing the College seal. He had therefore occupied the house, cottages and barns outside the gates of the monastery, and enjoyed arable, meadow land and woodland rights.

Eme alleged at the Court of Augmentations that he had been 'unquieted and perturbed' in his possessions by John Norris, gentleman farmer. Norris had been granted custody of Ashridge House, the former College of the Bonhommes, for 21 years from 19 November 1541. In the court, Norris alleged that Eme had stolen old doors, lead, iron and glass from the monastery. Eme replied that Elizabeth his wife, and his servants had been locked up in the monastery 'whereby Elizabeth is likely by such durance of imprisonment to die'.

When Ashridge was conveyed to Princess Elizabeth in 1550 Eme still occupied the Dairy lands. In 1575 'Le Deyrey' was a house with an old room adjoining called 'A Carte Howse'.

In 1690 a brick-kiln stood on the land, which was in the parish of Aldbury, and the owner was John Burton in the tenure of Michael Glenister. In 1693 John Burton sold 3½ acres to Richard Heath of Aldbury, maltster, including the kiln. Eleanor Heath, wife of Richard was buried in Aldbury in 1697. The initials over the Old Dairy are R.H.E. Burton sold the house to Job Gibson in 1697. In 1744 the owner was the Duke of Bridgewater and the occupier Daniel Puddefoot. His father probably lived there before him and it could have been ' a parlour, three chambers, a brewhouse and buttery'. Until 1779 it was referred to as 'Brick Kiln' or 'Kiln Farm'. It then changed to 'Dairy Farm'. In 1800 William Buckingham took the Dairy Farm under the Duke of Bridgewater. He also took over the Old Dairy meadows in Michaelmas 1801 from R. Bradshawe Esq., as well as the kitchen-gardens, hot houses and other outhouses.

In 1803 on the death of the Canal Duke, the 7th Earl and his Countess visited Buckingham and said that the Earl would require the Dairy Farm and gardens. Buckingham agreed to act as bailiff and moved to the Home Farm, Little Gaddesden.

The extent of the Dairy Farm was 40 acres, and there was a homestead, meadow and hop-garden.

In 1838 the Bridgewater Trustees administered the property which was occupied by Thomas Halsey and Joseph Swabey. There were two cottages and gardens. As time went on some of the

47

LITTLE GADDESDEN 1981

NOTES

Roads: This map does not distinguish between public and private roads. Many of the roads are not public rights of way.

Road Names: The names of some roads are not universally agreed. The names given are believed to be those accepted by most well-informed local residents.

Woods: Named woods are outlined, but other wooded areas have been omitted.

Parish Boundaries: The Civil Parish of Little Gaddesden and the various Ecclesiastical Parishes which lie within it are here shown for the first time on a single map.

KEY

═══	Roads (public or private)
▭▭	Drives and Tracks
– – –	Paths

Boundaries:-

- – · – · – Little Gaddesden Civil Parish
- – ·· – ·· – Gaddesden Ecclesiastical Parish (Little Gaddesden Civil Parish and Little)
- – ··· – ··· – Ecclesiastical Parish Divisions within Little Gaddesden Civil Parish
- – · – · – County boundaries adjoining Little Gaddesden, (which is itself entirely in Hertfordshire)

MILES 0 ¼ ½ ¾ 1
FURLONGS 0 1 2 3 4 5 6 7 8

THE MAP IS RULED WITH THE KILOMETRE SQUARES OF THE NATIONAL GRID

BUCKINGHAMSHIRE
BEDFORDSHIRE
HERTFORDSHIRE

LITTLE GADDESDEN CIVIL AND ECCLESIASTICAL PARISHES

Periodic Source of the River Gade (e.g. 1979)

Place labels:

- Four Ways Garage
- Four Acres Nursery
- Valley Farm
- HUDNALL
- The Growels
- Meadow Farm
- Butchers
- Church Farm
- BADGER WOOD
- Jansens Farm
- HOO WOOD
- The Parish Church of St Peter and St Paul
- Post Office Stores
- Bridgewater Arms
- Bede Court
- Village Hall
- Church Primary School
- John O'Gaddesden's
- Telephone Exchange
- Playing Field
- War Memorial
- Marian Lodge
- Beaney's (former rectory)
- Rectory
- Tudor Lodge
- Alford Memorial
- WITCHCRAFT BOTTOM
- GOLF COURSE
- Golf Club Road
- ALDERTON DRIVE
- ARDBURY LANE
- RINGSHALL DRIVE
- PITSTONE PARK COPSE
- SALLOW COPSE
- PITSTONE COMMON
- IVINGHOE COMMON
- LING RIDE
- BEACON ROAD
- Reservoir
- Fountain's Stores (until 1960s)
- Laundry (closed 1950s)
- RINGSHALL
- Swimming Pool
- Ringshall Lodge
- Deer Leap Garage
- Pump
- Hall Farm
- Ashridge Farm
- LEVI'S SPRING
- O'MALLEY'S WOOD
- Well Fm
- B4506
- A4146
- A4147

Reeves Green

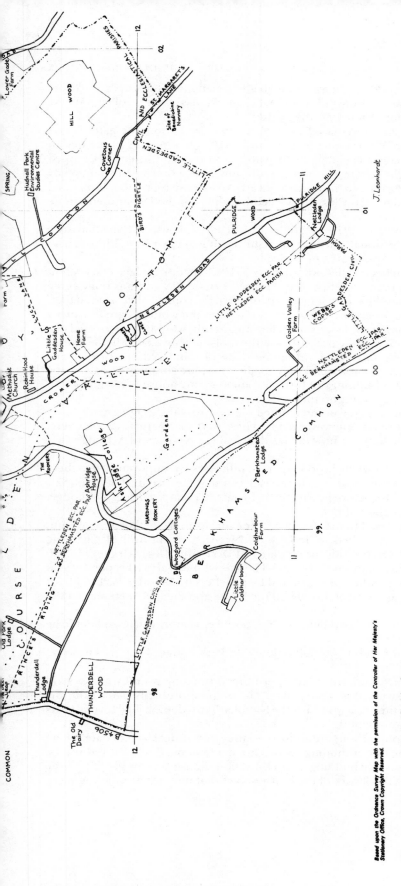

Fig. 14 Parish map of Little Gaddesden.

smaller farms were divided and labourers' cottages were made from them. The property became that of Mr Gilbert Stone, whose responsibility in Ashridge Management College Works Department still maintained a connection with the house.

Thunderdell Lodge. This Lodge probably replaced an earlier one and a monastic gate. It was designed by either James or Jeffry Wyatt between 1813 and 1819. Certain parts of the design figured in plans of the latter architect. The chequered pattern of stone and squared, knapped flints is not infrequent in East Anglia. There are casement windows. The porch is surmounted by a parapet. There are crow-stepped gables to the north and east. An extensive garden was planned by the architect. Thunderdell Lodge is in Class II of listed buildings of the Department of the Environment.

Forester's Lodge. This house was built in 1970 by Frederick's of Penn. It was a Canadian style prefabricated house, built by the National Trust for the Ashridge Ranger, Mr John Wilson, who came in 1957 from the Fountains Abbey area of Yorkshire.

Old Park Lodge. This is said to have been called King Henry VIII's Keeper's Lodge. The present building may be on the site of an older building, but it is itself dated 1619 and was built as the house of the verderer. This office was held by a solicitor involved in the control of the royal parks.

The chimneys are Tudor-style. There are dormer-windows and the windows are unusually high. One sundial on the chimney-stack faces south and apparently would have covered the hours from one to eight. The other is on the east face below the roof and above a two-light window and this may have covered the remaining hours. Additions in the 18th and 19th centuries of one storey, three windows and a gable at the north end were made. There are chimney breasts on the north and south walls. In the list of buildings of historical interest this house is categorised in Class II amongst buildings of regional importance.

The central tower allowed the verderer uninterrupted views across the grazing park.

This area was isolated before the golf course was made. There were many great oak trees here, and a local name is 'Oak Hill'. The house is now the residence of the secretary of Ashridge Golf Club.

Traditionally it had been the house of the head keeper, an office of such importance that there were 60 applicants before Seth Cox was appointed in the 19th century. He died in 1900. John Saw also held this position for many years before he died in 1914 aged 95 years, at Ringshall Lodge. Mr Ruffett was head keeper from about 1923.

A former keeper who lived here was Thomas Bamford. He came from Baileythorpe, Oakham, Leicestershire (formerly Rutland) and died in 1863 aged 74 years. In the will of Charlotte Catherine Anne widow of the 7th Earl of Bridgewater dated 24 December 1846, a legacy of £100 was left to 'My Park Keeper, Thomas Bamford'. His son Thomas who was also a keeper, lived at Nettleden in 1851. It was thought that he was murdered by poachers in Ashridge Park in about 1870. Walter Bamford, Park Ranger, lived all his life on the Estate and died 19 September 1899 aged sixty-five.

The house was called Forester's Lodge earlier in the 20th century, a name which was later to be adopted for the Head Ranger's House.

Three modern cottages built for Golf Club staff adjoin Old Park Lodge. They are known as 'Greenkeepers' Cottages'.

Coldharbour. The house at Great Coldharbour is a timber-framed building round which a solid shell of brickwork has been constructed at a later date. The original probably dates from the enclosure in about 1620. The fine timber barn which the National Trust demolished several years ago may have dated from the same period.

The farm buildings of Little Coldharbour are almost certainly a good deal later in date. There are, however, two walls in a range of outbuildings which are made of two-inch soft red bricks, which suggest that at least there was one building, a brick dwelling-house, on this site during the early 17th century. A study of the brickwork of the house shows that the earliest building was a single cell made of local brick. Traces of a round-topped garden or courtyard wall on the west wall indicate that it was some sort of lodge or gatehouse dating from the late 18th or early 19th centuries.

The main part of the house was added later, probably about 1860, for first floor joists that had been cut on a circular saw have been found, and the broad overhanging eaves are said to have been a feature of the work of Paxton.

In 1971 Mr David Wray made a number of alterations, though with due respect for the historical and architectural merits of the house.

Mr Wray, with a small team, was responsible for the restoration of the ancient windmill at Ivinghoe, said to be the earliest known mill of its type still in existence today.

Woodyard Cottages. During the last years of his life the 7th Earl of Bridgewater built Berkhamsted Lodge on a road running from Hemel Hempstead to Aldbury. He then made a woodyard and built two cottages. An earlier mention of a woodyard appears in 1603. In the evidence concerning the enclosure attempt by Lord Brownlow in 1866, heard before the Master of the Rolls who gave judgement in 1870, the erection of the Woodyard cottages is mentioned as being near the Park, the railings having been moved out a few feet to enclose part of the road into the Park. This alteration of the line of the road caused much dissatisfaction.

THE BRIDGEWATER MONUMENT.

The Monument stands 729 feet above sea level at the end of the long Drive which runs north-west from Ashridge House. The inscription at the base of the Monument reads—

IN HONOUR OF
FRANCIS THIRD DUKE OF BRIDGEWATER
'FATHER OF INLAND NAVIGATION'
1832

The Duke had died in March 1803, and in accordance with his will he was interred quietly in the family vault in Little Gaddesden church. He had been Duke since 1748 and was succeeded by John William, the 7th Earl of Bridgewater, who in his turn was succeeded by Francis Henry, the 8th and last Earl. Francis Henry had given instructions that an obelisk and urn should be erected in memory of his great ancestor. There was difficulty about such a memorial and Charlotte Catherine Anne, widow of the 7th Earl, still then living at Ashridge, did not wish for there to be an obelisk. Consequently the Monument did not have one.

In 1832 the Bridgewater Monument was erected. Lord Farnborough, Trustee to the will of the 8th Earl, arranged for the Doric Column 100 feet high, fluted, in granite, with 172 steps, to be built by Philip Newell of Pimlico. The cost was expected to be £700. Sir Jeffry Wyatville, who designed it, received £400 at this time. An inscription on a brass plate inside the monument reads—

THIS COLUMN WAS ERECTED CONFORMABLY WITH THE INTENTIONS OF JOHN WILLIAM EARL OF BRIDGEWATER ACCORDING TO THE TESTAMENTARY DIRECTION OF FRANCIS HENRY EARL OF BRIDGEWATER
AND WITH THE APPROBATION OF CHARLOTTE CATHERINE ANNE COUNTESS OF BRIDGEWATER IN HONOUR OF
FRANCIS THIRD DUKE OF BRIDGEWATER
WHO BY DEVOTING THE ENERGIES OF HIS MIND TO THE ACCOMPLISHMENT OF THE MOST SPLENDID WORKS OF INLAND NAVIGATION OPENED A NEW FIELD TO NATIONAL INDUSTRY AND RENDERED THE MOST IMPORTANT SERVICES TO THE COMMERCIAL INTERESTS OF HIS COUNTRY

For the Jubilee of Queen Victoria, Earl Brownlow made a design for fire buckets to be placed over the column for a beacon fire. It was to be lighted at 10 p.m. on 21 June 1887. 'These fires had good effect' stated Wright, the Clerk of Works, 'They were made to hang just below the cupola'.

The Monument is a focal point for thousands of visitors to the Ashridge Estate. It overlooks the London-Scotland railway line and one can watch the Inter-City express trains moving at 125 miles per hour beside the Grand Union Canal.

RINGSHALL ROAD

Greenacre. It was built by Louis Moore A.R.I.B.A. who resided here. His daughter Miss Jean Moore was Chairman of the Parish Council, and in her memory a clock was placed in the Village Hall. Clifford Baron, who lived at Greenacre from 1975, thought that — 'An appropriate name for this house would have been Deer Leap because old maps give the original Deer Leap immediately adjoining the fence near the gate'. It was later extended by Mr Godden in 1980.

Theccans. In 1936 Miss Bridget Talbot obtained permission for the building of some houses in Ashridge Park, subject to very careful regulations and limitations. Theccans was one of the first to be built. Louis Moore, architect, designed it in 1937 and Donald Lockhart of Berkhamsted built it for him. All the houses to be built were to have at least two acres of garden, and were to be in keeping with the character of the Park. The name 'Theccans' was chosen because it was an Anglo-Saxon word connected with a thatcher. *Thaca* is an Old English word for a 'roof of thatch'. *Thaec* means 'thatch', or material for thatching, and is used about places where thatching material (reeds etc.) is available. *Thak* is used both in Old Norse and in modern Scandinavian languages to mean 'thatch' or a 'thatched roof'.

On the death of his wife, Louis Moore took ¾ acre of his garden and built Greenacre for himself and his daughter.

Thunderdell. This was built in 1937 for Rhonda Keane, the actress, by Donald Lockhart, with Louis Moore as architect. In 1938 the architect bought the house, and let it to the Lockhart family. During the war three members of the family were on active service and open house was kept for those in the services. Dutch and Polish troops encamped nearby in the vicinity of the Monument availed themselves of this hospitality.

Just after the war Mr John Hobson acquired the property and extended it to about five acres. In June 1978 Mr Allen E. Fry bought Thunderdell.

There is a natural dell in front of the house.

Princes Riding. The house was designed by Louis Moore and built by Donald Lockhart Ltd. in 1938 for Mrs Blaikie. Rodinghead was then built for her and she gave Princes Riding to her daughter and son-in-law. The house was built in the style of a Dutch colonial dwelling. At the outbreak of the Second World War it was sold to Mr George Bishop, drama critic for *The Daily Telegraph.* In 1957 he published his autobiography entitled *My Betters,* which is a remarkable record of well known people whom he knew. It includes many personal anecdotes about Dame Edith Evans, Francis Thompson, Noel Coward, Charlie Chaplin, Sibelius, Moiseiwitsch, Somerset Maugham, Priestley, Walpole, Marie Tempest, Gielgud, Olivier, and Betjeman. Perhaps the one person whose friendship gave him very great pleasure was G.B. Shaw. These anecdotes are presented with intimate knowledge and in a kindly manner.

Later the house was sold to Mr George Macnab, surgeon of Westminster Hospital. It was a favourite venue for meetings of the Music Club and for musicians of renown. For many years elderly and infirm folk from London were entertained there.

Edward VI was said to have ridden along the Avenue from Ashridge House towards the site of the present Monument. He was at Ashridge in 1543 with his sisters, the Princesses Mary and Elizabeth, the latter of whom was to own the property after Edward became king and gave it to her. The Western Avenue was therefore known as The Princes Riding in 1762 and 1823, and the house takes its name from this.

The Old English *rydding* meant a 'clearing' or an area cleared of trees. Such a derivation could thus be older than our present understanding of the term.

Looking towards the golf course from the rear of Princes Riding, there are areas where the land formation is not unlike the old 'strip' system.

The Wood. Dr Cyril Ambrose Goddard who was in general practice in Wembley purchased the land for this house in 1937 from the Little Gaddesden Estate. The architect for the building was F. Heckinbottom A.R.I.B.A. partner of Louis Moore. Jesse Mead of Chesham was the builder. Dr Goddard moved in late in October 1952. He made plans for an extension of the dining-room and for a billiard room in 1955. Rayment of Potten End completed this work. One fireplace was constructed by Dr Goddard to illustrate the words— 'Let all the birds of the Wood rejoice before the Lord'. The birds were carved and coloured by him in authentic colours. He made the gardens a haven for bird life, and constructed a pond and a small waterfall. He planted trees and shrubs and carted many tons of earth to form a lawn.

In the parish he became churchwarden and sidesman, President of the Ashridge Golf Club senior Golfers Section, and President of the Gaddesden Society and the Over 60s Club. He was a Rotarian of many years standing. His contribution to the life of Little Gaddesden was immeasurable because of his great personal qualities. On his 90th birthday a garden chair was presented to him after the church service on Sunday morning. He died on Easter morning 1979. New gates to Little Gaddesden church were erected in the church porch in his memory, and there were also beautiful gifts of frontals, embroidery, and vestments.

In 1980/1 extensive alterations and modernisations were initiated by Mr and Mrs Buchan.
Ringshall Rise. Originally called 'Silver Birches' it was built for Mr E. Griggs in 1936 under the supervision of Harrison and Stevens, architects of London WC2. The name was changed to identify it more closely with Ringshall 'Rise', because it is built on a small rise on the B 4506, which passes the gate. The original site was one acre, but after its purchase by Mr Peter Foxall in 1953 a three acre plot was acquired north-east for the adjoining house.
Stag Wood. This was built in 1967 for Mr F. Hawley. The Ashridge Estate saw-mill was located on the edge of this site, and the mill operated before the houses Ringshall Rise and Stag Wood were built.
Bridgewater House. Formerly called Bridgewater Lodge and Shangri-La, this house was built for Henry Cotton, golfer, who designed the Ashridge golf course where he was professional. Cotton was born in Cheshire in 1908, the son of a Methodist preacher. In order that he could watch and perfect his golf strokes and stance he placed mirrors on four walls of his room.

This house was later occupied by Arthur Slater whose brother-in-law, Archbishop Trevor Huddleston, frequently visited the parish. Mr Slater built the adjoining bungalow for his family in 1965 in the grounds of the Lodge. Dr J. Ehrlich followed Mr Slater and the name of the house became Bridgewater House.

GOLF CLUB ROAD

Bridgewater Lodge. This was built for Mr A.R.O. Slater by Donald Lockhart Ltd. The architect was C.C. Handyside F.R.I.B.A. Mr J.L. Hughes acquired the property after Mr Slater.
The Beguine. Mr N.W. Valios built this house. The architects were H. Rolls and Partners, and Donald Lockhart Ltd. were the builders. When Mr Valios left in 1973 he was followed here by Mr T. Christoffersen.
Kestrel. A Colt cedar wood bungalow of modern design which was built in 1965 to blend with the landscape for Mr and Mrs R.G. Hodge.
Cottonwood. (formerly Nob's Crook.) This was built in 1936 as one of the first houses in the Park, for Mr Patterson, surgeon, of London. Nob's Crook was the name of the nearby spinney, and of the 8th hole on the golf course. There was a pond near the house.

Mrs Winifred Dorothea Patterson died 15 July 1970. Their son Ian an officer in the Royal Artillery had been killed in the Second World War. Miss Dorothea Patterson, a well-known artist, lived here. The name of the house was changed to Cottonwood because of the association of Mr and Mrs A Meyer with a similar place in North America, as well as local connections.
Pitstone Copse. This property on the lane to the Golf Club was built by Donald Lockhart Ltd. for Captain Downer in 1952. The architects were Peter Dunham, Widdup and Harrison. The house

faced Pitstone Park Copse. Mr J.A.D. Timms acquired the property when the Downer family moved. There was a small pond nearby.

The Hook. This house was so named as a place of repose for golf balls escaping the wrath of their owners seeking the adjoining 8th hole on the golf course. It was previously owned by Mr Peter Cox. From Mr Cox the property was acquired by Mr Stanley Broughton, former Deputy-Lieutenant of the county of Bedford. Mr Broughton was Captain of the Golf Club in 1973. He was Chairman of the Little Gaddesden Parish Church Restoration Appeal in 1978.

Marlesfield. In 1957 Mr H.L. Alexander invited R.K. Brett F.R.I.B.A. to plan this house. Donald Lockhart's were the builders. Later Mr J.D. McCracken bought the property.

Birch Wood. This house was built in 1960 for Mr D.C. Fletcher to the design of Humphrey Hamilton A.R.I.B.A. of Hall Park, Berkhamsted. The builders were Honours of Tring. Mr T.J.A. Green is able to write— 'The astonishing thing is that only 21 years ago, Mr Fletcher could buy an acre of land and put a family house on it with three double bedrooms, two bathrooms and the rest to scale for £12,000'. Mr Green was Captain of the Ashridge Golf Club in 1967, having come into residence in the early 1960s.

Kinross. Built in 1959 by Honours of Tring. There are approximately two acres, conforming with the original specifications of area under the Brownlow conditions of sale. Kinross is on Loch Leven, Scotland. The property, formerly belonging to Mr D.B. Irving, was acquired by Mr John Holloway in 1972 and six years later by Mr John Dahl.

Inyanga. Formerly called Tyrone, this house was named after mountainous Inyanga National Park in Zimbabwe, 68 miles from Umtali. Mr and Mrs T.I. Cameron moved from Rhodesia to Little Gaddesden after the O'Neill family left in about 1969, and they renamed the house after the estate left in trust by Cecil Rhodes.

Westcott. This house was designed by architect John Westcott Ball R.I.B.A. in 1956 for his own occupation. It was given the name 'Westcott' from his family name. He had the honourable distinction of being descended from Captain Westcott who fought under the command of Admiral Nelson at the battle of the Nile where he was killed. He was buried in St Paul's Cathedral, London.

> Among the senior officers the casualties were particularly heavy. Hood, Miller, Saumerez and Ball were slightly wounded, Captain Westcott of the Majestic was killed. His opponent in the Tonnant, Captain Petit Thouars having lost both arms and a leg, insisted on his trunk being put in a tub on the quarter-deck where he continued to fight the ship. Admirals Brueys and Blanquet were both wounded and nearly all their captains were killed or hurt.
>
> On 1st January 1801 Nelson was made Vice-Admiral. On 13th he set out for Plymouth, and at Honiton he enquired for Mrs Westcott, the mother of the only captain killed at the Nile. He found her, except for Government and Lloyds, in very low circumstances. 'The brother is a tailor, but had they been chimney sweeps it was my duty to show respect'. Mrs Westcott said that she had not received her son's Nile medal; Nelson with typical generosity gave her his own.

(Ludovic Kennedy's book on the Life of Nelson)

Pook's Hill. Built in 1962, destroyed by fire in 1962, and rebuilt in 1971, Pook's Hill was named after the 4th hole of Ashridge Golf Club, which was in turn named after the first professional of the Club. The house was designed by Peter Dunham, and his son supervised the rebuilding for Mr Patrick S. Whaley who was Rural District Councillor for the area and Captain of the Ashridge Golf Club in 1977.

RINGSHALL ROAD

Journey's End. At one time Mr John Mendl Finn lived here, and the house, because of its thatched roof, was called 'Thatchers'. For a short period Mr Benno Moiseiwitsch, the pianist, lived here. Mr J.P. Napier later owned the property. He died in December 1973. Mr W. Woods acquired it in 1974.

Sallow Copse. This house was formerly known as Canford and then as Lacy Hey. It is named after the copse on the opposite side of Ringshall Road which stretches towards Monument Drive. The

120 acres of Sallow Copse which is astride the 700 feet contour contained mature sweet and Spanish Chestnuts grown by The National Trust for young coppice shoots, for stakes. In the 1930s children knew the Copse as Soller Copse, though in 1825 it was called Sallow Coppice. The house received its present name when Mr Peter W. Harris acquired it from Mr J.M. Finn.

ALDERTON DRIVE

Canford. This was an earlier name of Sallow Copse. When the Aylwin family moved to this new house which they built in the grounds of their previous home, they transferred the name also. It is named after Canford, Bournemouth which had very happy associations for Mr and Mrs Hugh Aylwin. The architects of the present house built for Mrs C.W. Aylwin were A.W. Willis & Associates. The builders were Donald Lockhart Ltd.

Lacy Hey. The architect Mr F. Heckinbottom planned this house for himself, and later Donald Lockhart Ltd. extended it. Mr J.M. Finn acquired it from Mr M.L. Breedon who used to call it Green Glades. Mr Finn brought the name Lacy Hey from his previous house on Ringshall Road. He also used the name for his property at Canford Cliffs, Bournemouth.

Alderton Lodge. This property was obtained by Sir William Swallow on the death of Mrs George in 1964. In explaining the name of the drive, Sir William referred to the ancient craft of woodturning in Berkhamsted and Chesham, and quoted William Ellis, farmer and churchwarden of Little Gaddesden, that these two towns 'made more consumption of this wood [alder] than any other two towns in Britain, as is allowed by good judges'. The men in and around Berkhamsted could make a thin-walled bowl from alder which could be turned inside out without either cracking or breaking. Sir William was Captain of Ashridge Golf Club in 1976.

Heathlands. This was built in 1954 by Donald Lockhart Ltd and designed by R.K. Brett F.R.I.B.A. There are the statutory two acres in accordance with the original conditions of the Estate. The gardens, like others in the vicinity stretch down to the golf course. It was named 'Heathlands' after a Derbyshire county family. Mrs Alexander's maiden name was Heathcote.

Ringshall Beeches. This was built by Mr Ford who did not take up residence but sold it to Mr and Mrs Maclaren who added a wing to it. After several years they sold it to Captain de Normanville, the inventor of the overdrive gearing device for cars. In 1956 Mr L.H.K. Neil purchased Ringshall Beeches from him. The avenue of stately trees behind the house stretches down from meticulously-kept rose beds to the golf course.

Witchwood. This house was built in 1938 by Mr W.H. Wiggins of Watford for Mr Balfour. Later Mr W.S. Verrells resided here from 1946 to 1975. There is a small turret overlooking the beautifully planted garden and drive. The staircase is of solid oak, as are the floors.

Little Witch. Mrs Verrells built this house in a copse adjoining Witchwood, in a corner of her original garden.

The Conveyance of the Ashridge Estate is given below together with conditions that were laid down at sale. This extract concerning 'Beggars Roost', Alderton Drive is typical of the conditions set out in the conveyances in this area.

The Conveyance of 2 May 1928.

Vendors: The Trustees of the Ashridge Estate under the will of the Right Hon. Adelbert Wellington Brownlow, 3rd Earl Brownlow, to Edgar Creyke Fairweather of Westminster, and thence to Thomas Place of Northallerton, Yorkshire. The Ashridge Mansion and 1,157 acres . . . for £53,000. The purchasers were to preserve the trees known as the 'Queen Beech', the 'Giant Ash' and the 'Queen Victoria Oak' on the Ashridge croquet lawn.

The Conveyance 7 March 1936. Thomas Place conveyed to Cosmo Rose Cran, solicitor, and Kathleen Jessie Cran, his wife, the part of Ashridge Park between Ringshall Drive and the new road (Alderton Drive) that is now the area covered by Cherry Tree Cottage, Cherry Dell, Beggars Roost, and Priory Close. The price was £1,900.

Conditions imposed on purchasers.

a) No lorries over five tons to use the roads.

b) No trees to be felled if over six inches in diameter.

c) No washing to be visible.

d) No animals to be kept.

e) No dwelling-house to occupy less than an acre of ground, due allowance being made for coachmen and chauffeurs, and 1,350 square feet of floor space.

f) No wireless poles.

g) Nothing related to trade, manufacture, asylum, hospitals, charity, church or school or other illegal activity.

h) Nothing which may tend to deteriorate the value for the owners of the Ashridge Estates for residential property.

i) Payment of £10 per annum from 1 June 1937 for road maintenance.

j) Any new building, outhouse or alteration must have prior approval of the vendor.

Beggars Roost. This house was built for Mr Meredith by Donald Lockhart Ltd. of Berkhamsted. The name given was the same as Mr Lockhart's own house in Berkhamsted. It covered an area of 1.4 acres. The architect was R.K. Brett F.R.I.B.A.

In 1963 Beggars Roost was acquired by Mr L.C. Hopkins for £9,250. He was convinced that at that price there must be gold beneath the surface! He added the terraces (at a cost of £2,000) and in 1969 a summer lounge and 'Grandpa suite'. The architect for Mr Hopkins' extension was W.F. Johnston of Hemel Hempstead.

Cherry Dell. In January 1955 Mr Meredith sold 1.9 acres to Mr Jack Godwin for £575. Mr Godwin designed and built his own house with contract labour between July 1955 and April 1956. He named it Cherry Dell. Mr Godwin estimated the total cost including land, legal costs and services at £4,138.

Priory Close. Designed by Mrs Cosmo Cran, an American citizen. She bought 35 acres from the Ashridge Estate but the Second World War prevented this being developed. Priory Close was built just after the war by F.G. Whitman. Mrs Cran lived in Witchcraft Hill as it is now called. It is not known why she used the name 'Priory' for this area. Mr R.W. Stanes bought the house from Ralph Muda of Sarawak, heir to his uncle Sir Vyner Brooke, the White Rajah of Sarawak, who gave his territory to the British Government during the war. Anthony Brooke failed to regain his territory.

Mr Stanes and Mr Max Bemrose (Bracken Priory) founded the Little Gaddesden Conservative Association. Mr Stanes was a sidesman of Little Gaddesden church for many years.

Priory Cottage. This was designed by Mrs Cosmo Cran and built by Mr F.G. Whitman on a plot of land of two to three acres. It was extended by Sir Leslie Pott who acquired the property in 1961/2. When he moved to Becking Spring in 1974, Mr Peter Mann came to reside there.

Bracken Cottage. This was also designed by Mrs Cran and built by Mr Whitman. In 1981 Mr A.A. Berry began extensive alterations and improvements.

Priory End. The house was completed in 1956 for Mr and Mrs John Davies. The architect was D. Murray Evans, and the builder F.G. Whitman & Son. Part of a 'Living World' B.B.C. programme was recorded at Priory End in 1979 in which Clive Banks and Michael Clark reported on their visit to Mr Davies' loft where a colony of long-eared bats had settled. This type of bat is one of the most attractive species of the order Chiroptera, and is harmless to human beings.

RINGSHALL ROAD/ALDERTON DRIVE

Windrush. Originally there was one thatched cottage here, built by Mrs Cran in 1937. In 1947 it was purchased by Mr W.N.A. Smalley for retirement when eventually he would return from Hong Kong. Much of the planning for this house was therefore done in Hong Kong. He was to extend and develop both the house and site very considerably in the next two decades. The architect was Matthews of Lincolns Inn Fields, London.

Mr and Mrs Smalley were prisoners of war in the Far East during the Second World War, and their great courage during this period deserves our complete admiration. The gardens are a very attractive feature at the entrance to Alderton Drive from Ringshall Road. The River Windrush — 'the gentle Windrush' — is a Cotswold meandering waterway.

The Thatched Cottage. Between Windrush and the Thatched Cottage was another similar cottage which was burned down by the 'Fire-Raiser' and never rebuilt. The site is part of the Thatched Cottage property belonging to Mr H. Duncan who was the first man in Little Gaddesden to volunteer for the Local Defence Volunteers, the predecessors of the Home Guard during the Second World War. Mrs Duncan was attached to the Home Guard and was on duty twice a week at the Red House to be at the telephone should German parachutists land in the village. She was also the first person to volunteer for menial tasks at Ashridge when the Dunkirk wounded arrived. Mr Duncan played an important part in keeping Ashridge Golf Club open during the war, and in founding the Artisan Golf Club.

Blue Cottage. This was designed by Louis Moore for Elsie and Doris Waters (the comediennes 'Gert and Daisy') who, as they were entertaining the Forces during the Second World War, continued to live in London because of transport difficulties. They were to be followed by Colonel and Mrs Wynne Morgan, who planted the beech hedge.

The village was horrified at the blue tiles on the cottage, so Mr Moore invited his friend Sir Edward Lutyens (1894-1944) for a visit. Lutyens was thought of as an 'aristocratic-architect' whose houses were built along traditional English country house lines mainly for new families and business men of a romantic nature. He loved generous roofs and bold chimney-stacks. He designed the Cenotaph in Whitehall. Thus his approval of Blue Cottage was acceptable indeed.

Mrs E.E. Clayton ran her nursery school here from 1958 until 1970 after which her daughter Mrs Ernest Janes continued it in the Village Hall. Mr E.E. Clayton acquired the property which now stands in five acres, in 1953. Previously it was owned by Mr R.A. Corby.

RINGSHALL

The first extant mention of Ringshall occurs in 1235 where the spelling is *Ringeshale.* This form is also found in 1262. In 1314 and 1386 *Ryngeshale* is mentioned. In 1432 the form is *Rynnggeshole*; in 1448, *Ryngesole.* In 1660 it is *Ringsell*; in 1766, *Ringsal*, in 1825, *Ringsall.* By the end of the 19th century its spelling settled to the present *Ringshall,* although in the spoken word the aspirate has frequently disappeared.

The etymology of Ringshall is interesting. *'Hring's Healh', Hring* is found combined with different endings. *Hring* is probably a forename. It occurs in Kent as early as 762. *Healh* or *Halh* is used in a number of ways. In general it appears to mean a nook or corner of land. From this has evolved its meaning of a secluded hollow on a hill side, or a small steep valley on the side of a larger one. It also came to be known as a nook of land in the corner of a parish, and in some cases a detached part of a parish. Ringshall, Dagnall, Hudnall, and Northall all contain *'Healh'* and are nooks in the Chiltern Hills. Later in some places the word became identified with *Hall* as a place of residence or a manor house. This usage became more common after the Norman Conquest, and sometimes became confused with the earlier meanings (as above) of the Old English *Healh* and *Halh.*

Much of Ringshall was formerly in the ancient parish of Ivinghoe and thus belonged to the see of Winchester. In 1420 Ivinghoe was given by papal consent to the Bonhommes at Ashridge. It then became a vicarage and descended with the manor of Ivinghoe until Queen Mary gave it to the Bishop of Lincoln. This gift was shortly afterwards revoked and it reverted to the crown. Later it was granted to Lord Chancellor Ellesmere and from him it descended through the Earls of Bridgewater. The 1st Earl presented the incumbent of Ivinghoe in 1639.

It would appear that the Brownlows tried not to alter the traditional Hertfordshire village pattern, where a few cottages surrounded a farmhouse and its buildings. Houses were numbered in each of these hamlets but not across the whole Estate. In Ringshall there were two stages of building. The first was to the north of the Ivinghoe-Ringshall road; and the second, about a century later, to the south. This included the laundry building and five or six groups of semi-

detached cottages built by the 7th Earl. Each group of cottages had a common meadow and orchard behind it. There was a common bakehouse and domestic laundry behind cottage numbers 19 to 35 on the south side. Under the wash-house there was a soft-water tank and this took the water from the roofs of cottages 32 to 35. In the older group the pump and pump-house adjoined cottage numbers four and six. This was built before the mains water supply was laid on from Ashridge and thus is dated pre-1856. All the cottages had drinking water from the main reservoir behind Meadow Farm (still of 22 degrees hardness). The water was piped into individual wash-houses in each cottage where there was a sink, and to a copper in each outhouse. There was a kennel for the gun dogs and a few stables for ponies. Each cottage had a pigsty. The common drainage system took the waste from each cottage into self-cleaning pits in a field in the Ivinghoe road.
The Well. Standing beneath a strongly constructed shelter, the well was in use until Lady Marian Alford introduced piped water in 1858. In 1855 it was 250 feet deep. The mechanical apparatus is of the same period as the Canal Duke's work on the well at Ashridge. No one has claimed ownership of the well, but the former Little Gaddesden Preservation Society renovated it about 1966, but 'without obligation'.

The Brownlows encouraged the cottagers to care for their gardens. Some of the apple trees planted then still exist. They had planted a screen of trees of guelder rose, lilac, and bullace along the mainroad.

There were no entrance gates on the main road until after the 1928 sale, and entrance was from the common path in front of the cottages. The cast-iron diamond pane windows must be some of the earliest metal casements in cast-iron to be used in domestic building and probably date from about 1870. All the timber is from the Estate.

At the entrance to the common meadow there was an Estate workshop, where shooting carts, decoys and butts were made. This suggests that many of the residents were concerned with shooting and the maintenance of game. In 1927 the executors of the late Earl Brownlow offered interest-free loans to enable tenants to purchase their own properties, as well as 12 months' wages. In 1928 parts of the Ringshall area formerly in the parish of Ivinghoe were transferred to Little Gaddesden. There are still benefits available in this former Ivinghoe area from the earlier Ivinghoe charities.

Ringshall Cottages. Cottage numbers 3 to 13 were built earlier than 1820 and probably all have 18th-century work, some being restorations of late 17th-century cottages. Number 3 was used for a farm worker from Ringshall Hall Farm, and No. 4 for a farm worker from Wards Hurst Farm.

No. 6. As early as 1765, John and Henry Fountain owned houses in Ringshall, and Fountain's Store was kept in cottage 6 for several generations. Mr Arthur Fountain was responsible for much building work on older property and he worked on Ashridge House. He was for many years a chorister at Little Gaddesden church. His daughter and her husband took over the store after him, and their daughter, Mrs Stinton, transferred it to the Little Gaddesden Post Office in 1980. Cottage 6 was built later than No. 7, and has timbering in the roof, dating from the 17th to 18th centuries.

No. 7. This is one of the older timber-framed properties and much of its work is of the late 17th and 18th centuries. Floors on different levels suggest different stages of construction and the possible joining together of houses. From early maps we gather that there might have been a farm building here in the 18th century.

Timber-framing is exposed on the gable ends above the adjoining cottages. In the 1920s Tom Goodridge, a storeman at Ashridge, lived here. When the Estate was broken up, £125 was paid for this property. Mr Clifford Baron moved here from Greenacre in 1979. He was Captain of the Golf Club in 1959 and President from 1980.

No. 8. Arthur Clifton, whose father also lived here, was responsible for much restoration of older properties in the parish. He worked on John O'Gaddesden's House. Similarly, £125 was paid for this house at the Ashridge sale.

No. 9. Emma Saw came to live at No. 9 from Ringshall Lodge and also paid £125 for her house.

No. 10. Mr Smith bought this for £125.

No. 11. Mr Ginger, pensioner, bought this cottage for £125.

Mr Stephen J. Oakins, the postman, negotiated the purchases of these properties for the pensioners.

Nos. 12 & 13. There is early timber work on the inside of the rooms. Handmade locks and keys are of great interest. The porch of No. 13 is of local craftsmanship. The Garrett family lived here at the time of the sale. Cottage 13 cost £135.

Ringshall Laundry. One of several laundries known to exist at the end of the 19th century. It was occupied by the Goodman family after Elizabeth Whitman who had previously run the business. It was closed in 1981. The house was formerly known as the Egerton Arms Public House in the parish of Ivinghoe. At that time the houses on the Northchurch side of the Ringshall road were at the planning stage. No. 1 Ivinghoe Road was built adjoining the Laundry by Mr C.D. Williams. Mrs Williams was a daughter of Mr Goodman, senior.

No. 15. Mr and Mrs Wells of an old Ringshall family lived here. Mr D.N. Hepburn later acquired the house.

No. 16. Mr and Mrs W. Harmon lived here. He had been a member of the Metropolitan Police Force . For many years the Rector of Little Gaddesden conducted a monthly service here. Mrs Harmon's family had served at Ashridge for many years.

No. 19. Mr Buzzacott was Chairman of the Silver Jubilee Festival (1977) Committee in Little Gaddesden, who arranged a memorable week in the life of the parish.

Nos. 20 & 21. Mr R.B. Barrington extensively developed these two former cottages.

No. 22.(across the entry) The home of Mr John Milton the last of the original tenants who purchased their homes from the Ashridge Estate. He spent many years on the Estate.

No. 24. Mr Jack Mayling who had been churchyard gardener, school caretaker, and Rectory gardener lived here. Mrs Mayling who for many years held a monthly service here had formerly been a district nurse and midwife and had served in the Christmas Common area of Buckinghamshire. She was a much loved member of the Over 60s Club and the Women's Institute.

No. 25. Mr Thame worked for the National Trust for many, many years. He had a profound knowledge of the Estate.

No. 26. Mr C. Chapman who lived here had been decorated with the French Légion d'Honneur. He died in 1970. In earlier years this was the home of the Oakins family.

No. 28. Fred Hing, prominent in the British Legion lived here.

No. 29. The home of the Johnson family. Mrs Johnson was a founder member of the Women's Institute.

No. 32. Miss D.M. Rait Kerr, before living here was custodian and Librarian at Lords Cricket Ground from 1946 where her father, Colonel Rowan Scrope Rait Kerr C.B.E., D.S.O., M.C., had been secretary from 1939-52. Miss Rait Kerr and Ian Peebles published the official history of the M.C.C, *Lords 1946-1970.*

No. 33. Dr S.E.T. Cusdin has provided technical information about these houses. An architect specialising in hospital and medical aspects of his profession, he co-operated with Mr James Crooks, surgeon, of Meadow Farm, in the publication of *Demonstration Plans for Hospitals for Sick Children.* This work of 1947 was to be basic to the future of the Royal Children's Hospital, Great Ormonde Street. Dr Cusdin has also been concerned with hospital and university development in Hong Kong.

No. 34. Dr Ian G. Catchpole is one of the small number of those born in Little Gaddesden who have remained here after qualifying and marrying. He was formerly Chairman of the Sword and Keys Society and his wife was the secretary.

No. 35. Mr E.A. Janes, born and bred in Little Gaddesden, nourished his interest in nature and photography in the adjoining woodlands, and has done the photography for this book. Mrs E.A.

Janes succeeded her mother Mrs E.E. Clayton in her concern for the care and education of the infants of the village and she is head of the play group which meets in the Village Hall. Formerly Mr and Mrs Seth Janes lived here, and earlier still, the Saunders family.

Ringshall Cottages — Tenancy Agreement

This agreement signed by Mr A. Fountain of No. 5 Ringshall Cottages is typical of those made between the Ashridge Estate and their tenants in the late 19th and early 20th centuries.

Terms and Conditions

1. The tenant to hold the premises from month to month and pay the rent monthly if required, otherwise half-yearly (Lady Day and Michaelmas).

2. No lodger without written consent of the Landlord or Agent.

3. The bedroom windows, unless in case of illness, to be opened every morning from 8 o'clock until 12.

4. Every room to be lime-washed once a year, in May, at the expense of the tenant, the landlord delivering lime on the premises, on application.

5. All vegetable matter and refuse to be used or dug into the ground and not to accumulate in heaps or pits on any part of the premises.

6. No buildings to be erected on the premises by the tenant, and no existing buildings to be used for any other purpose than that for which it was built, without permission.

7. The Agent or Inspector to look over the whole premises as often as he may consider it necessary.

8. If these rules are strictly adhered to an allowance of one shilling in the pound will be returned on payment of the rent.

9. The tenancy commences on . . . and can be determined by either Landlord or tenant at any time giving to the other one calendar month's notice to quit. To be signed by the Agent and Tenant and witnessed.

Ringshall Hall Farm. Ringshall hamlet between Clipperdown and Little Gaddesden contained a farmhouse called Ringshall Hall Farm. It was appended to Ivinghoe which was in the possession of the bishopric of Winchester. It was purchased from the trustees of Thomas Squire and others on 20 May 1807 by John William, 7th Earl of Bridgewater. It was then annexed to the great Bridgewater Estate. At one time it was used specifically as breeding stables. For a great part of the 19th century it was farmed by a branch of the Janes' family. Mrs Potton, corn merchant, lived here for 20 years. The house had been restored in the late 19th century, and the Brownlow 'B' with the date 1872 is inscribed on it. During the war there were eight evacuees here.

Mr and Mrs Cullen acquired the property from Mrs Potton.

Ashridge Equestrian Centre. This land was obtained from Mr and Mrs Potton of Hall farm by Mr and Mrs Ellison of Benhay, and was used for stabling and breaking in hunters. Mrs Ellison ran an outdoor school for them and built the riding stables. In 1968 Mr and Mrs Craib bought the property and planned the new house. In the first instance it was intended to provide simply for their daughters' horses, but as requests for aid became more frequent, the idea for an Equestrian Centre developed and this has grown into a permanent centre of training where from eight to 12 students, both residential and non-residential prepare for the British Horse Show examination. The course lasts for about a year. Staff members are also trained, and riding instruction provided. Permission was obtained to use a cottage for staff. Part of the development in its early stage was the conversion of the outbuildings of Hall Farm. The architect whom Mr Craib used for Ashridge Farm was Raymond Andrews of Andrews, Downle & Kelly, and Donald Lockhart Ltd was responsible for the building in 1970.

Meadow Farm. This house was an Ashridge Estate property which was sold on the death of the 3rd Earl Brownlow. Dating possibly from the 17th century, there was certainly a building here by 1760, which was restored in the 19th century. The Hing family lived here at the time of the sale.

In 1928 Mr E.C. Fairweather sold the farm to Mr Francis Edwin Fisher of Duddenhill, Watford, who sold it a year later to Lottie Louise Elmslie. She sold it in July 1936, with Coppice Cottage, to Lady Gladys Williams, wife of Sir Owen Williams, for £2,200, and Lady Williams disposed of it in September 1936 for £1,050 to Mr James Crooks, surgeon of the Royal Children's Hospital, Great Ormonde Street, London. Mr Crooks had been largely responsible for the modern development of that hospital working to architectural designs with Dr S.E.T. Cusdin. He had been surgeon to younger members of the royal family and was made a companion of the Royal Victorian Order. He died in 1980.

The Coppice Cottage. This was probably a Jacobean cottage modernised in the 19th century. There is a pump dated 1709 in the house. White, the Ashridge keeper, lived here and bred pheasants in the 1920s in big wooden pens. He suffered greatly from poachers who stole the eggs and sometimes sold them back to him.

Sir Owen Williams resided here. He was responsible for the building of Wembley Stadium, and he later became a pioneer in motorway construction and the civil engineering of the M1 was his work. Sir John Betjeman stated that Sir Owen Williams' most prominent building was the Daily Express offices and printing house in Fleet Street, designed in 1931 with Ellis and Clark.

Later Mr and Mrs J. Purton lived here. In 1962 Mr A.W. Howitt acquired the property. In 1981 he was Master of the Merchant Taylors Livery Company. His chaplain was the former Archbishop of Canterbury, Lord Coggan, who, like Archbishop Robert Runcie, was an old boy of one of the Merchant Taylor Schools. Mr Howitt had the honour of presenting Archbishop Runcie to the Lord Mayor of London when he was invested a freeman of the city.

National Trust Cottages. These six cottages were erected by the National Trust for members working on the Ashridge Estate. Numbers 1 and 2 were first occupied in May 1939. Numbers 3 and 6 were built by Abbis and Hale of Rickmansworth in 1952.

Berrynarbor. This house is named after the pretty little parish in north Devon whose church possesses very valuable communion plate, and has an interesting squire's pew, like a cosy little room, with a fireplace. Berrynarbor in Devon was the birthplace of Bishop Jewel of Salisbury, a learned Anglican divine of the 16th century.

Ringshall End. This was built in 1929. Henry Christopher Bradby, for 36 years a master at Rugby School, lived here for 20 years after his retirement. He died in 1947 aged 79. A tablet to him and one to his wife were placed on the north wall of Little Gaddesden church.

Professor Charles R. Boxer F.B.A., Professor of Portuguese in the University of London, acquired Ringshall End in 1947. He had been a prisoner of war in Japanese hands 1941-45. He was an honorary Doctor of the Universities of Utrecht, Lisbon, Bahia, and Liverpool. He held a number of Portuguese decorations, wrote several books, and was a contributor to many learned journals. Mrs Boxer was formerly Emily Hahn.

Mrs Harvell was Chairman of the Village Produce Society and catering officer for the Over 60s Club for many years. Mr and Mrs Harvell came to live at Ringshall End in 1954.

Yeoman's. This house was built for Mr and Mrs G. Rogers in 1955 by Mr F.G. Whitman. It was later developed and enlarged by Mr Rogers, with the major work being done *c.* 1973. Mr George Rogers has the responsibility of mowing the Green.

Boundary Edge. The boundary between the counties of Hertford and Buckingham crosses Ivinghoe Road here. It is also the boundary between Ringshall, Little Gaddesden and Ivinghoe. In 1928 Edgar Fairweather who had bought part of the Ashridge Estate sold Ringshall cottage number 30 to Stanley Jones together with two other plots of land. Jones had the property built, and sold it to Mr Clarke in 1934. The house was then known as 'Meadow View'. After Clarke died, his widow sold it in 1957 to Mr McMinn, and the name was then changed to 'Boundary Edge'. In 1967 it was sold to Miss Brayshaw who in 1970 sold it to Mr N. Lymbery. The Lymberys built the second floor in 1973.

Ivinghoe Road. Traditionally known as Ivinghoe Road, in recent years a resident began to call it Beacon Road to the dismay of some, but acceptance of others.

7. *The Deer Leap to the Alford Cross*

THE ASHRIDGE LODGES

Ringshall Lodge (now the Deer Leap Garage). This was part of the Jeffry Wyatt reconstruction of Ashridge House *c.* 1817. It was at the entrance to the main drive from the north, which became a private drive after the 7th Earl had made the present main road from the Lodge corner down to the village. The Lodge is a Department of Environment Grade II building.

Little Gaddesden Lodge. Lately known as Tudor Lodge (see article), it marked the entrance to the Park from Little Gaddesden.

Peacock Lodge (Nettleden Lodge). This was sited on the ancient road from Ashridge to Water End, along which Princess Elizabeth was conveyed in February 1553 when summoned by Queen Mary to the Tower on suspicion of being implicated in the Wyatt rebellion.

Marian Lodge. Not named after a lodge like the others, but a residence.

Home Farm Lodge. At the entrance to the Home Farm.

Thunderdell Lodge. The work of James and Jeffry Wyatt (especially the latter) in about 1817 when work was being completed at Ashridge. Its design is not an uncommon one in East Anglia. It is probably built on the site of an older entrance to the Estate.

Berkhamsted Lodge. This was built by the 7th Earl of Bridgewater towards the end of his life on the old road from Hemel Hempstead to Aldbury. The pargetting on the present house which contains the Brownlow coat of arms is worth studying. The original pattern for this is in the Ashridge workshops. In 1980 this design was recoloured and renovated. It is similar to the work on numbers 20 and 21, Little Gaddesden. At one time it was possible to open the gates from the inside of the Lodge by means of a wheel connected with them.

Older couples who had served on the Estate moved into semi-retirement as lodge-keepers of Berkhamsted Lodge.

Deer Leap Swimming Pool. In the 1930s when it was first established, the Pool was run from the Garage, having been built by Mr Leslie Bedford who owned the property. During the war the Home Guard used the hut. It was later purchased by Mr John L. Constantine of White Meadows, Little Gaddesden. In hot summers the Pool naturally proved very popular and Little Gaddesden school children visited it regularly. The surroundings were pleasant, and later extensions were made and facilities improved. On several occasions attempts were made to establish a larger sports centre; a proposal which aroused considerable local feeling on both sides.

Deer Leap Garage. This was formerly Ringshall Lodge, and the Misses Saws are remembered as lodge-keepers. Their brother had been Head Keeper. The toll used to be one shilling.

The Oak House. Built between the wars by Mr Cuthbertson senior on his land. Dr Claud Morris, an anaesthetist from University College Hospital, London lived here, followed later by an Icelandic family, and then by Raymond Bird and his family. Mr P.E. Jones extended it considerably.

Silver Birches. This house was erected in 1966 by Mr E.W. Nightall and occupied by him in 1972 after his departure from Gaywoods.

Gaywoods. This was built in 1953-54 by F.G. Whitman for Mr Leek of Chudleigh to house Mantle, his gardener, though it was occupied and used in 1954 by Mr Mitchell as a pig and poultry farm. A year later its six and a half acres became a poultry breeding station owned and worked by Mr E.W. Nightall. Pedigree Rhode Island Red and Light Sussex birds formed the basic stock. There was a 5,000 egg incubator and 1,700 eggs were incubated weekly. The eggs were sold from the premises and through a packing station. Gaywoods was sold on Mr Nightall's retirement in 1972 to Mr Michael Laing. The house had been extended in 1963.

Chudleigh. Chudleigh was built in 1935 by Mr Fred Green and designed by his nephew. Mr Green was the brother of Sir Alan Green of Potten End. In 1952 when Sir Vincent Del Tufo bought Chudleigh, the house Gaywoods and Chailey Cottage were part of the estate. This was then divided, and now consists of six acres, including the wood on the far side of the valley, across Ringshall Drive. Chudleigh lies on the Exeter to Plymouth Road in a very attractive area of Devon. Lady Del Tufo has worked strenuously for the welfare of elderly people in Berkhamsted and Little Gaddesden.

Chailey Cottage. Mr L. Bedford of Deer Leap built this house initially as a gardener's cottage for Geoffrey Mantle, gardener to Mr Leek of Chudleigh, for £450. The house was later owned by the Rayment family. Mrs Rayment had pioneered the work of the Citizen's Advice Bureau in Hemel Hempstead. The house was named after a village of the same name about seven miles north of Lewes in Sussex where Mr Rayment had lived.

Dr Richard Edwards, Professor of Human Metabolism, University College Hospital, London, acquired the property from Mr Rayment. He modernised and extended it in 1979-80, and was one of the first residents to introduce the Scandinavian-style wood burning stoves for central heating. In 1981 the birds of the garden were recorded as part of a B.B.C. 'Living World' programme concerning the movement of local birds.

Saxons. Built in 1962-63 by Mrs Violet Hughes, possibly on the site of a Saxon settlement. Bits of Saxon tiles were ploughed up in the meadow during the Second World War when potato planting was being encouraged (1940). A Nissen hut on the site housed the Auxiliary Fire Service, and its engine was towed by the Hughes' Armstrong Siddeley car. Later the hut was used for village whist drives and Parish Council meetings. The architect was Willis of Berkhamsted and the builders Donald Lockhart Ltd.

From Saxons Mrs Hughes continued the public service which had characterised her husband's work in the area, especially on the Parish Council. Mrs Hughes' father was Mr Horace Nicholls, the official photographer to the nation during World War One. His photographs showing the part played by women during that war are remarkable studies, as also are those he took of Ashridge Park.

The Spinney. This was the first house built in the Park after the sale of the Brownlow Estate. It was erected in 1932 for Selby Hughes. The architect was Grice & Poulton, London, the builder was Wood of Wendover and the thatcher was Farman of Norwich. The land was bought from Mr Place of Northallerton who had purchased the land which the National Trust did not take from the Estate. It was called 'The Spinney' because of its situation. Later it was learned that this area was called Jenks's Spring after a former Rector, the Rev. David Jenks who kept a type of caravan here during his long incumbency (1829-69). In early days a nominal one shilling per annum tithe charge was paid to Queen Anne's Bounty (for clergy stipends).

Coneygarth. The spelling of Coneygarth has changed throughout the years. *Coneygarthe feld* is mentioned in 1543. *Koning Arc* was an earlier name recorded at the dissolution of Ashridge College. It was amongst lands from which sixpence an acre was paid to the crown (there were 30 acres). 'Coninger ffeilde . . . 40 acres' is the spelling and entry for Queen Elizabeth's inquisition of 1575. 'Coneygarth' literally means a rabbit-warren. The field to the north is named Coney Hill in an 1828 map of the area.

The present house was built by Mr Cuthbertson senior, between the wars. For a short time when the Froebel School had taken over Denison House, Mr G. Cuthbertson moved into Coneygarth. Mr P.W. Haydon, Rural District and Parish Councillor, Church Treasurer and lawyer lived here.

Hoo House, Hoo Wood. The Anglo-Saxon *Hoe* and *Ho* meant a spur of land, or the end of a ridge where the ground falls away sharply. It is used in Ivinghoe, Totternhoe, and Lilley Hoo. In Christian terminology *Hoh* and *Hough* denoted property belonging to the church ('Holy'), though there is no suggestion of that usage here.

This house was built by F.G. Whitman. For many years Leslie Lane, Parochial Church Council Treasurer and his family resided here. At that time it was known as 'The Cottage'. It was later extended and modernised by Mr S. Fraser-Beck and Mr R.J. Baker.

Farthings. This house was built in 1951-52 and was formerly called Norgael. F.G. Whitman was builder. It was greatly extended and modernised by Mr and Mrs J.C. Hill-Smith.

Springfield. This was built at the same time as Farthings by F.G. Whitman when wartime restrictions on private building were being relaxed. The site was originally known as glebe land. The two properties were solidly built to pre-war standards, with pre-war materials and roofed with pre-war shingles and tiles. It was planned to fit in with Little Gaddesden surroundings. There is evidence that there was originally a water tank for cattle grazing on glebe land, though at present there is no sign of a spring or boring.

Acorn Cottage and Glebe Cottage. These were formerly part of the Old Rectory estate which was sold in 1928 when the present Rectory was built. They were probably on the site of earlier Glebe cottages belonging to the 1744 Rectory. It is said that they were built to house the head and under-gardeners.

Acorn Cottage was the home of Mrs Alexandra 'Queenie' Thompson. After acquiring the property Mr F.A. Moody extended and modernised it.

Mrs May Rawdon-Smith lived in Glebe Cottage. Mr R.R. Slade extended and modernised it. Mrs Rawdon-Smith was correspondent to Little Gaddesden Church of England School governors, a position held at present by Mrs F.A. Moody.

Chittoe. This was at one time number two, Beaney Cottages. It is named after a tiny village in the Lacock area of Wiltshire. Built as one of two cottages by F.G. Whitman towards the end of the 1920s probably as service cottages of Beaney, which was the new name given to the former Rectory. For a time it was on loan to the R.A.F. Commander Howard Pain R.N. who had distinguished service in the Fleet Air Arm bought the property in 1951.

No. 1, Beaney Cottages. Built with the adjoining Chittoe by F.G. Whitman who owned them for a time and later sold them for £250. This property has recently been greatly extended by Mr Brian Morris.

Beaney, Ben Hay, Beany's, Godwin's, The Old Rectory. The frequent changes of this property's name indicate corresponding developments in the former Rectory estate. (see later note on the Rectories)

In 1878 a major reconstruction of the 1830 house took place. Godwin was at this time the architect for the stables, the parish church restoration and a proposed east window. He also designed Northampton Town Hall.

The area was in a state of terrible disrepair — the stables opposite the front door were tumbled down beneath an old oak tree, there was no drainage, and there was a stagnant pond behind the stables within five yards of the house, used by ducks and geese. To this 'fountain' villagers came for water in hot weather. The incumbent, Rector Lane, filled in the pond and made the present road to the stables. Extremely solid foundations were placed for the stalls. Rector Lane preferred to plant trees rather than to have a wall. The stables cost £600 of which Lord Brownlow paid two-thirds.

Extensive internal alterations took place in 1875 when the rector made an upstairs study. Roof slates had been bare and a new upstairs floor was constructed. He removed the pillars at the entrance to the house. In 1877 a new hot water system was installed together with a larder and outhouses. In 1879 he planted apple trees in the garden opposite the rectory door (Cox's orange, Dumelow seedling, new hawthornden, Keswick cod'ring, northern spy).

E.W. Godwin's obituary notices of 15 October 1886 say that he submitted designs for the rectory as well as for the stables, though these were never carried out.

In 1905 Rector E. Clarke planted a mulberry tree on the lawn and six standard apples and he added later a copper beech, an acacia (1910) and a laburnum (1915). The rockery, the holly hedge and the mountain ash had been planted by Rector Jenks. The trees were planted on family occasions. A manuscript in the British Library (Add. MS 5829 f198.6) gives a poem said to have been fixed to a fir or yew tree in Little Gaddesden Rectory garden.

During the Second World War the old parish room erected by Rector Hodgson and adjoining the Rectory was still being used by evacuees and Land Army girls.

After the sale, the Gibbs family who bought the house re-named it 'Benhay'. Susan the daughter married the founder of the Abbeyfield Homes and Mary married the Lord of the Isles.

The Rectory lands were conveyed to Mrs Dorothy Gibbs of Bush Hall, Hatfield by the ecclesiastical authorities on 10 November 1928 for £4,500. (See the article under 'The Rectory')

Later the Rectory lands were developed and Gatesdene Close was built in one part. Mr V. Ellison bought the property and later sold it to Mr Jack Overhill, who divided and modernised it, and provided new residential accommodation, including the former stable block. The Walsham family moved into 'Beaney' in 1982.

The Town Houses.

In 1617 Philip Power, churchwarden bequeathed his house and 10 acres of land to the poor. This charity became administered by the Philip Power Trustees, and the 'The Town Houses' was the name given to the property. They consisted in 1817 of — the house occupied by John Meager; the houses occupied by the widows; the houses at the top of the yard; the thatched cottage adjoining, occupied by Pates; and the barn and the wood barns.

An account of 1817 refers to the houses at the top of the yard—

> the south end wall is at least 4" out of upright, the timbers in front are in a decayed state, and the bricknogging tumbling out — the rafters, pulins and ceiling joints are much decayed & the roof appears to be falling in — the tiles also are much decayed and broken. The upper floor is in a very decayed state & being kept up only by a support nailed on one of the uprights is in great danger of falling in. There is no floor to the room occupied by Thorn's Family underneath and the floor of the room occupied by Rogers in which there is no fireplace or chimney is rotten and in danger of falling in. The bedroom over this is also in a very bad state, and the whole of the house is most filthy.

The dilapidated state of the Town Houses in 1817 was such that they would not last much longer. On 21 May 1821 Mr George Atty, clerk at Ashridge House, received a report from John Field which stated that the condition of the house recently occupied by John Thorn, and the part occupied by John Pates were both in such a decayed and dangerous state that it would be impossible to make them habitable. He recommended that they be taken down or sold, and negotiations took place with the Trustees of the Dissenters Chapel at Chesham for a sale or exchange of the property. The 'Pearrishmen' took an inventory of the goods of the old widows on their decease. Mother Hearkear on 7 January 1754 had — 'two cobbards, two tabels wrmin pan: heand isurns 1 pear of tongs one spit 1 dripin pan 1 beef fork 1 friin pan two beads 2 blankets and curtens 1 churst two boxes two peals two bearils one kittel one porrig pot:6:Chears 1 gridion'.

In contrast with the above record is another list of the possessions of widow Gould on 8 June 1775.

> 'A cherry tree table, a large square ashen table, a pull up clock with a head to it, pewter plates, a warming pan, two iron candlesticks, two chimney hooks, a gridiron, a pair of iron dogs, a small ironfender, a pair of bellows, a pair of tongs, a fire shovel, seven old chairs, a brass pottage pot, a brass skilot, a brass kettle, a large oak chest, one bedstead and curtains, one feather bed and bolster, one flock bed and bolster, one plain bedstead, a box on a stand, two blankets, one firkin barrel, a frying pan, a wood peel'.

This was a carefully written list, and one deduces that the writer was educated. It may have been prepared before she died, ready to pass to the 'Pearrishmen'. She may have been typical of those who ended their days in the Town Houses because they had no other means of support.

Under the Canal Duke (1748-1803) men who arrived late for work on Mondays on the Ashridge Estate were fined a half-crown. The proceeds went to the construction of new cottages which became known locally as 'Half-Crown Row'. The name Half-Crown Row was also popularly used of cottages in the Duke's Lancashire property. It would be interesting to know to which row this title referred . . . The Town Houses, Ringshall, or Ringshall Drive below Hudnall Lane end?

Numbers 1-4, Little Gaddesden.

The register of electors for 1930 gives numbers 1 to 63, Little Gaddesden as being 1 to 63 High Street. Numbers 1 to 4 were called 'The Town Houses', but their precise relationship with the buildings of the houses described in the 1820s is not clear. These four houses were for large families, having three bedrooms. Originally the present front doors were at the back and the houses fronted, it is suggested, on to an older road. Numbers 3 and 4 were reserved for the gardener and the coachman at the Rectory.

Number 2 went with the church farm.

Number 1 was reserved for a gamekeeper. Mr Stephen J. Oakins, later the postman, was born here on 20 February 1880.

5, The Old Forge. This was so named in 1921 when the Duncombe family went to live there. Wilfred Duncombe was the blacksmith at Ashridge. The bellows are behind the house and two weights from the forge are beside the door. Mrs Duncombe (Alice Wheatcroft) had come from Emsworth in Yorkshire to work in the Ashridge laundry as 3rd laundry maid and she later married Mr Duncombe. There were 25 servants in the house at that time.

October House. In 1838 there were two cottages on this site, occupied by William Foster. From the 1930s to the 1960s this was the home of the Liberty family. It was kept as a café for a time, and boys from Berkhamsted School stayed there during half-term holidays when their parents were away. Frank West, later Bishop of Taunton, remembered the iron poster bed.

The ancient pathway from the Rectory to the Church began here, part of which, made of brick, still remains. The village pound in the field nearby was associated with this house. The house was extensively modernised and restored by Mr Terence Indermaur Jones. He and his wife, Diana, were married in October, hence the name of the house.

Numbers 6 and 7. Little Gaddesden. When the Department of the Environment included a Class III category in the list of buildings of historical interest, this was included in that group. This house with its diamond-shaped leaded window-panes and casements is believed to have been built as a small square in 1760 under the Canal Duke. The bricks come from St Margarets. Lord Brownlow added the kitchen at the end of each part of the house and put in a small staircase about 1860. It became two three-bedroomed cottages. It had four rooms downstairs and four upstairs, an entrance hall and a staircase.

The Andrews family lived in no. 6 for many years as small farmers. Old Mr Andrews was the Ashridge tailor and he supplied the livery for Ashridge. There is a small area on the ground floor where he worked which is protected so that his feet should not get cold on the bare stone. Mrs Drewitt, his daughter, helped to run the farm. Before the first war she drove round the village in a pony and trap delivering the milk and eggs.

When Miss Burnett was working on the fresco at the east end of Little Gaddesden church she lived in cottage six. She worked in candlelight on scaffolding in the church. She had copied the fresco in the Palazzo Riccardi in Florence, and had achieved great success in the resulting copy in the Parish Church.

Mr W.E. Hurcomb who later occupied the property was a highly respected antique dealer. He numbered amongst his clients many whose names were very well known indeed, and included members of the royal family. He sold for Archbishop Temple (then at Manchester) all the silver which had been presented to his father when Archbishop of Canterbury. He also sold the private communion set belonging to the Rev. H. Lyte, author of 'Abide with me'. His *Life and Diary* is a remarkable record of anecdotes concerning his customers and the sales he made on their behalf. His daughter lived here, and the house became a single dwelling.

Dr Cassell converted the stable hayloft block into a music room in 1975-76 and it was opened with a violin recital on 14 March 1976 by Dona Lee Croft, an American violinist.

The house may have been built for a senior estate servant or used for the curate. The village street probably went behind the house and cottages 1 to 4, thence to Dagnall.

No. 8. In the 1930s Jesse Holland lived here. A century before in 1838 a man of the same name lived at no. 54 or one of the adjoining cottages.

No. 9. Walter Holland lived here during the 1930s.

No. 10. The date is uncertain but the property was probably built in the late 18th century. Joseph Buggey, carter at Ashridge, began his tenancy here on Lady Day, 25 March 1900. His mark (a cross) was witnessed by W.F. Wheatley, the Ashridge agent, and by J. Parsons. The house contained a living-room and a scullery downstairs with two bedrooms and an attic upstairs, and with a flush toilet outside. Soft bricks 14 inches long were used with lath and plaster partitions and it is from these bricks that we can date the structure to the period from 1784 to 1806.

Mr John J. Oakins, churchwarden for 25 years, Chairman of the Parish Council, and for 40 years crafts master at Berkhamsted School, moved here on 14 September 1935 on his marriage. Mr Oakins' symbol, an acorn, may be seen inscribed on some of his work in the Parish Church. Mr Oakins' father was village postman and churchwarden and his grandfather was a church official. Mr Oakins had purchased numbers 10 and 11 for £240 in 1935.

No. 11. The residence of Mr Stephen Oakins after his mother's death. His father, Stephen, had moved here from 26, Ringshall on 1 November 1915. Numbers 10 and 11 were extended by F. Whitman in 1933.

No. 12. Mr James lived here. He had been associated with a former Rector, Dr H.G. Woods who became Master of the Temple in 1904.

No. 13. The village plaiting school was originally held in this house. The 7th Earl when he came to Ashridge complained that the village boys only knew plaiting and lace making which their mothers taught them. The house was pulled down at the turn of the century and rebuilt.

Both numbers 12 and 13 were extended in 1965 by Mr G.E. Catchpole. Mrs Catchpole was born, and has always lived in number thirteen. For many years the building adjoining was a chandlers shop. Mr G.E.Catchpole became churchwarden of Little Gaddesden in 1973.

Their surname is of considerable interest. In the Domesday Survey of 1086 it appears as *Chacepol*; under Henry II it is *le Chacepol*; in 1221 *Cachepol*; Middle English as *Caccepol* and *Cachpol*; and Old Norman-French has *Cachepol* with the meaning 'Chase-fowl'.

On the eve of the Norman Conquest it signified a collector of poultry in default of money . . . a type of tax-gatherer. Yet by the 14th century its usage had become more generalised to mean an officer of the sheriff, especially one of the standing of a sergeant who would arrest for debt.

Church View. When Mrs Ward retired from the Post Office she built this house and named it Church View because of its excellent view across the meadows to the Church. The architect was Mr J.W. Ball F. R.I.B.A. of Westcott, Golf Club Road.

No. 14. A house formerly belonging to the Ashridge Estate. In January 1892 Mr A. Fountain put in a new window in the bedroom, worked on the flooring and plastered the barn. There had been an earlier building — perhaps even two cottages — on this site. At one time there was a shop here.

Ralph Kibby was born here. He began to play the Little Gaddesden organ at the outbreak of war in 1914 when he was only 13 and he continued playing here as well as Great Gaddesden and Ashridge College. He played at the College for 55 years. His father was Sam Kibby, and his service in the Boer War resulted in him losing a leg, after which he wore the old type of stump to get about. His son Simeon was in the choir — 'when as a tenor he let drive on a top note, as he frequently did, he bleated like a sheep'.

For many years this house was the residence of Mr and Mrs V. Ward who owned the Post Office and store. Mr Ward had been a great sportsman in his younger days and was goalkeeper for St Albans in the Isthmian League. His exploits were featured in national newspapers . . . the *Sunday Graphic* and *Daily Express*.

Gatesdene Close. This was formerly part of the Rectory lands which had been conveyed by the Rector, the Bishop of St Albans, the Archbishop of Canterbury and the Ecclesiastical Commissioners for England to Dorothy Elizabeth Gibbs, wife of Ralph Crawley Gibbs of Bush Hall, Hatfield in 1928. She conveyed it to Frederick George Whitman, farmer, of Hudnall Common Farm on 31 December 1949, together with numbers 1 to 4 Beaney Cottages. On 2 April 1954 F.G. Whitman conveyed various plots to purchasers who were to create an attractive cul-de-sac in this area. On the same day Whitman also conveyed lands which were to form the future Gatesdene Close. Plot five was conveyed to Mr Douglas Milward Ball who named it *Greyfriars.* This name was chosen because of a house in a London suburb which had been so greatly admired that both this house and one owned earlier by Mr Ball were given this name.

Through Mr Ball's interest Little Gaddesden obtained a set of handbells for the church. Mr and Mrs Heard succeeded the Ball family in 1981.

Number One. This house built by F.G. Whitman after the 1954 conveyance, was occupied by members of the Dunn family ('The Hatters') who had moved from Hudnall. Mr and Mrs C.A. Brighton succeeded to this property. Mr Brighton's lectures on 'Plastics in the Garden' proved very useful to members of the Village Produce Association.

Wood Ash. This name was given by Mr and Mrs Purton who had previously lived in Wood Vale, London.

Ash Riding. This perpetuates the name of an old drive, similar to Princes Riding, which appears on early maps including one of 1760.

Serenity. This land was bought from F.G. Whitman by Mr and Mrs K.A.M. Dickson in 1956.

Mr Whitman had worked with Mr Hobson Hill at West Common, Harpenden and he developed a similar architectural style. This revealed itself in the design of Serenity through a tile-hung upper storey, with 'eyebrows' over upstairs windows. He used old bricks, doors, locks and latches to give an 'established' appearance to the house.

Serenity was first occupied on 7 October 1957. The house was so named because of its clear views across the valley which give a feeling of tranquility. The garden has been a haven for wild birds, hedgehogs, weasels and frogs and in early years nightingales used to sing from the fir trees bordering Benhay.

There was a toad walk along which the toads moved to the natural ponds then in the area.

Windyacre has superb views across Ringshall Drive and valley.

In the planning stage Gatesdene Close was known as Witchcraft Close because of its proximity to Rosina Massey's cottage in Witchcraft Bottom. However a possible purchaser of this plot feared an unlucky association with the name witch, and so it became Gatesdene Close. For the derivation of Gatesdene see the article on Little Gaddesden and Ashridge. (see page 1)

The Post Offices. The old Post Office was housed at no. 15, a Brownlow cottage owned by Mr Bevan of Hemel Hempstead. His sister, Mrs Cobb, was Postmistress until Mr Ward succeeded her and rented the front part of the cottage from 1 April 1934 to 10 November 1947 when he and Mrs Ward moved to their new premises. The present Post Office which they built was the work of F.G. Whitman and local workmen, and designed by Mr Louis Moore of Greenacre, Ringshall Road. Since Mr and Mrs Ward's time the Post Office has been owned by Mr Barlow, then by Mrs Battel, and since 1980 by Mrs Stinton and Mrs Mountfort.

The signpost is the work of Mr L. Ouseley. The 'Telegraph Office' sign now to be seen was brought from the old Post Office in 1947.

In 1847 Mr George Tomlin, one of three tailors in the parish (Thomas Marriott and John Harvey were the others), simultaneously held the position of Postmaster. Letters were received at the office from Hemel Hempstead at 8 a.m. each morning; the despatch was at 5 p.m.

Edward Cutler was Postmaster in 1853. Mr Stephen J. Oakins was the postman for many years.

The Bridgewater Arms. The earliest part of the present building dates from the 18th century. The porch with its Doric columns and doorway with its fan-shaped over window are both early 19th century. One story says that part was built to house overflow guests or staff from Ashridge House. Another story says that it may originally have been a granary for Ashridge College of the Bonhommes, though evidence for this seems lacking.

There was a building on this site in 1760 and towards the end of the 18th century the Garrett family, later to become managers of the *Bridgewater Arms*, were extensive farmers. William Garrett farmed 135 acres for Mr Underwood, and Samuel Garrett farmed 24 acres for Mr John Garrett. In 1838 George Garrett farmed about eight acres of land known as Winnett's Meadow and Street Meadow, as well as managing the *Bridgewater Arms*. By then the land was owned by the Countess of Bridgewater, though John Garrett owned two acres of Badger Wood. However the date when the house became an inn could be either during the lifetime of the 7th Earl or perhaps even earlier, during the ducal period. The present Inn sign, a copy of an earlier sign, shows a ducal coronet. If this had been a copy of an even earlier one, then the date of the house would have been between 1720 and 1803 when the last Duke died.

Nathaniel Duddleston, farmer was said to have been the first licensee and he took over in 1815. Such a date might suggest that the *Bridgewater Arms* became important when the new road to the present Deer Leap was made, and when Ringshall Drive was then enclosed . . . thus removing some of the trade from the inn in Witchcraft Bottom.

In 1853-54 the school for Little Gaddesden was held in the *Bridgewater Arms*. The children clambered up the steps and in through a window because they were not allowed to pass through the door of licensed premises. More adults than children at first attended the school! The Inn stands on the old path from Studham to Northchurch and the Hertfordshire stile in the car park is of interest.

In 1880 Mr Norris was proprietor and licensee. He was dependent on the hay crop for his rent, and in this year there was a very bad harvest, which in addition to his home troubles almost took away his reason. He had a stroke and died on 13 September 1880. His funeral was held at the Baptist cemetery at Ivinghoe. A contemporary journal describes the funeral— 'The minister stood over the grave and after the corpse had been deposited he said "Ere's the remains of Muster Norris, Overseer of the Parish of Little Gaddesden for 35 years and a good man of business. We 'ope 'is soul's gone to 'eaven"'. That constituted the entire service! After Norris's death Mrs Norris had none to care for her 'but to prevent the disgrace of her going to the Union, her relatives consented to allow her something a week, and Lord Brownlow gave her a room at Hoar's the butcher's. She was conveyed there in the Rector's [C.G. Lane] brougham, as she dreaded the gaze of the village'.

In the 1920s Mr Geer a former engineer, was licensee. He first installed electricity both in the *Bridgewater Arms* and then in the Home Farm. He proposed to his future wife on the top of the Bridgewater Monument. He was father of Austin Geer, an aeronautical engineer.

In later years extensive improvements were carried out on the taproom, the stables, the outhouses and the garden cottages. The garden was enclosed and enlarged and for a time the village bowling green attracted much interest. The Trust House Forte Group acquired the *Bridgewater Arms* and for some years provided residential accommodation which was well used. Finally it was decided that the necessary reconstruction and fire precautions would be too expensive, and it was then divided into two parts: the Inn without accommodation owned by Mr W.W. Woods; and the new flats.

Early landlords included Messrs James Foster, G. Garrett, Arthur Norris (1847, 1867), Mr and Mrs Allison, and Vic Edge. Allison traded in second-hand carts and met a tragic death as he was driving to Berkhamsted in one when a bolt came out of the cart and he was dragged along behind it. The gate-keeper seeing the cart, opened the gate not realising that Allison was being dragged along, and Allison was killed.

Numbers 15, 16 and 17. These estate cottages probably all date from the mid-18th century. At the turn of the century they were owned by Mrs Vaughan and occupied by Captain Newby who farmed 22 acres. There is a memorial to Mrs Vaughan by Edward Physick in the parish church dated 1826. In 1838 the cottages were occupied by widow George, Thomas Kirby and John Clifton.

Number 15 was formerly the Post Office (see article on the Post Offices) and occupied by Mrs Cobb. Her husband was a veteran of the First World War having served in the Royal Navy as a boy. His father had been a coastguard. 'Old Cobbie' was in charge of a large contingent of sailors in the London Victory Parade.

Number 18/19. The timber-framing of this property could be late 16th to mid-17th century, and of the time of the 1st and 2nd Earls of Bridgewater. In 1802 the occupiers were Mr Marriott and P. Rogers. In the mid-18th century there were three cottages here occupied by James Meager, Anstiss Cooley and William Batchelor. An 18th-century addition was made on the south-east side. The meadow was known as Winnett's Meadow by 1838.

After the sale of the Ashridge Estate Mr Place established the Little Gaddesden Estate office at no. 18 and Mr H. Thoms was placed in charge. People who desired to purchase building plots had to apply to this office. Henry Thoms worked here until he moved to no. 16 next to Mrs Hing's cottage (no. 17). Mr Gordon Stock, the waterworks engineer under Mr Thoms, worked and lived at no. 18, and people came to the house to pay their water rates. Once a week a branch of Barclay's Bank was opened here. At one time when there was a local shoot the game was laid out on trestle-tables in the garden at the rear

Mr Owen Williams bought the house, and he considerably renovated and modernised it in 1950.

The Rectory. The present Rectory is the successor of houses for the rector which go back at least to before 1209. In that year Hugh of Wells, Bishop of Lincoln, in whose vast diocese Little Gaddesden was, wrote that there was a suitable house here for Julian the Cleric. If the present church was built on the site of its predecessors, and there is no reason to believe the contrary, a very likely place for such a house would be on the south side of the church. The Priest's pathway to the present south chapel door may therefore be very old indeed — worn down with usage, and leading from the house to the chancel.

In 1638 the Rectory contained a hall, a kitchen, a brew-house, a 'stayer case', a 'little studye' and three upper rooms or lodging chambers. In the yard there were two barns, a stable, a schoolhouse, a hog sty with nine or 10 bays, a little milk-house, an orchard, two gardens, a nursery, and a hop-yard. This would probably have been on the site of the present house, Benhay.

In 1682 when Thomas Henshaw was presented to the Rectory by the 2nd Earl of Bridgewater, the rectorial tithes were restored.

In 1780 the pond in the parsonage garden was cleaned, for the first time in 60 years. In 1835 it was again cleaned for David Jenks II, though 35 years later it was filled in and the road to the new stables was made across it (see Benhay).

In 1744 Rector Charles Tough built a new parsonage and brew-house. Scroop the 1st Duke provided the oak and valued it at over £50.

In 1830 the Rectory was rebuilt for James Horseman. It took over a year to build a 'very superior parsonage' (Horseman).

On 10 November 1928 the Rectory house, gardens and lands of 12 acres together with stabling and outbuildings were conveyed to Mrs Dorothy Gibbs for £4,500 including a further four acres. Mrs Gibbs conveyed them to F.G. Whitman for £9,730 on 31 December 1949 . . . the 12 acres plus the four acres containing numbers 1 to 4 Beaney Cottages.

The Present Rectory cost £2,960 in 1929 for the Rev. J.L. Barkway. The architect, who also built Aldbury Rectory, was C.H.B. Quennell. The harvest preacher at Little Gaddesden in 1885 had been the Rev. W. Quennell. The building was completed by H.Y. Matthews of Berkhamsted. H. Meager was general foreman, and Frank Hoare labourer. The carpenters were Messrs. Stratford and Langford. Mr John Oakins was the apprentice. During the building the Rector lived at no. 20. This was later to be occupied by the Pritchard, the Lane, the Heber, the Rabbetts and the Oakley families. Mr Pritchard owned the field between numbers 18 and 19 and the Rectory.

Numbers 20 and 21. In the middle of the 18th century there was a building here of two or more cottages. In 1902 the occupier was named Pitkin. In 1838 William Pitkin was the occupant. In the late 19th century Mr Worrall the schoolmaster said that near School Meadow four cottages were rebuilt, four having previously been pulled down. Mr F. Green states that the present nos. 20 and 21 were made from the previous four. These were erected in 1903 and were said to be the last Brownlow houses ever built. No. 21 was bought in 1928 for the policeman.

The pargetting on the front of no. 20 and the side of no. 21 is of interest. The coat of arms of the Brownlow family with the motto 'Esse quam videri' is shown on it, together with the initials 'B' for Brownlow and 'AB' for Adelaide Brownlow.

Mr Harry Temple, the carpenter, helped to build these houses. Before the First World War a Mr Willis lived here and then Mr Aylott from 1925 to 1930. Mrs Aylott watched the building opposite the Rectory, and remarked on 'the enormous cess pit'. Mr Parker lived here from 1931 to 1949, and the last policeman to live here was Mr A.A. Sherringham (1949-63). The third bedroom and electricity were added in 1937.

In 1963 the Rector negotiated with Hertfordshire County Council to obtain no. 21 as a school house. He had recently obtained their approval for a similar scheme elsewhere and the precedent was recognised. The policeman's house was built adjoining the Village Hall as a result of parallel negotiations between the British Legion, and the Parish and County Councils. Mr D.J. Prior lived here from 1963 to 1966 when Mr A.J. Williams followed him.

Number 22/23. Originally there were two cottages here with a central chimney made of two-inch bricks. The earliest date has been estimated at 1600. In 1802 the area was owned by Mr Meager and the occupier was Forster. In 1838 four tenants appear — John Clarke, Thomas Simmons, Adam Tomkins and William Clifton. Lord Brownlow added a room at each end (one of his customary additions to cottages) and a room at the rear of of twenty-three. An outer skin was thus built round the original cottages.

The shield on the chimney of no. 23 is an earl's coronet above the letter 'B' for Brownlow and the date is 1872. At the time of the Great War Jack Buggey lived at no. 22 and Mr Batchelor at no. twenty-three. In the early 20th century an addition of about three feet was made in Luton-blue brick, and at the same time an outhouse was built. In 1971 John Campbell added two rooms and a garage. Old timbers from a Suffolk barn and stock brick were used. When the Department of the Environment had a Class III in its schedule of listed buildings this was included in that class. Further modernisation was completed by Mr A. Hyde.

Number 24. There was a cottage here in the mid-18th century and at the end of the century it was occupied by a man named Morris. There were two occupants and therefore two cottages here in 1838. 'Frankie Rogers said that there were formerly two old cottages here [F. Green]. The second would be 25.'

In 1961-62 the present house was built for Mr Thomas Simmons and designed by A.L. Osborne F.R.I.B.A. Originally the house was planned for two elderly ladies. Opposition in the village to the possible house made them fear future unpleasantness, and so they sold it to Mr Simmons, a building contractor and ex-Mayor of Watford, who bought the plans, modified them slightly and built it. He moved in during 1962. There had been a public enquiry because of local objections to the building of the house, and the Little Gaddesden Preservation Society was active in opposition. However Mr Simmons succeeded in obtaining permission. He extended his land by purchasing a strip from no. 22/23 and built a new cesspit for it. 'To conciliate the Village' he replaced the old, dilapidated church notice-board with the present glass-fronted one, illuminated it and erected signposts for the church and Church Farm. He donated the land for the paving of Church Road. Once Mr and Mrs Simmons had lived here there was no ill feeling in the village.

The garden was planned by R.S. Ball of Watford. Mr Simmons built the oak fence round his garden to provide safety for the golden retriever which his successors were to bring with them. The house cost £12,000 to build plus an additional £750 to provide fittings for it.

Miss Margaret Crawford's rockery on the wayside on Church Road has become a feature of the parish and gives pleasure to passers-by throughout the year.

Number 26. It is suggested that the present no. 26 stands on the site of an older property in existence in the mid-18th century. It was a house not a cottage, and by 1802 Mr C. Buckmaster who was agent or steward at Ashridge owned and lived in the property. He was also church-warden. In 1838 it was occupied by Mary Buckmaster, his widow.

Number 28 was a butcher's shop in 1838 and was occupied by William Reeve. The chimneys of the house are worth studying.

26, Greenend. This house was built with no. 28 in 1850 to house Lord Brownlow's estate workers. There was an abattoir on the site of the present garden on the Rectory side of the drive which served the butcher's shop. The outhouse building form is visible in drought conditions.

Until 1929 Greenend was used as the schoolmaster's house. There had, as above, been a butcher's shop at the Rectory end and there was a grocer's shop facing the main road. The three houses were made into one for Mr Worrall the schoolmaster who kept the post office here in the former grocer's shop.

Later the armoury from the Manor House was moved to adjoin the school house here. Sutherland, Clerk of Works at Ashridge was in charge of the alterations. In the cellar of the former butcher's shop there were meat hooks in the ceiling.

Meriden Cottage. Numbers 27 and 28. No. 27 was lower than nos. 26 and 28. The interior reveals structural differences and upstairs there are different ceiling and roof levels. There are cellars and the older roof tiles still exist. Mr and Mrs Harry Temple lived in Meriden Cottage, and Mrs Temple took in paying guests. After Mr Temple died Miss Helen Cowdell lived in the house and was the local authority on animals and their care. The annexe at the rear was called the Harness Room because it was used by the Home Guard. Harry Temple gave woodwork instruction at his Hudnall Lane shed. His brother was said to be the best carpenter in England.

The gates of the parish church and Hudnall Chapel were the work of Harry Temple.

Sergeant-Major Ballam a well known figure at the turn of the century lived at 28. [See the Gazetteer].

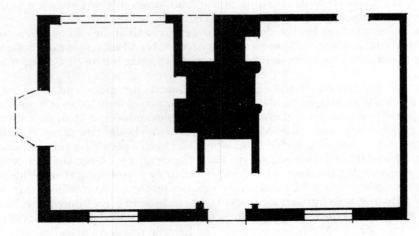

Fig. 15   Plan of Tudor Cottage.

Tudor Lodge. This house was variously known as Turl's Lodge after Tookey Turl, Park Gate Lodge, Fountain Lodge, Simmond's Lodge and Lady Marian Lodge. This last name was given because Lady Marian Alford made plans, which never materialised, to convert it into a residence for Miss Mac-Dougall. The space between the two main rooms is about six feet thick and may conceal an inglenook.

The Temples were lodge-keepers for the Estate and when the 1928 sale took place it was simply called 'The Lodge'. 'Tudor' was added either by the Brigsbury or the Beer families who later resided here. It has been known as Tudor Lodge since before 1939.

It is not unlikely to have been of 17th-century origin, and formerly was two cottages. It was part of Ivinghoe parish and when in the 1840s an ancestor of the Oakins family was to be married, he or she had to walk to Ivinghoe Church from this cottage for the ceremony. The schoolmaster John Worrall lodged here for almost six years when he first came in 1854.

RINGSHALL DRIVE

There was originally a main road down the valley through Little Gaddesden from Ivinghoe to Hemel Hempstead. The road was enclosed by the 7th Earl of Bridgewater when he made the present road from the former Rectory, now Benhay, to the present Deer Leap Garage site. Parallel to the old road, the present Drive became the private carriage drive to Ashridge House. The old road continued down the Golden Valley to Nettleden and Water End.

The former cottages date from the 17th century and have interesting chimney-stacks set diagonally, and there are also dormer-windows and protruding bay windows. Two cottages were formerly an inn (pre-1654) and hooks on which the sign hung could be seen in the late 19th century. The modern straight road succeeds an older driveway which meandered along the valley on the other side of Faerie Hollow and Witchcraft Hollow.

The Croft. Originally part of the Estate, the land from the Lodge to Witchcraft Hill was sold by Thomas Place of Northallerton. He sold the 'Croft' land to Julia Stonebridge for £120. Erected in 1934 this house was the second to be built in the Park. It was designed for Mr Stonebridge, agent to the Duke of Bedford at Woburn, by his son. The Croft was sold to Mr Farry, a London silk merchant in 1938 and in 1943 Mr C.H.G. Dunham bought the property. It was 1½ acres and was said to be a portion of a four acre plot sold for £200.

Faerie Hollow formerly *Witchcraft Bottom.* This was once three Estate cottages though the one to the north was burned out. Stumps of three old apples trees, one for each cottage could be seen at one time. The cottages were numbered 42, 43 and 44 and the road ran across the further side of the house from the present lane.

Wytchacre. Built after the breakup of the Estate it was for many years the home of Miss Hedges and Miss M.R. Wood, the latter of whom modernised it in 1979-80. It was built in 1934 by F.G. Whitman for £900. The architect was Newbury A. Trent of Chelsea.

Witchcraft Cottage. Built about 1933-34 for Mr Richard Oakley, school manager and local amateur historian, who was especially interested in John O'Gaddesden's House where he lived for a time. This formed 1¼ acres of the four acre site mentioned above. Mr G. Samford resided here and kept sheep. He was followed by Mr G.L. Wicks.

Witches Hollow. This was formerly the Inn on the pathway from Studham to Berkhamsted. The date when the *Bridgewater Arms* replaced this Inn, or whether they both existed for a time together, is not known. Later Mr Hart, Ashridge gardener and Mr T. Halsey, keeper, lived here as neighbours. Two semi-detached cottages were converted in about 1936 by Philip Brown of Ealing for Lady Waller.

Former residents include Major and Mrs Greer. Mr Greer did much important work for the Ashridge Golf Club. Mrs Greer, was Baroness Freytag-Loringhaven, and she fled from Russia at the time of the Revolution carrying her son and a revolver in her Russian muff. Each Easter morning she would greet the Rector after service with the traditional Russian Easter greeting.

For information about Rosina Jane Massey, the reputed witch, see the article on witches in the Gazetteer section.

Witchcraft Hill formerly known as *Bracken Priory*. Originally in the Estate numbering, these two properties were nos. 36 and 37, following no. 35 the end house at Ringshall. Mr Tom Hobbs was born at no. 37 in 1861. His mother was Caroline Simmons from Ringshall in the parish of Ivinghoe. Bob Hobbs was standard-bearer for the British Legion a century later.

The two semi-detached cottages were said to be Elizabethan.

Mrs Cosmo Cran bought about thirty five acres here in 1936 for development. After the war she called this house, now made into one dwelling, Bracken Priory. The 'Priory' name does not seem to have any connection with the Ashridge Bonhommes. The builder was F.G. Whitman and the thatcher was Farman of Norwich. Later residents have included Mr Scott, Mr (later Sir) Max Bemrose, Mr M. Saville, Sir Ivan Stedeford, and Mr N.P. Bailey.

Cherry Tree Cottages. Numbers 38 and 39 were later called by this name. Billy Munden and his wife adopted children and brought them up here. Frankie Rogers, sexton at the parish church, and his wife also adopted sons. Children brought up here grew with a profound knowledge of the countryside and the richness of natural life in this area.

At one time there was also a 'granny cottage' here.

In 1821 there were 17 cottages in the present Ringshall Drive area including two at the present Tudor Lodge.

THE ALFORD CROSS

The cross at the Little Gaddesden entrance to the Ashridge Estate was unveiled on Sunday 21 June 1891 in memory of Lady Marian Alford. Although the official spelling in documents was Marianne, the normal spelling was Marian. She was widow of John Hume Egerton, Viscount Alford whom she had married in 1841. He inherited Ashridge in 1849 two years before he died. Lady Marian was the mother of the 2nd and 3rd Earls Brownlow.

The cross in her memory is in the form of an 'Iona' cross because similar crosses marked the resting places of many of her ancestors. Iona, the size of Ashridge Park, is close to the Isle of Mull off the west coast of Scotland. St Columba built his monastery there. Missionaries went from Iona, and it became an educational centre for northern Britain with its Cathedral of St Margaret.

Lady Marian's father, the Marquess of Northampton, as a belated traveller took refuge at Torloisk where he was received graciously by Colonel McClean Clephane, and by his three daughters. The Marquess fell in love and married one of the daughters, and the McClean property thus came into the Compton family. Lady Marian was their daughter, and thus always had an affection for Iona and the faith vigorously upheld by the apostles of the north.

In front of the cross is carved 'Whosoever drinketh of the water that I shall give him shall never thirst; but the water that I shall give him shall be in him a well of water springing up into Everlasting Life'. Beneath the cross is a fountain and drinking trough for horses, and on the ground a small one for dogs.

At the service of dedication the Bishop of Ely, Lord Alwyne Compton, the Dean of York, Lady Marian's brother, and the Rector officiated. Lord Brownlow unveiled the cross in memory of his mother. Many of Lady Marian's friends and relatives had contributed. The cross in its design owed much to Mrs Wheatley who later sought to keep alive the memory of Lady Marian's goodness among the children of Little Gaddesden by distributing bags of sweets each year on the anniversary, to the children gathered near the cross.

Lady Marian was a very distinguished woman, her father was President of the Royal Society and her mother was said to be one of the most well educated women in England, and a friend of Sir Walter Scott. Lady Marian had a profound knowledge of art and was greatly influenced by her travels in Italy. As a needlewoman she made an altar frontal for the parish church and her exquisite needlework was seen in other churches adjoining the Ashridge Estate. She gained the assistance of Princess Christian and others to establish the Royal School of Needlework under Queen Victoria's patronage.

She was also a promoter of social benefits. She had water laid on in the Estate cottages in 1858, and personally designed alterations and modernisations for houses and cottages across the Estate. The east window in the parish church and the altar cross are dedicated to her memory. The panels of the white frontal there are parts of her wedding dress.

8. *Little Gaddesden C.E. School. The Church Road. Possible Earth Works.*

LITTLE GADDESDEN CHURCH OF ENGLAND SCHOOL

On 18 May 1854 John Worrall was appointed schoolmaster by Lord Brownlow and on 15 June 1854 he opened the school in the large room at the *Bridgewater Arms* Inn. Objections were raised to the children walking in through the door and tap room. Therefore they climbed through the window. A teachers' class was formed for the Sunday School, and the following winter an evening class was arranged for girls over 14 years. There were 130 children in the Sunday School and 90 boys in the Day School. On 5 June 1858 the new schoolroom was opened. The architect was G.E. Street R.A. His two earlier designs of 1854 and 1856 had been rejected. Street planned a quadrangle for the school with a Headmaster's house flanked by two wings of the school. Only one was actually built.

In 1858 a sewing mistress was engaged. A harmonium was bought by Lady Marian Alford. In 1863 Samuel Green became assistant master. Other assistants by 1881 included Messrs. Wilson, Attie and Roberts. In 1881 the Schools sub-inspector, Mr Baldry, said that the school was one of the 12 best in Hertfordshire.

In 1894 Mr Worrall who had been schoolmaster for 40 years was presented with an illuminated address and a purse of £40 by his old pupils. The Rector presided and the presentation was made by Sergeant-Major Ballam. Mr Worrall had been educated and sponsored from the age of eight or nine by Bishop Edward King of Lincoln, a bishop regarded by many as a modern saint. He sent Worrall to Chester Training College, and thence to Cuddesdon, the home of one of the church's most influential theological colleges, where Worrall taught. He then went to Shropshire, and from there to Little Gaddesden. Distinguished visitors to Ashridge used to visit him at the school.

On 31 October 1903 Mr Samuel Green completed 40 years at the school. He was given a purse of 20 guineas and a silver ring by past and present pupils. He was Mr Worrall's son-in-law.

Rector Dr H.G. Woods who came in 1900 from being President of Trinity College, Oxford, and who was to be Master of the Temple, was surprised at the good reports about the school, but reflected that these were being spoiled by irregular attendance on the part of some pupils. The 1906 Education Act was received 'peaceably'. The Rector, the Rev. Edward Clark prevented the alienation of the Bridgewater Trust which provided sums of money towards Christian education.

From 1904-18 there were consistently good reports from His Majesty's Inspectorate. Luckily there were not the scarlet fever closures of the previous decade during which 40 cases were reported at one time, and the school had to be closed three times. However the numbers attending dropped from 120 to about sixty.

Mr Green gave 51 years of unbroken service to the school, and was Headmaster from 1896. On his retirement in 1914 Lord Brownlow handed him a purse of gold containing £68 10s, as his age was 68 at the time. He had been schoolmaster, organist, choirmaster, and Sunday School teacher. After he retired he lived with his father-in-law John Worrall in Dagnall. Mr Worrall lived to the great age of 96, and was buried on 28 July 1922 in the west section of the old churchyard beside Charlton Lane, William Paxton and other worthy parishioners.

Mr D. Harrison succeeded Mr Green in 1914. Whilst he was away on active service from 1916-19 Miss Sapford took his place. Mr W. Woolfall served from 1921 to 1922 and was succeeded by Mr Parker in 1922. From 1924 to 1929 Mr W. Jones was Headmaster. In the 1920s the pupils assembled daily outside the school whilst the Red Ensign was hoisted. In 1925 the Rector the Rev. A. Bidlake wrote to the Hertfordshire County Education Committee about having a wireless set for the school. He was told that wireless had not yet proved itself sufficiently valuable to adopt it in schools.

In 1929 Mr Vicars Walker Bell was appointed Headmaster and he remained until 1963 when he proceeded to continue training for the Ordained Ministry which he had begun at Kings College, London in his student days. He was ordained priest to serve in the diocese of Exeter. As schoolmaster it was said by later commentators that he had been ahead of his time. Overseas visitors to England were directed to Little Gaddesden by the Education Ministry in London to see a rural school. During the war his methods won great admiration for their adaptability, ingenuity and practical application. In demand as a lecturer he also wrote books about his work, about Little Gaddesden, and also a number of detective stories and children's works. He played a leading part in the Home Guard and in parish affairs.

In 1963 Mr D.J. Pryor was appointed schoolmaster and remained until 1966 when he moved to a Lectureship at Matlock College of Further Education. Like his predecessor he trained for the Ordained Ministry and he was made a deacon in 1980. He is remembered by many for his great interest in amateur dramatic work.

In 1966 Mr Albert J. Williams was appointed Headmaster and under his steady guidance the school has achieved much, not only in the educational field, but additionally in those of sport, music and drama. Links with village events have also been fostered. Annual occasions such as May Day, the Inter-Village Sports, and the Hemel Hempstead Pavilion Music Festival have been important, as have the many school visits made. The School Hall, formerly the wartime canteen, is used for school meals and also houses the Library.

Extensions to the school were made in 1961-62 with an extra classroom and corridor. In 1965 a garage was built and a pottery room furnished. A television set was acquired. In 1979 a headmaster's study, a staff room, and a medical inspection or secretary's room were added. The school equipment, both inside and outside the buildings is of high standard and excellent quality. Much has been provided by the exceptional enthusiasm engendered by the School annual bazaar.

Long serving members of staff included Miss F. Wright and Mrs D. Drewitt. The school grounds and environment, the proximity of Ashridge Estate and the delightful rural setting must make this school one of the most attractive in England.

The Playing Field. On 26 July 1948 the Parish Council was authorised to purchase a playing field of approximately six acres adjoining the site of the old Village Hall at a price not exceeding £750. L. Moore was Chairman of the Council. One-third of the site of the old Village Hall was sold to Dr Rawdon Smith, the owner of John O'Gaddesden's House for £100 plus a donation of £100 towards the cost of acquiring the playing field. The cost of the land and the necessary work was later stated to be £1,240.

Hertfordshire County Council assisted in the maintenance of the field by regular mowing for the use of Little Gaddesden C. of E. School.

The new Pavilion was built by public subscription in 1974-75 at a cost of £5,879.49 and was opened on 21 July 1975.

The tennis courts were relaid in 1978-79 at a cost of £4,600.

THE VILLAGE HALL

A room adjoining the old Rectory stable yard was used for parish meetings for many years, there having once been a school classroom there as early as 1683. In 1861 the Rector established a reading and games room where chess and draughts were played, and where smoking was permitted. This new room was in the Manor House and was supervised by Sergeant-Major Balham. Evening classes were held in it.

In 1894 Lord Brownlow allowed John O'Gaddesden's House to be used as a reading room, and it was opened just before Christmas in that year. The 'Solar' was used, and marks of the burning caused by one of the lamps may still be seen on the beams.

In 1921 the first Village Hall was built on land given by Lord Brownlow. It was an old wooden army hut 100 feet long, bought from Gadebridge Park after the First World War needs had ended. George Liberty and Simeon Whitman dismantled it in Gadebridge and re-erected it on its site behind John O'Gaddesden's House. On Sunday evening, 2 May 1943, a fire-raiser (later seen to be a poor, deprived, mixed-up youth) set fire to it as he had done to the Golf Club, the Laundry and the Bridgewater Stables. People were said to be more frightened of the fire-raiser than of the enemy bombs! Mr Selby Hughes allowed the use of a hut at The Spinney for parish meetings.

In 1952 Mr Basil Phillips gave a strip of land, equal in area to the present police house, to the British Legion for a club house. At the same time he gave the adjoining larger piece of land, including the present police house site, to the parish for a Village Hall. The deed of gift was dated 26 February 1952. Later it was thought that it would be better to build the Village Hall next to the School. An exchange of land was agreed and the Parish Council became owners of the land from the school boundary to the present police house, the site of which became the possession of the Legion. This deed of exchange was dated 14 December 1956. The British Legion later sold their land to the Hertfordshire County Council, and plans were made to build a Village Hall and raise the funds. Amongst the instigators of this were Mr S. Block, Mr Selby Hughes and Mr J.T. Pritchard, who was already acting as Treasurer. The Parish Council sub-committee which was at work from 1954 concerning the future Village Hall comprised: Miss J. Moore; Messrs J. Oakins; V.W. Bell; H.V. Ward; and S.A. Block.

There was a plan in 1954-55 to build a brick building but the cost was too great. Eventually the Reema Construction Company, specialists in village hall construction gave an estimate for a prefabricated building. The contract was signed in April 1956. The first donation for the Hall Fund was received by Mr Pritchard on 17 February 1955. A government grant of £2,000 was promised and paid, and £2,000 was also borrowed from the National Council of Social Service, repayment of which was made over an eight year period by covenants. The remainder was subscribed by residents and societies. There was a small sum from insurance of the old hall. The Hall was completed and paid for by the end of 1957. The first letting, for a fee of 5s., was to Mr Block for the Ashridge Cricket Club.

A Trust was formed under the guidance of the Ministry of Education and the Hall was registered as a charity under the Act. It is run by a Management Committee appointed annually in accordance with specific rules set down in the Trust Deed. The organisations of the parish are represented on the committee.

Extensions were made in 1973 and an extra dressing-room cum storage room was built. The Drama Club have a repository at the rear of the Hall, and the Village Produce Association have an annexe in which they sell garden requisites.

The heating system has had several improvements made. The stage has been equipped with lighting suitable for major productions. A doctor visits Little Gaddesden and has a room for a surgery each week. The Hall is thus in daily use.

In 1962 gratitude was expressed to Mr Pritchard the Treasurer, and also 'to Mr John Oakins who takes the bookings, whose phone is never silent'. In 1981 Mr Oakins still took the bookings. One of the most important contributions to the quality of life in the parish is that made by the play school which meets on three mornings a week in the Hall. Mrs Valerie Janes is responsible for this, and she follows the memorable work of her mother, Mrs Clayton, in the area of professional care for the young.

CHURCH ROAD

Before 1854 there was an open meadow to the church. The roadway was a source of controversy earlier in the 20th century. At first it was closed, then locked, and after that it was fenced on both sides. At the Green end there was a carriage gate and a kissing-gate. A fence was erected in 1934 and the triangle near to the church and used now as a car park, was enclosed. The fence was uprooted.

At one time the way from the church to Hudnall across the Mill Field was greatly used. John Ash said that when he was a boy he helped to pull down a cottage (there were two or three there) by Mill Field.

In July 1894 Mr A. Fountain fixed a water trough in Church Meadow.

Policeman's House. This was built in 1964. The present School House used to be the Policeman's House until it was acquired for the schoolmaster.

Coronation Villas. These were built at the time of the Coronation of Queen Elizabeth II in 1953. A plaque is a reminder of this. Mr Colin Revell, Chairman of the Parish Council for many years, resided here. In 1981 his son Kevin cycled from Land's End to John O'Groats for charity.

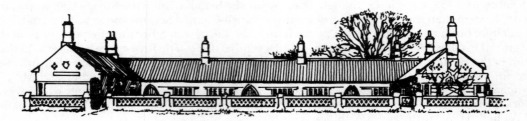

Fig. 16.   Bede Houses.

Bede Court. In 1862 'The Bede Houses' were designed by Lady Marian Alford, probably influenced by the work of G.E. Street, architect, and by almshouses on the continent. They were built in memory of her husband John Hume Egerton, Viscount Alford who died on 3 January 1851.

The Bede Houses were originally five or six cottages built for 10 widows, though these were later made into three dwellings. Completed by 1865 they contained 10 rooms in pairs, with garden attached. Ashridge gave two tons of coal per annum and 4s. per week to each widow together with medical attention.

In 1888 Princess Alexandra, while on a visit to Little Gaddesden church, also visited the Bede Houses during her stay with the Prince of Wales at Ashridge.

A bell was rung each day for prayers and as a curfew. This bell is now in the possession of the parish church. Special prayer books were provided for the Bedeswomen. There were rules concerning behaviour which were strictly observed.

On 1 August 1896, the Bedeswomen assembled at the Rectory to welcome Rector Hodgson and his bride after their two month's honeymoon.

The Bede Houses were sold with the Ashridge Estate, and as tenants died they were not replaced. The executors of the late Mr G.A.R. Mead offered the Bede Houses to the Council with some adjacent land for £14,000. The Council built 21 cottages, including one for a warden. The sundial from the Bede Houses was erected in Bede Court (the name given to the new buildings), two stone plaques one with the Egerton lion and the other with the initials MA for Lady Marian Alford, both surmounted by a Viscount's coronet and commemorating the original building in 1862, were preserved and placed on the present exterior. The yew trees are also from the original Bede Houses. In 1981 the Warden of Bede Court was Mrs Phipps.

The contract price for the land, building, Estate road, sewers etc., was £76,000, making a cost of £3,620 per dwelling. The Hertfordshire County Council was to make a grant for the warden's services. The architect was Charles Lee, F.R.I.B.A., of Kendrick, Findley & Partners. C. Laidman was Council Surveyor, C.S.L. Desborough was Clerk of Works and Willis Dawson Ltd., were contractors.

On 27 October 1969 Bede Court was officially opened. Officials present were the Vice-Chairman of the Rural District Council, P.E. Draper; Chairman of the Parish Council, Mrs Peter Foxall; and Rural District Councillor and Parish Councillor, P.W. Haydon. Cottage no. 11 (Miss Irene Wells) was used for a token opening ceremony. Prayers were said by the Rector (Canon H. Senar).

Lydiard Cottage. This was named after Lydiard Tregoze in Wiltshire, the home of the St Johns-Bolingbroke where the grandfather of Mrs Curtis-Philips, former resident here, had lived and had been buried.

Church Meadow. Excavation and observation of this site has produced the following information—
1. There was occupation in the Roman period, for blue-grey fragments of coarse pottery, dated to the Romano-British period, were identified. Jacquetta Hawkes examined and reported this. The fragments were deposited in Little Gaddesden School. The proximity of the Roman road from St Margaret's to Ivinghoe, to the west of this field, makes Romano-British occupation reasonable. The excavation was a limited one and took place about 1959-60.
2. There was no evidence from the area excavated to prove later occupation. However, an aerial view suggests that there was an earthwork here of an extent broader than the meadow itself, which is not Roman. This circular central earthwork could be the base of a higher earthwork or fortification which has gradually been levelled. It is surrounded with a low embankment stretching across the meadow and to the north of the church. The earthwork is rectilinear in shape, curved at the south end (nearest Church Road), and may have had an entrance at its east side . . . towards the church. In the north-west corner of Church Meadow, adjoining the west bank of the earthwork, there is clear evidence of more formal banks with straight lines. At the north side this adjoins the old village road from the present October House to Lamsey and Church Farms. It could appear that the east churchyard wall if projected to the north in a straight line, would join a bank on the old village road just mentioned. A small rectangular area, in the vicinity of a pond of perhaps later date is visible from the air. It is difficult to date this structure.

There are similar earthworks which were known as 'Motte-and-Bailey' works. These were mounds with an area between them, and perimeter banks. Some of them are dated to the period of the anarchy during the reign of Stephen 1135-54. Dissatisfied subjects erected these small fortifications. In some parts of the country they were more numerous than here.
3. Whether or not this was the site of a deserted medieval village has not been discovered. The existence of a medieval village in Little Gaddesden must be assumed, if for no other reason than that there was a parish church from at least the mid-12th century on the present site. Whilst the deserted medieval village has been traditionally said to have been here, there could well have been a hamlet possibly near the Manor House and Hudnall Corner.
4. *Bury Field, Great Bury Grove, Bury Grove.* The original meaning of 'Bury' is not connected with a burial place. Thus the derivation of these field-names near Church Meadow does not provide evidence that this was the burial place for the victims of the Black Death. *Bury* in Anglo-Saxon is used for a fortification place, and whilst it often means a pre-English earthwork, it can also mean a Roman encampment, or an Anglo-Saxon fortification (Hertingfordbury may have been built by Edward the Elder in 911). 'Aldeberie' or Aldbury, a Saxon settlement of the 8th to 9th centuries meant 'old fortified place' (See Mrs Jean Davis, *Aldbury*). 'Bury' is also used of a castle of post-Norman dating. Later it may mean a fortified house or manor.

In Hertfordshire the word 'Bury' is common with the meaning of a manor house, a place possibly fortified at some time. St Paul's Waldenbury, Kings Walden Bury, and Langley-bury are such examples. In the 13th century 'bury' became frequent in Hertfordshire.

Bury Field or Close could indicate the earthwork nearby as being Anglo-Saxon or of the 12th century. It could of course merely suggest that the areas specified belonged to the Bury . . . perhaps that of Richard de Bury mentioned later in 1432.

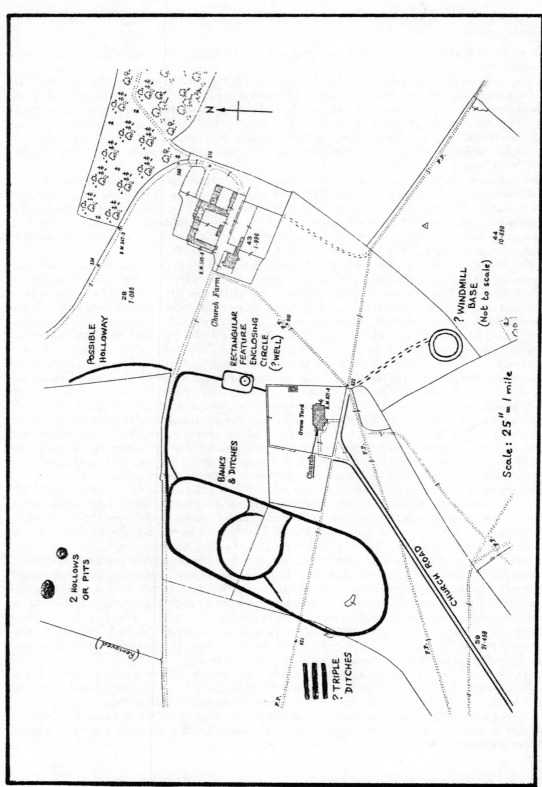

Fig. 17 Map of earthworks.

Church Farm. It was said that Little Gaddesden was unknown until the works of Hugh Ellis, farmer, made it famous. In 1732 he invented a four-wheeled drill plough and other implements. He had six or even eight horses spanning out in a row, drawing baggage wagons behind them, or he had a six-harnessed tandem. Sheep were plentiful on his land. A visitor Peter Kalm, from Sweden who published an account of his visit in 1748 described Little Gaddesden at that time, He said that Ellis only kept 20 cattle.

In 1733 Ellis published his *Chiltern and Vale Farming explained.* He was a pioneer in his knowledge of tilling, of manures and of clovers, turnips and farming composts. He was a pioneer readily understood, but locally he was suspect as a Londoner, a theoretician, a writer, a traveller, and a salesman. The comments of his contemporaries here seem to have been derogatory. His work on husbandry was republished in 1772. He wrote about recipes, medicines, and sneezing; the remedy for the latter being — 'Dose the body with a hearty drink of wine and other strong liquor until it is thoroughly heated'.

He farmed Church Farm (incorporating Lamsey) for 50 years and was buried here on 16 June 1758. He had six sons, one of whom, Phillip, a farmer, also became churchwarden as his father was at the time of his death.

Other farmers at Church Farm included — 'Peppercorn'; Benedict; Holland; George Underwood in 1852 (breeder of shire horses), (Mrs Roland Underwood was noted for her cream, but her recipes died with her); George Stanbridge, whose day-to-day diaries reveal the constant struggle of life on this farm; and James Whitman.

Some short extracts about miscellaneous events taken from the diaries of G. Stanbridge follow. William Munden buried on 12 September 1882 aged 60.

'He was one of the best workman Mr Underwood ever had. He was a man not contented with doing his work in a moderately ordinary manner. As a ploughman . . . we know from the number of first prizes he had gained . . . he was unsurpassed.'

12 April 1892.

'Fy Skinner was married yesterday, and the curate forgot about the wedding. Old Joe had to go to Dunstable to fetch him. He had gone through the churchyard while they were all there, and he wondered what the doors did open, and yet it did not occur to him to go and see.'

25 December 1892. Xmas Day.

'I got up and had breakfast and then went to Church at 8.30 a.m. to the early celebration, fully choral. There were a lot there.'

8 March 1896.

'The Rector, Mr. Hodgson, sent me ten pounds yesterday as consolation for the loss of the heifer last October, which died from the effects of yew poisoning obtained through the Churchyard gate being left open when the workmen were putting a new heating apparatus down. Lord Brownlow gave five and he gave the other. I had suggested to him a settlement of the sort a few weeks ago, whereby we loose the difference of £18.'

12 July 1896. Sunday.

'Lady Brownlow's coachman called with her old pony and put up while she was in Church. I had to give them all beer. Liberty came for some milk for a girl who fainted in church. So instead of a rest I had to be at the back door most of the time.'

26 July 1896.

'I went to church at 8 a.m., about a dozen of us there. A curate from Berkhamsted celebrated. Then breakfast, then changed clothes . . . put on flannels!!!'

15 July 1909.
'Collyer took 2 pigs to H.H. with old Kitty (horse) and he was back at 3 p.m. After he had his dinner he and Janes had a horse and cart each and carted the Parson's grass out of the churchyard up to the Rectory for him to make it into hay up there. His man only came to ask me at 3 p.m.'

1916.
'Zeppelin raids, rebellion in Ireland. Anthrax amongst the church farm cattles . . . therefore carcases burned and buried'.

Sunday 21 May.
'The first morning of daylight saving. We put the clocks on an hour. It seemed strange all day. We went to church and had meals the same, consequently we were an hour before our usual time.'

2 September 1916.
'The Policeman brought order revoking our anthrax restrictions after being closed up nearly four months; Church Meadow, Home and Pond.'

3 September
'An enemy airship came over last night, frightened our sheep, so that they broke the hurdles down and some got out. They were frightened in the night hearing a Zeppelin overhead.'
Newspaper report 13 Zeppelins last night over east counties.

In June 1948 the farm covered an extensive acreage when it was put up for auction by the St Andrew's Steam Fishing company. It was bought by Mr C.G.H. Dunham and Mr W. Brown of Lamsey Farm, Dagnall, who resold it in lots later in 1948. The bulk of the farm was sold to Mr Basil Phillips who sold it to the Bonar Law Trust. Mr Brown kept the field south of Badger Wood and Mr Dunham retained Hoo Wood. Hoo Wood consists of 90 acres of larch, young ash, Turkey oak and assorted pine. A right of way was retained through Lamsey Farm from the Dagnall Road. George Mead acquired the farm in 1952. An account of Church Farm in 1965 follows—
'The Church Farm lands are inclined to be cold and they crop later than some. They are seldom free from winds.
320 acres arable, produce wheat, barley, oats, potatoes, cattle green food.
30 head of cattle being fattened for beef, chiefly Angus and Hereford Shorthorn crosses.
A dairy herd of Shorthorns. Milk was transported daily to a Surrey dairy. The sheep were Clun Forest. Foxes, 8 left the corn during cutting.
Hens were kept in deep litter. Eggs went to a packing station at Leighton Buzzard. No pigs. Badgers from Badger Wood damage the corn.
There were wild rabbits in Hoo Wood.
6 hares in March in Church Road meadows. Harvest Home on 20 October.'
In 1972 a number of the fields belonging to the Farm were sold including three on the Little Gaddesden to Deer Leap Road beyond the Town Houses.
Field House was built in 1960. The architect was Peter Dunham of Dunham, Widdup and Harrison. It was the home of Mr John Mead, farmer of Church Farm. The three *Gable Cottages* built for the Farm in 1960, 1963 and 1967 were designed by the same architect as Field House.

9.   *The Parish Church of St Peter and St Paul*

The parish church stands in the meadows one-third of a mile from the village street. It has a commanding view northwards along the old road to Leighton Buzzard. Trees converge, as pathways do, on to the ancient site. The north-west corner buttress of the tower stands on a large piece of prehistoric Hertfordshire pudding-stone. At all times of the year the view from the top of the tower is magnificent.

The date of the first church here is not known. That there were Christians in Gaddesden is shown when a Christian seal of the mid-9th century was found in Ringshall Drive, as well as by gifts to St Albans Abbey in 942-46 by Aethelgiva who gave Gaddesden 'to St Alban' himself, and by Godiva who gave a towel and a chalice to the Abbey.

The first specific mention of a church here comes when the Archbishop of Canterbury, Thomas à Becket, gave the rectorial tithe of Little Gaddesden to the monastery of St James, Northampton in 1161. This presupposes that there would have been a church here dating from Saxon or Norman times, and a rector.

In 1178 a matron of Gaddesden was cured at Redbourn by the relics of St Amphibalus by lying on the spot of his translation.

In 1209 soon after he became Bishop of Lincoln, Hugh of Wells while enquiring about houses for the clergy, noted that there was a suitable house for Julian the Cleric, adjoining the church.

The ancient pathway to the east end of the church from the lane may have been the rector's path to the church. It has been worn down below the surface of the surrounding churchyard.

The ground to the west of the church is obviously an area of former habitation, and Roman remains have been found there. Aerial photographs show an earthwork which may be indicative of occupation during the troubled days of Stephen (1135-54).

Local tradition however states that the Black Death was the cause of the church standing on its own, the inhabitants having died or abandoned their holdings when the disease struck here. The Grey Death of 1361-62 would almost certainly have been the cause of incumbency changes at Little and at Great Gaddesden. In spite of this it would appear that the following century saw rebuilding in the parish church. The north arcade may have been the work of two masons from the quarry at Totternhoe, Philip Lessy and William Farele, who were working in the area in the late 14th century. They could also have been responsible for the tower arch and work on the tower and window. Dr Eileen Roberts quotes a document of November 1392 when Lessy and Farele contracted to build the tower of Houghton Conquest, All Saints, at 10s. per foot of the foundations and 13s. 4d. per foot above the foundations (together with six quarters of wheat). The estimated total of this would be £40.

Dr Roberts notes similarities in their work in Hertfordshire churches. Of these Little Gaddesden is the nearest to the Totternhoe quarries from which the tower base came. The north-west buttress of the tower stands on a piece of Hertfordshire pudding-stone.

The Parish Chest. This ancient chest has seven locks, six of which are padlocks. Its date is not known, though the earliest chest at Oxford University is dated 1411-26 and there are similarities to the Little Gaddesden chest, although clearly the Oxford chest is earlier. It also bears similarity with one of the chests in Kings College Chapel at Cambridge which was said to have been filled with gold and given to the College by Henry VI or VII between 1446 and 1515.

In 1441 it was confirmed that Little Gaddesden church had been appropriated to St James. Northampton. That religious house appointed the most distinguished of the medieval incumbents, John Hunsden. He was in bishop's orders, having been bishop of Llandaff since 1458. He continued to be Bishop of that diocese from the time of his appointment to Little Gaddesden in 1473 until his departure in 1479. He invested William of Wallingford as Abbot of St Albans, after officiating at the funeral of Wallingford's predecessor.

The visitation of John Longland, Bishop of Lincoln in 1530 shows that the chancel at Little Gaddesden was 'ruinosus', and that the Rector, John Wyatt, was living at his other parish of Oakley, Bedford. He promised to do the repairs for Michaelmas. Henry VIII came to Ashridge at Christmas in this year. Prince Edward and the Princesses Mary and Elizabeth were at Ashridge in 1543. Perhaps they worshipped in this church.

The Rectory was valued at £11 12s 8d in 1535. Four years later it is recorded that there were four bells in the tower, which had a small spire.

John Wyatt remained as incumbent during the troubled years of the 1530s. He died in 1545. At the visitation for King Edward VI in 1552, the church contained three bells (possibly the fourth mentioned above was the priest's bell) two chalices, four vestments of red velvet, damask and silk, two red silk copes, one alb and one linen surplice.

There is a name scratched on the pillar by the lectern which could be 'Frances Combes 1569'. The Combes family of Hemel Hempstead was connected with Ashridge at this time. Frances Combes was born about 1554 and thus could have been 15 when the name was inscribed. A Richard Combes of Hemel Hempstead bought possession of the Ashridge Monastery buildings in 1557. His son Francis succeeded him in 1595, and he was succeeded by his son, also named Francis, 'an enemy of the ministry', who died in 1641.

The first of the parish charities inscribed on a large tablet in the tower was established by Elizabeth Winchester in 1597.

The coming of the family of Sir Thomas Egerton, Baron Ellesmere, to Ashridge in 1604 was the beginning of the long association between the church and Ashridge House. His beloved grand-daughter is recalled by the monument on the south wall of the church ('The Red Lady'). This monument was brought from St Martin's-in-the-Fields when the old St Martin's was taken down in 1730. At first it was erected to the right of the present organ.

The church suffered during the commonwealth. The Rector, Barnabas Holway, was ejected, though his wife remained in the Rectory. Cromwell's soldiers came on 13 June 1643 and broke into the Bridgewater vault where the Earl's wife and daughter were buried. This vault lay beneath the present chancel and had been extended in 1635 by the Earl. There were 10 steps down to the vault. The tombstone of his daughter, Anne, now lies before the altar in the south chapel.

The silver chalice is probably from early in the 17th century, and the flagon perhaps, by Thomas Brown, is dated 1636. In 1649 the 1st Earl died and the 'Great Monument' was erected on the south side of the chancel. The south sanctuary window was thus blocked up until the restoration of the 1870s. The coats of arms at the base are—

Left: Sir John Egerton, 1st Earl of Bridgewater. His motto inscribed is SIC DONEC.
Right: His arms impaling those of his wife Frances (Stanley, Earl of Derby) SIC DONEC   SANS CHANGER.
Above: The arms of the 2nd Earl of Bridgewater impaling those of Elizabeth his wife (Cavendish, Marquess of Newcastle) SIC DONEC   CAVENDO TUTUS

In 1875 it was removed to its present position to the east of the vestry door.

In 1658 the Rev. Thomas Fossan was appointed to the Rectory by Richard Cromwell, the Lord Protector. He was an unsuccessful schoolmaster of Berkhamsted School. Thomas Henshaw succeeded him in 1682, the Earl of Bridgewater restoring the rectorial tithe to the parish.

Above the main doorway to the church is the monument to the 2nd Earl. He had been prominent in the preparations for the 1662 Book of Common Prayer. The tablet records that after the death of his wife 'he did sorrowfully wear out 23 years, 4 months and 12 days' before he died in 1686. He had been responsible for this wording as also for that on the 'Great Monument' to his father which is now on the right of the vestry door. 'A dutiful son to his mother the Church of England in her persecution as in her greatest splendour. A loyal subject in those worst of times when it was accounted treason not to be a traitor.' His mother's epitaph on the same memorial states 'She married seven of her daughters richly and honorably. She died religiously 11th March 1635, and she reigns triumphantly for ever'. John the 2nd Earl's own wife is recalled on the same monument: 'Transcendentally vertuous lady, now glorious saint. On June 16th 1663 she exchanged her earthly coronet for an Heavenly Crown'.

The churchwardens accounts date from this period and throw light on the society of the 17th century. Details are in the Gazetteer.

The death of the 3rd Earl, K.B., in 1701 is recalled on his monument on the north side of the South Chapel, adjoining that of his first wife. Her memorial is a masterpiece of the inscriber's art. Her coat of arms at the head of the memorial remains as it was after her death in 1669. The memorial to his second wife, Jane, daughter of the Duke of Bolton, is on the left side of the vestry door. Before 1875 it was on the north side of the sanctuary. Their son Scroop became the 1st Duke of Bridgewater in 1720.

Scroop's first wife was Elizabeth, daughter of the 1st Duke of Marlborough. She died of smallpox in 1713, as did her son at Eton five years later. Their memorial is to the left of the vestry door. Scroop provided timber for the new Rectory of 1744 for the Rector, the Rev. Charles Tough, who was also Rector of St Paul's, Covent Garden and who was buried on 29 June 1754 'in the aisle leading to ye Bell free, his feet near ye cross isle, his head under ye gallery'. There is no memorial to Scroop here, although he is buried in the vaults. He was succeeded by his brother John, who two years later was to be laid beside him. Scroop's widow Rachel survived him until 1777, when she was laid to rest at her husband's left side.

Francis, the 3rd Duke and the 'Canal Duke', succeeded in 1747. He was buried in the vault at the apex of the triangle of the three Dukes of Bridgewater (see the diagram in the Gazetteer). His monument with the only ducal coronet in the church is on the south wall of the South Chapel above a former fireplace. He was buried on 16 March 1803. The dukedom lapsed with his death.

He was succeeded as 7th Earl by his cousin General John William Egerton, son of the Bishop of Durham. He was an active parishioner and became churchwarden, residing at Ashridge which he had built. He employed James Wyatt to take down the south wall of the Church in 1810-12. His head and that of his Countess are carved on either side of the porch. The South Chapel was completed in 1819, being closed at its west end, from the south aisle, and becoming a Bridgewater mausoleum. Francis Bernasconi was employed in 1817 to work under Jeffry Wyatt on the chapel ceiling. He decorated many royal palaces and great houses. He was at Ashridge in 1813-15 and was paid £879. In 1814-18 he worked also on the great screen in York Minster. He was at Buckingham Palace in 1820, and in 1825 he was occupied on the altarpiece at Westminster Abbey.

It is probable that Jeffry Wyatt also designed the south aisle of the church although the earlier wooden arch on the north side of the aisle has customarily been attributed to James Wyatt.

In 1875 the west wall was removed, and an arch was built and the chapel was opened. It became the vestry. A wooden arch coloured to resemble stone, which attracted many visitors, was made to span from the pulpit to the tower wall. It was replaced by the south arcade in 1875.

The 7th Earl was responsible for the sale of the old bells and their replacement in 1820 by two new ones, made by Briant of Hertford.

Sir Richard Westmacott was responsible for the very fine monument to the 7th Earl and his Countess on the east wall of the Chapel. It was called 'The Midday Rest' but it has been thought by many to have been intended as a family monument inspired by Florentine work. The inscription appears to give a genuine appraisal of the life and work of one who laid the foundation of the Ashridge Estate for the remainder of the 19th century.

Francis Henry, the last Earl of Bridgewater lived in Paris, and was regarded as an eccentric English aristocrat, though respected for his scholarship if not for the fact that he was a Prebendary of Durham Cathedral and Rector of a Shropshire parish. His monument recounts that in his will he left £8,000 to be divided between scholars who would write of God's work as revealed in creation. His monument, also by Westmacott, shows him surrounded by the works of nature. He had been responsible for initiating the Monument in the Park to the Canal Duke. His own bequest for a very large monument to himself in Little Gaddesden church was unacceptable to the Rector, David Jenks, and also to the widow of his predecessor. It was not until 1832 that the present memorial to him was erected . . . and the date of his death had to be recut in the memorial. He was buried in 1829. His manuscripts were left to the British Museum.

The Silver Paten was presented to the church in 1831, although its hall-mark dates it as 1781.

The Lectern Bible is dated 1832 and has been in use regularly since that year.

When Lady Marian Alford came to Ashridge in 1849 she showed considerable interest in the parish church and its interior. A new organ replaced the choir and band which had been in the gallery. The *Ancient and Modern Hymn Book* was introduced, and working with her son, the 3rd Earl Brownlow, and the Rector, the Rev. C.G. Lane, many alterations took place. The cost of the major restoration was £2,105.

The east wall was moved further east; the gallery was removed; the Wyatt Arch was replaced by the present south arcade; and the South Chapel was opened to the south aisle and church. The new pulpit was given by Lady Marian Alford and its figures were made by Mrs Watts at Compton, and presented by Miss Noyes. The east wall was also decorated with a fresco copying one in the Palazzo Medici Riccardi in Florence. Stained glass windows were placed in memory of Mrs Maberly, Charlton Lane and Miss Elizabeth Noyes. A small window was inserted in 1878 in the north-west corner to commemorate the late 19th century restoration. This is the oldest window in the church, dating from 1534, and originating in Germany.

The reredos was made as a memorial to Rector Lane's first wife. The three steps in the sanctuary coloured black, red and white, as well as the lanterns, were of this period. The Maw's tiles bear the symbols of St Peter (the cross upside down and the crossed keys), and of St Paul (the sword of the spirit), the patron saints of the church.

The east window was the memorial of Lord Brownlow to his mother, Lady Marian Alford, and the altar cross is Lady Brownlow's memorial to her. The stools are the work of 'Thompson the Mouseman' from Kilburn, Yorkshire, while John Oakins was responsible for the cabinet and for the credence table. The parish Roll of Honour commemorates those who died during the two world wars, and the Royal British Legion standard is in the Chapel. The parish chest is in the north choir aisle, and the reading desk by the pulpit is the memorial to Enid Goddard. A faculty for electric light was obtained in 1939 but light was not installed until after the war.

The South Chapel was created out of the Bridgewater Mausoleum which had been used as the vestry, in 1963, and in the same year the church was redecorated. In 1972 the new south door was made. In 1965-67 the new vestries were built, and silver communion vessels and altar ornaments were presented at this time.

A new pathway from the tower to the vestries was made by Mr Jack Pannell using coping-stones from the former wall which divided the old churchyard from the west ground.

The Remembrance and Gifts Book was presented in 1974. Nearby is a tablet to Henry Bradby 1868-1947, for 36 years a master at Rugby School.

A major restoration took place in 1978, and a new set of six bells was installed, being dedicated by the Right Rev. Robert Runcie, Bishop of St Albans and who became Archbishop of Canterbury in 1980. A set of handbells was acquired in 1980.

A *History and Guide Book* to the church first published in 1974 was enlarged and republished in 1980. New porch doors and a lantern were erected in 1981.

Finally it should be added that a parish church, for all its historical interest, is best seen when used as a place of worship. Perhaps during the midnight communion at Christmas, when the interior is illuminated by innumerable candles and the lights from the Christmas tree; or on Easter morning with the diocesan flag upon the tower, with choristers singing Easter carols, with every corner decorated with flowers, and with parishioners kneeling, called to church by Easter joy bells. Or even on an ordinary Sunday when Christians meet on the first day of the week before their Lord.

10.   *The Green. John O'Gaddesden's House. The Manor House.*

The Little Gaddesden Green. Traditionally the Little Gaddesden Feast was held on the Green on the Monday after St Peter's Day, 29 June. It deteriorated in the late 19th century into an annual orgy for which people came from other parts, and 'scenes of indescribable wickedness' took place with fights, brawls and drunkenness. Tents and stalls were erected and the school had a half-holiday. After 1878 its former revelries seem to have been better controlled. In 1881 there were more booths and caravans than previously and consequently 'much animation', but 'all went well'.

The Green was sold with Ashridge Estate and in parts fences were built around it, which caused much controversy. The Parish Council now watches most carefully the use and condition of the Green. Trees are planted and seats provided to mark important occasions, such as the Silver Jubilee in 1977.

In the middle of the 18th century Peter Kalm, a Swedish naturalist, visited Little Gaddesden (26 March-15 April 1748). He described the houses in the village being in a row against the common land. Holly bushes were hung with the washing, and the women wore red cloaks with pattens on their feet and straw hats. The houses were built with brick, with stone lower courses and limewashed upper walls. The roofs were tiled, but the cottages and the outhouses were covered with straw thatch. The houses had little hedges separating the gardens.

In the middle of the 18th century there was no indication of a continuous road along the Green as there is today. In front of John O'Gaddesden's House there was a lane stretching as far as the present Yew Tree Cottage and apparently turning at the group of houses there. There does not seem to have been a marked lane until near the present Denison House, from which a broad path or lane then extended to Hudnall Lane. This was the only way available for the houses on the Green at this time. Just beyond the corner of the present Hudnall Lane, near Kingham's Meadow this path met a path coming up from the Golden Valley. The road then went to Pulridge.

By 1802 it would appear that the present road along the Green was in existence as a lane. At the same time there was a clear way, probably a sizeable path, on the site of the present path along the whole length of the Green. Seven paths across the Green were visible by 1802. At Hudnall corner this path crossed Hudnall Lane and continued parallel to the road running towards Pulridge, as far as the triangular entrance to Robin Hood.

A later Estate map from the early part of the century does not indicate any such path along the Green as that immediately in front of the houses, though an earlier map does show a lane from the Green going for two fields in the direction of the church, but on the south (i.e. Hudnall) side of John O'Gaddesden's House and parallel to where the present Church Road goes. This lane would have crossed the present playing field. It is suggested that the present pathway along the Green has strong foundations, and that parts of it must be over 200 years old. Alongside the pathway there was a narrow brick edging.

At the sale of the Estate Mr Cuthbertson bought the Green from Mr Fairweather. He placed posts and chains as boundaries, thus marking it as private property. The Hertfordshire County Council bought the Green, and leased it to the Parish Council. Mr Basil Phillips bought the border on the Ashridge side.

The War Memorial. The Memorial opposite the Little Gaddesden entrance to Ashridge Drive, and at the end of the Green outside John O'Gaddesden's House was erected in 1920-21. The design is Italian, and Mrs Wheatley, wife of Lord Brownlow's agent and cousin of Lady Brownlow, brought back from Italy both the concept and some of the material. Harry Temple made the oak truss which carries the roof. At each end a bottle is built into the ridge containing information placed there when the Memorial was erected. The small cameo-type ornaments are Italian.

The names of the 29 men from Little Gaddesden who died in the two World Wars are inscribed on the Memorial.

Each Remembrance Sunday a ceremony takes place here, before which, 29 poppies are placed at the foot of the memorial by the Royal British Legion. A wreath from the Legion and one from the Women's Institute are placed beside them. Two minutes silence is observed during the ceremony and the Berkhamsted Brass Band plays the hymn 'O Valiant Hearts', and 'Last Post' and 'Réveillé'.

The Royal British Legion takes care of the Memorial and restored it in 1974-76.

Little Gaddesden May Song

Hertfordshire Folk Song

Arranged by
DOROTHY ERHART

1
And now comes in the month of May.
The spring-time of the year
And I am come to your house
To taste of your strong beer.
And I am come *etc.*

2
And if you have got no strong beer
We'll be content with small,
So take the goodwill of your house
And give God thanks for all.
So take *etc.*

3
We have been rambling all this night
And best part of the day,
And now I am come to your house
To bring you a branch of May.
And now *etc.*

4
A branch of May I have brought you
Before your door it stands,
'Tis but a sprout, but it's well budded out
In the work of our Lord's hands.
'Tis but *etc.*

5
Our time is short, we must be gone,
We can no longer stay,
God bless you all, both great and small,
And send you a joyful May.
God bless *etc.*

Fig. 18 Little Gaddesden May Song.

LITTLE GADDESDEN MAY DAY SONG

A Hertfordshire folk song written down by Miss Dorothy Erhart after hearing it from an old resident, Miss Susan Garrett, at the Bede Houses and was sung on May Day. It was published by the Oxford University Press together with another song which she sang called 'The Spotted Cow'.

JOHN O'GADDESDEN.

John O'Gaddesden was born about 1280 and died either in 1349 or about 1361. The name appears variously as Joannes de Gaddesden, Joannes de Gadesden, John de Gatesden, Jone de Gabeshede, and Joannes de Gatisden. John was a student at Merton College, Oxford. He may have entered as a boy in 1294 and would have proceeded to study for his first degree in about 1300. He graduated as a Bachelor of Medicine in 1307 and as Doctor in Medicinis in 1309. He also graduated as a Bachelor in Theology. He was resident in Merton College in 1314 and became a Fellow of Merton in 1320.

His book 'Rosa Medicinae' as he entitled it, or 'Rosa Angelica' as it became known, was probably written during 1314. It was printed in Pavia in 1492, in Venice in 1502 and in Augsburg in 1595.

The date of his ordination to the priesthood is not known, but in 1320 John de Gatesden was Rector of Chipping Norton which, like Little Gaddesden was then in the diocese of Lincoln. In 1333 he was Canon of Chichester. On 1 August 1342 he was appointed a Prebendary of St Paul's Cathedral with the stall of Wilsland. On this appointment he was to resign the living of 'Cheping Norton'.

A John of Gatesden gave information to Henry III in 1236 about the daughter of Raymond Berringer. He was sent by Henry to Alphonsus, King of Castile to appease his complaints about English merchants.

A John of Gaddesden was entered in the Book of Benefactors of St Albans Abbey, in the list of laymen admitted to the fraternity of the Abbey as an honorary member of the Chapter.

Of considerable interest is the fact that a John of Gaddesden signed the Foundation Charter of the College of Bonhommes at Ashridge in the year 1283 when the College was established. Was this John the father of the physician and priest?

Chaucer (1340?-1400) spent some time at Berkhamsted Castle, and it was possible that when there, he heard of John O'Gaddesden whose work he was to mention in the Prologue to the *Canterbury Tales*. It has been said that Chaucer used O'Gaddesden as the model for the 'Doctour of Physick'. Chaucer's doctor was said to be fond of his fees and Gaddesden was reputed to be like-minded, and the appropriate quotation would be—

'For gold in Physick is a cordial
Therefore he lovede gold in special'

John was said to have received a large fee from the Barber Surgeons' Guild for a prescription in which the chief ingredients were three frogs! Nevertheless he had poor as well as rich patients, and he gave them prescriptions they could afford.

Chaucer's doctor was grounded in astronomy, John does not appear to have any knowledge in this field. Chaucer also says 'His Studye was but litel on the Bibel'. Is this Chaucer's characteristic criticism of clergy who did not live up to the standards of his 'poor parson of the toun'? Or did Chaucer use local traditions about him? In the Annals of Merton College it states that just as the College produced famous philosophers, theologians and astronomers, so in medicine it produced Gaddesden.

He served Edward I and attended one of his sons, probably Thomas de Bretherton, for smallpox and wrapped him in scarlet cloth in a bed with scarlet hangings. John was court physician to Edward II. The date and place of his death is uncertain. Did he die of the Black Death like many of the clergy of England? A doctor-priest was especially vulnerable to plague.

The heiress of John was sold by her husband Ralph, Lord Carroys to Sir William Pannell, and there were discussions in Parliament about this.

Rosa Medicinae. Gaddesden said that he chose the name *Rosa* because a rose has five sepals and his book had five parts; and as the rose excels all flowers, so his book excels all treatises on medicine. He believed in medicine being a mystery with information being withheld from the uninitiated.

The book begins with an account of fevers, and passes through diseases, remedies and injuries. Finally there are remarks on diet and cooking— 'For hypochondriacs, quicksilver water cures pox, king's evil, leprosy, itch, gout, rheumatism, scurvy, worms, bugs in the bed'. He used religion in medicine— 'Write the words on the jaw of the patient . . . In the name of the Father and of the Son and of the Holy Ghost, Amen. Rex Pax in Christo Filio, and the pain will cease at once'. 'When the Sunday Gospel is read, let the man sign his tooth and his head with the sign of the cross and say a paternoster and an ave for the souls of the father and mother of St. Philip without stopping. It will keep the teeth from pain in the future and cure them in the present.' 'For epilepsy roast a cuckoo until it can be powdered. Blow the Powder into the patient's nostrils and the patient will recover. He may wear a cuckoo suspended from his neck. The cuckoo will attract the epileptic "materia" to itself, for the cuckoo has epilepsy every month. For nose bleeding. "In the Name of God . . . Wash the patient's shirt, pouring out the water nine times upon it, straining the water through it and then give the shirt to the patient." For the King's evil. Before being touched for it, apply snails and licquorice first.' He also gives instructions for keeping the body and the breath sweet smelling.

It was said that the *Rosa* gives a fair picture of an English physician of the 14th century. He was a man of education, academically well qualified, and acquainted with the work of his predecessors. He was an accurate observer, and had a shrewd understanding of human nature. *John O'Gaddesden's House.* It has been suggested that the present house is on the site of an earlier house, possibly of a Manor House of Little Gaddesden (the house now known as the Manor House at the other end of the Green was the Manor House of the Lucies). However this is conjecture as evidence is lacking, as also is early dating for the naming of this house after the priest-physician.

The Manor of Little Gaddesden was given to Ashridge College of the Bonhommes on its foundation in 1283 by Edmund, Earl of Cornwall. A John O'Gaddesden signed the Foundation Charter of the College. As the later priest-physician was aged three or four at the time, this might have been his father or grandfather. The present house is on a site dating back to the 15th century, and in an area where there has been habitation for many centuries.

The close-set timber in the walls and the small, narrow red bricks of the chimney-stacks show its age. Of the original house of the 15th century, probably only two rooms remain . . . the present dining-room and the small bedroom above it. The original building has been greatly enlarged by various additions. The ground floor is overhung. It shows rich-brown timbering. The original daub has been replaced with brick nogging overlaid with whitewash. The small sitting-room on the ground floor was panelled in Queen Anne's day or a little later. It has a formal Tudor fireplace from Ashridge, decorated with roses, passion fruit and two shields of the crossed keys of St Peter and the three swords in pile of the Paulet family. The Solar or medieval hall is a room 30 feet by 18 feet. It has a fine beamed roof, lighted by three mullion windows, and a fireplace set in Jacobean oak panelling. In the 19th century the ceiling had been covered, concealing the old woodwork, and cutting off the heads of four wooden figures, a priest, a doctor, a lawyer and a merchant. These heads were replaced by plaster heads by Lawrence Tanner who worked at Westminster Abbey. He did not wish to deceive future generations by replacing them in wood.

On a map of 1762 the house appears as a square with a courtyard in the middle. At the turn of the 18th century it had three sides round the yard. In 1838 William Fountain junior occupied the house and three acres of meadow, and the property belonged to the Countess of Bridgewater.

During the 19th century the house was occupied for long periods by caretakers. The schoolmaster John Worrall, who had lived opposite since 1854, described it as a farmhouse with an orchard. John Rogers was here from 1889 to 1890. The Brownlow family allowed the house to be used as a village reading and games room. The charring of the timbers on the underside of the main beams in the Solar was caused by oil lamps hung above the billiard table.

In 1920 Lord Brownlow decided to use the house as a residence for an aunt, much to the dismay of the local people. However he died in 1921 and the house became the property of the

Trustees. In the 1930s Mr and Mrs Pocock were caretakers. The house was bought by Dr Rawdon Smith for weekend use and he rented it to Captain Richard Oakley from about 1932. During the war Rawdon Smith lived here and the wrought-iron gates came from his London home. He extended the property in 1948 and later, buying some land from the former Village Hall which adjoined his land. He employed Frank Jennings as architect, and used local craftsmen including Stephen Oakins, Arthur Clifton and Richard Fountain.Bill Green also assisted with the work. It took four years to find and dismantle the pieces required . . . ancient door latches, nails, windows, glass, fire stacks, and wrought-iron casements. It took 18 months to erect them.

The final work came from four sources. Firstly Hawstead in Suffolk, four miles from the Abbey of Bury St Edmunds which had been dissolved . . . and the yeoman's house at Hawstead was being built in the mid-16th century, possibly from Abbey material. The great tie-beam in the Solar with its king post, and the ceiling both show traces of tinctures of Elizabethan date, spandrels with wyverns, acanthus leaves, and carved shields.

The second house was Wrestlingworth Manor in Bedfordshire. This was built later than Hawstead. It provided material for the kitchen wing, part of the roof, ceilings and paving stones. It may date from the period of William and Mary.

The third house from North Essex provided the 16th-century fireplace in the bedroom in the library wing.

The fourth contribution came from Lex Priory in Essex and was part of the main staircase of 1540. The remainder of the staircase is a modern copy of that style.

The pine panelled room had its paint removed and water which had seeped on to the solid earth floor had been said to make the room cold. A new oak floor was put in.

Dr Rawdon Smith died in 1957 and Dr Parker bought the property in 1958 and came to live here. Much specialised work was needed on the house. Central heating had caused shrinkage. An archaeological colleague of Dr Parker confirmed that the dining-room was the oldest part of the house, and that the depression in the cellar was part of an old ice storage hole. The green glazed bricks of the hall panels are of local glazing-type, fired by brushwood (a potter's glaze). The date could be anywhere between 1560 and 1770. The upper storey with its cement pargetting on a geometrical design is later and a similar effect can be seen at nos. 20 and 21 Little Gaddesden and Frithsden. Windows with leaded lights, some with original fastenings, are set in oak mullions. The double doors at the south entrance and the single door are of massive oak. The roof is tiled. Near the north end is a chimney-stack with two octagonal shafts, and at the back a third surmounts a crow-stepped gable. One stained glass window bears a coat of arms of the Dormer family. This family lived at the Manor House.

During the 1970s an American industrialist Mr William Warner resided here . . . and he took great care and interest in the property.

The Lord Mayor of London, Sir Peter Gadsden, and the Lady Mayoress paid a visit to the House and to Ashridge in 1980.

Numbers 31 and 32, The Green. This was originally a hall house and a single building dating from the 17th century. Later, it was divided into two small cottages, and upstairs rooms were constructed. The two cottages appear on maps of 1762, 1802 and 1838. No. 31 was graded III on the Department of the Environment list of scheduled buildings and was described by the Hertfordshire Planning department as being '18th century or possibly earlier'. 'One storey with an attic, three windows, tiled roof, one gabled dormer window, red brick, half-hipped roof, casement with diamond shaped leaded windows.'

In 1802 Mr Maberly of the Manor House owned the property including one acre with orchard, and it was occupied by Doggett. The widow of the 7th Earl of Bridgewater owned the property in 1838 and the cottages were occupied by widow Marriott and Joseph Smith.

William Buckingham who died in 1829 having resigned as Steward at Ashridge three years earlier built two cottages and they were occupied by widow Marriott and 'Beard the Bear'.

Mr and Mrs Patterson lived in No. 31 in the early 1900s. 'She was a tiny little woman who wore elastic sided buttoned boots. He was a huge man of six foot or over with a great beard. He frightened young children, perhaps unwittingly'. The Bevan family lived here a little later, and their daughter was village Postmistress.

Miss F. Wright who was school teacher at Little Gaddesden C. of E. School until 1923 lived here with her sister who was almost blind and kept house. Miss Wright spent all her life in the school and she died in 1948 aged eighty. After her death Mr and Mrs L. Richardson rented the house from 1947 and Mrs Richardson senior lived here. Dr Rawdon Smith bought these cottages from Mr Cuthbertson at the break up of the Estate. Mr Cuthbertson had bought all the Estate cottages which had not been sold to tenants. Mrs S.F. Richardson remained in No. 31 until 1980. Number 32 had been the home of four successive chauffeur-gardeners for Dr Rawdon Smith.

The cottages were sold to Mr and Mrs A. Browne in 1974 who planned to make the two cottages into one, as was the original building.

Norwood Cottage. This house was built in the orchard of John O'Gaddesden's House. The name Norwood appears in the earliest registers of Little Gaddesden church.

Number 25. On 19 July 1949 Peregrine, Lord Brownlow sold the land to Harold Ansell. He sold it in July 1954 to Fred Harrowell, builder, who built the house and sold it in September 1957 to Alec Thornton the first owner/occupier. He sold it in December 1961 to Miss Margaret Elizabeth Griffiths. On Miss Griffiths' death in January 1976 it passed to Miss Margaret Clift. Thus for 14 years it was the residence of Miss Griffiths who was Senior History Mistress at Berkhamsted School for Girls, and a highly esteemed historian. The bells of Little Gaddesden church were installed in 1977 in her memory, and in thankfulness for her work and life. They were dedicated on 5 November 1978 by the Bishop of St Albans, the Right Rev. Robert K. Runcie M.C., M.A. the future Archbishop of Canterbury.

Numbers 33-37. 'The New Houses' were built in Mr Reeves' meadow in 1869 by Lord Brownlow for Estate workers at the cost of £1,000 for the five. They were then called 'The New Cottages'.

No. 33 has its front door at the side. The other four are in pairs facing the terrace. A communal path leads from the steps down from the terrace to the front gate. It is believed that there should have been a No. 38 similar to 33 but when it was realised that there was a right of way at that end the building was stopped, and the terrace looks unfinished. Mrs Halsey used to live at No. 36, alone, and used to sit at her front door. Bill, Nell and Nance Munden lived next door. Bill was a First World War victim crippled with arthritis. Nell and Nance ran a hand laundry in a small separate room in their backyard. They carried their heavy baskets to the little drying-ground behind the playing fields where the garage now stands. They said that at one time eight of them lived in their cottage which had no bathroom. There were three bedrooms.

Mr W.K. Kibby was living at No. 33 when Mrs Stout bought it for £1,200. The weekly rent had been 6/3d. No. 33 has the date 1869 on a shield. The Estate cottages all of which were well built were sold, in 1928 by the Trustees to Thomas Place who subsequently sold them.

Lady Marian Alford and Lord Brownlow were active in designing cottages for their Estate, and these cottages were designed by Lady Marian herself, who made detailed drawings of each room. This was just after she had completed the work on the Bede Houses.

White Meadows. This house was built by Mr John L. Constantine, formerly a builder, of Berkhamsted, for his own family. He was sidesman of Little Gaddesden church and a Governor of Little Gaddesden School. Tradition says that there was once a 'gentleman's residence' adjoining Mr Reeves' meadow and it had been called White Meadows. Dr Allen acquired the property in 1980.

Number 38. There was a house on this site in 1762. It had a garden, and was in front of Small Meadow. It was owned by Mr Maberly of the Manor House. In 1802 it was occupied by Mr Fisher. In 1838 it was owned by the Countess of Bridgewater and occupied by Mr William Atty, one of the Atty family who served the Estate faithfully for over fifty years. William was a clerk at Ashridge. His relationship to George Atty is not clear.

This house was reserved for important officers of the Estate. Mr Johnson the overseer and foreman of Ashridge lived here. On the sale of the Estate in 1926 it was occupied by Mr H.C. Thoms who represented John D. Wood, an estate agent of London who had bought the land for building development at Ashridge. Mr Thoms worked at the Little Gaddesden Estate office. His daughter Mrs Richard Hollings and her husband lived here until 1970. Mr Hollings served for 30 years in the Hertfordshire Special Constabulary and reached the rank of Commandant. He was honoured with the Silver Jubilee medal in 1977. Mr N. Webster acquired the property from Mr J.R. Pilkington. Mrs Webster re-established the Little Gaddesden Brownie troop in 1980.

Number 39/40 Yew Tree Cottage. There was a property here in 1762 though in 1802 and 1838 it appears as two cottages and in 1838 David Marriott and Edward Oak lived in them. They are older cottages which probably date back to the 17th century and the time of the 1st or 2nd Earl of Bridgewater. Mr J. Wright, Clerk of Works to the 3rd Earl Brownlow, lived here. He put into practical terms the designs and plans of the Earl and Lady Marian Alford. Wright thus made a considerable contribution to Little Gaddesden and the parish owes him a great debt.

After the Second World War Mrs Dieter ran a small country club here. It was then sold to Mr Richardson, who was killed in an air disaster in 1962. Later it was bought by Mr David Hamilton-Russell. At one time the Whitman family had a laundry at the rear of the house. This was Grade III when the Department of Environment included that category in their schedule of historical buildings. The casement windows have diamond-shaped leaded panes. The gabled porch dates from the 19th century. There are three gabled dormers.

Number 41, Alford Cottage. The device on the external wall has a Viscount's coronet and the monogram MA for Lady Marian Alford and is dated 1867, which places it among the building projects of the Bede Houses period. In this year the 2nd Earl Brownlow died and he was succeeded by Lady Marian's second son who became the 3rd and last Earl Brownlow. Lady Marian and Lord Brownlow designed new properties and altered old ones.

Designs for cottages, school houses, staircases, windows, garden seats, inglenooks, chimneys, metal work, and gates, were submitted to Joseph Wright to execute. This house is an extension of an older property, earlier than the Brownlow period. The shield marks the reconstruction.

There were several ale houses and inns in Little Gaddesden and there was a public house here where Mr Reeve's son lived. He was the son of Mr Reeve of Reeve's Meadow (the butcher in 1838). Mr Pattison followed him in the mid-19th century. A lane ran between No. 42 and Alford Cottage.

Number 42. In 1838 there were two or three cottages here occupied by William Simmons who owned the property, and also by Charles Thorn and Lucy Jackson. In 1802 a cottage in this area was occupied by a man named Thomas Scrivener, but the exact site is not clear. Thomas Edwards and Martha Clifton lived nearby.

Lady Marian Alford personally designed this house as 'the Grocer's Shop'. The porch was one of her special designs, together with the projection of the windows. This became the 'Old Post Office', and was called Miss Pratt's Shop because Miss Pratt owned it. Her grandmother had established the shop in 1867. There was a pitchpine telephone box here. The Post Office was at the opposite end to the drive. The Brownlow sign (the Pheon) may be seen on the wall at the Hudnall end of the house.

The shop was closed in the 1960s. Finally the building was sold and Mr E.C. Turney modernised the interior as a private residence.

Number 43, Three Chimneys. The name of this house has been changed according to the number of the chimneys. It stands on a site which probably once had a building of a much earlier date. There is internal evidence of a 17th-century one-up, one-down cottage. There is a very old, oak beam in one of the present downstairs rooms. There was a cottage here in 1762 and in 1802 Mr Groom lived here. For a time it was the gardener's cottage for Denison House. A gate to No. 44 was used by the Youngs who were concerned with the gardens. Mr Young later moved to 4, Ashridge Cottages. When Mr Drewitt acquired No. 44 he bought also the right of way across 44 and the garden behind No. forty-three.

The Little Gaddesden Maypole was traditionally held on the Green opposite this house. There was a procession of St George and the Dragon, and at one time George Wright and John Young were responsible for collecting the donkey for the procession from Great Gaddesden Vicarage. The proximity of one of the public houses may have had something to do with the siting of the event. The May festivities are now held in the grounds of Little Gaddesden School.

Number 44. There was a building here in the mid-18th century, possibly of two cottages. At the beginning of the 19th century Mr Meager owned and rented the property to Mr Symonds. Mr and Mrs Drewitt lived here for many years, the former being the accountant at Ashridge and his wife being a school teacher at Little Gaddesden C. of E. School. Her father who lived at No. 6 was the Ashridge tailor.

Number 45. In 1802 the property was owned and occupied by Mr Hurdnall (Hurndall?) and a man of the same name was here in 1838. Mr G. Atty who had been Clerk of Works to the 7th Earl and to the Countess after her husband's death, lived here. At different times he and his family had lived at No. 38 and also near the present Little Gaddesden House.

A later Clerk of Works, Mr Phillips lived here. Another resident was Mr Wilson, a London bookseller. There was a small boarding school called 'The Endowed School' here with never more than six pupils, and their teacher John Wilson became one of Mr Worrall's teachers. He had lived in this house before 1847. His daughter Lucy married Thomas Phillips, dentist, in 1859. It became the home of Mr Francis Cory-Wright.

Numbers 46, 47, 48. Until 1926 there were three or four old cottages each with two rooms upstairs and two downstairs. This was called the 'Bothy'. They were gardeners' cottages for Denison House, but were in fact older than that house. Mr Gentle, Head-gardener lived here. On 14 April 1926 Richard Fountain began to pull them down. On 24 April he dug up the foundations. On 3 September he began to build a new cottage for Mr Blake. The three cottages were eventually built and at various times Mr Richard Wells and his wife Ella lived in each of them. Considerable alterations were made to No. 48 in 1980 by Miss Mary Wood. In the vicinity of these houses, in the 19th century there was a long building, possibly three or four cottages. The tithe apportionment map for 1838 states 'Robin Hood and Little John Beer shop'/'Three cottages and garden'. The occupants were James Tomlin, James Rogers, William Turner and widow Andrews.

Before and after this time the *Robin Hood* Inn was beyond Hudnall Lane towards the Home Farm. There had been a brewery attached to Denison House, as to the Rectory and other larger houses. The proximity of the May Day Festival on the Green nearby, together with the wording of the May Day Song 'I am come to your house to taste your strong beer', may suggest that there was need for refreshment in this area.

Denison House. A substantial house stood on the site of the present house in the mid-18th century. It was owned by the Duke of Bridgewater. At the end of the century it was occupied by Mr Fox. In 1838 it was described as a dwelling-house, yard, garden, brew-house and malt-house. It was occupied by William and John Jennings.

Before the Denison family lived here the house was called Marian Lodge after Lady Marian Alford who was largely responsible for its rebuilding. It was reconstructed in the 1850s and a shield dated 1864 over the porch on the drive side of the house bears the Pheons and the Brownlow 'B'. This was one of the earliest of the properties of the Alford-Brownlow régime as they proceeded to create 'the first Garden Village in Hertfordshire', perhaps after the style of the 'Model Village' at Edensor in Derbyshire on the Duke of Devonshire's Estate at Chatsworth. Paxtons worked at both places. One of the great cedars in the garden may date from the work of 'Capability' Brown in the 18th century. Former residents included Mr Mayling, the Misses Fordham, Miss MacDougall, Colonels Elliot and Ellis. Col. Arthur Ellis was equerry to HRH the Prince of Wales (Edward VII) in 1872.

In 1882 Mrs Denison resided here. Under her guidance the house became a centre for exquisite embroidery of the highest quality and skill. Each year soft cloth woven here was sent to

Queen Victoria. For a time there was a school here. A cottage was pulled down to enlarge the garden. Mrs Denison's companion bred sheepdogs and goats. Mrs Denison died aged 91 in 1916.

Mr and Mrs V. Sunman lived here. Later it was owned by Mr Cuthbertson, a London stockbroker, and his family. At one time he was offered the house, cottages and outhouses for £10,000. He kept dogs, and spent much time with them in the extensive kennels at the rear of the house. He was also a very able horticulturalist, and his borders were extremely well kept. Baskets of vegetables and flowers were sent weekly from here to his London house in the Albany, and to Bushey his other Hertfordshire home. These hampers were the responsibility of Mr Blake, his agent.

In his earlier days Mr Cuthbertson had won the London to Brighton walk organised for the business men of the city of London. His son Geoffrey was to follow his father's athletic footsteps by gaining a 'Blue' in cricket and becoming Captain of the Nottinghamshire County Club. He also played for Little Gaddesden.

Mr Cuthbertson also purchased other property in Little Gaddesden. During the Second World War he moved to another house in the village and allowed the use of Denison House to Froebel College, Roehampton when they were hurriedly evacuated to here and to Offley Place, Hitchin. The large cellars were quickly whitewashed and 100 students and staff slept there in what became an extensive air raid shelter.

Later the house was divided. There are now four dwellings. On the former land there are now eight houses in addition to Denison House.

Mr John H. Lewis son of a former High Sheriff of Anglesea moved to Denison House from Gaddesden Hall in the late 1950s. He became a member of the Hertfordshire County Council and a prominent educationalist, as well as being a greatly-loved member of the local community. He was a former Welsh hockey international. Mr and Mrs Lewis moved to Denison Cottage in 1982, and Mr and Mrs C.M.S. Rennie succeeded them.

The Coach House. This was the Coach House to Denison House. Gee was the coachman to Mr Woodward. Strickland was the chauffeur to Mr Cuthbertson who drove a Hispano-Suizza. Major General E.N.K. Estcourt, Principal of Ashridge College 1958-62 converted the stable building into the present house, and for a time resided here before moving to the Vyne, Basingstoke.

Marian Lodge Estate. Modern development began here in the early 1950s. Mr Basil Phillips was responsible for much of the work. In 1952 he built Pedley. He gave this name to other houses in which he resided because of the pleasure that Pedley Hill had given to him in the past. He sold the land on which Orchard End and Applegarth were built.

Applegarth was the home of the Rev. Alfred H. Strand formerly the Rector of Aldbury who moved here after resigning that living. He made a considerable impact on this parish. The Havilland family followed, and then the Grants. 'Applegarth' is a house in Aldbury formerly a farm and the home in 1690 of the town crier. (See Mrs Davis' 'Aldbury') F.G. Whitman built the houses. The Osborn family moved into Pedley in 1973. They came here from Kenya.

In 1959 Chiltern Mead was built by the Courtenay-Broome-Russell family. Later it was owned by the Walkers, and the Broome-Russells moved into Barn Cottage. This had previously been a gardener's cottage, and later was called 'The Studio' after Mr Phillips converted it. Tithes had been levied on it. Early in the century it had been thatched, but this was removed.

The adjoining property 'Ostlers' was acquired by Christopher Greaves an artist and was later owned by Norman Young.

Lutece. This house was designed by Mrs Bullock when she and Mr Bullock came to reside here in 1960. The staircase is 18th century and was originally in a house of that period in Grosvenor Square, London. The fireplace is of late-18th to early-19th-century origin. The double entrance gates were formerly the entrance gates to Hemel Hempstead Churchyard gardens. The small gate is from the 18th century. The name was chosen because Mrs Bullock was of French extraction. The heart of France is the Ile de France on which Notre Dame stands. This area was the headquarters of the Lutecii tribe before the arrival of Julius Caesar and his Roman armies. Lutece thus has marked the family association with France.

Number 49. This house appears in the 1762 map. In 1802 it was occupied by Messrs. Horn and Hervey. In 1838 the house and garden were occupied by John Harvey. The Countess of Bridgewater was the owner. Mr J.T. Pritchard has said that when the house was purchased in the 1940s Major Wykeham-Musgrave who had been agent to the Ashridge Estate said that he understood the cottage to be between 375 and 400 years old. This suggests a 16th-century date. The single storey addition at the north end was built in the 1870s when the Brownlow family were improving their cottages, and developing their concept of a garden village.

At the south end a drawing-room with a bedroom and bathroom above were added by Mr Munro Cuthbertson, son of the owner of Denison House, for his own use. This was built by Matthews of Berkhamsted and John Oakins was the apprentice. The first woman B.B.C. radio announcer, Sheila Borrett, lived here in the 1930s.

On the front wall of the old part is a metal plaque about which the Sun Insurance Group provides this information— 'It is a 'Sun' fire mark number 209530 which indicates the number of the policy issued in June 1764 to one Thomas Groome, Carpenter of Little Gadsden in the County of Hertfordshire on his houses and offices only for a sum not exceeding £100. Premium 3/-. Renewal Date Midsummer 1765. Agent–Capon'. In 1849 Ashridge House was insured by the same society for £20,000, premium £54 4s.0d.

In 1856 Mr Wright came to Little Gaddesden to instal the new water-pumping engine. He came from Shevington, Suffolk. His son Walter E. Wright and grandson George were born in this house. There is a photograph of an elderly lady in the former porch (where is now the front window) with her spinning wheel, a typical 19th-century feature of cottage life.

One interesting feature of the exterior of the older frontage is the buttresses.

The Red House. The house was known in former years as the Holly Bush Lodge, and the holly hedge still runs along the front of the house. Standing in the centre of the houses on the Green in the 18th century it had extensive gardens. It belonged to the Duke of Bridgewater and was occupied in 1802 by Mr Fox. In 1838 John Adsetts lived here. He also had 11 acres of meadowland. The rubbed-brickwork is especially decorative and is similar to the Ashridge Pumping station of 1858. The brick plaque on the exterior has a large 'B' for Brownlow with an earl's coronet and the date 1870.

This is a residence with outhouses rebuilt under the Alford-Brownlow aegis, and suitable for the central workshops for the vast estate. There were about thirty workshops for blacksmiths, wheelwrights, plumbers, painters, well-sinkers, carpenters, builders and plasterers. The bell rang daily at 8 a.m., noon, 1 p.m. and 5 p.m.

In the traction-house shed there were two steam engines which worked the steam plough. This was one of the Colonel Wheatley's institutions. Two engines were needed for Pulridge Hill. The engines were housed in the large barn at the top of the drive. The shed has a part cut out of the ceiling for the funnel. The men on the Estate had a colourful way of expressing themselves. One instance is given of old Mr Groom who drove the Ashridge Steam Roller— 'If Colonel Wheatley had had the faintest idea that my steam roller would climb a tree, he would have expected me to drive up it, and then go birdnesting among the branches'. Colonel Wheatley was responsible for the 28,000 acres of the Brownlow Estate. Mr J. Wright the Clerk of Works worked from here.

Miss Noyes whose stained-glass window is in the north choir-aisle of the parish church lived here. The window is probably a true likeness of her. She was related to the Halsey family from Great Gaddesden and cousin to the poet Alfred Noyes. 'As Miss Noyes walked along the Green with her "poms" or drove along in her carriage, she insisted that the village boys should salute her, and the girls curtsey. This was expected by the Gentry before the Great War.'

Colonel Wheatley whose green Napier was AR1, had his headquarters here. He cycled to Ashridge, and the brick path he used can still be traced across the field and down to the Golden Valley.

Mrs Wheatley helped to work altar frontals for Little Gaddesden church. A cousin of Lady Brownlow, she was prominent in the arrangements for the Alford Cross and War Memorial on the Green.

Spencer Block, lawyer, sportsman, Chairman of the Parish Council and of the Village Hall Committee lived here. He had been a Cambridge Blue in four sports, a Surrey County Cricketer, President of Ashridge Golf Club and an England Hockey Player.

The Block family were followed by Mr and Mrs Grieff O'Neill who came here from St Albans. *The Waterworks.* In 1858 the Ashridge Waterworks was constructed. The well was 275 feet deep. The stone bears the date 1858. The original steam engine only ceased working in 1930. In 1856 Mr Wright came to instal the new pumping engine. He was later to be killed on the pump wheel. The building was a Victorian one and the Dacorum Council refused permission for it to be pulled down when the Rickmansworth and Uxbridge Valley Water Company wished to do so. However plans for a new Waterworks were approved, at a cost of £30,000, in 1978.

The provision for piped water for each cottage was a great achievement for 1858, and Lady Marian Alford was remembered with great gratitude for this. Joseph Whitman a native of Ringshall died aged 70 years having served 51 years as machinist and engineer at the Waterworks. *Number 50.* There was a lane across the Green in the 18th century between No. 50 and the Red House. It appears that the property now No. 50 was parallel to that lane. Other houses along the Green were also built like that (e.g. 31-32). Ann Cox lived here in 1838.

The Brownlow shield on the exterior gives the date 1875. When extensive alterations took place in which Mr Arthur Clifton was concerned, evidence of 17th-century work was revealed. At one time this was a butcher's shop. Mr Thorn, Ashridge Farm overseer, lived here and later it was the home of Mr Jack Yewdall who became clerk to the Parish Council.

Number 54. This timber-framed house with casement windows is, like No. 50, one of the older houses on the Green. It was suggested that there were plans for three cottages identical to the older part of this one. There had been three buildings between the present 50 and 54 in the 18th and 19th centuries. At the beginning of the 19th century the occupants were Cox, Hennings and others. Part of the land was leased by John Lamport from the Ashridge Estate. In 1838 the occupants were William Pratt, Timothy Garratt, Sarah Hurndall, James Buckthorn and Jesse Holland. The older part of 54 dates from the 17th century. Lord Brownlow made additions in 1912, and this must have been amongst the latest work which he initiated. The Austin family came here in 1907. It had been a grocer's shop. Stanley Austin added to the house and developed it. He was made President of the local branch of the Royal British Legion in 1968.

THE ADELAIDE CROSS

The Cross may be seen from the Front Entrance Porch of Ashridge House when looking up through the avenue of trees to the village Green. It was once said that this avenue was created because the Countess of Bridgewater, wife of the 7th Earl, wished to be able to see her mother's house on the Green from her own house each morning. This is a pleasant but perhaps inaccurate story . . . though one wonders if there is a kernel of truth in it. The inscription reads—
IN REMEMBRANCE OF ADELAIDE WIFE OF ADELBERT 3rd EARL BROWNLOW
DAUGHTER OF HENRY 18th EARL OF SHREWSBURY AND TALBOT
BORN 1844 MARRIED 1866 DIED 1917
At the base— MERCY AND TRUTH HAVE MET TOGETHER
RIGHTEOUSNESS AND PEACE HAVE KISSED EACH OTHER.
The Cross stands near the Manor House where Lady Brownlow's relatives had lived and at the opposite end of the Green to that where her beloved mother-in-law, Lady Marian Alford, was also remembered by a Cross.
Ancient Cross. In 1825 there was an ancient cross at the south corner of the Green. The exact site is not known. It was thought to be a place on an old Ivinghoe-Little Gaddesden boundary.

BONFIRE NIGHT 5 NOVEMBER

Guy Fawkes' night was celebrated vigorously in the 18th and 19th centuries in Little Gaddesden. The church bells were rung and the ringers were paid for their work. A massive bonfire was erected outside the Manor House on the Green. It was built by the Ashridge Estate staff. The climax came when the great barrel of tar containing the Guy at the top caught fire.

This end of the Green was noteworthy for the great variety of wild flowers in the days when cattle were grazing there, and there was no traffic to disturb them.

THE MANORS OF LITTLE GADDESDEN, LUCIES, ASHRIDGE

In 942-46 the Lady Aethelgiva left Gadsden to St Albans Abbey. By 1065 Edmer Ator (Attile) held the manor as an outlier of Berkhamsted. It came into the hands of Humphrey ('Hunfrid holds Gatesdene') under Robert of Mortain by 1086, according to the Domesday Survey. It remained there until the treason of the 2nd Count of Mortain. It then came into the hands of King Henry I. Henry visited Dunstable and Berkhamsted. It is known that he rode across the Common. He passed through Little Gaddesden. The manor remained in royal hands for many years.

Early in the 13th century it was held by the Broc family, sub-tenants of the royal manor of Berkhamsted. In 1204 Eva de Broc sold one half of her manor of Little Gaddesden to Simon de Wieleston. At her death the other half passed to her sister who was married to Geoffrey de Lucy. Simon's share passed to his son Thomas. Thomas gave this to Edmund, Earl of Cornwall.

King Henry III (1216-72) who had inherited the lands from Henry I's time gave them to his brother Richard who gave them to his son Edmund, Earl of Cornwall. Edmund gave the manor of Little Gaddesden to the new College of Bonhommes at Ashridge with Geoffrey de Lucy's agreement. The manor of Ashridge was given to them by Ulion Chendit. At the Dissolution the manor of Little Gaddesden passed into the hands of Henry, Earl of Essex.

In 1544 Sir William Parr, Earl of Essex, and brother of Catherine Parr, consort of King Henry VIII conveyed the manor of Little Gaddesden and Lucies to Robert Dormer and William Jakeman. THE DORMER FAMILY was one of great antiquity in Buckinghamshire having settled there under the bishops of Winchester. Sir Robert Dormer, thrice High Sheriff of Buckinghamshire and Bedfordshire under Henry VIII, received the manor of Wenge (Wing) at the Dissolution, part of the lands of St Albans Abbey. In 1552 he was succeeded by his eldest son, who in the reign of Philip and Mary was given a licence to retain 30 men wearing only his livery. His 2nd daughter was Maid of Honour to Queen Mary. This was the illustrious background against which the present 'Manor House' was to be built or rebuilt by Sir Robert Dormer in 1576. A stone tablet over the bay window on the south wall is inscribed —

A.D. 1576

E.E. (or E.B.)

A R-D

He was to succeed his father in 1585 and to become a baronet and baron in 1615. His son by his wife Elizabeth Browne, daughter of Viscount Montague was to be the 1st Earl of Carnarvon. He was killed at the battle of Newbury in 1643. He was overlord of Hudnall.

In 1602 the manor of Lucies was conveyed to John Eames and Robert James by Queen Elizabeth. They sold it to Lord Ellesmere at Ashridge. On 21 October 1604 the Manor House was conveyed to Lord Ellesmere.

One question to be answered is where the sites of the Manor Houses were, both in the 13th century and later. Clearly the site of the present Manor House was in the centre of a hamlet. Other ancient sites could include John O'Gaddesden's, the Church Farm, the vicinity of the former Rectory, and Hudnall Farm.

Little Gaddesden parish church, c. 1808.

Ashridge College from the south.

3. Thunderdell Lodge.

4. (*below*) Old Park Lodge.

5. (*right*) The Bridgewater Monument. ·

(*above*) Princes Riding towards Ashridge House.
e Deer Leap.

(*centre right*) Alderton Drive (a private road).

(*bottom right*) Ringshall Cottages

(*below*) Ringshall Cottages

10. (*top*) Ringshall Lodge and Deer Leap Garage

11. (*centre*) The Town Houses, Little Gaddesden.

12. (*bottom*) Benhay, the former Rectory.

3. (*top*) Little Gaddesden cottages, 6-13.

4. (*centre*) Wood Ash, a Whitman house.

5. (*bottom*) Little Gaddesden Post Office and Stores.

16. The *Bridgewater Arms*.

17. The Rectory, Little Gaddesden, 1981.

18. The Alford Cross and the entrance to Ashridge Park.

19.   The north end of the Green, with Church Road, Ashridge Park entrance and the road to Ringshall.

20.   Ringshall Drive

21.   Little Gaddesden Church of
England School.

22. The parish church from the south.

23. Bede Court.

24. The Chapel and Westmacott Memorial.

25. The Chancel, Little Gaddesden parish church

26. (*left*) The Parish Chest.

27. (*below left*) War memorial on the Green.

28. (*below*) The Dutton-Egerton Memorial, Little Gaddesden parish church

29. (*above*) John O'Gaddesden's House.

30. (*right*) Numbers 31 and 32 The Green.

31. (*below*) The New Houses, Numbers 33 to 37 The Green.

32. (*above*) Yew Tree Cottage.

33. (*left*) Number 42 The Green.

34. (*below*) Number 43 The Green (The Three Chimneys) with Number 41, Alford Cottage in the background.

35. Denison House.

36. Number 49 The Green.

37.   The Red House.

38.   The Adelaide Cross with Numbers 50
and 54 The Green in the distance.

39.   Number 54 The Green.

40.   'Jarman's Coffin', The Manor House chimneys.

41. The Manor House.

42. The Manor House. An interior view.

43. Robin Hood Cottages with Robin Hood House.

44. Little Gaddesden House.

45. The Home Farm House.

46. (*right*) The Dovecot.

47. (*below*) Cromer Wood House.

48. Ashridge Cottages.

49. Cromer Close.

50. (*above*) 'Quinacres'.

51. (*left*) The Methodist church and Chapel Close.

52. (*below*) Numbers 1 and 2 Hudnall.

53. (*above*) Hudnall Farm.

54. (*right*) The lane to St Margaret's from Hudnall.

55. The Hudnall Park Environmental Study Centre.

56. The Golden Valley.

57. Ashridge Management College from the north-east.

58. The Annunciation, Ashridge College Chapel.

59. (*above*) Ashridge College Chapel.

60. (*right*) The Rose Brass, Ashridge College Chapel.

61. Heads from the pulpit.

ASHRIDGE COLLEGE CHAPEL

62. The Tudor Portcullis.

64. A miniature from a stall.

63. The Haynes Family Arms.

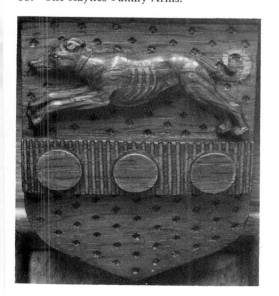

65. Pargetting.

66. (*below*) Herkomer House door.

67. (*centre right*) The old Post Office Shield. (Number 42, The Green).

68. (*bottom right*) Number 49, The Green, Fire Insurance Plate.

69. An illustrated page (self-portrait?) from a manuscript of Simon de Wederore of Tring.

70. Dury and Andrews' map of Ashridge College *c.1766 (reproduced by courtesy of Hertfordshire County Record Office).*

71. Earthworks west of Little Gaddesden church: an aerial view (*reproduced by courtesy of* Aerofilms *and Mr W. Brooker*).

72. (*top left*) The *Bridgewater Arms* sign.

73. (*above*) The 7th Earl of Bridgewater from the church porch.

74. (*left*) Buckingham the steward of Ashridge under the 7th Earl (from the original in the possession of Geoffrey Buckingham, Wilmslow, Cheshire).

75. An aerial view of Ashridge, *c.*1928 (*reproduced by courtesy of* Aerofilms).

76. An aerial view of Ashridge, *c.*1981 (*reproduced by courtesy of* Aerofilms).

77. Ashridge Golf Club.

78. Ashridge Golf Club.

THE MANOR HOUSE

This ancient building stands back from Gaddesden Green at the Hudnall Lane End. It is turretted above its Totternhoe stone walls. At each end of the main frontage is a square projecting turret which reaches above the main roof. At the apex of the north-west gable there is a stone clock dial, divided up and with figures. The divisions are repeated on the inside of the wall. There is an oak staircase in the turret. The stepped gables, Dutch-style, were common in Hertfordshire in the early 16th century. They were to be seen in buildings flanking the former Ashridge House before the 19th-century rebuilding.

There is a projecting bay window between the two turrets, extending to the second storey. The windows have stone mullions and transoms. The stone tablet over the bay window, dated 1576, probably refers to Robert Dormer and his wife Elizabeth (Browne). It could be that E.E. (not E.B.) means Elizabeth of England [see below]. On the front wall is a leaden drain pipe with the date and lettering—

16E 84

I.M.

The M. may stand for Maberly, a family which lived here for several generations.

Part of the earlier wing of the house is half-timbered. It could appear that between 1862 and 1900 a fire had destroyed one wing and more. The chimneys are interesting, especially the one known as Jarman's Coffin, because of its unusual shape and position. The roofs are of old tiles. At one time the house was believed to have been called 'The Priory'.

The dining-room in the Manor House has an Elizabethan fireplace of 1576 set below the royal coat of arms of Elizabeth I. This was in accordance with a special privilege granted to the Dormer family allowing them to use the royal arms. A contemporary painting of Princess Elizabeth formerly on part of a door was discovered in the cellar of the Manor House in the 1890s when workmen were installing a boiler for Mrs Wheatley. It had probably been taken down there during or after the Crimean War when the dining-room was used as an armoury for the local militia. It was identified and later erected on the dining-room wall, framed and with a small light.

The Princess Elizabeth had left London on 6 December 1553 accompanied by an escort of 500 gentlemen on horseback. About ten miles out she sent back for vessels and vestments for use in the Holy Communion service. She arrived in Ashridge but was not to remain there long. Her sister Queen Mary believing the story that Elizabeth was implicated in the rebellion of Sir Thomas Wyatt sent 200 soldiers to Ashridge summoning her to London. Elizabeth said that she was too ill to go, but it was of no avail, and she was transported by stages to the Tower entering on Palm Sunday 1554 by the Traitor's Gate. Wyatt repudiated any suggestion that Elizabeth had been implicated before he was executed. Elizabeth was sent by barge on 19 May 1554 to Woodstock via Richmond. Her second night was spent at Sir William Dormer's House at West Wycombe. The later privilege of using the royal arms of Elizabeth may have resulted in part from the hospitality she received at this time.

In the painting of Elizabeth she is seen at Ashridge being approached by the soldiers in February 1553/4. They had allowed her to wait until the following day before taking her away. Her room had been a small one above the cloister. There she had been preparing baby clothes for her sister when she was believed to be expecting a child by Philip her husband. Some tiny socks for an infant were left behind at Ashridge. These, with Elizabeth's hair brushes and high-heeled shoes, were preserved. In 1928 they were withdrawn from the sale of the Ashridge Estates by Lord Brownlow's trustees. The flowers and the blossom in the picture suggest spring or summer, but the arrest was in February. The journey must have followed the road down the Golden Valley, thence down 'The Lady's Mile' to Water End, and on to London.

In a woodcut in a manual on hunting by George Turbeville in the 16th century, Queen Elizabeth is portrayed wearing a hat ribbon and pendant, and robes, not dissimilar to these worn by the Queen when she was at Ashridge as the Princess. The portrait could thus be a little later in the century.

In the dining-room there is also wainscotting which came from Ashridge College, probably from either the College Chapel or the Refectory. A large banquetting table of the 16th century or earlier, previously used as a carpenter's block, also came from Ashridge.

The Solar above the dining-room is a little larger than the dining-room. It was also the work of Sir Robert Dormer and has its original mantelpiece. A profile carved above one mantelpiece is said to be of Dr Friend. His connection with the Manor House is not known. There is a bust to a Dr Friend in Christ Church Library at Oxford.

Whilst Ashridge was a royal residence it is likely that the Manor House was the residence of the royal steward of Ashridge. During the time of the 7th Earl of Bridgewater the Maberly family resided there and in 1802 farmed 244 acres of the surrounding land.

In the time of the last countess who died in 1849 it was used as an Estate Office. During the Crimean War it was used as an armoury for the local volunteers, and after Sergeant-Major Ballam was wounded in that war he became responsible for it.

The Cautley family occupied the house after this until 1882 when Colonel Wheatley became agent to the Estate. During the 19th century parts of the house were used for the armoury, lending library, reading room, and night school. When Colonel Wheatley married Miss Annette Cust on 21 February 1887 at St Peter's, Eaton Square, London, the Dean of York, cousin of the bride, officiated. The new Mrs Wheatley was cousin to Lord Brownlow. They moved into the Manor House. The house was restored for Lord Brownlow. Colonel Wheatley ran the Estate with great devotion. His ideas were forward-looking and to many local men revolutionary. His car was a two seater Napier with yellow spoked wheels. Its number was AR 1. He died on 29 May 1932 and Mrs Wheatley died on 3 October 1932.

On the death of Lord Brownlow the Manor House was bought by his niece Miss Kathleen Talbot, grand-daughter of the 18th Earl of Shrewsbury and Talbot and daughter of the Hon. Alfred Talbot of Little Gaddesden House. She founded the Village Produce Societies of England, and was National President. She was prominent in the establishment of the Hertfordshire Rural Music School and the Little Gaddesden Choral Society. Her friend who also lived at the Manor House, Miss Dorothy Erhart, had an outstanding collection of musical instruments which she demonstrated to visitors to the Manor House when it was open to the public.

Miss Talbot's ashes were placed beneath a Cherry Tree to the north-east of the nave of the parish church, and Miss Erhart's ashes were later laid there.

At the top of the garden there was a cowshed, stables, cottages and greenhouses. The yews were planted in 1899. Before the 1939 war the topiarists had made three figures . . . faith, hope and charity. Later they made a schooner, which became a sea-lion. A peacock and a camel's head were also fashioned.

For a time a retired clergyman the Rev. Canon Rollo Meyer resided here. He was a noted gardener and a national expert on roses.

On the death of Miss Erhart the Manor House became the property of Mr Graham-Stewart. For its internal features this house is in Grade IIx of the Department of Environment's list of buildings of historical and architectural interest.

No. 55 Little Gaddesden. Part of the south-east wing of the Manor House which contained the offices is now detached to form a separate cottage known as No. 55. It is of lower elevation than the main portion. It is timber-framed refaced with brick on the north side, but with some timbering with red-brick infilling exposed on the south-east side. The casement windows have small square-leaded panes. This, with the Manor House, is in category IIx of the list of graded buildings. Nineteenth-century additions to the north-east form a separate house.

Tree Tops. 'Tree Tops' faces the Green, and siding on Hudnall Lane, is adjacent to the Manor House and was formerly part of the Manor Orchard. The building was a school-room for Ashridge apprentices who came to learn various trades, mostly studying in the evenings, and finishing with social events. They paid a penny for a cup of tea. When this use was discontinued the building was used to house coaches. There is a brick courtyard beneath the grass immediately in front of the building. Later it became registered as a Market Garden. In 1968 it was bought from Miss Dorothy Erhart by Mr J. Peasnall and was extensively renovated, permission being obtained for a drive opening on to Hudnall Lane.

11. Hudnall Corner to Pulridge Hill. Cromer.

HUDNALL CORNER

Situated at the Ashridge end of Hudnall Lane, with the road going south to Nettleden and north towards Ivinghoe, this could have been an important place in the village. The proximity of the 'Manor House' and the cottages and buildings in the area, together with the clear marks of the old strip system method of farming behind the present Kingham's Meadow all suggest that there was a small hamlet here. There was also an ancient cross at this end of the Green.

In the 18th century it appears that the present road along the Green was not then established throughout its length, but that from Hudnall corner a lane ran down into the Golden Valley and along to Ringshall Drive. There was a lane immediately in front of John O'Gaddesden's House and stretching just beyond Yew Tree Cottage. Nearer to Denison House it broadened again and followed the lane of the present pathway along the Green to Hudnall. By 1802 this pathway was clearly marked and the present road along the Green also appears.

After the Black Death the Hudnall Lane area may have grown in importance if, as local tradition states, the parish church area was left after the inhabitants moved away. The Manor House could have been the home of the Lucies, and the house would have become the centre for cottages and ancillary accommodation. On the Kingham's Meadow side there is evidence of cottage property in the mid-18th century, and a small number were known as 'Town orchard and cottages'. In 1838 Thomas Pangbourne lived here. The three acre meadow belonged to James Kingham. Traces of what could be old earthworks have been noted in the meadows behind the Manor House.

KINGHAM'S MEADOW.

In 1854 there was a small white house here, a workman's cottage. The present house was built in 1858. A Brownlow tablet is on the exterior wall. The chimneys were said to be copies of some at Hampton Court Palace. Mr George the Head Clerk at Ashridge lived here, then Mr Hodgson, and then Mr Joseph Parsons, who left a fortune stated to be £50,000. He had been responsible for all the Ashridge linen and its marking, and had been head of the Estate Office. The house is named after the meadow in which it originally stood. The tree in front of the house is a Swamp Cypress (*Taxodium distichum*).

On the death of Earl Brownlow in 1921 the house and land were bought from the trustees by Miss Bridget Talbot of Little Gaddesden House. On 28 April 1932 she conveyed it to Gertrude Grimke Drayton and Lilian Bartlett for £1,000. In 1938 Miss Talbot bought back 19 perches. It was then known as Hudnall Corner Cottage.

After the deaths of the two ladies in 1941 and 1944 the property was purchased by Elsie Dunphy for £3,725. At that time it was known as 'Kinghams'. She sold it in 1947 to Martha Simpson of Nettleden Farm for £5,500 and she conveyed it to John Simpson in 1955. By then it had received its name of 'Kingham's Meadow'.

Mr Arthur Wooster came here in 1967, and since then much modernisation has taken place especially in 1976.

58, 59, 60, 61, 62 Little Gaddesden. Cottages were marked here in 1762 and perhaps there were more at an earlier date. In 1802 they are shown adjoining the *Robin Hood* Inn. In 1838 the occupants, from Hudnall Lane end, were Joseph Impey, Jesse Fowler, George Norwood and William Fowler, senior. Each cottage had its own garden, and they were all Estate cottages belonging to the Countess of Bridgewater. There was a dew pond between 58 and Hudnall Lane.

58. At the beginning of the 20th century the Simmonds family lived here. *58* and *59* have been made into one since 1955. The Poole family lived here and were followed in about 1969 by Mr Bliss ('News at Ten'). In 1972 Mr W.T.N. Allen acquired it, but did not reside here until 1976. However he was associated with the development of the Cricket Colts from 1972. In 1930 John and Emma Simmonds lived in 58.

60 has signs of having been two cottages. Floors are on different levels. The inner portion near 61 has old timber and beams which indicate a date contemporaneous with the oldest part of Robin Hood House. Walter Lamb who lived here at the turn of the 20th century was a well-known character who drove one of the Ashridge ploughing engines. Cyril Cornelius and Daisy White lived here in 1930.

61. In the 1940s this cottage had old oak-mullioned windows and diamond-paned lattice windows. These were removed before 1950. There was a very old attic and staircase, with a cellar of the same date . . . probably late-Tudor, as in Robin Hood House. It has different levels from 60 and 62 on either side. In the garden of Robin Hood cottage 61 is a filled-in spring. The level did not go down during the 1971 drought. William and Alice Newman were here in 1930.

62 has been said to be 300 years old which dates it at the end of the 17th century, during the time of the 2nd and 3rd Earls of Bridgewater. It has a kitchen with two ranges and a large store room behind, which could have been a bakehouse. In 1950 there was an old pump working in the kitchen, but this was taken to Cornwall on the sale of this cottage.

There is a reservoir of rain water beneath the cow-shed at the rear of the cottages, now covered in, and which used to supply Robin Hood House. There was another well.

In the earlier grading of houses by the Department of the Environment, 60, 61 and Robin Hood House were in the category Grade III now no longer used.

ROBIN HOOD HOUSE

Formerly the *Green Man* and the *Robin Hood* Inn. In the *Jornal de la Chambre* 1324, the name Robyn Hood is included with A. Henri Lawe, Colle de Ashruge (25 April 1324) and Jack Ede, Coll Ashruge (21 August 1324) in royal payments.

The cellars were said to date from 1578, about the time of the building of the Manor House. On 26 March 1748 Peter Kalm, a Swedish naturalist visited Hugh Ellis the farmer of Church Farm. He arrived at 6.00 p.m. and stayed at the *Robin Hood* inn. He commented on the open door with windows on either side. The entrance was then in the front of the house. There was a high-backed seat beside the fire. Woods of high and thick beeches were below the house. There was a saw-pit there and one of the trees he noticed had 162 sap rings when cut across.

Francis, 3rd Duke of Bridgewater, the Canal Duke became the owner of racehorses. His most famous horse was the Cullen Arabian bred in 1757. The Duke's racing colours were blue silk and silver. His stable companions were the Duke of Cumberland, a 2nd son of King George II, and the 4th Duke of Queensberry. In 1746 he was auctioning hunters from Ashridge stables. 'At the sign of the *Robin Hood* on Little Gaddesden Hill, Herts . . . to meet the cost of canal construction' (from Sutherland Estate papers).

In the field behind Robin Hood House and Nobody's Bottom in a 1788 plan of Little Gaddesden there was an ancient tarred, half-timbered cow-house and stockyard built on staddle stones to keep out the rats. This old cowshed which must have belonged to the Agricultural College days was burned out in an act of arson after the 1945 war. An 18th-century plan showed the layout of the *Robin Hood* as a prosperous inn of coaching days. On the south side were stabling and workers' cottages, and an entrance to the inn yard coming in from the road. These buildings must have been extensive. The late Mrs Dora Drewitt told of her mother as a little girl talking of the days when highwaymen frequented the Inn and caused much dread by their uncouth appearance and foul language. There was a bakehouse turned into a stable, which might have been an old kitchen.

In 1802 the Duke of Bridgewater owned the property and it was occupied by T. Buckthorp.

The 1838 tithe apportionment map places the 'Robin Hood and Little John Beer Shop' on Gaddesden Green near the present Denison House.

In 1855 John, 2nd Earl Brownlow reconstructed this house. This included the present porch. His shield with 'B' surmounted by an earl's coronet bears the date 1855. This is one of the earliest of the Brownlow reconstructions. In 1867 Lord Brownlow decided to pay for a curate to assist the ageing Rector, the Rev. David Jenks. The Rev. C.G. Lane was appointed, and the Chaplain's House became the former 'Robin Hood'.

Later it was occupied by Miss Fanny Halsey from 1870 when Lord Brownlow gave her a 21 years lease until her death in 1885. He then leased it for seven years to Miss W. and Miss L. Brooke (1893-1900) for £50 per annum.

Whilst Little Gaddesden House was being built, Robin Hood was probably used as an Estate Office. For a time it was used as a school for young gentlemen. The Hon. Alfred Talbot, father of Miss Kathleen and Miss Bridget Talbot was educated there. It was arranged as a long hall or schoolroom. The present stone-flagged hall was the butler's pantry.

At the turn of the century, Mr Murray-Smith lived there. His wife was the daughter of Dr Bradley, Dean of Westminster, and thus sister-in-law of Rector H.G. Woods of Little Gaddesden (1900-1904). Later Mr Wykeham-Musgrave purchased the property and he obtained four acres of Cromer Wood at the north end to make a wild garden and provide a bridleway into the park from opposite No. 58 and Robin Hood Farm. Many bulbs and herbaceous plants suitable for naturalisation were planted in green lands between little meandering pathways. From one of these at the head of a small ravine could be seen a bridge constructed for Lady Brownlow to drive around the Estate in her phaeton. The bridge was made of brick with a stone coping. The single arch spanned the hollow made by glacial action, which the pudding-stones at the cottage gates confirm. The bridge is now smothered. The former views from this area are now obstructed by the overgrowth of trees and shrubs.

In 1928 there was a specification for electric lighting. An altered apportionment dated 1930 shows Robin Hood House as 1 acre 9 square perches, and owned by Major Wykeham-Musgrave. He was churchwarden with Mr Stephen J. Oakins.

In 1945 the house was bought by Mr and Mrs Wade. During the 1939-45 war it was used by Belgian refugees in the charge of nuns, one of whom was an artist. A large studio was built between the present front door and hall and the Gig-house. The Gig-house had an ancient vine, and shoots still exist. In 1949/50 the house was bought by Mrs Shepherd. Later it was the residence of Major Eric Buller-Leybourne-Popham M.C., an Old Harrovian and descendant of General Buller. Mrs Bridget Buller-Leybourne-Popham was a very accomplished horsewoman. She rode side-saddle to the great pleasure of Little Gaddesden people. It was acquired by Mr K. Fulton in 1973. The fields behind the house were Dip Well, Appletree Close and Great Meadow.

LITTLE GADDESDEN HOUSE

A Victorian country residence originally built in 1859 by Harris of Berkhamsted for Lord Brownlow. There is no evidence to suggest that this was the 'Gaddesden House' mentioned in 1604. Mr G. Atty, Lady Bridgewater's agent lived for a time in a small white house halfway between the present house and the road. Mr Paxton who served as agent under the Brownlows lived here in a small house until Little Gaddesden House was completed, and he then moved in. Paxton was nephew to Sir Joseph Paxton who built the Conservatory at Chatsworth House for the

Duke of Devonshire and later Crystal Palace. He took the lead in laying out the new churchyard extension, where he was buried. He also gave the lectern to the parish church. 'He left a fortune'. He served as agent for 28 years until 1882. He died in 1886.

The House was used partly as an Estate Office and partly as a school. It became the home of one branch of the Talbot family, and the Hon. Alfred Chetwynd Talbot (1848-1913) younger son of the 18th Earl of Shrewsbury and his wife Emily Louisa Augusta, eldest daughter of the 5th Baron Walsingham, lived here. In 1900 Alfred Talbot had a bicycle accident and after his recovery he publicly gave thanks at service in Little Gaddesden church. It was he who nominated the Rev. Edward Clark to Lord Brownlow as Rector to succeed Dr Woods in 1904.

Humphrey Talbot, the eldest son founded the Little Gaddesden Band. He died suddenly on his wedding day, 6 February 1944. Mrs Talbot died in January 1912 and Bishop Talbot of Winchester officiated at her funeral. In 1913 Alfred Talbot died. He was the favourite brother of Lady Brownlow and a man of great public spirit who devoted himself to Little Gaddesden. His daughter Miss Kathleen Talbot moved into the Manor House. Miss Bridget stayed at Little Gaddesden House and her property, Kiplin Hall, Northallerton, Yorkshire. The house was occupied by Miss Bridget Talbot, but on her death it was not possible to finance the capital requirements and restoration work which would be required if the house, as she had hoped, was to be used as a charitable establishment for children. It was sold and the buildings were restored by Messrs. E.J. Waterhouse who converted the property into nine freehold residences. The work was completed in 1978. The original drive was replaced by one nearer to Hudnall Lane. Little Gaddesden House was one of the first houses to be fitted for gas lighting.

MISS BRIDGET TALBOT, O.B.E.

Daughter of the Hon.Alfred Talbot and Emily Louisa his wife, and grand-daughter of the 18th Earl of Shrewsbury, she owned Little Gaddesden House.

In 1914 Miss Talbot was a member of the Belgian Refugee committee. Refugees were to come to Robin Hood House. In 1916 she joined the Anglo-Italian Red Cross and stayed until 1919 with this organisation, receiving the Italian Medal for Valour, for her services. In 1920 she received the O.B.E. Between 1920 and 1922 she founded a Committee to aid Russian refugees and began a co-operative farm colony in Asia Minor. In 1932 she went to Russia with Lady Muriel Paget's mission. In 1937 she sailed on the four-masted ship *Pamir* to Finland and on her return in 1939 she began the National Labour Enquiry into the state of the Merchant Navy.

She invented the electric torch for lifebelts. Because of her insistence that automatic electric light should be fitted on life jackets and rafts, Parliament made the fitting and its adequate provision on rafts and life-saving equipment compulsory for all Merchant Navy, Royal Navy and R.A.F. personnel.

Before becoming involved with refugees in 1914 she had begun the cultivation of co-operative gardens on waste lands in this country. The Ministry of Agriculture later adopted her scheme. In 1950 she was defeated as a Liberal candidate for Bermondsey.

The Ashridge Estates were saved from major private development because of her alertness and persistence. She was responsible for conditions being imposed on the sale of Ashridge property to preserve the beauty of the area. The National Trust owes a great deal to her activity when she heard from her cousin of the impending sale for development.

She was Lord of the Manor of Scorton, Yorkshire; Hereditary Governor of Scorton Grammar School; Vice-President of the Red Ensign Club; Honorary Member of St Dunstan's Governing Committee; Honorary Officer of the Roman Grenadier Guards to which she was appointed after the battle of Monte Santo in 1917; and a member of the National Labour Council.

Miss Talbot had taken an active part in preserving the village community especially in its traditional patterns. She personally organised the annual May Day Procession on the Green with St George and the Dragon. This ended annually with her casting sweets to the children of the village. She had presented a pageant at Ashridge about the life of Elizabeth I just before the Great War, and this had been the swan song of old Ashridge. Later she tried to persuade Edward, Prince of Wales to take Ashridge for philanthropic purposes or for a Commonwealth College. She wanted to make the Home Farm a land training settlement for the unemployed. She was deeply concerned about the poor and the right use of wealth. She hoped that Little Gaddesden House would be used after her death for philanthropic purposes, but this was not practicable. She died on 30 November 1971, mourned for her long and active life, and to be remembered locally in innumerable personal anecdotes.

The Chesham Electric Light Company wrote to the Berkhamsted Rural District Council for permission to erect overhead cables to carry the current to Little Gaddesden. The route was to be underground to the Hollow and across the Common from Northchurch to the village. 'But this was an extraordinary waste' said Miss Talbot. 'Little Gaddesden' she said 'was a pretty place and every possible step should be taken to prevent the spoiling of a lovely village. Why should we spoil England when only three people in the village wanted electric light'. But members were told that the final decision rested with the Electricity Commissioners. Miss Talbot wrote to *The Berkhamsted Gazette* in August 1929 about this.

The Garden Cottage Peachey's Stores. This was originally the cottage for the gardener at Little Gaddesden House. Mr Pinnock lived here. His son Edward has his name on the War Memorials on the Green and in the parish church for he was killed when serving in the Great War on H.M.S. Black Prince. Later it became a shop beloved of the children who delighted to buy their sweets from Mrs Peachey a Scottish lady, daughter of a Scottish schoolmaster who had been a pioneer missionary in the China Inland Mission. The children loved to have their pictures and drawings on Mrs Peachey's walls, respected her as she taught them 'good manners', and benefited from her remarkable command of the English language. Mrs Peachey who came here with her husband in 1954 had been a nurse and also was a qualified English teacher.

Deer Leap Horticultural Works. This property is on the site of the former Home Farm buildings. It began in association with the Deer Leap Garage and Mr Gordon Huxtable. Mr R.A. Brooks was the manager and he was followed by Mr and Mrs Wilson and their son. The Bungalow was built in connection with the Horticultural Works.

The Bothy. This house was built by Mr J. Waterton in 1970, the architect being Peter Robinson A.R.I.B.A.; the former gardener's bothy and outbuildings being converted into stables. The land was part of the kitchen-garden of Little Gaddesden House which was purchased from Miss Talbot in 1969.

Home Farm Cottages. No. 1, adjoining the Horticultural Centre was modernised by Mr G. Huxtable and included a 'granny' flat. At the beginning of the century Mr Fred Mead lived here. He was the chauffeur who kept Colonel Wheatley's Napier AR 1 in superb condition. Mr Mead was unable to drive, but sat in the 'Dickie' seat in the open air even in rain and storm, whilst Colonel Wheatley was at the wheel, and within the hood.

THE HOME FARM

In the middle of the 18th century this was the Home Farm of the Duke of Bridgewater's Ashridge Estate. After his death in 1803, the 7th Earl moved William Buckingham the farmer at the Old Dairy from 1800 to be farm bailiff and to reside at the Home Farm. Buckingham was to be one of a trio with Clarke and George Atty who were to run the Estate. He progressed during the next 23 years to become agent and steward of the Estate, although the two titles were not to be used consistently before the death of the 7th Earl.

Buckingham's three children were born at the Home Farm and were brought up there. John Henry was the elder son and was greatly favoured. When he left school he began work for a short time in the Estate Office. He made a painting of the Home Farm, now in the possession of a relative in Australia. After the death of the 7th Earl (whose will had been witnessed by

Buckingham, with the rector of Little Gaddesden and Atty and Clarke on 1 April 1823) he seems not to have been in favour with the widowed Countess, who preferred Clarke's assistance. Clarke worked in her service and that of the late Earl for 55 years. On 21 May 1825 Buckingham gave notice 'to quit the concern altogether', and George, the Nettleden Farm, on Lady Day 1826.

In 1807 the Home Farmhouse was known as 'Mr Buckingham's house'. It had a frontage of 48 feet 10 inches. Adjoining it on the Pulridge side was a brewhouse (18 feet 6 inches) and beyond that a malting-house and a drying-house. The house was at an angle to the buildings on the road side. These were 332 feet in length, with a 35 feet entrance. There was an old garden on the Pulridge side. Facing the house the buildings on the roadside were — on the right . . . the Wheeler's shop, the Men's Mess Room, the brewhouse, the coals and a privy and a woodhouse. Later this block was divided into the stable servants' mess room, the stable and the cart-house. On the left of the entrance . . . the stable. Later . . . the labourers' mess room, hackney stable, ox shed and hay house. Another cart-shed and ox-shed went at right-angles to this at the left-hand side end. Beyond that was a strawhouse and barn and an outhouse for the threshing machine. Jeffry Wyatt was responsible for many of the alterations to the Buckingham Home Farmhouse and these outbuildings.

In 1841 there were more alterations. Mr and Mrs Pitkin were at the Home Farm when this happened. Tudor-style gables were added. By this time there were no buildings adjoining the house at the Pulridge End.

The house bears the Brownlow shield, dated 1877. This probably marked the major 'face-lift' when the house had a completely new 'skin' of bricks with new windows and lintels. The oldest evident structure is the north-west chimney which has much smaller and older bricks than any visible on the rest of the house. It is thought that the two front rooms (facing S.W.) and bedrooms above are part of the original house. The eaves were originally a couple of feet lower (the bedroom windows appear to be dormers from the inside) and the roof now has attractive curved gables as a result of the eaves being raised without modification to the crown of the roof. The various thicknesses of the internal walls might be interpreted to indicate that the house was enlarged by five separate extensions, one of which included digging a basement. At various times it has been split up into two cottages, and then rejoined, so there are two staircases. The clock was made by John Thwaites of London and like the Ashridge tower clock is dated 1804.

In the painting of the house as it appeared in 1820 by the artistic John Henry Buckingham, son of the Ashridge steward and diarist, it is shown as a much larger house. The only parts identifiable are the belfry, clock and the north-west chimneys. The overall size and shape is quite different, and this confuses accurate assessment.

Late in the 19th century the Brownlow Estate rented the Home Farm to George Underwood and then to his eldest son. This was when the house was made into two cottages. It was later acquired by Cooper, McDougall and Robinson, Agricultural Chemists. A very high standard of stock breeding took place. Many national trophies were acquired and visitors came from all over the world. 'Shep' Bunting who was responsible for the sheep on the Farm was photographed for many important journals.

When Cooper, McDougall and Robinson left, it became again a farm. Later it became a private residence, in the 1970s.

The outbuildings were converted into modern luxury dwellings, preserving the character of the former homestead.

Ashridge Cottages. The Davidson Cottages in Cromer Wood. Sir John and Lady Davidson (later Viscount Davidson of Little Gaddesden . . . and Lady Davidson, Baroness Northchurch) commissioned the architect, Clough Williams-Ellis, who was working at Ashridge, to design six cottages for families on the break up of the Ashridge Estate. They were built in 1929 by Matthews.

Sir Frederick Gibberd writing the obituary for Ellis stated 'Not for him the R.I.B.A. Gold Medal or the R.T.P.I. Medal. His great gift was his sensibility to the environment as a whole'. It is very interesting to know that these cottages had such a distinguished architect. At Ashridge he was responsible for enclosing the Conservatory so that it provided the modern Dining Hall.

Buyurun. This house was one of a pair of houses built by F.G. Whitman in 1961/2 and was bought by Mr Leslie G. Johnston. The name 'Buyurun' is Turkish for 'Welcome'. Mr Johnston was born in Turkey and Mrs Johnston was also there for some years before they came to England and to Little Gaddesden. Mrs Johnston has twice been president of the Women's Institute and Mr Johnstone twice chairman of the Drama Club, their positions overlapping at one period.

Morles. When Mr and Mrs Thorne acquired this property in 1962 they named it after his family's farm in Cheriton Fitzpaine, Devon where Mr Thorne had been brought up. Mr Cyril Jack Thorne was sidesman at the parish church and became stewardship chairman, and for many years stewardship recorder.

The Dovecot. The Dovecot was known as the Dove-House and its design for 400 birds was prepared by Jeffry Wyatt in 1821. Its width was to be 17 feet 10 inches with an internal measurement of 15 feet 6 inches. The base was to be 5 feet and the wall-height from the base 25 feet. The roof moved to a point from the top of the wall about 17 feet higher. At the apex there was a form of ventilator exit, surmounted by a weathervane.

The Dovecot was converted in the mid-1970s into a private dwelling and was named Gade House by Mr T. Muddiman.

In the Department of Environment lists of Buildings of Special Architectural or Historic Interest this building is listed in Grade II, those buildings of regional importance.

Bailiffs and West Pulridge The Duke of Bridgewater owned several small properties here in the mid-18th century and Mr Garrett rented the land from him. Fifty years later Daniel Simmons rented land in this area. Mr Murray Smith who lived at Robin Hood House c. 1900 was responsible for building in this vicinity. In 1930 Walter and Hilda Prudhames lived here. Formerly one house it was called Pulridge House, and as such was built for one of the officials at Ashridge House.

Mr J. Overhill lived here, and the house was divided and named Pulridge House West and Pulridge House East. When Colonel Day came he changed the name Pulridge House West to Bailiffs to avoid confusion with West Pulridge, and to preserve the connection with the Ashridge Home Farm. Professor Wallace Peters preserved the Pulridge House association by keeping the name East also. Both houses have been modernised and extended by the present owners. Colonel Day became parochial church secretary in 1973 and churchwarden in 1980. Both houses have very attractive views.

Cromer Wood In the time of Henry VIII Cromer Style is mentioned. 'Cromer' means crows mere or lake. There are pigeons rather than crows here today and there is certainly no lake. The derivation is thus uncertain. There were buildings here in 1762 and 1802, and in 1838 cottages were occupied by David Simmons, John Pratt and William Pitkin, all familiar family names in Little Gaddesden. The main part of the house was formerly two cottages. Mr Joseph Rogers lived at the road end. He was responsible for the lights at Ashridge House. It was a whole day's work trimming the lamps there. He was remembered for his remarkable black beard. At the other end of the house lived David Clarke the very able craftsman whose work became widely known. He was head house carpenter at Ashridge. Mr Worrall the head teacher at Little Gaddesden C. of E. School lived here. He married the sister of Mr George from the Ashridge Estate staff. Miss Wright also lived here. The Halsey family lived in the cottage at right-angles to the Cromer Wood House, and in 1930 this was known as Cromer End. The Townsend family lived for many years at Cromer Wood House which became known as 'Townsend's'. Jim Townsend was in great demand for auditing the accounts of village societies. Later Mr Michael Walsham bought the property which seems to be becoming named 'Walsham's'. In 1982 the Walsham family moved to 'Beaney'.

Old 'Shep' Bunting who was featured in many agricultural magazines and journals lived at Cromer Cottage. These cottages were a 19th-century restoration of older cottages. Mr Murray Smith was responsible for some work in this area, and was probably the builder of Bailiffs and Pulridge House.

Cromer Close was built in 1949 and Mr and Mrs T. Sears moved into Number 19 on 24 September 1949. In the garden of 19 there are remains of the flint road which ran from the Park Road to the sheds where the sick animals from Ashridge were kept, near the present Ranch House. The Cromer Woods are opposite the Home Farm.

Gilbert of Berkhamsted was the builder of Cromer Close for the Berkhamsted Rural District Council. Cromer Close has been fortunate in having excellent gardeners whose work gives great pleasure, and who have also won many prizes at local horticultural shows. The contribution to the life of Little Gaddesden made by residents of Cromer Close has been immeasurable. Dr Colin Andrews, the local doctor was bred here and attended Little Gaddesden C. of E. School.

Stags End formerly Shangri-la. This was built in 1946 by Geoffrey Horrod with his war service grant. He kept poultry and bred pheasants, had a market garden and did carpentry. Mrs Horrod was the local hairdresser. The property was sold and then renamed Stags End. Mr Horrod also built *Deerdyke* and *Woodlands*. The latter was extended in 1970.

The Ranch House. The sick animals from Ashridge were kept in sheds near the present Ranch House. A road ran from the Park to the sheds and flints are still found along the way. There was a steam engine at Cromer Farm (Ranch House area). This was used to drive four mills for grinding barley and crushing oats. There were other farm implements kept here and an early steam-driven sheep-shearing machine. This was the farm for the flocks of sheep and Scottish cattle which Lord Brownlow grazed over Ashridge Park, which was enclosed by the high deer fence. The present house was built in the early 1960s and Mr Francis Hock owned it. It was built on the site of the disused farm laundry building. Later Mrs B.M. Bennett daughter of Canon Glossop of St Albans lived here with her daughter. Canon Glossop had made an outstanding contribution to the Cathedral, Diocese and City of St Albans, especially during wartime. He is buried in the Cathedral churchyard. Mr L.A. Traherne acquired the property from Mrs Bennett.

Quinacres. This was built in 1939 by Mr Sinclair, a surgeon and Harley Street specialist, who called it 'Forres' after a house in Scotland. It was bought in 1945 by H.R.L. Shepherd Q.C. who sold it in 1949 to Mr Desoutter, founder of the firm which made compressed-air drills with the trade slogan, 'The little horses'. He gave the house its present name. It was sold to Mr D. Marriott, and then to Mr R.J.G. Forestier-Walker, architect. He designed and built the new wing of this house. His bravery during a fire at the house is recalled when he might have lost his life to save his daughter. Mr and Mrs M. Essex and Mr and Mrs Birch came to Quinacres after the Forestier-Walker family moved to Buckinghamshire.

West Pulridge. This was built for Captain Tyrer on a seven acre site in 1937. It was bought by Mr F.G. Hawley in 1949. In 1967/8 Mr Donald (later Sir Donald) Hawley acquired it from his father. Three acres at the rear giving access to Ashridge Park were bought in the 1970s. Sir Donald and his family left after he had been appointed High Commisioner in Malaysia. Mr J. Kelly followed in 1980. The views across the Golden Valley from houses along this road give great pleasure.

Roseneath formerly St Anthony's. Built in the late 1930s by Mrs Henrietta Stokes. It was sold to Mr Maurice, Managing Director of Procea Bread.
Dr Rawdon-Smith lived here.

Torwood. This was built in 1940 by Mrs Henrietta Stokes, who named it White Walls. It was changed to Torwood by Mrs Fraser-Beck.

Tanglewood. Built but not occupied by Mr Holmes, lawyer of Berkhamsted. It was occupied by The Rev. C.E. Wager, Rector of Little Gaddesden when he resigned the living, until his death. Mrs Wager continued to live here. It became a sanctuary for bird life. Considerable alterations and additions were effected during the 1970s by R. Clayton Smith.

Peacock's Wood. 1939 summer. The original house was built by Matthews of Berkhamsted for £800. It was designed by Mrs Irene Foord-Kelcey, artist and sculptor, and her son R.D. Foord-Kelcey. In 1953 they designed a second house adjacent to the first. It was built by Bedford of Potten End for £2,090. Mrs Foord-Kelcey lived here and had her studio here, giving great delight to her many visitors. Park Pulridge Wood had been the Pheasantry of the Ashridge Estate. The name of the wood, Peacock's Wood is associated with this. Mr Foord-Kelcey is the earliest of those who having built their own property continues to reside there. Purchasers of land in this area had to agree to the stipulations laid down by the Ashridge Estate trustees.

ASHRIDGE ESTATE. VENDORS' STIPULATIONS

1. No hut, building, or erection, without written consent.
   No caravan, house on wheels, or other removable form of habitation permitted.
2. Purchaser to provide drainage system which shall include a septic tank.
3. Previous consent required for any building with in area of the plot.
   No brick walls shall be erected in place of boundary fences.
4. Every building to be erected in a most substantial manner with sound materials of good quality, of approved character and appearance.
5. No building to be erected without prior approval of the owner.
6. Purchaser to prevent unnecessary damage to Ashridge Estate roads. He shall protect existing trees and hedgerows on or adjacent to the land.
7. Consent required for laying of garden or tennis lawn on or adjacent to the land.
   No tree exceeding 6″ in diameter or boundary hedge below 4′6″ in height shall be cut down.
8. Agent of the Owner to have free access to see the work.
9. The building shall be used for a private dwelling place, but not for trade, business or manufacture of any description, or for the reception of private patients, or as an asylum, hospital or charity institution or for the purpose of any public body or society or as a church, chapel, school or mission hall or as a place of public amusement or sport or for any illegal or immoral or noisy or noisome purposes, and no dwelling to be used for any purpose save that of a private dwelling into separate tenements or flats. Provided that nothing in this stipulation shall prevent private rooms over any garage or stable for a chauffeur or coachman with or without his family.
10. No building or extension without approval.
11. No wireless poles, no washing or laundry shall be exposed in view of any adjacent plot. Nothing to be done to deteriorate the value of such land or of the Ashridge Estate as a building estate for residential property.
12. No sign, notices or advertisements shall be exhibited on the land or building or of any wall, fence or gate save the name of the house or number and name of the street.
13. The Owner shall be able to vary the stipulations in this schedule in writing with the consent of the registered proprietor of the land.
    The purchaser shall within one year of the transfer erect a post and wire fence 4′6″ high and also plant and maintain a hedge of evergreen shrubs or beech or thorn on the purchaser's site along the whole of every boundary except the boundary next to the road which may be a post and chain fence and shall not prevent the hedge reaching 4′6″ and shall at all times maintain such hedge at between 4′6″ and 6′6″ in height. No hedge shall be nearer the carriageway than 21′ from the centre of the carriageway.

Nettleden Lodge. This was an ancient Lodge on the main road which runs from the Lady's Mile at Water End, up the bank above Nettleden church, crossing the Roman Road and running towards the Golden Valley. Roman remains of minor interest in themselves have been found along the Golden Valley. As recently as 1962 this drive was walked. The pathway down to the Lady's Mile was exchanged by the farmer for another pathway by arrangement with the local authority. Subsequently the Golden Valley was closed at the Nettleden End.

In 1932 there were two cottages for farm staff and in 1933-4 Mr and Mrs Mantle, gardener lived there. In the late 1930s the Lodge was extended and converted by Dr Hare who ran it as a nursing home. In the 1940s it was a children's home for evacuees, organised by the Soldiers, Sailors and Air Force Association (SSAFA). George Buckingham, younger son of William Buckingham, agent to the 7th Earl of Bridgewater farmed Nettleden Farm. He left there on Lady Day 1826.

12. Hudnall Corner. Hudnall. St Margaret's Lane. The Environmental Centre. Grovells

HUDNALL

The name appears—
c. 1200 HUDENHALE
1227 HUDENHAL
1278, 1287, 1299 HODENHALE
1309, 1348, 1367, 1376, 1432 HODENHALE
1480 HUDNALE
1550 HODENHALL PARK
Elizabeth I HUDNOLL
HUDA'S HEALH (Old English usage 5th-7th century).
The name HUDA is found in the 9th century when an ealdorman of Surrey under King Aethelwulf of Wessex was killed in battle with the Danes in 853.
For the 2nd syllable HEALH see the derivation under RINGSHALL. (see p. 57) HEALH can mean a nook of land in the corner of a parish, and in some cases a detached portion of a parish. This could be appropriate when one recalls that Hudnall was a detached part of the parish of Edlesborough for many centuries. However it could be that this detaching post-dated the name of the hamlet. Later the word HALL for the chief residence may have superceded the earlier meaning.

On 24 August 1323 Sir Henry Spigurnell, lord of the manor of DAGGEHALL endowed a free chapel in the parish of Edlesborough, at Dagnall.

At Michaelmas 1479, 100 acres of land, 10 acres of meadow, 20 acres of pasture at 20s. rent in Edlesborough, HODENHALL and Northall were used in endowing the advowson of DAGENHALL, All Saints Chapel.

This endowment of the Chapel of Ease to Edlesborough church at Dagnall could have been the origin of the land being the isolated pocket of of Edlesborough parish which was moved into the parish of Little Gaddesden and diocese of St Albans by an order in Council of 1973. This area covered the greater part of Hudnall. The area had been annexed to the civil parish of Little Gaddesden by a local government order of 25 March 1885.

In the time of Henry VIII there were proceedings in the Court of Augmentations in which HODENHALE PARK was mentioned as being let to John Norreys Esquyer.

The lordship had belonged to the College of Ashridge until its dissolution. Edward VI conveyed HODENHALL alias HUNDENHALL to his sister the future Queen Elizabeth I in 1550. It was occupied at that time by Robert Eme. In 1575 it contained eight acres. It passed under the crown to the Dormer family. Robert Ist Earl of Carnarvon of the Manor House, the son of Sir Robert Dormer held his court baron at Hudnall on 28 October 1633 when he received the homage of his tenants. He was to die at the battle of Newbury in 1643. From the Earl of Carnarvon it passed to Elizabeth, wife of Philip Earl of Chesterfield and thence to Sir William Stanhope K.B., and from him to the Dyson family. Jeremiah Dyson, clerk to the House of Commons in his will, caused it to be sold. Thomas Poynder bought it. It was sold to the 7th Earl of Bridgewater on 14 May 1808 and remained in the Ashridge Estates until the death in 1921 of 3rd Earl Brownlow.

HUDNALL METHODIST CHAPEL

In 1838 a girl in Dagnall was converted and came to Hudnall. From 1838-45 a barn was rented at 1s. per week, and members paid 2d. per week. In the early days a Methodist minister went to Hudnall and preached in the cart-shed on Glenister's Farm to a few adherents. The services were taken alternatively by Hemel Hempstead and Ivinghoe people. The Ivinghoe people fitted up the shed with seats and furniture, but then there was disagreement with the Hemel Hempstead people and the seats were removed. They were replaced by planks put on bushel baskets. Glenister's Farm was taken over by the Ashridge Estate, and the Farm House was pulled down and the Methodists turned out. So they met on Hudnall Common with the clouds for a roof and only a six foot fence screening them to enclose their meeting. A new owner of Hudnall Farm allowed his kitchen to be used. He was a leader in Methodism. This lasted for several years, and again they met in a farm and then in a cart shed. A request for a barn at the Home Farm was refused.

Eventually Lord Brownlow had the Chapel erected on Hudnall Common near to the present Hudnall Farm. It cost £120 and the rent was £6 6s. per year, later reduced to six pounds. This Chapel was opened on 1 December 1888. This was a great change from the 90 Sundays when worship had taken place in the open air.

Over a 50 year period the Chapel was the property of an earl, a butcher, a farmer and a doctor. At one time Methodists were not allowed to hold a service at the same time as a parish church service. The Rector, the Rev. Charlton Lane who had tried to establish a Sunday evening service in Hudnall in 1868 had been greatly saddened by the division of Christians in the parish.

Mr James Purton was in charge of the finances of the Chapel for 40 years. For the same length of time he was gardener at the Manor House. He died aged 83. Mrs Purton was Chapel caretaker.

THE NEW CHAPEL (HUDNALL METHODIST CHURCH)

At length it was decided to build a new place for worship and meeting, and land was purchased in Hudnall Lane at the end nearest the Green. The cost of the new building was to be £1,500. By the time of the laying of the foundation stone, £1,100 had been raised by local effort. At the foundation ceremony £263 15s. was collected. The service and ceremony was conducted by the Rev. F.G. Gatehouse and the Rev. B. Owen. There was a congregation of 400 people. After the ceremony there was tea in Little Gaddesden Village Hall for 350 people. A second collection brought the total to £300. This was on Whit Monday 1939. The builder of the new Chapel was Mr F.G. Whitman who was also steward. His son Master George Whitman on Good Friday 1940 presented the key for the opening to Mrs Lawson wife of the Rev. W.H. Lawson, superintendent minister for the Dunstable circuit. She opened the door in place of Mrs Abraham of Dunstable who had recently died.

The total cost was £1,532, and Mr C. Philips-Cole was the architect. The gates are of the same design as those at the parish church, and were made also by Harry Temple of Little Gaddesden. *Chapel Close.* In 1934 Berkhamsted Rural District Council set about erecting council houses and numbers 1-10 were built from about 1936 and completed by 1938. Numbers 9 and 10 were built by F.G. Whitman. At the same time Mr Cuthbertson began to build near the new council houses. Numbers 1-4 were built about 1935; numbers 5-10 were built about 1933. These were named 'Hudnall Lane', and this proved a little confusing when houses lower down the lane also used the title. The new Dacorum Council purchased land from the Methodist authorities in 1975 and built three new cottages — numbers 11, 12 and 14; no number 13 was built.
Standard Works Vanguard Works. Originally a laundry belonging to Mr Fred Whitman, it was sold during the war and bought by Goodman and Van der Vieren's for a factory as their London factory had been bombed. Later it was taken over by Stephen's Ink, and amongst other stationery requisites made here were Vanguard Staplers. It later became part of the John Dickinson Group. It was closed in 1980 and a new factory was established.

Conifers. This house was occupied by Mrs Van der Vieren and it was then called Dulwich House. Later acquired by Mr B.D. Gregory it was renamed Conifers.

Greenfield. This was built for Mr and Mrs Marks in 1948 by F.G. Whitman to the designs of Mr Heckinbottom of Berkhamsted.

Waveney Cottage. Mr and Mrs S.A. Moyse were the first residents here. They built it in 1949. They named it after the River Waveney in Suffolk because of their love for that county and especially for Beccles. F.G. Whitman was builder.

Field End. This house was built for Mr Norman Warren. Subsequently it was acquired and considerably extended by Mr P.W. Harris. Later alterations were made by Mr Gartside. After he moved south, Mr W.A. Gillespie and his family came here.

Kent House. This house was built by F.G. Whitman for himself in about 1933. The three similar houses to the east were built for three of his daughters. They all passed on the freehold.

The spinney to the west of Kent House was formerly the parish boundary and county boundary between Hertfordshire and Buckinghamshire. It might have consisted of an old track but Mr Richard Wyatt Bagshawe the authority on Roman roads in these parts, and co-author in *The Viatores,* whose residence Kent House is, does not think that it was of Roman origin.

Green Leas. The first of the houses built by Whitman for his family. It is interesting that Mr C. Miller (Hedges), Mr R.W. Bagshawe (Kent House) and Miss Amanda Glenn (Green Leas) were all educated at Rugby School.

The Cottage. The second of the Whitman houses. It was bought by Mr W. Brooker, Director of Aerofilms. He presented to Little Gaddesden church chest a series of photographs of the houses of Little Gaddesden taken from the air which provide a remarkable record of the parish in the 1970s. The photograph in this book of the deserted medieval village was given to the author by Mr Brooker.

Hedges. The third house built by Mr F.G. Whitman. For many years it was the home of Mr and Mrs Charles C. Miller. Mr Miller a former member of the Indian Parliament was secretary to the Parochial Church Council for many years. His use of the English language was memorable. Dr C. Honeyborne bought the property from Mrs Miller.

West Tower. This house was completed on 30 June 1956 and occupied by the Bradfield family on 4 July 1956. The architect and builder was F.G. Whitman. With the adjoining house 'The Hawthornes' it has a tower. This is the western of the two.

The Hawthornes. This was built as a pair with West Tower. It was formerly called 'East Tower' and later 'Stanfield'. There is not a local field known to have a name related to this. Mr Lee, senior, moved in here in 1976 followed by his son's family.

Greenholt. This house is situated on a plot originally part of an orchard belonging to Hudnall Common Farm. It was built in 1957 by Mr F.G. Whitman, constructed of brick and tile and was first bought and occupied by Mr and Mrs Jack P. Harvey in April 1957. The name is a compound of 'Green' (the first impression of the local countryside) and 'Holt' (a wood or shelter). Hudnall Lane at the time looked like a wooded burrow with trees meeting at the top, arched over the road. Like most of the houses in this vicinity it was originally in the parish of Edlesborough. The ancient tithe was bought out about 1960 from the tithe commissioners who had taken over the tithe from the church authorities in the 1930s.

Upper Gade. This was called 'The Boys Home' and 'Countess Brownlow's Home'. It was provided by Lady Brownlow, wife of the 3rd Earl Brownlow as a home for 12 invalid children from London. It was in existence in 1875.

Mr Ferguson-Davy and his wife were in charge at one time of the children, all of whom were convalescents. They attended Little Gaddesdon C. of E. School. A glass bowl with the Ferguson-Davy coat of arms is on display at the Victoria and Albert Museum.

In 1884 a weekly service took place at the home. Mrs Jarvis who had been Matron for 11 years suddenly succumbed to the influenza epidemic and died within three days. There had been the worst frost for 50 years just before the epidemic. Later Mrs Cooper was matron. Mr A.D.Veall modernised the property in the 1970s.

THE PLUM TREE, UPPER GADE, BUTCHER'S SHOP AREA

Plum Tree Cottage. This house is believed to date from about 1590. It was extended and restored by Mr M.N.M. Viney in the 1970s, who had acquired the property in 1970. Mr Geoffrey Tandy the previous owner was scholar, broadcaster, church chorister and cricket umpire. In earlier days Fred Liberty, keeper of the Ashridge Estate lived here. There is a plum tree in the garden.
Mr Tandy spoke strongly against the use of 'Hudnall Common' for the lane to St Margaret's and for addresses. It was an affectation of 'suburbia'. Hudnall was adequate, historical and traditional.

To the north of Hudnall Lane. In 1802 Thomas Godman mentions a homestead and close where Mr Mason and R. Glenister were tenants, of an area 1 acre 3 roods. In 1874/5 there were four tenements recorded here, owned by Lord Brownlow. Matthew Simmonds and three others lived here. This was probably the area on which Mr Cheshire's the butcher's shop now stands. Mr Fred Janes, the butcher used to be centre site. (In 1791 it adjoined Hawridge Wick.)

Adjoining this in 1800 was a cottage and garden occupied by Robert Asstint. A longer building, nearer Hudnall Lane was occupied by George Brooks. There was a cottage, garden and orchard.

There was another cottage to the south-east of this one.

In 1875 the schoolroom of 'Countess Brownlow's Home' was on the site of the building formerly occupied by George Brooks. There was a tenement and garden occupied by Elizabeth Simmonds on the lane side. This was in the vicinity of numbers 5 and 6, the present Hudnall House, the residence of Mr C. Osborn-Jones.

Across Hudnall Lane on the lane to St Margaret's the cottages were—
the first, on the corner. James Rogers
the second, in the meadow. Mr Ambrose.

Mrs Simmonds was tenant of the next cottage. Elizabeth Simmond occupied this cottage in 1875.

The numbering of the cottages began from Hudnall Farm and extended to the present butcher's shop across the Hudnall Lane.
Kaim End. Miss Bartram had wanted to build a house near Hudnall Farm and on the site of the former Methodist Chapel because of the solid foundations. However this was regarded as common land. She wished to build on the other side of the lane but with the same result. Finally she purchased a field on the opposite side of Hudnall Lane from Mr Janes the butcher who had acquired it from the Ashridge Estate. She had been secretary to the Cooper McDougall's. She built Kaim End using F.G. Whitman, in about 1929. She named it Kaim End which is Scottish for 'The house at the top of the hill'. In the late 1940s Colonel Maffatt bought it from her. When she built the house the lane stopped at the drive gate, and the footpath from there led to the parish church. In 1953 it passed to the Dunham family and in 1970 Mr G. Dunham sold it to Mr R. Frater.
Dial House. An equatorial dial by the sculptor Henry Moore stood outside *The Times* office in Printing House Square, London. In the back garden of Dial House is a copy of the original made in bronze, reduced in size, and made for Mr John Moffatt. When Mr and Mrs Moffatt came to take possession of their house in July 1971 and were pondering a name, their daughter Elizabeth suggested 'Dial House', and the name was accepted with much pleasure. The house was designed and built by Mr G. Brightman.

THE GROVELLS [Originally Crovells]

In May 1928 Edgar Creyke Fairweather of 54, Abbey House, Westminster bought from the Ashridge trustees 9,283.586 acres for £146,250 with a stamp duty of £1,462 10s.

Colonel Monro Cuthbertson bought from Mr Fairweather 686 acres for £12,160 10s.5d. in 1928. Colonel Cuthbertson sold 83 acres for £490 to Mr G.G. Keen butcher of Hemel Hempstead in 1935. In 1935 Mr Keen sold 53 acres for £575 to Mr H. Elbourn of Rickmansworth. In 1938 Mr Elbourn sold 12½ acres for £250 to Mr F.G. Whitman. Mr Whitman built houses and sold them to the tenants of the Grovells estate.

In 1929 3,000 acres of the Ashridge Estate were sold to Mr Fisher of Watford for £21,000. It was said that 105 cottages were added in order to encourage the completion of the conveyance. This land was on both sides of the road from Fourways to Dagnall, and a large area in Studham.

Grovells. The 10 houses in this cul-de-sac were built by Mr F.G. Whitman over several years beginning 1948-50. The field on which they were built was called 'The Grovells field'.

The field to the south of Grovells was called 'Matthews Meadow'. Before 1930 there were allotments near where the Grovells' houses now stand. Evidence remains in patches of wild raspberries. There was a small house, and stones from this were seen up to 1950. A yew hedge still grows. On the north of these houses Grovells field slopes down to the Leighton Buzzard Road. In this part there used to be Becking Spring. Across the road in Milebarn Farm field there is the source of the River Gade, rising from a spring that often may be seen bubbling away.

Meadow Farm was formerly 'Matthews Meadow'. It was built in 1963 and former occupants were Mrs Ward, Mr and Mrs Allen (1960), Miss P. Lowe (1961-71) and Mr and Mrs Inskip until 1977, when they were followed by Mr and Mrs Marshall.

Red Mays. It was named because of the red may trees on either side of the gate. It was built in 1953 for Mr and Mrs W. Downing, and on part of the former 'Matthews Field'. Mr and Mrs K. Reiss came here in 1958.

The New House. This house was built for Mr G. Cruickshank in 1955. It is one of the two houses in the Grovells in which the original owner is still living in 1982. The views across the valley from the gardens on this side of the road are amongst the finest in Little Gaddesden.

Woodpeckers. This house was built in 1953 for Mr and Mrs S. Ives who also are the original owners of the property. The woodpeckers in the garden at the time they were considering the name, determined its name.

Becking Spring. 'The Beckings' was the name of a field towards the Leighton Buzzard road. Spring may mean a copse, wood or a well. The name 'Beck' is found as a family name (Henry La Becke) in the time of Henry III). Antony Bec, Bishop of Durham was associated with Ashridge College. How much one would like to stretch one's imagination and suggest a connection here! The house was built for Mr and Mrs Morris in 1953. In 1961 Mr and Mrs G. Ruscoe were here, and then Mr and Mrs Peter Mitchell for 10 years from 1964. Sir Leslie and Lady Pott came here in 1974. Sir Leslie had been in the Diplomatic Service having served as H.M. Consul in Marseilles and previously at Istanbul, Bombay, Alexandria, the Middle East and Russia. He retired to Priory Cottage in 1962.

Fairfield. This house was built in 1953 for Mr and Mrs Owen. Mr and Mrs Hayward lived here with their three sons. Mr Hayward was the first headmaster of Cavendish School, Hemel Hempstead and a strong link was forged with the school at Little Gaddesden to the mutual benefit of both communities. Later Wing-Commander and Mrs Handley lived here. In 1975 Mr and Mrs Huggins came here and in 1979 Mr and Mrs Pike. In recent years much work on the fabric has taken place.

Beech Corner. This was formerly Carlton House and then Carlton Cottage. It was built in 1948/9. The beech hedge determined its name. It was originally a cottage with two rooms upstairs and two downstairs. It was occupied by Mr and Mrs W. Whittaker and then by Mr and Mrs Chapman in 1959. After that Mr and Mrs Kruger occupied it until 1980 when it was acquired by Mr and Mrs Stanley. Mr and Mrs Kruger had extended and modernised the house.

Greenways was built in 1953 for Mr and Mrs Cole who were followed in 1955 by Mr and Mrs G.E.F. Bailey. The house was built mainly from second-hand bricks, old tiles and old oak window frames from a demolished house at Watford. This was in accordance with the desire of Mr F.G. Whitman, that ancient craftsmanship should be preserved and incorporated into modern houses. The brickwork was done by Mr Fountain of Ringshall who was aged about seventy at the time.

During a quarter of a century Mr and Mrs Bailey have been active members of the community, serving in very many ways. Mrs Bailey was secretary to the Parish Council and for many years secretary to the Lady Caroline Egerton Trust. Both have been heavily committed to the Drama Club and Mr Bailey has been a very active member of the Art Club.

Walnut Cottage. So named because of the walnut tree in the garden. Major and Mrs Whybrow occupied this house when first built in 1954. Subsequently Mr and Mrs B. Shelton lived here from 1956 to 1964 when Mr and Mrs W. Davis moved here.

Highfield. This house was built in 1954 and was occupied by the Spittle family until 1960 when Dr and Mrs L.H. Turner bought it. They subsequently extended it within the limitations imposed by the conditions under which properties in the area were governed after the Ashridge Estate sale. There is one acre of land belonging to the property. Dr Turner was prisoner-of-war for three years in the Far East.

Herkomer House. The exact reason for the name is not known, but the front door is beautifully carved. Sir Hubert van Herkomer (1849-1914) was a British painter, born in Waal in Bavaria, and brought to Britain by his father in 1857. His father was a Bavarian wood carver of great ability. In 1866 Hubert began to study at the South Kensington schools and exhibited at the Royal Academy in 1869. He was elected A.R.A. in 1879 and R.A. in 1890. He was a member of the Royal Society of Painters in 1894. He became Slade Professor at Oxford in 1885. He founded Bushey 'Herkomer' School in 1883 and built 'Lululand' Bushey in 1885 (since demolished). He had three pictures in the Royal Academy' *Found* in 1885; *Charterhouse Chapel* in 1889; and *The Council of the British Academy* in 1907. He became an honorary D.C.L. of Oxford in 1907, and K.C.V.O. in 1907. He died at Budleigh Salterton on 31 March 1914. A photograph of him appeared in *The Hertfordshire Countryside* for August 1967.

This house was built by F.G. Whitman. Mr George Whitman lived here before moving to Marlborough.

Hudnall Common Farm. In the 18th century there was a pond marked in this paddock. Before 1960 there was an orchard here. In the 19th century there were nine buildings in this area where St Margaret's Lane and Hudnall meet. This was the residence of F.G.Whitman to be remembered with lasting admiration as the builder of so many houses in Little Gaddesden.

1 and 2 Hudnall. The present house (2 Hudnall Common) was formerly number 2 of three Ashridge Estate cottages rebuilt probably c. 1840. The half-timbered overhanging upper storey suggest that the façade may be part of a much older structure, perhaps of the 16th-17th centuries, and thus one of the oldest properties in the parish.

The original cottages were of the standard two up, two down, Estate pattern. The downstairs of both cottages have had their partition walls removed to form two large reception rooms. A single storey kitchen was added at the back which joined the main structure to the cottage shed which had served the housing of the pig or goat. These sheds have now been incorporated into the main downstairs structure.

The two cottages numbers 1 and 2 were bought as one lot at the Ashridge Estate sale. Tradition has it that the present sitting-room was a sweet shop in the 1930s. It was also said that the house was called 'Look after the hunt' dating from when the fox-hounds met on Hudnall Common.

That the cottages are two of the oldest structures in Hudnall is supported by the numbering. This began with these two cottages and stretched along and across Hudnall Lane.

The lath and plaster walls are covered with lining paper, but the roof space has exposed lath and plaster walling. The structure of the beams in the roof space suggests a former use as an attic bedroom. The cottages were probably thatched.

In the 1800s there were two buildings here. On was L-shaped with the top of the 'L' nearest the lane. Opposite the upright was another building which may have been a cottage. George Brooks occupied a cottage here with garden and close. Wade's orchard was adjoining in 1792.

In 1868-74 four tenements are figured with gardens here and they were occupied by William Beeke and others, the land being one acre.

Mr and Mrs C.I. Mansfield Clark lived here before moving to Hudnall Farm. They were followed by Mr and Mrs R. Westmacott *c.* 1969.

Bury Orchard. This house on its two-acre site was the first built by F.G. Whitman *c.* 1931 adjoining his own farm land. Jubal Jones, who was born in the year of Queen Victoria's Jubilee, and Arthur Fountain helped with the building. There were foundations of old cottage property and of a small lane found by them during the work. The house was first inhabited by a clergyman, named the Rev. A.G. Hodgson.

In 1941 Lt. Colonel and Mrs P.C. Field bought the property. Colonel Field had served in the R.A.M.C. in the First World War in Egypt and the Sudan and the Second World War in France. He was the president of the Little Gaddesden British Legion. Mrs Field who grew up in Great and Little Gaddesden recalled having luncheon at Ashridge House and meeting Lord Brownlow there, when a very little girl, and then being allowed to sit beside George the family coachman, and drive down the Golden Valley, and Nettleden Lodge being respectfully opened as she drove through. She recalled local names at Hudnall such as Luck Lane, Becking Lane, and riding along Birds Pikle. Her family nurse was Nurse Cutler from Ringshall.

Hudnall Cottage. A pair of semi-detached cottages was built in 1935 by F.F. Pearce of Berkhamsted to accommodate workers at Hudnall Farm. Originally Mr and Mrs Keith Geater lived here. About 1960 Mr and Mrs G. Parsons from Hudnall Farm gave number 1 to their son as a wedding present and the name was changed to Hudnall Cottage. It was altered and extended in 1964 and sold to Mr J.H.N. Francis who became treasurer of the Gaddesden Society of which Mrs Francis was for many years the secretary. A clock was presented to the Village Hall in memory of Mr Francis. The driveway was originally the tradesmen's entrance to Hudnall Farm.

Hudnall Farm. This house was probably the principal residence and farm house of the hamlet of Hudnall from very early days. It has many features of architectural interest. It may have been built on or near an old well. There were extensive orchards here in the 18th century. In the early days of the 1800s the buildings were substantial. A courtyard was enclosed on three sides with an entrance on the fourth side near the lane. The building projected on the south side. Nearby on that side was a building almost as long as the house. Further along St Margaret's Lane, but probably belonging to the Farm were other buildings of some size. In the same period there was a pond on the side of the house adjoining the lane. In 1878 the area of the homestead was 1 acre, 3 roods. It was owned by Lord Brownlow and farmed by George Underwood one of the major farmers of the end of the 19th and beginning of the 20th centuries. He farmed 500 acres. The water trough was fixed by Arthur Fountain in July 1894.

At the end of Brownlow days the farm was occupied by Mr H. Fern. It was bought by Mr Murdoch who wished to enclose the Common but there was opposition to this. Later Mr McGarry and Mr Edwards owned it. At one point the land was sold for £10 an acre. Farmer Hoare farmed the land. Later the Heathcote family cultivated apple orchards, specialising in Cox's Orange Pippins. There were 26½ acres of apples trees, with a few pear and plum trees, blackcurrants, raspberries and strawberries. Spraying went on through the year. At harvest time the apples were taken to the large barn for grading and packing. It was in this barn that King George VI had luncheon with his officers during the Second World War. He had come to visit the wounded at Ashridge, and then he visited Hudnall Farm on a very private visit. Only the people at the Farm were aware of his coming. Mr and Mrs Parsons and later Mr Blandford-Newson owned the property.

The 1st Earl of Carnarvon, son of Sir Robert Dormer of the Manor House, Little Gaddesden held his court baron at Hudnall on 28 October 1633 when he received the obeisance of his tenants. He was killed at the battle of Newbury 10 years later. The court might well have been held at or near Hudnall Farm. Mr C.I.M. Clark has carefully preserved this historic house.

STARSWOOD, BRAMBLEDOWN GATE, MASCALLS.

Eight acres adjoining the house now known as Kingsley Mount were divided into five plots after the 1945 War, and these three houses were built by F.G. Whitman in 1956/7. They are on top of a little Chiltern Hill and therefore have the maximum depth of clay — at least 30 feet — over the chalk.

Starswood was formerly The Denes but was given the name by Captain and Mrs G.H. Ashby who came here in 1959. Starswood is a loose translation of the South African university town of Stellenbosch near where Mrs Ashby was brought up. Van der Stel was one of the early Dutch settlers of the Cape. The trees on the Starswood boundary were once a hedge in which grew oak, field maple, hawthorn, holly, elm, and hornbeam. The ditch at Starswood is maintained. The land was formerly said to be 'worn-out farmland'. This has been changed by skilled gardening and landscaping. Drainage is poor. There is a wartime air raid shelter in the garden. Captain Ashby gave outstanding service to Little Gaddesden. Mrs Ashby wrote the 'Country Notes' for the *Parish News* each month which were an important part of Little Gaddesden life. Mrs Ashby left for Oundle in 1982.

Brambledown Gate. Mrs Seton writes from Canada— 'The land belonged to Lt. Col. McBarry of Piccotts End. At first there was one house here called Grove House. Later Brackenfield, Tamarisk Cottage, Kingsley Mount, Starswood and Mascalls were built by Whitman. When Colonel Seton met him he was given the price. There was no contract, no paper signing. The price on completion was exactly as agreed by word of mouth. Originally there was a straight drive at right-angles to the road. Whitman said that he made it like that because of the mountain ash tree at the entrance, which was a guard against witches. He also put a small ornamental brick in the front upper wall for good luck'.

The Setons moved into the house in April 1957. It was then called 2 Coppice Close. William their son aged seven suggested the name Brambledown Gate. Colonel Seton was an author and a soldier. He and his family spent much time extending the gardens and resiting the drive.
Mr and Mrs J.M. Feeney acquired and extended the property.

Mascalls. This house named after an adjoining field was the home of Mr and Mrs Kenneth Clarke. Mr Clarke was a golf enthusiast and Mrs Clarke a very highly valued member of the community. The lantern in Little Gaddesden church porch was in his memory. The house was extended, and altered considerably by Mr L. Thorne and by Mr N.R. Cooper.

Hither Coppice. This house with its stabling was the home for many years of Mr John Kidd. In 1971 a field of this name was on the opposite (east) side of St Margaret's Lane.

Cherry Cottage. This house was built by Mr F.G. Whitman and was completed in August 1939 for Mr G.H. Webb. It was sited in part of the small wood called Ladygrove. The area of 2.8 acres was purchased from Mr J. McGarry of Hudnall Farm. It is named Cherry Cottage because of several forest-sized cherry trees in the front of the house. Exquisite embroidery is made here.

Wood Cottage. There have been four owners of this property. Marion Dawson Trail, wife of Dr Trail, purchased it on 8 June 1939 for £1,250. Geoffrey Stafford Hall, oil technologist bought it for £6,000 in December 1949. It was acquired by Colonel Charles Bertram Blinco M.B.E., Bank Manager, Deputy Lieutenant of Bedfordshire in November 1960 for £7,500. He was a specialist in tomato growing. In July 1975 John Heald Bean O.B.E., Ph.D., Geologist, purchased the property for £40,000.

Langside. Mr Dunn of Ladygrove built cottages for his staff. Mr and Mrs Gibbs lived in one and Mr and Mrs Halsey and their daughter lived in Langside. The Gibbs' cottage became known as

Birchwood End, and Mr Halsey's became Langside. Mrs Halsey, a greatly respected member of the monthly Ringshall Group and of the Over-Sixties Club, moved to 10 Hudnall Lane. Later Mr A.W. Fulton bought the property and modernised it. He was a very gifted Scottish business man. In recent years further alterations and modernisation has taken place. Mr J.S. Hilton came here in August 1976.

Ladygrove. Mr F.G. Whitman built this house for Mr McGarry in 1934 on a site of 5½ acres. For many years it was the home of members of the Dunn family ('The hatters'). Mr Dunn built adjoining cottages for his staff. Later he moved to 1, Gatesdene Close. The Bouet family lived in Ladygrove and later, Colonel and Mrs Antony J. Wheatcroft and their family made their home there. The name derives from the local beech wood. Was the wood planted on an older site in succession to earlier trees here? Had the name anything to do with St Margaret's nunnery perhaps as part of the monastic estate used for prayer and meditation?

Kilbracken. This house, like Kingsley Mount and Tamarisk Cottage was built by F.G. Whitman. Earlier residents were Mr Kelly and Mr and Mrs Wykeham-Musgrave. It was built in the 1930s. When war broke out the Wykeham-Musgraves moved from Robin Hood House and brought several of their domestic staff. They kept pigs, and on weekdays these were cared for by a man who came in to do odd jobs. On Sunday he was not employed. However the cook refused to allow Mrs Wykeham-Musgrave to prepare the pig food in her kitchen. So a hot-water pipe had to be laid and placed against the outside of the house for the preparation to be done. This house is probably unique in having an outside hot water-tap. Colonel and Mrs Corby moved here in about 1952. Colonel Corby is President of the Little Gaddesden British Legion and of the Parish Council. A 'granny flat' has been made here.

Spinneys. This house was built by F.G. Whitman in 1937/8. It has been greatly extended and modernised by Mr and Mrs Donald F.G. Clarke.

High Beeches. This house was built a little later than Spinneys, also by F.G. Whitman. When for many years Mr and Mrs Hames and Miss A. Hern lived here it was a natural bird and wild life sanctuary. Later Mr and Mrs Nunn and their family moved here.

Kalkudah (formerly *Magamba*). In 1958 Mr and Mrs Oswald Wynn returned from East Africa and built and named their home Magamba because of their association with Magamba in the former Tanganyka. Mr Wynn was a prominent member of the St Albans Diocesan Conference. In 1967 Mr and Mrs H. Lucas returning from Ceylon (Sri Lanka) renamed it Kalkudah because of associations there where Mr Lucas had been a tea-planter and Mrs Lucas a nurse.

The Cottage. This F.G. Whitman house has been greatly altered and extended in recent years.

Raglens. This was so named by Mr and Mrs How who kept kennels. 'Raglens' was the registered kennel prefix for their Manchester terriers.

This was the first house built on this stretch of the lane. F.G. Whitman laid the foundations with the help of Mr Arthur Fountain and as it was to be a 'Hurlingham' house the superstructure was completed by the 'Hurlingham' firm. This was done for Mr Boots and the house was first named Littleover (Derbyshire). Mr How next came to live here. The house was altered completely inside and outside by Mr Heywood. In 1963 Mr T.M. Hart acquired the property and subsequently extended it. There is garden all round the house.

Covetous Corner. It is believed that this formerly belonged to St Margaret's Priory. A story told locally is that annually processions took place across the monastic land and that sermons were preached at each corner, and that this was the corner where covetousness was dealt with.

Three buildings appear here in the early years of the 19th century. Two were occupied by John Newman and William Maynard and the third by William Chennells. In 1875 there were two tenements and William Purton and one other lived in them.

1 Covetous Corner. When Mr and Mrs C.G. Leggett arrived here in 1928 they were told that the property was 230 years old, thus dating it to about 1700, the time of the 3rd Earl of Bridgewater. Mr and Mrs Leggett met on the Goodwood Estate where they worked for Charles 8th Duke of

Richmond and Gordon until 1924, when they went to Australia for four years. Mrs Leggett's father ('Bill' Batchelor) was a keeper on the Ashridge Estate with Mr Cox at a time when the punishment for poachers was two months in prison. At one time the farmer at Hudnall Farm began to enclose part of Hudnall Common and a big gate and smaller ones were erected. Cooper's intimated that they were going to padlock the gates. Consequently on Sundays Mrs Leggett assisted her husband in removing the stakes and protecting the rights of the commoners, the land having been common land for the statutory 40 years.

Amongst her treasures Mrs Leggett possesses a letter sent by Queen Alexandra to her friend Lady Brownlow, and which was given as a very special gift to Mrs Leggett. Recently Mrs Leggett was greatly admired for her courage when a burglar broke into her home, told her to remain absolutely still whilst he searched an adjoining room. She slipped quietly out, unlocked the door, returned to bed when he peered in, and then when he moved into another room she left and raised the alarm. He was apprehended by the police near Pedley Hill.

2 Covetous Corner. Of similar age to No. 1. Mrs Barrett bought it and lived here intermittently. Mr Pratt a gamekeeper lived here. During the war four families of evacuees were here. Finally Mr Richard Webb came and extended the cottage very carefully. He was an accomplished artist.

Meadow House, Covetous Corner. Formerly owned by Mr Kenneth E. Lobban who ran the 'Meadow Nurseries' and visited the local markets and Little Gaddesden houses with his produce. Mr and Mrs D. Faulconer followed, but the nursery was discontinued. Mr Faulconer played a great part in the establishment of the Little Gaddesden Colts Cricket Club and in the work for the new Sports Pavilion. This house was the last to be built on this old lane along which the Romans of former days had marched.

Pest House Field. This is the name of the field in the south-east corner of the parish on the Great Gaddesden boundary to the east of Wood field.

ST MARGARET'S

St Margaret de Bosco de Ivinghoe was the name of the priory which from early times was associated with the parish of Ivinghoe and the bishops of Winchester. The ancient kingdoms were very extensive and Ivinghoe was at the extreme end of the kingdom, the diocese of Winchester being conterminous with the kingdom. The lands endowing the priory were given by William Gifford, Bishop of Winchester for nine religious women. He died in 1129. Bishop Henry de Blois of Winchester confirmed the establishment in 1160. He was brother of King Stephen. He was Abbot of Glastonbury from 1126-71 and Bishop of Winchester from 1129-71 holding the two offices together. He died on 6 August 1171 and was buried in 'Ivinghoe church in the County of Bucks where he founded a Nunnery, the manor belonging to the See of Winchester'. Amongst the benefactors were Milo Heiremut and William Pichenstorre.

In 1280 King Edward I gave land in Mursley (Merewe), Buckinghamshire to the Prioress and nuns 'for his soul and for his ancestors'. Ten years later he was staying at Ashridge over Christmas a month after his wife Queen Eleanor had died.

The foundation was one of St Benedict. There were five nuns of whom two were professed and three were novices. Three were 'desyring'. There were four servants of whom two were hinds. There were two women servants. This was at the end of the monastic days. The value at the first survey was £13 3s. 4d. and at the second survey £19 8s. 9d. This was at the time of the Dissolution in the 1530s. At that time the bells, lead and other buildings were valued at £8 10s. 6d. and the moveable goods £1 13s. 4d. There were seven acres of woods of about twenty years growth. Speed gives the revenue at the time of the Dissolution as £22 6s. 7d. and Dugdale £14 3s. 1d. In 1537 Henry VIII gave the site to Sir John Dance and there was a lease to John Verney for 21 years at a rent of £1 15s. 8d. per annum, and also to John Mercer. In the year 1260 the community was called that of St Margaret de Gatesden.

Browne Willis writing in the early 1700s says that a small but neat modern house stands where the nunnery stood. The only thing recorded of the old edifice was a stained-glass window with a coat of arms . . . 'Gules, a dragon pierced in the back with a sword, in his mouth a crucifix'. The interest of this lies in the dedication to St Margaret.

St Margaret of Antioch in Pisidia was a popular medieval saint. She was a reputed martyr of the Diocletian persecution. She was the daughter of a pagan priest and she rebuffed the advances of a Roman official who then denounced her as a Christian. The ordeals she suffered included being swallowed by Satan in the form of a dragon. The stained-glass window would therefore show the emblem of St Margaret of Antioch, patron saint of the community.

Prioresses.

Isolda occurs about 1250. She died in 1262.
Cecilia. Elected 1262 on the presentation of the Bishop of Winchester. She died in 1274.
Maud de Hoccliff. Presented by the Bishop of Winchester, 11 February 1274. She died 1296.
Isolda de Beauchamp. Elected 17 September 1296.
Sibilla de Hamstead. Resigned 1340.
Maude de Cheyndry (or Cheyne). Elected 1340. Her name occurs in 1341, and then there is a space until—
Elenor Crosse, died 1467.
Elenor Tyms. Elected 2 June 1467.
Elizabeth Wyvill. Died 1534.
Margaret Hardwick. Elected 31 August 1534. She was prioress at the Dissolution.

In 1802, it was later stated, the buildings were almost entire and the decorated Refectory remained (Kelly 1887). In 1806 the property was sold to George Catherall.

The Meacher family farmed the land during much of the 19th century. Edward Augustus Meacher was farmer in 1864 and George Meacher in 1895. In 1841 there were 22 houses with a population of 125 in St Margaret's.

HUDNALL PARK, HUDNALL PARK ENVIRONMENTAL STUDIES CENTRE.

In the 1875 tithe map for Edlesborough Hudnall Park was the name of a field abutting on St Margaret's Lane and adjoining Covetous Meadow. The modern houses Spinneys, High Beeches, Kalkudah, The Cottage, and Raglens now occupy part of the field. Hudnall Park, the residence built by Miss Kathleen Duncanson was built on Upper Tem field. Her property was to include the wood, Whitfield Spring and later part of Hill Wood. These were added in 1936-38. Miss Tooms a friend of Miss Duncanson bought 60 acres for her, to prevent building development.

The mansion was built in about 1933 by F.G. Whitman, to stand in the fields. The white exterior is plastered. The corners in many places are rounded with windows in the curves. The sunshine roof is flat and was used for sunbathing. The windows are latticed with rectangular panes. Originally the kitchen was upstairs and a service lift was used to convey food downstairs to the dining-room. This was Miss Duncanson's method of reducing cooking smells in the living-rooms.

Miss Duncanson was the daughter of a Berkhamsted draper. She was born in 1885 and was educated at Berkhamsted School for Girls. There she met Clementine Hosier, later Lady Spencer-Churchill, wife of Sir Winston Churchill. Their friendship lasted all their lives. She became a nurse, having trained at Kings College Hospital, London. Later she became matron of the Beaumont Nursing Home in Beaumont Street, London W.1. Many 'Royals' became her patients, as well as Sir Winston Churchill. She became part owner of the Home and had Hudnall Park as her country residence. The Home was seriously bombed during the 1945 war and several of her nurses were killed. In 1945 the Council of King Edward VII's Hospital for Officers bought Beaumont House and opened it on 15 October 1948. Sister Agnes the Foundress in 1899 was remembered in the name of the Hospital, but many people still refer to the Hospital as Beaumont House and tend to link Miss Duncanson with the present Hospital rather than its predecessor. For a time Miss Duncanson was a patient in the new hospital. There had been a tiny but very attractive Chapel there which was in regular use.

In 1941 she sold Hudnall Park to Mr J.T. Agelasto, but bought it back later. For a short period in about 1946 Mr Herbert James Rae and his wife lived there. In 1946/7 Miss Duncanson built the Lodge for her chauffeur. In 1958 she bought numbers 5 and 6 Hudnall, two cottages which she filled with antiques. She resided there off and on until finally she had to move to a nursing home. She died in 1974. In the meanwhile the Cade family, coal merchants of London purchased Hudnall Park. They added the bungalow in 1967.

After the death of Mr and Mrs Cade the property was acquired by the Hertfordshire County Countil in 1971. Part of the upper storey had been made into a flat, and the north end had been enclosed, large picture windows having been constructed. A flat-roofed garage had been added. The Cade Rolls Royce was a familiar sight along the lane.

The County Council adapted the house and garage with minor structural alterations to provide a residential field centre for parties of Hertfordshire students from Colleges and Secondary Schools. They named it 'Hudnall Park Environmental Studies Centre'. The opening course was in 1972. At first there had been some local controversy about the new establishment, but this vanished very quickly as the value of the centre was observed and the work of the wardens was recognised with admiration.

Mr Peter Pain came in 1972 and he was succeeded by Mr John Leonhardt in 1977.

Many residential courses are now held throughout the year. Emphasis is laid upon the field work and its analysis in the well equipped 'laboratory'. For many of the visitors recognition of trees and shrubs, flowers, birds and mammals is a beginning, it is hoped, of a lifelong fascination. The deer in the Ashridge area, their feeding, their browsing on the bark of trees, their prints and the sight of them moving is carefully investigated. This is a unique opportunity. The woodlands and hills, the bird and insect life, squirrels and badgers, the River Gade with the possibility of investigating the invertebrate creatures, as well as swans and coots . . . all this in summer or winter provides great interest, as well as the profitability of studying together and learning together. Detailed study of various creatures and their ability to survive in winter time has been an absorbing subject for many. Mapping of areas and analysis of the work and its assessment provides a growing library of information for students of all ages.

The centre works with the National Trust. In one area on Hudnall Common endeavours are being made to restore a small part of chalk grassland vegetation and its associated wild flowers. Ivinghoe Hills are regularly visited. Practical conservation, biology, geography, local history and many allied subjects are studied communally. This must be an important part of the educational work of the county. The enthusiasm noted when parties and groups from the centre are met by local inhabitants is infectious.

PART FOUR

13.   Gazetteer and local memories.

ASHRIDGE BOUNDARIES

Old English boundaries were marked in certain instances by ash trees, and the name became incorporated in place-names. Several Hertfordshire pudding-stones could mark an early boundary stretching from the Golden Valley through the quadrangle (laundry yard) at Ashridge to Aldbury.

The Bishops of Oxford and St Albans were dining at Ashridge some time after 1877. They were at opposite ends of the table. The question arose as to who should say Grace. The Bishop of Oxford said, 'This is my diocese, I should.' 'Not so,' said the Bishop of St Albans, 'the kitchens are in my diocese. No correct blessing, no food'. This was ecclesiastical banter. The Bishop of Oxford was in his own diocese, but the Bishop of St Albans was also in the Oxford diocese, because the actual lines of the boundary went across the quadrangle further west than he thought, and the kitchens were in the Oxford diocese.

The boundary at that time was between Buckinghamshire and Hertfordshire as well as being the ecclesiastical boundary.

The main rooms of the College, including the Chapel, were in the parish of Pitstone (Nettleden being a hamlet of that parish) and in the Oxford diocese. However to the west from the quadrangle the buildings were in the parish of Berkhamsted in the diocese of St Albans.

Although Nettleden and Berkhamsted are both now in the diocese of St Albans, the parish boundary still exists ecclesiastically.

Both parishes and Pitstone and Ivinghoe were for many centuries in the diocese of Lincoln and the College of the Bonhommes was in that diocese throughout its history.

The question arises as to what the origin of the interest in the College was which was shown by bishops of Winchester.

The diocese of Lincoln was formed when Remigius, Bishop of Dorchester moved his see from there to Lincoln in 1075. The see of Dorchester had been a sub-division of the vast diocese of Winchester. Winchester was founded in 635 and Dorchester in 680. Ivinghoe and Pitstone on the Icknield Way were both in the old diocese of Winchester, which included the land of the Chiltern-seatas, in Wessex. Berkhamsted was in Mercia.

Despite the change from Winchester to Dorchester in 680 and then to Lincoln in 1075, the bishop of Winchester still maintained his ownership of the manor of Ivinghoe and the advowson of Ivinghoe church. He gave the advowson to Ashridge College in 1420 and during the 15th century was generous towards the College. Pitstone advowson had been given to the College in 1381 'cum capella de Nettleden'. Thus the association between this area and the bishops of Winchester dates back to the time before the foundation of the College of the Bonhommes and when Ivinghoe and Pitstone were in the ancient kingdom of Wessex.

This boundary across the quadrangle, the backyard of the College, which still exists ecclesiastically may date back to the division of England into the ancient kingdoms, and when Wessex and Mercia adjoined.

ASHRIDGE ESTATE OFFICERS
Ashridge Agents and Bailiffs

ROBERT CLARKE

Born in 1758 and died in 1841, he was agent and auditor to the 7th Earl of Bridgewater and later to his widow, Charlotte Catherine Anne. He had served them for 55 years. Lady Bridgewater erected a tablet in his memory in Nettleden church.

He served General Egerton before working on the Ashridge Estate and earldom, and was 45 years old when he came there.

Clarke signed as agent in 1808, although this title was not much used in the days of the 7th Earl; nevertheless the duties were meticulously observed. With the Rev. J. Horseman, G. Atty and W. Buckingham, he witnessed the 106-page will of the Earl.

WILLIAM BUCKINGHAM

He came in 1800 to the Old Dairy Farm, but the 7th Earl moved him in 1803 to be bailiff and to reside at the Home Farm. Soon after he began his new responsibilities, the four year system of cropping was adopted . . . wheat, turnips (roots), barley and hay, then back to wheat or oats in the fifth year. Many of the trees on the Estate today are the result of Buckingham's extensive planting. His varied work even included such duties as looking after the details of the funeral of Mrs Haynes (Lady Bridgewater's mother) in May 1813. He arranged for her to be laid out; to be measured for her coffin; for the coffin to be made; for the cutting of the way through the shrubbery towards the Church Road, and then to provide breakfast for the bearers. He organised the sale of Mrs Haynes' property. He looked after the health needs of people on the Estate, and also their general welfare. He was also an officer in the Ashridge Yeomanry Cavalry. He kept a set of diaries which reveal the extent and the thoroughness of his dedication to the House. He had seen it built; the completion and the entry of Lord and Lady Bridgewater on 11 October 1814; and later the work on the Orangery and Great Porch.

During the last decade of the Earl's life, Buckingham's responsibility for the Estate reached its zenith, especially when Robert Clarke was away visiting other estates belonging to the family. When Clarke was present there were indications in the diaries that he acted without full consultation with Buckingham, his subordinate.

In Buckingham's hands were the arrangements for the funeral of the 7th Earl on 30 October 1823. After the Earl's death, it would appear that Buckingham's influence declined, for he was not in favour with the widowed Countess, nor with Robert Clarke. Buckingham resigned in 1826 and bought a freehold property on the Green from the Maberly's of the Manor House, much to Clarke's dismay. Buckingham fenced in his land and made alterations to it. The property was large enough for Buckingham and his wife, his son Henry and his wife; as well as his son George, and Mary Norris.

In 1828 he purchased for John Henry an alehouse abutting on to the Green and called the *Robin Hood*. At the rear of this they built a brew-house and malthouse and fitted it with brewing equipment. They had the legal right to draw water from a well in Witchcraft Bottom. It could be that this right was challenged by the Countess, and as a result John Henry had to leave his father's properties, and the Bridgewater Estate took them over. John Henry left Little Gaddesden and his beer-house and died in 1881. His father was buried on 12 December 1829 in a vault beneath the south aisle of the church and adjoining the Bridgewater vault.

His late employer, the 7th Earl had mockingly said to him that one day they would knock at the dividing wall and consult about Estate business!

GEORGE ATTY

He was the treasurer and accountant at Ashridge and in charge of the office there. He worked in the team of Clarke, Buckingham and himself. Atty was ultimately responsible for the Estate books; he signed documents during the life of the 7th Earl and in 1852 one still finds his signature, perhaps for the last time.

In her will dated 24 December 1846 Charlotte Catherine Anne, widow of the 7th Earl of Bridgewater bequeathed to him the sum of £1,000, and the same amount to his younger son Robert Clarke Atty to be invested until he was 21 years of age.

George Atty was also to receive an annuity of £400, and his wife Eleanor was to receive this if he predeceased her.

JAMES ATTY
He was also a servant of the Estate and was surveyor, being so named in the Ivinghoe Enclosure Map of 1856.

WILLIAM PAXTON
He became agent at Ashridge in 1854 and remained in office until 1882 when he resigned. He died in 1886 and was buried at Little Gaddesden church aged 68 years.

He was nephew to Sir Joseph Paxton, creator of the Crystal Palace, and who had been responsible for much work at Edensor, the parish in which Chatsworth House, the home of the dukes of Devonshire lies. Edensor became the first model village, with picturesque groups of cottages of different periods. William Paxton was associated with this work at Little Gaddesden and in helping to make the first Hertfordshire Garden Village here. He was churchwarden and was responsible for laying out the churchyard pathways, building up the flint walls and caring for the fabric. He gave the lectern at the restoration of the church. His tombstone is at the west side of the old churchyard in a row of servants of the church and parish.
He was succeeded by Colonel Wheatley who lived at the Manor House and is referred to under that heading.

GARDENERS
Ashridge Estate Memories

Richard Buckland Lowe, formerly at Kew, was head gardener for over 20 years. He died in 1910. He was churchwarden at Little Gaddesden where he was remembered for his top hat and morning coat, always worn to church and on important occasions.
Mr C. Wells was also remembered.
The kitchen-garden at Frithsden had 30 greenhouses and the rear of the Manor House was also Estate garden. The Park roads were hand-weeded and former workmen from the Estate helped in this work. The rockery was made from Hertfordshire pudding-stone, brought from all parts of the Ashridge Estate. Tunnels, groves, love-boxes, tea houses and the fuschia house were creations largely of the 19th century.

There was a skating pond and the long pond which were used by ducks and swans. The fish pond was from the monastic days. There was a lavender walk. The Monks' Garden had Bridgewater and Brownlow coats of arms in colour. The fountain was modified from the original design by Repton. Lord and Lady Brownlow were assisted by Lady Lothian (her sister) in much of the planning of the garden. It was said that from the Monks' Garden there was the old pathway to the Chapel of the original College.

HEAD GARDENERS AND STEWARDS OF THE GARDENS
1858-82 Mr Sage. He moved to Belton.
Richard Buckland Lowe — died 1910.
E. Robertson.
Mr Andrews was foreman.
Mr Savidge.
Charles Wells.

1934 Robert Moore.
1958 Andrew Jackson.
1966 Malcolm Lingard.

THE HEAD KEEPER

The head keeper was very important. Mr Cox came in May 1885. John Saw, who died in 1914 aged 90, was another. They wore a green-grey uniform of magnificent quality and made by the local tailor. In the shooting season, men on the Estate who went beating were clad in white smocks and red caps so that they could be seen. The head keeper had the care and killing of the deer as well as the rearing of pheasants and partridges, and the responsibility of the shoot. When the season was in for the venison, the carcases went to Smithfield Market.

Villagers were allowed to buy from the keeper sixpenny-worth of offal, liver, head and hearts. The money was the keeper's perquisite.

At Christmas, every family had a joint of home-killed beef two pounds for each adult and one pound for each child. So joints of 13-14 pounds were not uncommon.

Hares were made available for tenants; also young deer at 5s. Deer skins were given to be made into mats, and many Ringshall cottages were well carpeted with these.

At blackberry time the schoolmaster told the children that so many pounds were needed at Ashridge House, so they took tins, collected the blackberries and took them to the house where the cook gave them 2d. after weighing the fruit.

THE LAUNDRY

There were four laundry maids who were up at 5.30 a.m. and at work at 6 a.m. They finished work at 9 p.m. with breaks for meals. There were many guests throughout the Brownlow period; these included dignitaries of the church, the deans of York and Canterbury; the bishops of Lincoln, Oxford, Ely, and St Albans; the families of the Marquess of Northampton and the earls of Shrewsbury and Talbot into which families the earls of Brownlow had married. Many statesmen were guests including prime ministers. Disraeli was very fond of Ashridge. The Duke of Wellington was godfather both to the 3rd Earl Brownlow and to Lady Brownlow.

These visitors required great respect and attention, and provided interest for the staff. Food was excellent and plentiful for the staff and provided they observed the strict rules, they were treated with kindness. Laundry maids had a fortnight's holiday per year with 2s. 6d. over their wage for 'beer money'. Alice and Ethel Wheatcroft came from Yorkshire. Alice became Mrs Duncombe and retired to Little Gaddesden.

'Lord Brownlow never wore a shirt twice'. On one occasion when he was going away for several weeks, his many shirts were washed, boiled and starched, and ironed; each shirt front was polished with the polishing iron. Just after the work was completed the evening meal was announced and several of the laundry maids opted to have theirs 'picnic-style' in the laundry. The meal included raspberry pie and they did not bother much about the moths and insects flying about as they ate. After the meal they suddenly noticed that all the shirts were specked with raspberry which had been flecked from the insects wings. They had to stay up all night to prepare the 24 shirts again for the morning.

The Brownlow livery at Ashridge was blue. White stockings and buckled shoes were worn. Cockades were worn at the appropriate times. Golden buttons with an eagle were engraved for a special visitor, but normally buttons with the Brownlow 'B' beneath an earl's coronet were worn. The livery was made by the tailor who lived at 6, Little Gaddesden. Mr Francis Green spoke of Viner, the head coachman, in plum livery and white silk stockings, with a grey wig and three-cornered hat, driving the State barouche, with two powdered footmen standing at the back for such occasions as the State Opening of Parliament.

Edward Viner, coachman, died in 1912 after many years of service to the Brownlow family.

ASHRIDGE FAMILY MOTTOES

SIC DONEC. This motto can be seen in the Principal's sitting-room at Ashridge and elsewhere in the College, and on the Canal Duke's Memorial in Little Gaddesden church. It is the Bridgewater motto. The 2nd Earl Brownlow assumed by royal licence in 1853 the arms and surname of Egerton, as heir to the Bridgewater Estates. He also obtained a licence dated 6 July 1863 to use the name Cust after Egerton, and to bear the arms of Cust quarterly in the first quarter with those of Egerton. He died 20 February 1867.

The motto appears as SIC DON*I*C on the sign at the *Bridgewater Arms* Inn in Little Gaddesden. Its meaning is 'Thus, until'.

'Thus' says this motto to the various branches of the noble family which bears it . . . 'Thus shall you ever be, prosperous and honoured for your virtues which raised you to such prosperity UNTIL the virtues which raised you to such prosperity pass away, for then both your fame and fortunes shall perish'.

ESSE QUAM VIDERI. This appears on the ceiling of the Principal's sitting-room at Ashridge. This is also a Bridgewater motto. The 3rd Earl Brownlow, quoted by Lady Marian Alford, translated it 'To do, not to talk'. 'To be, rather than seem to be' is another translation.

NIHIL HUMANI ALIENUM. This is one of the mottoes of the family of the earls of Shrewsbury and Talbot. This is also on the ceiling of the Principal's sitting-room at Ashridge. It thus helps to date the ceiling to after 1868, the year when Lady Brownlow married the 3rd Earl. She was daughter of the 18th Earl of Shrewsbury and Talbot. The motto can be translated — 'Nothing concerning man is a matter of indifference to me'.

OPERA ILLIUS MEA SUNT. On the Principal's ceiling. A Brownlow motto. 'His works are mine'.

TECUM SALUS. On the Principal's ceiling. 'May you be safe and sound'.

SANS CHANGER. The motto of the Stanley family earls of Derby. This appears on the Great Monument in Little Gaddesden church, marking marriages between the Egertons and the Stanleys. 'Without changing'.

CAVENDO TUTUS. The Cavendish family motto. The dukes of Devonshire and the dukes of Newcastle (the wife of the 2nd Earl being of this family). 'Safe by being cautious'.

THE HISTORY OF THE COLLEGE OF ASHRIDGE

This monumental history by the Rev. H.J. Todd, Chaplain to the 7th Earl of Bridgewater was issued in two editions. The 1823 edition was produced shortly after the death of the Earl. The total cost was £3,613 9s. 3d. and each copy cost £18 11s. Two hundred were printed.

The binding on the presentation copy for King George IV cost an extra £6 10s. A list of those to whom copies were sent included the King; the Dukes of York and Clarence; the Duchess of Gloucester; Princess Augusta; Princess Sophia and Princess Sophia of Gloucester; the King of France; the Archbishops of Canterbury and York; the Dukes of Bedford, Buckingham, Devonshire, Montrose, Northumberland, Buccleuch, Wellington; the Marquesses Ailesbury, Chandos, Camden, Ely, Lansdown, Salisbury, Stafford; the Earls of Aberdeen, Amhurst, Brownlow, Liverpool, Powis, Spencer, Surrey, Verulam, Willan, Winchester and Jersey. Many others included Learned Societies, and the Bishops of Winchester, Worcester, Lincoln and St Asaph.

The total number on the list was 141 'to whom copies were given'.

The drawings were by F. Mackenzie and the engraving by Le Keux. Pages extracted from one copy, coloured and framed, hang in the main north corridor.

PAYMENTS AT ASHRIDGE

1830	Peter Sermon, Watchman, his wages	£27 17s. 3d.
	2 greatcoats for watchman	£2. 15s. 0d.

Wm. Greenhill, postman, for letters to and from Ashridge for the year	£20. 0s. 0d.
The Chaplin's (sic) salary	£100. 0s. 0d.
To Joseph Impey for assisting with the stables when Prince Leopold was at Ashridge	10s. 0d.
Keeper's wages. Thos. Bamford	£60 0s. 0d.
Elizabeth Bodkin for repairing the leather shoes of the horses when rolling the pleasure grounds	3s. 6d.
For Farm produce for the Household:- Butcher's meat	£950 0s. 0d.
24,966 quarts milk	£416 2s. 0d.
1236½ bushels of malt for brewing	£505 5s. 11d.
3786 eggs	
32 turkeys	
550 pigeons	£14 5s. 0d.

1843	A year's Noble charged on the site of the premises of the late Earl, to churchwardens of little Gaddesden	6s. 8d.
	John Adsett Clerk of Works ½ year	£63. 10s. 0d.
	George Atty, local agent ½ year	£220 0s. 0d.
	John Osborne for destroying rats at the Home Farm and other places	£2 2s. 6d.

In 1856 a year's rent of cottages was between £2 12s. and £3.

A house and orchard were rented at £6-£9.

Ringshall Hall Farm rent was £240, and the Ringshall cottages between £3 and £3 10s.

MEMORIES OF ASHRIDGE

These are a selection of anecdotes of the House, gathered from local sources.

The oak on the croquet lawn has a board on it designed by Earl Brownlow to say that it was planted by Queen Victoria in 1823. If that date is correct, she was then Princess and her hostess was Charlotte Catherine Anne whose husband the 7th Earl died on 21 October in that year. The Princess was then four years of age.

The Brownlows prevented the railway going along the line of Hemel Hempstead, Dagnall, Leighton Buzzard, and so it went through Berkhamsted. Special arrangements were made for the family when they travelled by train. They had a Coach House adjoining Berkhamsted Station on the Castle side.

In 1865, Edward, 2nd Earl Brownlow came of age and there were great festivities. Balls and parties were held. 'Hundreds of turtles were decapitated and some time after were seen wandering headless around the back yard'. There were free barrels of beer for those who worked on the Estate.

In 1879 the harvests were very bad, and the farmers pleaded for reduced rents. The Duke of Bedford had granted a half year free of rent, but the Rothschilds, who had bought Cheddington, doubled the rent, and the Macnamaras, of Studham and Whipsnade, largely increased rents.

Princess Mary of Teck was frequently at Ashridge and took part in the theatricals which were a part of Ashridge life. Her daughter, the future Queen Mary, came out at Ashridge at a ball. As children she and her future husband had enjoyed playing games on the roofs of the House.

The mother of Mr Francis Green of Dagnall had frequently carried messages between the future king and queen when she was lady's maid to the Princess. The Prince and Princess of Wales (later King Edward VII and Queen Alexandra) stayed at Ashridge in 1887. When he was king he came here for the shooting. Mrs Harmon related how when her parents were farming at Lamsey and a barn was used for the luncheon at a royal shoot, King Edward's cloak was wet and brought into the kitchen to dry. 'It was black lined with red silk, and beautiful to handle.'

'King Edward VII was the first to have the operation for the removal of his appendix. Lord Brownlow was the second, but he was the first to survive.' During a visit to Ashridge, Queen Mary, seated near the entrance to the present Dining Hall when asked about the menu said that nothing gave her as much pleasure as red currants and cream.

Christmas Time. The Christmas tree in the grand Hall was 60 feet high and had 300 candles. There were two very fine candelabra each with 250 candles. The servants were invited to look down from the balconies above the staircases. Presents were handed out from the Christmas tree. In 1881, every girl received a warm red cloak and every boy a worsted waistcoat.

The Estate was 15 miles across. There were always 15 men occupied in repairing the churches on the Estate. One man was totally occupied keeping fences in order. From 500 to 800 people were employed on the Estate.

The Titanic. Phoebe, one of the Ashridge maids, was taken by one of Lady Brownlow's friends to America. Both perished in the sinking of the *Titanic* on 15 April 1912. A total of 1,513 out of 2,224 drowned on the *Titanic.*

General Kitchener was at Ashridge on the Sunday before the 1914 war broke out. During tea he received a message of great importance which necessitated his immediate departure after reassuring words to his hostess.

The Herts. and Beds. Territorial Army unit was in camp at Ashridge on 3 August 1914. Within a few hours camp had been broken and 'by 6 a.m. all had disappeared'. War was declared on that day, the 4 August, 1914.

Each year on Michaelmas Day Lord Brownlow had chains put across all the ways leading to Ashridge House, at each lodge entrance. One set was put at the Monument at the top of Brownlow Road, another at the top above the field running down to the Lady's Mile at Nettleden. There was originally a carriage-way down this field. This was done to preserve the private rights of the Estate.

On the death of the 3rd Earl Brownlow all the workers on the Estate were given one year's wages. This enabled many of them to purchase their own houses from the Estate trustees. It is interesting to note that when the College had been dissolved in 1539 one year's wages had also been paid as part-compensation for those displaced. The former brothers received life pensions.

In Brownlow days the Golden Valley was pure lawn, kept down by rabbits and deer.

In 1921 Ashridge House had but two bathrooms.

James William Rogers who was 87 in 1936 had completed 50 years as roasting cook.

At the end of the Brownlow era there were about twenty-five servants in the house.

Before electricity it was said that it was a day's work for one man to trim and fill the oil lamps. Mr Rogers was lamp man.

Ice for the House was preserved in the Ice House in the grounds. This was a deep cavern dug into a bank with three doors to insulate it against heat. At the extreme end is a pit 30 feet deep. Blocks of ice were placed between layers of straw and thus were kept until needed in the summer.

In 1914 the Coach House was taken over for the Red Cross. Previously it had been the scene of an Annual Horticultural Show for all the villages on the vast Ashridge Estate. For a time in 1922 it was resuscitated but only for Little Gaddesden. Prize winners in that year included the names: Saunders; Temple; Clarke; Rogers; Welling; Williams; Batchelor; Austin; Buggey; Mayling; Holland; Liberty; Saunders; Heels; Jones; Drewitt; Halsey; Carpenter; Pratt; Stow and Bierton. The teas for the 1922 show were looked after by Mesdames Andrews, Drewitt, Duncombe, Wright, Nash, Holland, Mead, Bierton and Rogers.

In 1923 when the Ashridge Trustees wanted £300 per acre from Berkhamsted Association Football Club, the Berkhamsted Golf Club was allowed to purchase the land at £6 per acre.

One-half of the Ashridge Estate was bought for £40,000, one-half of this being given by a private donor. By 1934, £70,000 had been spent on the Estate.

Amongst those in recent years who have given long service to the College in its varying capacities have been:
  Mr Herbert H. Reasbeck, Accountant.
  Mr Reginald E. Bond, Clerk of Works.
  Mrs Jarvis, Housekeeper.
  Mr J. Gibling, Porter.
All began in the 1929-1930 years and were at Ashridge until the 1970s.
Mr and Mrs F. Jarvis continued their association with the College after their retirement, Mrs Jarvis caring for the floral arrangements and Mr Jarvis as Chapel Warden.
    The first Ashridge College tie was designed in 1931 by the Principal. It was green to represent the Ashridge lawns, grey for the habit of the Bonhommes, and white for the association with Elizabeth 'The Virgin Queen'. This tie was later replaced by the modern College design bearing the Ashridge symbol. This is obtainable against a navy blue or red background.

PICTURES BY OLD MASTERS

These were amongst those sold on 4 and 7 May 1923, being the property of Adelbert Wellington, 3rd Earl Brownlow. They were sold by Auction at Christies.
Italian & Spanish Schools
Works by Niccola dell Abbate, Sofonisba Anguissola, Giovanni Bellini (*The Adoration of the Shepherd*; perhaps by Vincenzo Catena), Gentile Bellini (*Portrait of Bartolomeo Colleoni*).
Of the school of Giovanni Bellini. *Madonna and Child*
Bordone, Bronzino, Carracci. Works by Annibale and Lodovico Carracci
Cima da Conegliano. *The Holy Family*
Domenichino. *St Sebastian*
Dossi Dossi. *St William*
Giorgione. *Venus & Adonis*
Benvenuto di Giovanni. *Lives of St Augustine & St Jerome*
Guercino. *St Jerome, St William*
Lorenzo Lotto. *Portrait of a Gentleman*
Bernardino Luini. *Holy Family*
Sebastiano Mainardi. *St Catherine*
Maratti. *The Annunciation*

Moroni. *A Gentleman*
Murillo. *A Crucifix*
Elisabetta Sirani. *The Magdalen*
Lo Spagna. *St Catherine*
Il Tintoretto.
Christ Curing the Paralytic
Portrait of a Senator
Portrait of a Gentleman
Portrait of a Doge
Removal of the Body of St Mark
Titian.
St Catherine of Alexandria
The Emperor Caligula
The Emperor Titus
The Presentation of the Virgin
Philip II
Head of the Doge Andrea Gritti
Miracle of St Anthony
Venus and Adonis
The Doge Antonio Grimani
Umbrian School
Madonna with Child
Velasquez
A Pope receiving a deputation
A cavalier and his charger
A marriage ceremony
Veronese
Portrait of an Admiral
Portrait of a Sculptor
Zurbaran *Portrait of a monk*
Dutch & Flemish Schools
L. Backhuison *A Man o' War*
Baptiste
Flowers in a basket
A vase of flowers
Aelbert Cuyp. *The Maas at Dordrecht*
Jan van Huysum
Mabuse. *Mary Tudor*
Van der Meer. *A town on a river*
Rembrandt. *An elderly Jew seated*
Sir P.R. Rubens
The Flight into Egypt
The Annunciation
The Discovery of Achilles
The death of Hippolytus
The two captives
Moonlight
Jacob van der Ruisdael
Landscape
A rushing stream

A harvest landscape
A rough sea
Van Slingelandt. *Lady with a mandoline*
F. Snyders
The fox and the stork
A study of dogs
D. Teniers
Archduke Leopold William
A man shooting wild duck
Cardplayers
Sir A. Van Dyck
Anton Triest
The Crucifixion
Head of an old man
Head of a nobleman
Portrait of Ferdinand de Boisschot
A man's head
Van de Velde
British & Dutch fleets
Men-of-war in a storm
Firing a salute
Boats becalmed
L. Verschuier. *Rotterdam*
Italian School
Campidoglio. *Fruit*
Dapperheit. *Flowers*
Granacci. *The Massacre of the Innocents*
Guido
A lady holding a dove
Ecce Homo
Lanfranco. *St Peter*
Mola. *Hagar*
Raphael. *A Boy*
Sassoferato. *Head of the Virgin*
Tempesta. *The Flock*
Titian
A child wearing a necklace
Bacchus and Ariadne
Di Tivoli. *A horse*
Marcello Venusti. *The Procession to Calvary*
Dutch & Flemish Schools
Bechey. *Market*
Van Bloemen. *Tivoli*
Bogdani. *Fruit and Birds*
Cuyp. *A hen and chicken*
School of van Ruisdael. *A river scene*
Ferg. *The Forge*
Miel. *A Herdsman*
Mytens. *A Cavalier*
Ravestyn. *A Lady*

Rombouts. *A road through a forest*
Swanevelt. *A Landscape*
French School
Claude
A pastoral
A bay
The Flock
A Landscape
Tivoli
Greuze. *La Crûche Cassée*
Charles le Brun. *Aurora*
G. Poussin. *A woody stream*
English School
Ernest Bird. *Louis XVIII*
E. Gill, 1854 *View from Ashridge*
George Jones. *Waterloo*
Charles Marshall. *Welsh Alps*
Proctor. *Daniel*

AMENITIES, CRAFTS AND TRADES
1932

Baker	Wersel Gadsden of Dagnall (until 1981)
	Groom (Potten End)
Blacksmith	Wilfred Duncombe
Butcher	Fred Janes
Coal (& wood)	Saunders
Groceries	Miss Pratt and Miss Cheeseman
	Fountain's
	Douglas Cutler (on bicycle)
Laundry	Jim Whitman
	Mundens
	Goodman's
	Garret sisters
Post Office	Miss Bevan and later Mr Harold Ward
Milk	Mr Bert Andrews, etc.
Poultry and eggs	Janes
Riding School	Angel
Tea Gardens	Fred Hing
	Mrs Liberty
Vegetables	Bert Andrews

AMENITIES, CRAFTS, TRADES, BUSINESS
1981

Aerial Photographs	Mr W. Brooker
Agricultural work	Mr G.I. Rogers
	Mr W. Moore
Laundry	From Berkhamsted, and Watford
Milk	Express Dairies
	Roy Haldane 'The Whistling Milkman'
Music teaching	Mrs D. Thorn

Newspapers	Delivery, Post Office
Police	Police House, Church Road (Herts. Constabulary)
Phone boxes (public)	(Bedford area) Village Hall
	Hudnall corner
Parish Council	Little Gaddesden
Parish Church Services	Sundays 8, 9.30, 6.30 and on Notice Boards
Plumber	Mr G.E. Catchpole
Photography	Mr E.A. Janes
Post	Collection daily (except week ends) 9.45 a.m. and 4.45 p.m.
	Boxes at Post Office
	Hudnall Corner
	Hudnall Lane
	Cromer Close
	Pulridge Hill
	Ringshall
	Ringshall Road
	Ashridge College
	Delivery each morning
Printing	Mrs Thorn
	Messrs Francis & Carnegie
Publications	*Gaddesden Diary* (Quarterly)
	Parish News (Monthly)
Schools	Little Gaddesden C. of E. School, Mr A.J. Williams, Headmaster
	The Play School (Village Hall), Mrs E.A. Janes
Stations	Berkhamsted & Hemel Hempstead for Euston-Scotland line
Stores	The Village Stores & Post Office
	Mrs Stinton and Mrs Mountfort
	Mrs D. Cocks
Advertisements (from manure for sale to sheets lost from washing line)	The Post Office Notice Board
Building and Contracting	Mr G.E. Catchpole
	Mr B. Freake
	Messrs How
	Mr P. Francis
	Mr G. Mayling
Baker	Grooms (Potten End)
	Gadsden (Dagnall)
Butcher	Mr Cheshire
Chapel	Dunstable Circuit (Methodist)
Diocese	St Albans
District	Dacorum (Hertfordshire County)
Doctor	Visits Village Hall weekly (notice of times in Village Hall)
Electricity	Eastern Electricity (Hemel area)
	Mr Mogg
	Mr Mooring
Fire Brigade	'A' Division, Hertfordshire. Queensway, Hemel Hempstead

Footwear	Regular visits paid to Little Gaddesden by Mr James from Edlesborough
Garages	Deer Leap (Mr G. Huxtable)
	Four Ways
Greengroceries	
Horticultural Machinery	Deer Leap Hort. Engineers (Home Farm)
	Mr Wilson
Library	County library visits. Times in Gaddesden Diary
Inn	*Bridgewater Arms*
Infant Welfare Centre	Village Hall
Registrar of Births,	*The Bury, Hemel Hempstead*
Marriages and Deaths	
Transport	Buses from Berkhamsted and Hemel Hempstead. Times in the Gaddesden Diary
Water Authority	Rickmansworth & Uxbridge Valley Water Company Ltd
	Thames Water Authority

DETAILS OF THE BELLS
Treble: Note G, Diameter 2ft. 0½ins., Weight 3–1–14
"THIS RING OF SIX BELLS WAS FORMED IN MEMORY OF ELIZABETH GRIFFITHS, 1977
TAYLOR LOUGHBORO 1977"

Reproduction of two Jubilee crown pieces, obverse and reverse have been impressed.

2nd: Note F, Diameter 2ft. 2ins., Weight 3–2–14
"JOHN BRIANT HERTFORD FECIT 1820

RECAST 1977

TAYLOR LOUGHBORO"

Recast from the heavier of the two previous Little Gaddesden bells.

3rd: Note E-flat, Diameter 2ft. 4ins., Weight 4–0–14
"JOHN HODSON MADE ME 1654"

4th: Note D, Diameter 2ft. 6ins., Weight 5–1–23
"PRAYE YE THE LORD 1630

RECAST 1977

TAYLOR LOUGHBORO"

5th: Note C, Diameter 2 ft. 7½ins., Weight 5–2–27
"W. ATTON + ROBERT + ATTON

+ MADE + MEE

+ 1611 +

THE FOUR LARGEST BELLS CAME FROM CHELLINGTON CHURCH BEDFORDSHIRE
RECAST 1977
TAYLOR LOUGHBORO"

Tenor: Note B-flat, Diameter 2ft. 9½ins., Weight 6–1–16
"SANCTA KATERINA ORA PRO NOBIS I + D"

The mark is probably that of John Daniel c. 1450

Priest's Bell: Note C-sharp, approx

Diameter 1ft. 9ins., Weight 1–3–23

"JOHN BRIANT HERTFORD FECIT 1820"

The bells were dedicated by the Lord Bishop of St Albans, the Right Rev. Robert Runcie M.C., M.A., on Sunday, November 5 1978

CASUAL JOTTINGS

in 1178 a matron of Gaddesden was cured at Redbourn by the relics of St Amphibalus by lying on the spot of his translation.

In the 17th century at Harvest time at Ashridge Estate, 5d. per day was paid.

Harvest. At 4.30 a.m. on the morning after the last stook was carried from the fields, a family would glean, and then take home the gleanings. The living-room was cleared of furniture and the grain was threshed on the floor. The grain was then put in sacks and carried to the miller for grinding and the family bread for the year was provided.

About 1829 a man died of an adder bite in the lane formerly running between the *Bridgewater Arms* and Witchcraft Bottom.

CHARITY BENEFACTIONS

1597	Mrs Elizabeth Winchester of Ringshall. For the poor and to educate poor fatherless children. She died 25 March 1597. 6s. 8d. per annum.
1617	Philip Power bequeathed his house and land for the poor. He was churchwarden at the time of his death, September 1616. £12 19s.
1679	The Earl of Bridgewater purchased an annuity on the marshes of Dagnall for the poor worth £4 10s. p.a.
1707	The Rev. George Burghope gave in his lifetime £30, the interest to be divided equally between the rector and the poor. The rector was to preach a sermon each 26 May, on mortality. This was the day of Burghope's death. The money was to be distributed on that day. The sermon was discontinued after the First World War.
1724	Mr George Alsop gave £420, the interest for the poor.
1792	Lady Caroline Egerton gave £50 for the poor, the interest being £2 15s.

In 1836 coal was given costing 33s. 6d. per ton.

In 1837 bread was given costing 10d. per loaf.

In 1855 the income provided firewood, blankets and flannel.

In 1861 the sale of Power's land brought in an addition to the charities.

1869 recipients must have lived a year in the parish and not have more than £1 a week income.

In 1876 coal was given to 116 persons (40 had one ton and others five cwt.). Others received bread.

In 1878 blankets were given to 50 persons.

In 1894 after a prolonged strike coal was 'exceptionally dear at £1 15s. per ton'.

In 1895 the income from these charities was £73 6s. The charities were consolidated under the title 'The Lady Caroline Egerton and other Charities'. In 1980 the income was £160.

The Lady Caroline Egerton was the sister of the Canal Duke of Bridgewater. In later years the gifts in kind have been replaced by monetary gifts at Christmas.

The Bridgewater Trust

The Lady Charlotte Catherine Anne, widow of the 7th Earl of Bridgewater left for the education of young people on the Ashridge Estate £5,997 10s. 8d. The income in 1980 was £270 in total. The Estate beneficiaries stretch from Potten End to Billington and from Great Gaddesden to Long Marston and Puttenham.

Church Acre

This acre on Church Farm brought in a small annual figure until it was transmuted into land on which are the new west ground of the churchyard and the church car park. This was the 'Town Acre' belonging to the church (17th century).

Churchyard Maintenance

There was a sum of £3 p.a. for this in the time of the Rev. David Jenks II (1829-69). This has been lost.

Ivinghoe Charities

Francis Saywell of 'Wardhurst' by his will dated 28 August 1631 'gave 20s. per annum to the poor of Ivinghoe parish for ever, the most part to be distributed to the poor of Wardhurst and Ringshall by even portions, one half at the beginning of Lent and the other part at Whitsuntide, to be distributed by the Churchwardens with the consent of the Minister, out of his freehold lands tenements and hereditaments in Wardhurst'. Much of Ringshall was formerly in the parish of Ivinghoe. This is the reason benefits still accrue from the Ivinghoe Charities to Ringshall.

Little Gaddesden Church

There was an annual sum of a noble a year charged on a certain house in the parish, the donor unknown, for church ornaments (probably pre-Reformation).

CHURCHWARDENS

1635, 1639, 1640 William Maletrott (who also signed himself Maletrot) signed register sheets with the Rev. B. Holway.

The 'Bishops Transcripts' . . . copies of the baptisms, marriages and funerals were kept from 1604-1812 except for 26 April 1641 to 1665. The Churchwardens' Accounts provide information of day-to-day matters in the 17th, 18th and 19th centuries.

In 1758 Hugh Ellis who had farmed here for 52 years and had also been churchwarden died. He was buried on 16 June.

In 1808 the 7th Earl of Bridgewater was warden. A century later Lord Brownlow held the same office. Roland and Thomas Underwood, father and son, held the office at the turn of the century. John Oakins warden 1956-80 also followed his father Stephen in the office.

GADDESDEN FEAST

Held annually at St Peter's Tide (29 June). It was of ancient origin but became 'a horrible orgy'. The 'roughs' from all parts gathered at the *Bridgewater Arms*, six or seven men stripped and had a fist fight until only one remained standing (*c.* 1800).

DECORATIONS

In recent years decorations have included:

Geoffrey E. Moore	C.B.E.
Dr John Bean	O.B.E.

Vicars W. Bell	M.B.E.
Gerald Ashby	O.B.E.
R.A. Corby	O.B.E., T.D., D.L.
C.A.B. Brighton	M.B.E.
James Crooks	C.V.O.
Dr S.E.T. Cusdin	O.B.E.
Dr D. Bleackley	C.M.G.
Charles Blinco	M.B.E.
John Hobson	C.B.E.
Antony Hopkins	C.B.E.
Colonel J.J. Day	C.B.E.
Colonel F.W. Johnston	M.B.E.
J.R. Ede	C.B.
Miss B. Talbot	O.B.E.
Miss K. Talbot	M.B.E.
Owen T. Williams	C.B.E.
Cdr. H.E.H. Pain	D.S.C.
Sir Donald Hawley	K.C.M.G., M.B.E.
Sir Leslie Pott	K.B.E.
Sir Ivan Stedeford	G.B.E.
Sir William Swallow	Kt. Bach.
Sir Vincent Del Tufo	K.B.E., C.M.G.
Sir John Davidson	P.C., G.C.V.O., C.H., C.B.

became Viscount Sir John Davidson of Little Gaddesden 11 June 1937.
Lady Davidson D.B.E. became Baroness Northchurch, 13 January 1964.

DOMESDAY SURVEY 1086

The following are the contents of the Survey of Little Gaddesden:
Mills – none
Swine – 50
Hides – 5
Team lands – 3
Villeins – 5
Borderers – 2
Serfs – 1
Teams . . . demi – 1
Men – 2
Tenant-in-chief 1086, the Count of Mortain
Under-tenant 1086, Hunfrid
The Saxon holder in 1065 was Edmer Attile
Little Gaddesden was a Berewick in Berkhamsted
Value in 1065 – £4
Value in 1086 – £2
For tax purposes 5 hides = 600 acres. Compare Great Gaddesden where there were 6 hides valued at £22, and 500 hogs.

FIELD NAMES

Field names with dates when they appear:
Windmill Field Mills are mentioned 1284, 1705, 17th century owned by Eames
Badger Wood, 1840

NINETEENTH-CENTURY FIELD NAMES IN LITTLE GADDESDEN AND HUDNALL

This is a composite map based on the maps and schedules dated 1838 for Little Gaddesden and 1868-74 for Edlesborough. Modern kilometre grid squares have been added to give the scale and help locate sites. Some modern roads and the Roman Road have also been added as shown in the key. The parish and county boundaries are now considerably altered. All the areas that were then in Edlesborough and Ivinghoe Parishes were in Buckinghamshire, and their records are kept at Aylesbury. Some mis-matches along the Little Gaddesden-Edlesborough boundaries may be due to the different dates of the sources.

J. Leonhardt

KEY

–·–·– Parish Boundaries

×××× Position of roads built subsequent to the source maps

···· Course of the Roman Road, No. 169B, described by R.W. Bagshawe and R.H. Reid, where following a defined feature.

° ° ° ° The same, undefined.

Fig. 19 Nineteenth-century field names map.

Charlewood, 1323 – In Hodenhole. Henry de Hodenhole witnessed a grant for All Saints, Dagnall. This was part of the endowment of the chapelry there.

Cromer Wood, Cromerstyle, Henry VII.

Hill Wood
    Hullefield, 1402
    Hullelond, 1494
    Hill, 1660

Hoo Wood
    Le Hoo, 1530
    Hoo Lane, Hoo Grounds, 1638

Lamsey, Lamsey Lane, 1638

Manor House. This may have been the home of Richard de Bury, 1432.

Barrells Field, Barrell acre 1638
    Barrell Field, Little Barrells, Great Barrells, 1752.

Birds Pikle, Birds Field. Pightel is a small field or enclosure.

Hardens Hill, Hernes Hill, Henry VII.

Harness Hill, Round Acre, 1752

Picked Meadow, Picked acre, 1638

Picket close, Peacked acre or Cadding, 1752.

South Field, 1638, 1752; South Feild Close, 1752

Coney Hill, Coneyhill, 1532

The Lye, Lie Field 1638, Lye Acre, 1752. Church Close 1752

North Field, North Feild 1638

Readings, Ruydyng, 1406. Grett and Little Redyng 1532, Reddings 1559. The word meant a clearing.

Street Meadow, Street Furlong, 1651

Well Field, Wellfeild 1650

Wick Meadow, Le Wyck 1532

Fields in the Hudnall area—

1772 Upper Becking and Lower Becking

1791 in a Hudnall Farm survey—

High Oaks Field, Stony croft, Upper Beeching, Garretts Close, South Croft. There was also a common field containing strips named Lye Common and this was to the rear of the *Robin Hood* Inn.

Hither Coppice Field was on the east side of St Margaret's Lane.

Homesdens, 1752. Hempstead Highway, 1752

1980. Fields along the Leighton Buzzard boundary were Mile Barn field, South field, White's Close, Step Furlong, Big Field, Barrells.

Ashridge Estate Field Names

Princess Elizabeth who was given Ashridge by her brother King Edward VI conveyed certain fields in 1556 to Richard Combe or Combes of Hemel Hempstead. On a parish church pillar adjoining the lectern on the north side is a small scratching of a name which could be Francis Combes 1569. Richard Combe, above, was succeeded by his son Francis in 1595, and he was succeeded by his son in 1626 who was described as 'an enemy of the ministry'.

The fields conveyed included—

Hodenhale Park.

One meadowe lying behind the Dairie Howse.

One meadowe called 'The Launde' lying behind the stable. (Launde in Middle English meant an open space in the woodland.)

Tuthill Ffields, Parke Ffielde, Conygar Ffielde, Turnors Ffielde, Fyve Acres, Lose Ffeilde, North

Woode, the Bushie Parke, the South Woode, Hamond Hill, Stepmother Wood, Thorney Grene, Hard Hill.

After Elizabeth became Queen she conveyed other lands, including Turner's Close, Bushe Parke and Hamond's Hill. In 1575 she conveyed Stepmother Wood, Hardhill and Thorney, Northwood, Southwood and Hamonds Hill.

St Margaret's Land. Fields mentioned in the conveyance of land after the Dissolution 28 Henry VIII, 1537, to John Verney.

Colyers, Chappell Feldys, Longreding, formerly called Northfield, Stony-close, le Bekynfeld, le Netherwyke.

FUNERALS

Francis, 3rd Duke of Bridgewater

'The Canal Duke' had requested that his funeral would be a simple one. His burial took place at Little Gaddesden church on 16 March 1803. 'As his body did not show signs of decay the funeral was postponed so that his relatives could attend. The procession from London to Little Gaddesden consisted of—

The hearse and feathers with six horses,

His Grace's carriage with six horses,

Three mourning coaches with six horses each,

Ten outriders and the usual retinue of mutes and other attendants'.

(quoted from Hugh Malet, *The Canal Duke,* 1977).

The Funeral of the 7th Earl of Bridgewater

On 30 October 1823, he was interred in the Bridgewater vault at Little Gaddesden church. William Buckingham's Diaries record the order of the cortège from Ashridge at 11 o'clock:

'Park keeper

6 keepers on foot

2 porters on horse.

The valet with coronet on cushion (on horse)

Two porters on horses with staves

Plume of feathers

Hearse and six horses (5 bearers; own men).

1st Mourning Coach with:

Sir A. Hume,

Sir C. Long,

Earl Brownlow'

Viscount Clive (servants behind).

2nd Mourning Coach with:

General O'Loghlan,

Three Chaplains viz. Revs. Horseman, Jenks and Drake,

(servants behind).

3rd Mourning Coach with:

Mr Clarke,

Dr Steel,

Mr Wilson (servants behind).

4th Mourning Coach with:

Mr Ruddy,

Horn,

Hemming,

Gossleton,

Torbran and Pointer.

5th Mourning Coach with:
     the Cook and house servants.
Carriages followed with servants behind, viz. the Earl of Bridgewater's, Sir A. Hume's, Sir C. Long's, Earl Brownlow's, Viscount Clive's, Earl of Verulam's, Marquis of Salisbury's, General O'Loghlan's, Rev. Pechell's.
Self (W. Buckingham), Atty, Adsetts and Mr Head, Churchwarden attended the church and yard to let those in which we thought proper. George Buckingham and about 70 assistants to keep order. Service began before noon and ended before 1 p.m.'
The custom at this period was that people of high social standing would attend a funeral in the official mourning coaches, but their personal coaches followed empty with their servants walking behind. The first empty coach being that of the person departed. When unable to be present some people would send their own coach empty, to show their respect and sympathy.

LITTLE GADDESDEN CHURCH VAULTS

The Bridgewater family interments, in two sections of the vaults beneath the east end of the church, are as follows—

Section one
1. Lady Caroline Egerton, 1792; 2. Francis, 3rd Duke of Bridgewater, 1803; 3a. Francis Henry 8th Earl of Bridgewater, son of the Bishop of Durham and Lady Sophia Egerton, 1829. The last Earl; 3b. Elizabeth, 1st wife of Scroop, 4th Earl of Bridgewater and after her decease 1st Duke of Bridgewater, 1713; 4. John 2nd Duke of Bridgewater, 1747; 5. Scroop, 1st Duke of Bridgewater, 1744; 6. Rachel, Duchess of Bridgewater and 2nd wife of Scroop, 1st Duke of Bridgewater, 1777; 7. Unknown; 8. John Lord Brackley, son of Scroop and his Lady Elizabeth, 1718/19; 9. The Hon. John Egerton, sixth son of John 3rd Earl of Bridgewater and his Lady Jane, 1707; 10. Jane, Countess Dowager of Bridgewater, widow of John 3rd Earl of Bridgewater, 1716.

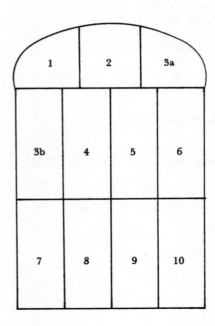

Fig.20   Little Gaddesden church vaults (section 1)

Section two

1. Mrs Elizabeth Haynes, 1813; 2. Samuel Haynes Esq., 1811, parents of Charlotte Catherine Anne; 3. Charlotte Catherine Anne, Countess of Bridgewater, 22 February 1849; 4. John William, 7th Earl of Bridgewater, her late husband, 23 October 1823.

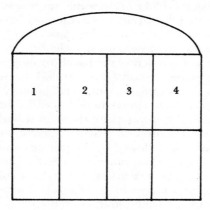

Fig. 21   Little Gaddesden church vaults (section 2)

Section three [including the above]

The 8th Earl of Bridgewater, the last of the line, died at his Hôtel Egerton in the Rue St Honoré in Paris. In his will he asked to be interred decently and privately in the family vaults at Little Gaddesden church. His agent in Paris, G. Barbier wrote to Ashridge asking that the necessary arrangements for mourning coaches and the hearse to be made and for the body to be met at Dover. He adds, 'The necessary precautions will be taken here that the coffin shall not be opened

Space for
two coffins

Mrs Haynes	Samuel Haynes	Charlotte, widow of 7th Earl	7th Earl
Coffin of bones	8th Earl		

Fig. 22   Little Gaddesden church vaults (section 3)

by the Custom Officers in this country, and I request that you take the necessary steps to ensure that a similar evil be avoided on its being handled at Dover'. George Atty wrote, probably to the Rev. Dr Tatham saying that at least six underbearers were required, and that the funeral could come via Lamsey Lane. The vault was opened at the church and precautions were taken to prevent any idle curiosity of visitors. Lady Bridgewater suggested the place where the coffin should be laid. She was anxious that the vacant space adjoining her husband's coffin should be available for her own burial. This would then leave four spaces for future interments in this area of the vaults. Black sealing wax was used on correspondence.

Viscount Alford M.P., eldest son and heir of the Earl Brownlow to whom Ashridge had been bequeathed by the Earl of Bridgewater died on 2 January 1851, having only lived at Ashridge for two years. 'The funeral took place on Monday sen'night (13 January 1851) in the church of Little Gaddesden. The first mourning coach contained the widow of the deceased, Lady Marian Alford with her two youthful sons, the Earl Compton and the Hon. Charles Cust. The second coach contained Lords William and Alwyne Compton, Viscount Cranley and Mr C. Tower. There were seven coaches. The seventh coach was followed by the private carriages of the deceased and of Earl Brownlow. The procession from the Mansion was headed by upwards of 70 of the tenantry of the estate on horseback, two and two. On reaching the church the coffin was conveyed within the sacred edifice. The body having been placed in the chancel the service was read. The body was then lowered into the family vault, and the mourners retired.'

Later Lady Marianne (sic) Viscountess Alford petitioned the bishop of the diocese, Lord George Murray, Bishop of Rochester (Ashridge was at that time in that diocese) for the removal of the body from Little Gaddesden vault to that of the Brownlow family at Belton church, Lincolnshire. The Bishop gave his permission under his seal on 23 May 1851. The coffin was removed to Belton on 26 June 1851, the Hon. Charles H. Egerton and Sir Edward Cust, executors, attending, and the Rector of Little Gaddesden, the Rev. David Jenks confirming the removal. Lord George Murray of Rochester was the last bishop to wear his wig in the House of Lords.

There have not been any interments in the Little Gaddesden vaults since that of Viscount Alford.

Inscriptions in the South Chapel, Little Gaddesden Church

> To the infant son of Dr Henry Stanley
> 'Tibi gnate uso
> Lucis brevi fuso
> Citoque hic concluso
> (Misero me deluso)
> Hoc memoriale
> Breve et cordiale
> Carmen Tripedale
> Saxulumque quale
> Curto non stet male
> Longum nisi nihil vale'

> (To my dearest son whose brief light here has so soon been spent.
> Have pity upon me, mocked indeed I am.
> This memorial, this little tiny stone, its three-foot long lament
> So short it is, but from my old heart's depths.
> Let not your few years here have been in vain.
> One final word. Farewell.)

The Epitaph to the Canal Duke

> To the Memory of
> FRANCIS
> Duke and Earl of Bridgewater
> Marquis of and Viscount Brackley
> He was born 21st May 1736 and died 8th March 1803
> He will be ever memorable among 'Those who were honoured in their generations and were
> the glory of their times'
> John William, Earl of Bridgewater erected this memorial
> Impulit ille rates ubi duxit aratra colonus
> (He sent barges across the fields which once the farmer ploughed)
>   H.M.P.
> J.W. Comes de Bridgewater.

The Bridgewater arms is surmounted by a ducal coronet. The motto is the Bridgewater 'SIC DONEC'.

GADDESDEN

Gat = goat or kid; Denn, den and denu = valley.
The place-name appears in documents with the following spellings—

812	Saxon Charters – 'Gaetesdene'
c. 942	Aethelgiva left 'Gadsden' to St Albans Abbey
c. 946	Godiva de 'Gadsden' left one mark and a towel and 20s. for making a chalice, to St Albans Abbey.
1086	Domesday Survey – 'Gatesdene'
1162-70	Thomas à Becket, Archbishop of Canterbury, granted (Little) 'Gaddesden' to St James, Northampton. This implies the presence of a church and priest here.
1205	Curia Regis Rolls. – 'Parva Gatesdenn'.
1281	Calendar of Patent Rolls. It is 'Gaddesden' and 'Gatesden'.
1286	Edward I granted the manor of 'Gatesden Parva', also spelt 'Gatesdene Parva', to the rector and brothers of Ashridge.
1441	'Guetsden'
1602	'Gadesden' manor was in the gift of the crown.
1605	The manor of 'Little Gaddesden' was conveyed to Lord Ellesmere.

For a time the River Gade was known as Gaete's Stream, and then Le Frereswater (The Friar's stream). The Friars Stream at Kings Langley was known as Blackfriars.

GENERAL DE GAULLE

During the Second World War General de Gaulle resided at Rodinghead as his country retreat. Mme. de Gaulle, and their daughter Elizabeth, their son Philippe and Jockey their ever-busy Skye Terrier lived here when Elizabeth was not at school and Philippe not serving with the Free French Navy on active service.
The General loved long walks over the hills. Mme. de Gaulle was one who shunned the limelight and loved her home and her family. Her younger daughter's governess lived here also in 1939.
   Rodinghead was built by Lockhart's of Berkhamsted; Louis Moore A.R.I.B.A. was the architect. Mr Donald Lockhart was instrumental in obtaining a gardener for the de Gaulles. Mme. de Gaulle was not a little surprised at differences between English and French gardeners.

On a visit to Potten End on an official occasion the General expressed some desire for the Croix de Lorraine to be flown.

Later Colonel F.W. Johnston resided here . . . the property being situated on the boundary of the Potten End and Berkhamsted parishes. Colonel Johnston received the award of the M.B.E. for his outstanding work for young people in Hertfordshire. Later Professor G. Manners lived here.

GHOSTS AND WITCHES

Jarman

'Jarman's Coffin' is the name given locally to a structure on the chimney-stack at the Manor House. Jarman lived there in the 18th century. He was said to have been crossed in love, and then he committed suicide. The ghost of Jarman was said to ride a blue horse without a head. As midnight struck on Ashridge clock he rode it to Bluepit Pond opposite the Manor House. Sometimes he disturbed the deer and shone on them. He also had two white horses which he was said to water on the Green.

In the 19th century Lady Worsley stayed at the Manor House with her aunt Mrs Cautley. As they sat in the stone-walled drawing-room on the first floor, all the lamps flickered and went low. 'Don't worry', said Mrs Cautley, 'it is only old Jarmy passing by'. He passed by on one particular day in the year. Jarman played tricks with the lights (and is still said to do so). At some time he had become troublesome and it was decided to lay him. Seven parsons assembled and the service of exorcism began. Jarman managed to extinguish six of the seven candles, but the seventh stayed alight, and from that moment Jarman gave little trouble.

Myers Lambert. A former resident at the Manor House, Mr Maberly told of an event about 1870 when Myers Lambert had done 'something worse than usual'. The Parish Clerk told him that he must come to church next Sunday and be prayed for. So he appeared and was duly prayed for by the parish in the public service.

John Saw, Head Keeper at Ashridge, lived at Ringshall Lodge. He was a fine tall man with white whiskers. He attended church in a green coat with brass buttons and a sugar-loaf hat. He told of Joe Swaby an under-gamekeeper who lived near the Bridgewater Monument. One day his savings disappeared so he visited the 'Cunning Man' of Wigginton. The 'Cunning Man' told him that they had been stolen and who had done so. '"Would you like to go home, high or low?" "High, if you please".' In a moment he had been whisked away across the wide valley to his own doorstep, right at the foot of the Bridgewater Monument.

Rosina Jane Massey

She was the wife of Gerald Massey a writer and journalist befriended by Earl Brownlow. They lived in Witchcraft Bottom in the 1850s. Rosina was reputed to be a dipsomaniac and to have strange powers. On one occasion she went out collecting woodchips. When rebuked by the woodmen she cast a spell on them so that their axes remained fast in the trees until she was able to help herself to the woodchips. She had a row with a local farmer and cast a spell on his cattle so that they gave no milk. She was reputed to have a hurdle on which she rode. On windy nights she took it from the end of her garden and rode to Studham. Her three-legged stool was said to run errands for her. She was said to charge unauthorised tolls on horses and carts and to bewitch those who did not pay, until they did so. After trouble with the baker she bewitched his loaves, which fell out of his cart and were spoiled. When a gamekeeper ordered her out of Hoo Wood she cried 'Roll out, roll out your pheasants' eggs', whereupon they did so, rolling into the ride, and were broken. She was seen to conduct her cups and saucers round her table in sprightly dance with hands outstretched.

She died in 1866 having prepared herself with a candle to light her through death's darkness, a penny for the toll, and a hammer to knock at heaven's gates. She was buried in the parish church yard. She was only 33 years old when she died, and was buried on 25 March 1866. A cross marks her grave.

In 1872, Mrs Draper going from the Armoury towards Mr Paxton's House saw the appearance of a man, a huge man, dressed like a watchman, lantern in hand, opposite Robin Hood House, and in front of her. She watched from under her umbrella . . . there was a slight drizzle. It did not speak, its form rustled and leaves moved in the wind. She ran away, but later an old man said 'it was old . . . I've seen him many times just there. He is supposed to have murdered his wife some years' ago at the Amoury'.

In 1954, an elegant gentleman's ghost was seen in glorious two-dimensional technicolour at 8.30 a.m. when friends were being seen off at the front door of Robin Hood. It was daylight outside, but the electric light was on in the hall. The figure came out of the swing door leading from the kitchen into the former 'flower room' but used then as a farm office. The man was tall and wore a chestnut curling wig of Charles I or Restoration period. His pink cheek could be seen and his nose, but not his other features. He was wearing a bottle green doublet and full breeches, black thigh length boots with the upper half (wide tops) turned down.

Another ghost was heard in a first floor bedroom by a guest, who was disturbed by a female presence with rustling skirts. She was later seen by a relative who described her as rather a middle-aged Germanic type in a yellowish gown, full-skirted with a square-cut necklace. The dress was trimmed in black.

In 1912, Mr W.B. Gerish of Bishops Stortford published *A relation of Mary Hall of Gaddesden, reputed to be possessed of Two Devils 1664*. Mary Hall lived in Little Gaddesden where her father was blacksmith. She was 'a civil, fair-conditioned Maid, who in the fall of the leaf in 1663 became possessed of two spirits, who she beheld first of all in the shape of two Flies coming down the chimney at her'. She then suffered from convulsive fits and ejaculations which decreased somewhat when she held 'stinking suffumigations' over her head. Being slightly invigorated she next heard strange noises, cats mewing, dogs barking, bears roaring, and a voice spake to her ear, 'pus cat'. 'What a Cat, nothing but new'. As she got no better she was sent to Dr Woodhouse of Berkhamsted, who was known for his cures of people bewitched. He was not successful. Mary's spirits had suggested that Goodwife Harwood had sent them. Mrs Harwood refuted this. Mary was then seen by Mr Saunders, an astrologer and chiromancer, again without success. Finally, Dr Drage of Hitchin was unsuccessful and he dismissed the idea of consulting an Amersham man Redman, who he said had served in prison for malpractices. There is no record of Mary having been cured.

HERTFORDSHIRE

Old Hertfordshire was dominated by hamlet-based villages. The hamlet was the single farmstead, often in a clearance of woodland, for except in the extreme north, the county was well-wooded. When the Anglo-Saxon invasions took place there were no establishments of large villages or agriculture on a wide scale. Hamlets with farm buildings, farm houses, outhouses and the small parish church began with clearings in the forests.

In 877 a group of the Danish armies annexed the eastern part of Mercia. This was formerly the land of Offa II King of Mercia and re-founder of St Albans Abbey, who was said to have died in this part of the land which they took.

If the Danish frontier was moved forward in 891/2, then the name Dacorum may find its origin in this. 'Dacorum' . . . the hundred of the Danes. Little Gaddesden was in Dacorum hundred, but Berkhamsted of which Little Gaddesden was an 'outlier' was in Tring. Tring may have been a third or thirding of the Danish hundred. (Tredung 1086 DB Treunge DB).

'Danish hundred' may have been in contrast to the English hundreds of Buckinghamshire and Bedfordshire adjoining them. Place-names do not suggest much Danish occupation in this area.

Dacorum – The name is found—

    1086 (Domesday Survey) DANAIS DANEIS
    1160 DANEISHDR

1161 DANSHDR DANESHUNDRED
1196 (DE) HUNDREDO DACORUM
1248 HUNDREN DACOR
1303 HUNDREDUM DACORUM
DACORUM = of the Danes. Danish

Hertfordshire Quarter Sessions (See also under Inns)

1639   Thomas Cooke labourer, and Agnes Eames, widow, both of Little
                 Gaddesden had severally kept an ale-house without a licence for
                 three months.

1640   Thomas Cooke and Thomas Iverye, both of Little Gaddesden,
                 husbandmen, for keeping ale-houses without licence.

1640   Thomas Cooke and Robert Ratcliffe, labourers of Little Gaddesden
                 broke into the house of John Alee at Berkhamsted and stole a
                 petticoat at value 10d.
                 Thomas Cooke of Little Gaddesden, labourer, stole 13 sheaves of
                 wheat value 10d. the property of William Mallitrott of the same.

1655   John Potter late of Little Gaddesden, butcher kept a common ale-
                 house without a licence.

1655   John Sibley, labourer, for poaching with a gun in Frithsden Copse in
                 Little Gaddesden, the property of the Earl of Bridgewater. Guilty and
                 imprisoned for 12 months.

1682   William Clarke, bricklayer of the parish of Wigginton, has occasion
                 to remove himself and his family from the parish of Wigginton to
                 Little Gaddesden, and the parishioners of Little Gaddesden refuse to
                 receive him into their parish and let him settle there without a
                 testimonial and certificate from the parishioners of Wigginton.
                 Certificate that the parishioners of Wigginton will at any time take
                 them back into their parish.

1694   Petition of Edward Green of Little Gaddesden, an old maimed
                 soldier. His father lost all for King Charles I. He is now aged 79,
                 cannot maintain himself. He prays benefit from the Act to provide
                 for old maimed soldiers.

Higglers & Badgers

April 1678 at the County Session
                 Higglers and Badgers not renewing their licences this Easter session,
                 included William Stainer of Little Gaddesden, higgler.

Higgler   One who higgles in bargaining. An itinerant dealer, especially a carrier
                 or huckster who buys up dairy and poultry produce and supplies
                 in exchange petty commodities from the shops in town, 1637

Badger   *c.* 1500
                 One who buys corn and other commodities and carries them
                 elsewhere to sell, a cadger, a huckster.
                 A cadger was an itinerant, a carrier, especially one who travelled
                 between town and country carrying butter, eggs and shop wares.
                 One who gets his living by begging or questionable means. A
                 hawker, a street seller.

10 July 1826
Indictment of William Brown an idle and disorderly person, late of Kings Langley, who entered
the wood of Little Gaddesden Hoo with intent to destroy game and armed with a bludgeon and
other offensive weapons.

HISTORICAL MONUMENTS COMMISSION

Secular buildings include:
>   John O'Gaddesden's House
>   Robin Hood House
>   Ashridge
>   Old Park Lodge
>   The Manor House

Religious buildings:
>   The Parish Church

INNS

>   The *Bridgewater* [the only survivor]
>   *Witchcraft*
>   The *Robin Hood*
>   The *Egerton Arms*
>   *Alford Cottage* Site
>   *Thavies* Inn
>   The *Green Man*

There was a *Robin Hood* and *Little John* Beer House on the Green in 1838 Tithe Survey.

In 1794 Mary, daughter of David and Catherine Taylor of *Thavies* Inn was buried.

The names of publicans in the 19th century including those at The *Bridgewater Arms:* William Bennett, 1819, 1811. Nathaniel Duddleston, 1815. James Foster, 1824. George and Mary Garrett are noted in 1835 and 1841. Arthur Norris, 1847. 1867. The Allison Family. Buckingham, Ranger, Edge.

KALM – 26 March 1748 (See Church Farm)

He came from Sweden to see the farming in Little Gaddesden. He describes the village and the Green. The houses in the village were in a row against the common land. Holly bushes were hung with the washing. The women wore red cloaks with pattens on their feet. The houses were built of brick with stone lower courses, and the upper walls were lime-washed. The roofs were tiled but the cottages and the outhouses had little hedges separating the gardens.

Kalm notes a Mr Williams as being the best farmer in Little Gaddesden. He said 'Chalk is seen in many places between St Albans and Hempstead spread out on a field as a manure. They intended to plough it down'.

He visited Ashridge and noted 1,000 head of deer. The house, stone built, had four aspects. He saw the well with the great wheel, and the snow pits. He says that the great chimney (inglenook) in the house had room for four stools. He noted the bundles of furze. These were cut for burning in the open kitchen hearths when carcases of animals and birds were roasted on long spits.

LITERARY ASSOCIATIONS

Geoffrey Chaucer (1340?-1400)

The very beautiful Ellesmere *Chaucer* which has the familiar paintings of the pilgrims was believed to be in the Library at Ashridge House. There is a supposition that this manuscript belonged to the Bonhommes, and that after the Dissolution it was for a time in the hands of the Combe family of Hemel Hempstead who obtained the House on lease from Queen Elizabeth I. From the Combe family the manuscript may have found its way back to Ashridge in the same way as another manuscript, made by the Bonhommes and entitled 'Flos Decretum'. This manuscript bears the legend 'Ex dono Richardi Coombe armigeri'.

Sir Thomas Egerton, Lord Ellesmere, was known to be a patron of the arts, and Francis Bacon states this. He was greatly interested in the works of Chaucer. Francis Thynne, son of William

Thynne, editor of Chaucer's works dedicated to Sir Thomas his *Impressions of Chaucer's works*. The Librarian at Ashridge, the Rev. H.J. Todd took the Ellesmere *Chaucer* to Bridgewater House in London for new binding.

The contents of Bridgewater House devolved on the future 1st Duke of Sutherland. The manuscript is now in the Huntington Library in California, but the British Library has a very fine copy, made in 1911.

This indicates the richness of the original libraries of Ashridge House.

The Canterbury Tales probably appeared about 1386. As Commissioner of the river bank between Greenwich and Woolwich, Chaucer probably saw the Canterbury pilgrims. He also was aware of the Shrine of the Holy Blood at Hailes, for he mentions this in the Pardoner's Tale. 'By Goddes precious herte, and by his nailes, And by the blood of Christ that is in Hailes'. He mentions John of Gaddesden in the Prologue to *The Canterbury Tales*, and it is possible that the Doctor of Physick owes something to John. Chaucer spent time as Clerk of the Works at Berkhamsted Castle and no doubt had heard about John and his reputation. It is not unlikely that the people of these parts spoke after the fashion of Chaucer's language.

John Skelton 1460-1529

> Of the Bonehommes at Ashge beside Barcanstede
> That goodly place to Skelton most kynde
> Where the sang royall is, Christis blood so rede,
> Whereupon he metrified after his mynde
> A pleasanter place than Ashridge it harde were to finde;
> As Skelton reherseth with words fewe and playne
> in his distichon made in verses twayne.

Fraxinus in clivo frondetque viret sine rivo
Non est sub divo similis sine flumine vivo
From *The Crowne of Laurell* by John Skelton 1523
An ash tree on the hill is crowned with leaves and flourishes
Under heaven there is not its equal, and yet there is no brook nor living stream.

Skelton, poet, rhetorician, translator was ordained priest in 1498 and became rector of Diss. He was hated by the Dominican monks for his satire, and his invective caused him to seek sanctuary in Westminster Abbey, fearing arrest. There John Islip received him until his death on 21 June 1529. His reference to his reception at Ashridge, in the poem printed in 1523 may refer to more than a kindness at a passing visit. It could reflect a period of peace and trust in the church whose earthly condition so much appalled him. As an admirer of Chaucer he would have known his association with the Berkhamsted area. Whilst sharing Chaucer's critical attitude to the worldliness of monks and friars, he could value the Bonhommes . . . and knew the area well enough to recognise the absence of a good water supply!

William Shakespeare

There is a story that Shakespeare wrote the words of the Memorial on the south wall of the parish church which commemorates Lady Elizabeth Dutton (The Red Lady). The immediate reaction could be cynical. However, there could have been a remote connection between Shakespeare and Gaddesden.

Thomas Hesketh's Players

In the will of Alexander Houghton of Lea Old Hall, Preston, who kept a household company of players, he made a bequest when he died in 1581 'of the music and instruments and the playe clothes to his brother Thomas, or if he will not keep the Players, to Thomas Hesketh of Rufford'. The properties went to Hesketh. Alexander Houghton in his will charged Thomas Hesketh 'to be friendly with Foke Gillome and William Shakeshafte nowe dwellynge with me'. Each of these men was to receive a year's wages and a share in the tontine bequest. (In 1581 Sir Thomas Hesketh was in gaol) . . . so Shakespeare may have left Rufford until life was normal.

By 1587 Thomas Hesketh had an active group of players again and the household books at Knowsley Hall, Lancashire, the home of the Earls of Derby, record that the Hesketh Players entertained at Knowsley in Christmas week 1587.

In 1582 Shakespeare had married Anne Hathaway. His daughter Susanna was christened in May 1583, and the twins Judith and Hamnet in February 1585. About this time he left Stratford for the stage. By the end of 1588 he was in London with Lord Strange's company. This company was an amalgamation of two smaller groups. The first of these had been centred on Lathom House, Lancashire and Knowsley under the patronage of Lord Strange. Strange was Lord Derby's heir. The second group came from the Earl of Leicester's group when he died in 1588. It has been assumed that Shakespeare came into Lord Strange's players from Leicester's players. However in view of the will of Alexander Houghton it could be that there was a connection there. Sir Thomas Hesketh died three months before Leicester and his players may have disbanded or have been transferred. The only remaining glass in Rufford Old Hall bears the coat of arms of Stanley, the Earl of Derby.

Now Lord Strange, Lord Derby's heir, owned land in Great Gaddesden and this area, so there was a local connection between Gaddesden and Strange and this may have extended through his players .. and so to Shakespeare. Moreover, Sir Thomas Egerton married the widow of Ferdinando, the 5th Earl of Derby, and Egerton's son married the daughter of Ferdinando. His Countess is mentioned on the stone set before the altar in the south chapel of Little Gaddesden Church. So there were connections between Strange, Derby, Egerton and Bridgewater which could have extended to Shakespeare.

The verse concerned:

> 'Who tho' of tender years yet did excel
> In virtuous living and in dying well
> Here rests in peace of whom 'tis truly said
> She lived true spouse and widow, dyed a maid'

The writer of the Memorials to the Dutton family said that this was written by Shakespeare 'as a conjecture'.

Massey The Poet

He followed the Rev. C.G. Lane at Wards Hurst Farm ('The Lonely House'). He had been educated in a charity school in Tring, thence he moved to a silk mill in Tring. He next became a page boy at a girls' school in London. He was an avid reader and self-educator.

He wrote poetry ('Marred by socialist views' . . . Rev. C.G. Lane). He came to the notice of Lord Tennyson. He became attracted to Kingsley and Maurice and the Christian Social Reformers and Tom Hughes. He wrote for *The Daily Telegraph*. He married the daughter of a professional man from the north of England. She was a medium and he became a spiritualist, having been an atheist. She was impractical. He fell in debt. Lord Brownlow gave him £100 and he went to Wards Hurst because Lord Brownlow thought that the isolation would remove temptation from him. After that he went to another Brownlow provided house in London.

John Milton

The 1st Earl of Bridgewater was patron of John Milton. With Henry Lawes the Royalist musician, Milton wrote *Comus* in 1654. The Earl, his Countess and children took part in the Masque which was acted in the Hall at Ludlow Castle to celebrate the Earl's appointment to be Lord President of the Marches. The idea was probably first conceived in the gardens of Ashridge. It romanticises in poetic form the disappearance of the Lady Alicia Egerton, daughter of Lord Bridgewater who had been lost in the forest near Ludlow.

In 1930 the Ashridge Players performed *Comus* under the patronage of the Rt. Hon. Stanley Baldwin, future prime minister. Arthur Bryant was the producer. Mr Baldwin stayed at Red Lodge when he was at Ashridge. The later dining-room was used as Mr Baldwin's bedroom.

THE LOLLARDS

On 15 June 1381 Ashridge was attacked by Wat Tyler's mob as St Albans was, and the Rector was forced to grant privileges. John Ball was executed at St Albans. Robert Bartlet a wealthy farmer was kept for seven years a prisoner at Ashridge. He was not only branded on the right cheek, but confined for 14 weeks in the Bishop's prison, probably at Woburn where 'he was so cruelly treated with cold, hunger and irons that after coming out of the said prison he was so lame in his back that he could never go upright as long as he lived'. In the persecutions of 1506/7, his sons were summoned to the visitation of the Bishop Longland (Lincoln) at Amersham.

Harding was the last English Lollard to be burned. This took place at Chesham. The Vicar General of the Bishop (Longland) was assisted by the Rector of Ashridge, Thomas Waterhouse, in Harding's trial.

Some Lollards were condemned to perpetual penance and to life imprisonment, including at Ashridge. A Lollard from Little Gaddesden was indicted at St Albans and executed there. (NB. The Rector of Ashridge in 1287 had claimed the right of gallows, tumbrel and pillory.)

On 14 April 1515 Attwater, Bishop Of Lincoln, sitting at Missenden imposed penance on Thomas Hardynge and his wife Alice, for heresy. Every Corpus Christi day they were to walk barefoot to Ashridge bearing a taper of wax.

Sir John Cheyne, a large landowner in the area, Thomas Cheyne, and Thomas Drayton, Rector of Drayton Beauchamp were imprisoned for Lollardy. Ashridge came into the hands of the Cheyne family after the Dissolution.

MILESTONES

Two milestones were erected by the 7th Earl of Bridgewater (1803-23), one near Cromer Close, 28 miles to London, and one on Pulridge Hill, 27 miles from London. The Cromer Close milestone was cleaned and the lettering re-carved by the authority of the Dacorum Council in 1979, instigated by the Rural Heritage Society.

NAMES

Names of monks at the dissolution of Ashridge College in 1539, with their pensions:

*Thomas Waterhouse, Rector. £100 p.a.
Thomas Hyll, £10
Elyas Bernard.
Michael Draper. £10
John Hatfelde (senex) £8
Robert Hetchingham [or Hychyn]. £7
Richard Gardyner. £7
William Knyghton. £6
*Rychard Bedforde. £6
*Edward Peacock. Novyce £2 13s. 4d.
*Roger Birchley [or Byrchelye]. £6
*William Downham. £6 13s. 4d.
Richard Sawnders. £5 6s. 8d.
*John Axstyll. £5 6s. 8d.
*William Brook [or Broke]. £5 6s. 8d.
Joseph Stepneth [or Slepnethe]. £8
Richard Canaan [or Canon]. £6
*William Young. £6 13s. 4d.

*These were still receiving their pensions in 1553. The pensions were paid on Lady Day and Michaelmas.

In 1554 the state of ex-religious priests was reported on in the diocese of Lincoln. At that time there were still Ashridge pensioners including—

Thomas Waterhouse, the former Rector who still received a pension of £100 p.a. and 50 loads of wood from the Ashridge Estate. He became Vicar of Quainton and was buried in Hemel Hempstead church where a brass was placed on his tomb.

William Downham. He graduated B.A. in 1541; M.A., in 1543. He married. He became Rector of Datchworth, Herts and in 1552, Chaplain to Princess Elizabeth, and Bishop of Chester in 1561. He died in 1577. His pension was £6 13s. 4d. His living was worth £14 13s. 4d. p.a.

Roger Birchleye had a pension of £6. He became Rector of Ayot St Peter. He married. His living was worth £7 per annum. Clerical marriage was legal after spring 1549. A pension of £5 was adequate, if not high before 1545. Most ex-Bonhommes had more than that, as shown above.

Richard Hanger (not in the 1539 list) was a former Bonhomme from Ashridge. He had a pension of £6 and became Rector of Souldrop (Sulthrop) Bedfordshire, worth £9 p.a.

NAMES IN LITTLE GADDESDEN

These names are found in the 17th, 18th and 19th centuries. It is of interest to note that the occupations and also the frequency with which sons followed their fathers in the same work.

Parish Church Registers

The names on page one of the 1681 register are— Lofty, Westcot, Thorne, Bulmer, Freeman, Norwood, Hall, Harris, Kingham, Tedder, Groom, Hill, Field, Humphreys, Henshawe, Clark, Moores, Ironmonger, Gage, Potton and Rickson. This is the earliest register.

Early names of interments in the Church

1612	John Eames was buried in the chancel.
1621	Bartholomew Holloway sepult: in chancel. (He was the Rector's son and the Rector had the right of burial at the east end.)
1625	Anne, 10th daughter of the 1st Earl of Bridgewater was buried in the vault
1635	Her mother Frances was buried there.

The eight earls of Bridgewater, three of whom were dukes, together with their families are buried in the vaults at the east end.

Names and occupations in the 19th century

1813	George Horn, butcher (also recorded in 1840).
	Theophilus Hemmings, wood bailiff to the 7th Earl of Bridgewater.
	Maria Horn, straw plaiter
1814	Charlotte Catherine Anne daughter of the Rector, James Horseman (she was named after the wife of the 7th Earl).
	John Lamport, farmer
	William Temple, glazier.
	Richard Perry, footman to the 7th Earl.

In 1814 there are recorded, a cleaver, a cordwainer, a 'plaisterer', a joiner, and a shopkeeper (Thomas Lamport).

Tailors at the time are James Tomlin, 1821 and Henry Harris, 1823.

1821 Christopher Buckmaster, churchwarden.

1822 William Wood, shopkeeper.

1826 James Gaddesden & William Simmonds, bakers.

Those named *Gentlemen and Esquire* in the 1820-30 period include:

George Atty, Francis Carleton, William Norris Franklyn, John Henry Buckingham (licensee for a time of the *Robin Hood* Beer House) and son of William Buckingham, bailiff of the Ashridge Estate.

1803-29, Robert Clarke, agent and auditor for the Estate. He served the Estate for 38 years having also served General Egerton the future 7th Earl for 17 years before they came to Ashridge.

George Atty, treasurer and accountant at Ashridge. He signed documents in 1830 and continued to do so until 1852.

1830   Nehemiah Cooley, village blacksmith. He died in this year. His son Charles became a clerk at Ashridge.

Thomas and Elizabeth Andrews had four children, George, William, David and Harriott. David Andrews married Lydia Surman in 1830.

1837   Mary-Anne daughter of William and Hannah Okins was baptised.

1839   Elizabeth Mead, daughter of William and Hannah Oakins of Ivinghoe, baptised. (Ivinghoe probably meant either the Ringshall or Ringshall Drive areas).

1839   William Temple, plumber
        William Reeve, butcher

1839   William Stanner, 'plaisterer'

1843   William Fountain, butcher

1844   George Tomlin, tailor, son of George Tomlin, tailor
        Thomas Andrews, tailor, son of Thomas Andrews, tailor
        James Potter, bricklayer

1845   William Rogers, shoemaker, son of James Rogers, shoemaker
        Mrs Ann Cox, grocer

1849   Charles Rogers, shoemaker

1850   Stephen Temple, glazier, son of William Temple, glazier

1850   Munden

1855   Edward Cutler, butcher, postmaster, shopkeeper

1856   William Reeve, butcher, son of John Reeve, butcher

1859   John Hervey, parish clerk was buried. A John Hervey was parish clerk in 1808

1859   Thomas Phillips, dentist. He married Lucy, daughter of John Wilson, schoolmaster

1861   Charles Cross, butcher

1862   Thomas Andrews, tailor, and parish clerk
        George Lingard, stonemason, son of William Lingard, stonemason

1873   Rosamund, daughter of Ralph Pattison, gamekeeper
        William Cheshire, baker at Ashridge

1879   Ann Elizabeth, daughter of Thomas Andrews, parish clerk
        Ann Allsop
        William Ghost, postmaster
        Miss Agnes and Miss Ann Fordom, drapers
        Stanners & Son, builders

1880   Richard Wells, plumber, son of Richard Wells, plumber. They laid lead on the roof of the parish church tower.
        Jane Wardle, teacher of needlework

1880   John Wardle, stonemason
        William Simmons, foreman of the Estate

1881   Edwin Andrews, son of Thomas Andrews, tailor. He married Elizabeth daughter of Sergeant-Major Ballam, veteran of the Crimean War.

1883   William Dell, postmaster
        Thomas Brandon, butcher

1884   Walter Bamford, park keeper

1887   John Sutherland, clerk of works at Ashridge

1896   Stephen Temple, painter

1900   Seth Cox, Head gamekeeper

Names in 1932 – Duncombe, Oakins, Ward, Andrews, Richardson, Wright, Wells, Ellen, Liberty, Austin, Halsey, Bunting, Reasbeck, Sears.

Names in Ringshall 1672-1932

1672-78   Thos. Ambrose, Elizabeth Alice Cooke, Frances Portress, Judith Blackett, Philip

Lovett, Sarah Messenger, Alice Bishop.
1683   Edward Quarrington, Elizabeth Portress
1686   Joseph, Sara, Jacobus, fil; Henrici et Sarae Fountain de Ringshole. Bapt. 26 Sept., 1686. Anne Potter
1688   Maria filia Johannis et Mariae Clifton de Ringshole. Bapt. 17 June 1688
1688   Edwardus filius Edwardi et Juditha Halsey de Ringshole. Bapt. 24 June 1688
1693   Ann Hurst. William Lodge
1702   30 December Thomas Cobb and Jane Okins
1705   Rebecca Norwood. John Rawlins
1709   8 January, Frances Okyns
1820   Richard Oakins
1861-75 Ralph Pattison, Gamekeeper. Ann Pattison. William Cutler. John Waterton. Jesse Spicer.

Names from a Ringshall Notebook 1877-98
These are deaths
1877   Richard Dean. Mrs Wells
1879   James Lanes. Ruth Simmons. Priscilla Putifoot. Richard Fountain. Matthew Hobbs. Thomas Fountain
1887   Fanny Wharton
1888   Mary Clarke
1889   Samuel Windmill. Mary Gareth. Rose Rogers
1890   Job Curl. George Draper. John Matthews
1891   George Garrett. David Saunders. George Fountain
1892   Emma Cox. Charles May. Thomas Hobbs. Eliza Edward. Edward Room. Thomas Andrews
1892   The Rector, the Rev. C.G. Lane
1893   John Garrett. Thomas Tame. Mrs Cob
These are marriages from 1878
1878   Edward Hoar. Joseph Blogg
1889   George Jones. John Clifton. Thomas Clarke
1891   James Halsey. Thomas Fenn. Charles Tripp
1894   Charles Allison. John Garrett
1895   Mr G. Stanbridge. Mr Chapman
1896   Robert Jones. Elizabeth Whitman
1899   George Collins, bricklayer. No. 32. c. 1900 Thomas Rogers, No. 4 Cobbler for Little Gaddesden and Dagnall. He was also well known for his hedge-laying and his organ playing at Dagnall.
1932   Ringshall names included—
        Milton, Mayling, Cato, Maunders, Goodman, Clifton, Cocks, Fountain, Rogers, Orange.

Names in Ringshall
Ringshall names appear in Dagnall in the 19th century—
1853   Batchelor
        Cripps, farmer
        Cutler, wooden shovel maker, farmer, grocer, draper
        Gadsden, farmer, straw-plaiting schoolmistress, baker
        Janes, blacksmith, publican
        Rogers (Daniel and William), shoemakers
        Ginger, farmer
        Jones, grocer

In Edlesborough 1847 the one entry under Gentry, apart from the Rev. W. Wroth, vicar, is Mrs Ginger.

Names in the Witchcraft Bottom Area 1797-1869

1797	James and Mary Watertun of Whitchcraft Bottom
1798	Thomas and Hannah Kirby of Whitchcraft Hill
1799	May Field, Whichcraft Hill
	Clerk Timberlake
	Martha Hares of Whichcraft Bottom
	Mary Anne Herbert of Whichcraft Bottom
1800	William George of Whichcraft
1802	William and Mary Simmons of Whichcraft Hill
	John Puddefoot of Whichcraft Bottom
1803	Joseph Norwood of Whichcraft
1806	Justice Horn of Whichcraft Bottom
1847	Samuel and Jane Andrews of Witchcraft
1856	Joseph Glenister of Witchcraft Bottom
1858	Daniel Horn of Witchcraft Bottom
1869	Catherine Fowler of Witchcraft Bottom

There were 17 cottages in this area at the beginning of the 19th century.

Names In The Witchcraft Bottom Area or Ringshall Area but included in the Registers as of Ivinghoe (some may be of Ivinghoe as now known)

1752	Frances Oakins
1784-1800	Simmonds, Dean, Clarke, Mortimer, Hawkins, Warren, Ivorman, Clack, Brown, Clayton, Roome, Draper, Ludgate, Puddefoot, Mills, Wood, Timberlake, Bateman, Hawkins, Horne, Inwood, Norman, Wright, Cox
1745	Fary
1748	Chalk
1810	Rogers
1812	Justice

Names in Hudnall 1654-1894

1654-57	John Garrett, Daniel Cooke, Margaret Andrewe, Sara, daughter of Isaac Seeare, Richard Sawell of St Margaret's
1673-1678	Alice Seeare, William Seeare, Isaac Seeare, John Besouth, Catherine Lacely, Hannah Bigg, Henry Morris
1683	Elizabeth Hill
1690-1697	Robert Warr, Mary Freeman, Daniel Whitlock, Thomas Church, Ann Howell
1709	John Thorn
1775	James Rogers, Mary Barton
1841	Matthew Simmonds, Elizabeth Simmonds, William Beake, William Purton
1875	Edward Meacher, Matthew Simmonds, George Underwood, William Beake
1894	Joseph Janes, butcher

NONCONFORMITY

1622	Presentment at Hertford, 30 Sept., Henry Pratt, carpenter of Little Gaddesden for having absented himself from the Parish Church.

The primary episcopal visitation of Robert Sanderson, Bishop of Lincoln to the Mursley Deanery 1662.

Edlesborough parish. Richard Young of Hudnall was presented for not repairing to the church and for frequenting conventicles.

John Russell and Samuel Branch of the same parish were similarly presented

1686   Presentment of Samuel Hall of Little Gadsdin, blacksmith . . . for not attending church.

20 June 1778. There were places registered for Nonconformist worship in Little Gaddesden. These included dwelling places and offices belonging to Robert Austin.

12 December 1812. The dwelling-house belonging to Robert Austin was certified for Protestant dissenters by John Crosby Sheppington, Minister.

See the account of the Methodists in Little Gaddesden in the article on the Chapels (see page 111).

THE PARISH CHURCH c. 1860-1917

On the south wall above the hymn book cabinet is a monument to Anne, daughter of Gervas Norton of Kettlethorpe in Yorkshire. It is inscribed — 'In search of health she accidentally passed a few days in this parish and found benefit from the pure air, fixed her residence here where she expired on 13th day of April 1796 in the 73rd year of her age'. The monument is by Ashton of Marylebone St., Piccadilly.

The first stained-glass window inserted in the Church was in memory of Mary Ann Maberly formerly of the Manor House. She was buried 25 January 1814. A note against the entry in the registers states — 'I have been told that the hearse containing Mrs Maberly's body took three weeks from Bath to Little Gaddesden owing to snow drifts'. F.H. Hodgson, Rector, 17 December 1898. A further addition was made—

'This is verified 21 June 1964. The Diary of William Buckingham, Steward of Ashridge, 8th January, 1814, "I wrote to Lord Bridgewater to inform him of the death of Mrs Maberly. Very heavy snow falls. 25th January, 1814. I went with Lord Bridgewater on pony to Frithsden and on the Berksted to meet Mrs Maberly's funeral".' H. Senar 21 June 1964

Reflections towards the end of the century about church behaviour tell of the years before 1860 when services were a monotonous duet between the rector and the clerk. There was no reverence and very little kneeling. Holy Communion was celebrated four times a year. There were no weekday services. Labourers walked into church with their hats on, took them off when they reached their pew, sat throughout the service. However, the oldest bowed at the Gloria, as did Rector Jenks and the Clerk. Hats were put on at the end and the congregation marched out to the sound of the clarinet played from the gallery.

In 1855 a singing class for the church choir was established at Ashridge Chapel. The choir had an outing to the Crystal Palace, the creation of Joseph Paxton, uncle of William Paxton of Ashridge. The Rector, the Rev. David Jenks (1829-69) did not approve of choral offices in parish churches, although he valued greatly the Cathedral choral services.

In 1863 there was a barrel organ in church and several instrumentalists including a clarinettist. Funerals were brought into church through the main west door. The preacher changed his robes for the sermon. 'In the clerk's pew there was a bottle.' The vaults were visible.

A new order began with the advent of the Rev. C.G. Lane. Surpliced choristers were trained by Mr Worrall, the surplices being worn for the first time for the funeral of Mrs Lane. Choir suppers and outings became regular features of church life. In 1871 the *Ancient and Modern Hymn Book* was introduced. It was to be used until 1960 when it was replaced by the *English Hymnal*. The harmonium was played by Tom Andrews the tailor for Ashridge. It was discarded when a new organ was provided, mostly by donations from the Ashridge and Rectory families. The new organ cost £111.

Harvest Thanksgivings. The idea of these spread rapidly and Little Gaddesden was early in their observing, and in church decorating. Lady Marian Alford's designs for the floral decoration were on an extensive scale. One year she was dissatisfied with the result, and ordered all the decorations to be stripped and the work begun again. Another year she based her designs on the work of Della Robbia. After the Harvest services a great Harvest Supper took place. In 1872, 300 people sat down to the meal in the church meadow. King's the caterers of Berkhamsted took care not to supply any beer where there was no ticket forthcoming. Men were given three pints, boys and women two pints. In 1885, 600 were present in the Monks' Barn for the Harvest Home.

The church restoration began in May 1876. Lord Brownlow was determined to use Godwin's designs. With the approval of the Bishop of Lincoln, Little Gaddesden parishioners were allowed to have morning service in Ashridge Chapel. The Bishop of Oxford in whose diocese Ashridge Chapel was, licensed the Chapel for Holy Communion. 'In spite of fear of the great incursion of Huns and Vandals from Berkhamsted, no difficulty arose.'

In the parish church the Bridgewater family had sat in their family pews on the north side of the choir stalls. They had permission to bury beneath this part of the chancel. The Brownlow family also sat in this part of the church. A solid foundation for the carriages was made outside the west door in what is now the churchyard west ground.

In 1876 the Parish Magazine was begun. In the following year the black-painted list of parish charities on a board in the tower was replaced by the stone-carved tablet. In 1880 the total offertories were £41 7s. 8½d. Churchwardens appointed in that year were Earl Brownlow and Mr George Underwood.

In 1885 a concert was given to provide new lighting for the Church. This is the origin of the wrought-iron lampholders for the oil lamps. The vestry table shows burn marks where the lamp glasses were placed when the lamps were being trimmed.

Magazine matter had to be sent in by the 25th day of the month. The printed magazines for the Deanery were completed and circulated by the first of the following month. Holy Communion was celebrated every other Sunday. A full choral service was sung every Sunday evening with an anthem on Sacrament Sundays. Mr Worrall the schoolmaster was still in charge of the music and the choir.

The Church restoration cost £2,105 14s 9d. The Maws and Minton tiles cost £104 7s. ½d. The cost of cementing and levelling the church paths and the building up of the flint walls was extra to the restoration cost. William Temple carved the beams and chancel symbols with the emblems of St Peter and St Paul, making them to Lord Brownlow's designs. In 1881 the Church was officially reopened. In 1887 a new altar frontal was dedicated on Easter Day, made by Lady Marian Alford. She died in 1888. The East window was her son's memorial to her, and the Altar Cross with its beautiful miniatures was Lady Brownlow's memorial to her.

In 1895 the Hon. Alfred Talbot of Little Gaddesden House set on foot a Village Memorial to the Rev. C.G. Lane, dividing up the parish into districts for the collectors. Thirty-two pounds was collected and the chancel lamps were the memorial. It had been hoped that sufficient money would be forthcoming to build a Lych-Gate. When the memorials to the late Rector were dedicated in 1895 the lesson was read by the Headmaster of Eton (Dr Warre). The Dean of York, Dr Purey Cust was the preacher.

In 1895 the new heating system ('The Apparatus') was installed and was pronounced a great success. The ducts and grilles are still in place. In 1896 a bridegroom placed the wedding ring on his bride's right hand by mistake. He was chafed for it and told that his marriage was illegal. The rector stated officially in the Parish Magazine that the marriage was valid.

The President of Trinity College Oxford, Dr H.G. Woods, whose wife was the daughter of Dr Bradley the Dean of Westminster, was inducted in 1900, and remained for four years, leaving because the climate here was unsuitable for his wife. He entertained the choir to tea and dinner at Trinity College for their annual outing. He brought distinguished preachers, including the Bishop of Hereford, the Bampton Lecturer, the Rev. R.E. Bartlett and the Dean of Westminster, who wore the ribbon of the Royal Victorian Order with which he had been invested after the Coronation of King Edward VII. The Choir of the Temple Church accompanied by Sir Walford Davies visited Little Gaddesden in 1904.

Afternoon services took the place of evening services except on full moon Sundays from November. The rector's gate into the churchyard was always kept unlocked. This is probably an ancient pathway entrance, and could date from a time when the Parsonage adjoined the Church. The death of Queen Victoria was marked by the tolling of the bell, the draping of the Chancel screen and the playing of the 'Dead March in Saul'.

An evening offertory was introduced in 1905.

In 1907 Andrew Rogers was the veteran member of the choir. He had been carpenter at Ashridge House for 50 years. As such he played a part in erecting the choir stalls designed by Lord Brownlow and copying the medieval stalls adjoining them.

In 1916 Mr Harrison, schoolmaster, was called up and Ralph Kibby aged 13 years took his place as organist. He played at Little Gaddesden and Great Gaddesden and 50 years later he was still playing the Ashridge organ for College services. In 1917 the Confirmation candidates included wounded soldiers resident at Ashridge.

PARISH COUNCIL *Foundation*

In 1894 by the Local Government Act a new order affecting the life of rural society was created. In every village numbering 300 a Parish Council was to be elected. The powers formerly exercised by the churchwardens and overseers except things pertaining to the church and its services were to be delegated to the newly created council. 'Great things were expected to enhearten village life and unearth the talents of the sons of the plough and give to village life a new conception of greatness'.

'The Fabian Society and noisy agitators tried to set class against class, and denounced the tyranny of the squire and the parson [the Rector's parish magazine notes]. In our quiet village the election passed quietly'.

Lord Brownlow was elected to be Chairman and five nominees were elected unopposed. Roland Underwood, Robert Pratt, Charles Allison, George Whitman and Ralph Patteson.

At the Parish Meeting in 1896 the Rector (the Rev. F.H. Hodgson) was elected Chairman and the five councillors elected above were re-elected. In 1897 the Rector was elected Chairman and five were elected to serve. R. Underwood, R. Pratt, G. Whitman, H. Temple and G. Wright. In 1901 the Rector was elected as Chairman. The five members were S. Green, R. Pratt, R. Underwood, G. Whitman and R. Patteson. In 1903 R. Underwood resigned as Parish Council clerk after many years.

List of Chairmen and Clerks to Little Gaddesden Parish Council.

Chairmen

1894-1896	R. Underwood
1896-1900	Rev. F.H. Hodgson
1900-1905	Rev. H.G. Woods
1905-1919	Rev. E. Clarke
1919-1923	Rev. T.E. Goodge
1923-1924	R. Jones
1924	H. Talbot
1925	R. Jones
1925-1928	Rev. A.D.M. Bidlake
1928-1934	Major Wykeham-Musgrave
1934-1937	W.B. Stonebridge
1937-1946	F.S. Hughes
1946-1949	L. Moore
1949-1952	Major Wykeham-Musgrave
1952	F.S. Hughes
1952-1955	S.A. Block (co-opted)

1955-1958	S.A. Block (co-opted)
1958-1961	S.A. Block (co-opted)
1961-1963	S.A. Block (co-opted)
1963-1973	C.D. Williams
1973	J. Oakins
1973-1975	Mrs E. Foxall
1975-1980	C. Revell
1980- —	R.A. Corby

Clerks

1894-1910	R. Underwood
1910-1911	H. Wells
1911-1926	J.C. Phillips
1926-1932	C.W. Samways
1932-1934	? Rendell
1934-1937	C. Ferguson-Davie
1937-1939	T. Hansford
1939-1946	L. Moore (deputy to T.W. Hansford – recalled 1939-1943 to Navy Service)
1946-1952	H. Reasbeck
1952-1955	H.L. McCaul
1955-1961	C.D. Williams
1961-1963	J. Yewdall
1963-1972	Mrs D. Bailey
1972-1975	Mrs M. Williams
1975-1978	Mrs P. Creed
1978- —	L.G. Ouseley

PATHWAYS AND LANES

1530, Le Chepingewaye. Cieping = Market way as in Cheapside. 1530 Greeneweaye. The Green. 1601, Le Howewood, Lucas Hill, Cockroads Close. 1638 Berry Lane. This was probably the lane running past the Manor House. In 1638 Fuller in his *Worthies of England* says 'Surely no county can show so fair a bunch of Berries for so they term the fair inhabitations of Gentlemen of rank which are called Places, Court, Halls and Manors in other shires'. In Hertfordshire Bury or Burh is very common in the sense of manor. 1638, Hoo Lane. 1778, Rigg's Lane. A well is mentioned there. *Pulridge Hill.* In 1881 the Rev. C.G. Lane gives the spelling as Poultridge. This was said to be constructed by the 7th Earl of Bridgewater (1803-23). Local people said that the name was given because of the need to have extra horses to pull carts up the hill.

Ringshall Road to Berkhamsted. This road too was said to have been made by the 7th Earl.

The Dagnall Road was also said to be the work of the 7th Earl.

He also made the road from the old Rectory (now Benhay) to the Ringshall Lodge. It could be that in some of these places he was building on earlier foundations.

Ashridge Rides and grass paths. Princes Riding is believed to have been so named after Prince Edward (afterwards King Edward VI) who rode here. This ride and Ash Riding, together with other Estate avenues and pathways were to owe much to the widow of the 7th Earl who occupied Ashridge from her husband's death in 1823 until her own death in 1849. She is credited with widening, improving and creating new pathways. In 1841 when Lady Marian Alford visited her and they went to a Ball in Berkhamsted they were guarded by outriders with loaded pistols for fear of being robbed as they passed through Berkhamsted Common.

In the spring of 1880 a new iron fence was put round the Park. This may still be seen along the park side of the Green, behind the present Rectory and along to the Hertfordshire-stile by the *Bridgewater Arms* car park. It appears in other parts of the park also.

The recognised pathways may be seen in the local maps. A few comments may be added here. The 'brick path' ran from the Green. Parts of the brickwork can still be seen by those who walk from the Adelaide Cross down into the Golden Valley. Colonel Wheatley cycled down this path. From opposite the Old Rectory, beside the present October House there were the ways leading to Dagnall and also to the Church Farm. The latter was an important lane. At one point it took a sharp right-angle turn. It went to Lamsey and also to the Church Farm. Perhaps one wonders why no evidence has yet been found of an offshoot direct to the parish church.

The present Church Road is a 20th century construction, and was the cause of considerable friction in the 1930s. Pathways to the Church include those from near the telephone exchange, and from Hudnall. It could appear that trees were planted in avenues centring on the Parish Church during the 19th century.

In 1896 Lord Brownlow made a new road to take the traffic away from the frontage of Ashridge House. A similar plan is projected today.

The Golden Valley.

This has perhaps the most interesting and romantic history of all the ways in this area. It is possible that there was a very early lane here running from Nettleden towards Ringshall . . . and from Hemel Hempstead to Ivinghoe in the wider areas. Roman pottery has been found here. The Golden Valley is the traditional way along which Princess Elizabeth was conveyed towards the Tower of London when in 1553/4 her sister Queen Mary summoned her to London and sent soldiers to convey her. The road went along the valley from Ashridge along the side of the hill . . . as seen today from Pulridge Hill, and over the crest of the hill above Nettleden, across the field (until the 1960s there was a pathway straight down to the Lady's Mile) and on to Water End. A gap in the hedge on the horizon as seen from the Lady's Mile looking towards Ashridge can still be seen. This is the way the young Princess was taken. No doubt Cromwell's troops rode this way with the horses and silver and treasures they had stolen from Ashridge when they attacked the House in 1643. It has also been used by the Ashridge families as the backcloth to their drama productions. It was possible in 1962 to walk to Nettleden along the Golden Valley from Ashridge.

Hudnall Area. In the late 18th century the lane from Hudnall Lane which passed Plum Tree Cottage and the butcher's shop turned downhill towards the Hemel Hempstead road and at that end of the lane it was called Becking Lane.

From the lane towards St Margaret's a lane curved away to the right beyond Hudnall Farm and was called Luck Lane in 1792. That name was also used in the 1920s.

LITTLE GADDESDEN VILLAGE POLICEMEN (since 1916)

1. 1916-24   George Williams
2. 1924-25   "Jock" Gray (worked from Berkhamsted)
3. 1925-32   Ernest George Aylott
4. 1932-49   Thomas Parker
5. 1949-64   Alfred Sherringham
6. 1964-68   Edward Goodwin
7. 1968-75   John Dunham
8. 1975-78   Paul Dumpleton
9. 1978-80   Gavin Murtagh
   1980- —   Richard John Abraham

Policemen Williams to Sherringham (except for Gray) lived in what is now the School House. The present Police House was built 1963/4.
The Hertfordshire Police Force has been in existence since 1841.

POPULATION OF LITTLE GADDESDEN

		Men	*Women*	*Houses*
1831	494			
1841	454	231	223	83
1851	386	182	204	83
1871	383	183	200	90
1881	373	168	205	85
1898	378			
1901	617			

(Inc. 40 families from Ivinghoe living in Ringshall area)

The list below is compiled from the Register of Electors issued each year in February and calculated at the previous October. It does not include children and those who are persons from abroad (very few in number .. perhaps half a dozen) who do not have a vote.

1965	791 (351 houses inc. 44 council houses)
1970	861
1971	891
1972	886
1973	862
1974	870
1975	875
1976	882
1977	853
1978	855
1979	859
1980	861

Little Gaddesden C. of E. School during this period had between 60 and 90 children on the roll, but at times up to one-third have resided outside the parish boundary. A very rough estimate of infants, children, teenagers at school, and young adults who have left school and do not appear on the electors' role would be about one hundred and twenty. The population increased after the former Edlesborough area in Hudnall was transferred to Little Gaddesden in 1885, and Ringshall from Ivinghoe at the same time.

The acreage of Little Gaddesden in 1841 was 910 acres. In that year there were 18 houses in Hudnall with a population of 92 there. The acreage was 668 acreas. Ringshall in 1841 had 48 houses with a population of 217.

PUBLIC RECORD OFFICE

The P.R.O. took over the buildings opposite Ashridge House in August 1951. The first documents arrived in September 1951. The records were moved to the new Records Office at Kew in 1978/9.

During the war (1939-45) Ashridge and the later P.R.O. buildings housed patients and staff from University College Hospital and Charing Cross Hospital. After Dunkirk the 51st Highland Division and the 11th Hussars were at Ashridge. From 1946-51 there was Little Gaddesden Training College for Teachers, firstly for men and then from 1947 for women also. There were 270 students trained there and 21 teaching staff.

LIST OF INCUMBENTS

1209	Julian
1215	Albanus (deacon)
1239	John
	William (died)

1276	August 7	Roger de Dukingham
		Robert (died)
1293	October 15	Richard de Heyford (resigned)
1294	April 14	Adam de Hangendchenthouton (sub deacon) (resigned)
1309	May 4	William de Aulay de Rothersthorpe (died)
1311/2	February 4	Robert de Morton (chaplain) (died)
1357	October 7	William Lille of Slipton
1361/2	February 11	Walter West of Dagenhall (resigned)
1377	May 31	John Dolimere
		John Bulmer (resigned)
1383	October 8	John Crothyn (resigned)
1384	July 6	John Okynden
		Thomas Appleby (resigned)
1410	November 3	John de Kyrkeby
1446	June 11	Henry Gustarde (resigned)
1459	March 28	Robert Browne
1463	August 25	William Evotte (resigned)
1472	February 8	Robert Fraunceys (resigned)
1473	October 18	John Hunsdon, S.T.P. Bishop of Llandaff 1458-1476 (resigned)
1480	September 1	Thomas Bramston (resigned)
1488/9	January 10	Robert Wylde (died)
1503	April 27	Ralph Nelson
c1518		John Wyatt (died)
1545	August 10	Miles Hadley, LL.B.
1558		Thomas Pickering
1573		William Wyndesor (died)
1576		Thomas Windsor
1604		Samuel Hackshaw, Curate
1612	May 1	Barnabas Holloway, M.A. (ejected April 1644)
1645	April 15	Thomas Gray
1646/7	January 10	William Adamson
1650		Thomas Draper (evicted)
1655	September 7	Richard Lee (resigned)
1658/9	March 18	Thomas Fossan, M.A. (conformed 1662) (died)
1682	December 6	Thomas Henshaw, M.A. (died)
1691	October 6	George Burghope, M.A. (died)
1713		Ralph Eddowes, M.A. (died)
1728/9	February 18	William Coleman, B.A. (died)
1743	April 27	Charles Tough, M.A. (died)
		(Also Vicar of St Pauls, Covent Garden)
1754	October 17	David Jenks, M.A. (died) (Curate from 1743)
1794	February 6	Samuel Jackson, M.A. (died)
1796	March 19	Thomas Gilbert, M.A. (deprived for non residence)
1805	April 2	Henry James Todd M.A. (resigned)
1813	March 16	James Horseman, M.A. (resigned)
1829	April 30	David Jenks, M.A. (resigned). He died Nov. 1 1869.
		(Also Rector of Aldbury, 1818-1862)
1870	January 16	Charlton George Lane, M.A. (died)
1893	April 20	Francis Henry Hodgson, M.A. (resigned)
1900	February 6	Henry George Woods, D.D. (President of Trinity College, Oxford,

1887-1900), Master of the Temple 1904) (resigned)

1904	November 17	Edward Clark, M.A. (resigned)
1919	January 14	Thomas Sydney Goudge, M.A., D.S.O. (resigned)
1924	June 3	Arthur Danvers Melanchthon Bidlake, M.A. (resigned)
1928	April 28	James Lumsden Barkway, M.A.* (later Bishop of Bedford 1935-
		1938 and of St Andrews 1938-1949, (resigned)
1934	April 17	Charles Edward Wager, B.A. (resigned)
1953	June 11	Robert Campbell Paterson, B.A. (resigned)
1959	September 5	David John Theodore Bickerton, B.A.* (resigned)
1962	February 2	Howard Senar, M.A., B.D.* (resigned Sept. 1982)

* Canon of St Albans

Some Rectors of Little Gaddesden

Thomas Fossan. His father was a merchant skinner of London. Thomas was born in 1635, educated at St Mary's Axe School and Magdalene College, Cambridge. He went to Cambridge in 1651 and became B.A. in 1654. He was admitted to Gray's Inn in 1654. He abandoned law, and was ordained. He became Master of Arts. On 18 March 1658/9 he was instituted Rector of Little Gaddesden and conformed in 1662. He was appointed Headmaster of Berkhamsted School on 14 January 1662/3. He continued to reside at the Rectory at Little Gaddesden. He was accused of neglecting the work of the school, nor had the scholars been taken to church or have daily prayers. The number of pupils which earlier had been 144, had been 70 when Fossan became Headmaster but by 1668 there were ten. He resigned after an official complaint had been made against him in 1668. He continued as Rector of Little Gaddesden until 1682. He died in 1686 and was buried at Berkhamsted on 28 March.

1794-6 *Samuel Jackson.* He is to be remembered for his beautiful writing in the Church Registers.

Gilbert, the Rev. Thomas, son of Thomas Gilbert, M.P., of Cotton, Staffordshire, gentleman.

Educated at Brasenose College, Oxford, B.A. 1794, then M.A., of Cotton Hall Staffordshire. He was born about 1762. He was inducted as Rector of Little Gaddesden 19 March 1796. He was of the same family as John Gilbert who worked with the Canal Duke of Bridgewater, and it was the Duke who presented him to the living. Thomas Gilbert senior was Chief Agent to the Duke. He was known for his work for Poor Law reform. The Rev. Robert Gilbert, curate of Ivinghoe, 1773-75, was cousin of Little Gaddesden's Rector. He was much given to horse-racing and games of chance.

There was considerable correspondence with the Bishop of Lincoln about his non-residence, and finally he was deprived of the living as a result of complaints made by the 7th Earl of Bridgewater. Various stories about Gilbert have been told. A local tradition at Cotton, his Staffordshire home, said that Gilbert fled to France about 1807, that he shot a man and that it was not known whether this was deliberate or accidental. The Gilbert family are buried in Alton churchyard on the Talbot estate in Staffordshire. Another story says that Gilbert became Clerk to the Privy Council. He was said to have died in France about 1842. On 2 April 1805 *Henry James Todd* was presented to Little Gaddesden Rectory by the Earl of Bridgewater. He was Chaplain to the 7th Earl, who preferred him to Settrington in Yorkshire. He later became Canon of York and Archdeacon of Cleveland before moving to Lambeth Palace to be Librarian to the Archbishop of Canterbury.

He wrote the great *History of Ashridge,* publishing it in two editions, the first in 1813 and enlarged in 1823. Only 200 copies of this work were published. They were given mostly as presentation copies. Todd also edited a new and enlarged edition of *Johnson's Dictionary.*

The Rev. James Horseman was inducted 16 March 1813.

The Rev. David Jenks. Rector 1829-69. He was the last of the Jenks family which had provided rectors, vicars and curates in this part of Hertfordshire and Bedfordshire for 200 years. He was nephew of the Rev. David Jenks who was Rector of Little Gaddesden 1754-94.

'Mysterious Disappearance. The Globe Newspaper, February 1839

Hemel Hempstead, Berkhamsted, Tring and the villages adjoining have been thrown into an unusual state of excitement by the sudden disappearance of the Rev. David Jenks, Rector of Little Gaddesden who has been lately appointed to the office of Rural Dean by the Bishop of Lincoln. It appears that the Rev. gentleman had during the last two or three weeks laboured under extraordinary depression of spirits, arising from some slight embarrassments into which he had been plunged by unforeseen circumstances.

On Monday 21st instant Mr Jenks left Gaddesden by the London and Birmingham Railway, in order to come to some arrangement with regard to his affairs. On arriving in London he went to an hotel, ordered dinner to be prepared in the course of an hour, left his carpet-bag and went out promising to be back in time for dinner. From that time he has not been heard of, and not the slightest clue to his discovery has been found.

We are informed that Mr Jenks, in addition to the Rectory of Little Gaddesden, holds also the Rectory of Aldbury in Buckinghamshire and is Chaplain to the Countess of Bridgewater.'

Mr Jenks' movements after this episode are not clear. However, he continued as Rector of Little Gaddesden for another 30 years. He died in office aged 84, and his burial stone is the monument surmounted by a cross beneath the south exterior wall of the tower.

In his younger days he was a very able horseman and a capital shot. He understood the habits of the game he was pursuing. He remembered the planting of the trees on the village green, and the park opposite the Rectory (now Benhay), and also when there was no carriage drive to Ashridge. He would not countenance any change to the liturgy. He used Tate and Brady Hymns and a barrel organ in the gallery at the west end of the church until his death. He was opposed to chanting in a village church, although he approved highly of Cathedral services. 'He never spoke unkindly of anyone. Shrewd, lively, playful, genial, showed kindliness to God's creatures, fond of children, clear blue eyed.' 'The artist Millais was greatly impressed with the vigour of the old Rector when he heard him preach. A very rich voice in reciting the liturgy even at 84'. These are comments from his successor the Rev. C.G. Lane. When Lady Marian Alford presented a harmonium to Little Gaddesden School in 1858, it was suggested that it be used in church on Sundays, but Rector Jenks objected and it was not so used.

The Rev. Charlton George Lane — 1869-92: He was born on St Barnabas Day, 11 June 1836 at Kennington where his father was for many years the Vicar, and close to the Oval Cricket ground. He went to Westminster School where for five years he played in the cricket XI and in 1853 he was captain. He passed to Christ Church, Oxford, where he was known as the Admirable Crichton of the University because of his ability to change his sport. He rowed three times for the university, twice at Putney (1858 and 1859) and once at Henley (1859). He played four years in the university cricket XI, being captain in 1860. He won the university racquets, played five years for the Gentlemen v. Players and was asked to captain the first English XI proposed to be taken to Australia . . . indeed the first to be taken to the colonies.

He was at the same time member of the select fraternity at Oxford known as the 'Hogarth Club' of which Millais, William Morris, Holman Hunt, Burne-Jones, Rossetti and Maddox Browne were also prominent in the Pre-Raphaelite movement. He was an artist of no mean attainment. Whilst at Christ Church he came under the influence of Stanley (later Dean Stanley) and valued greatly his lectures. He took his degree in 1860 and then acted as tutor to the future 2nd and 3rd Earls Brownlow, thus laying the foundations of a lifelong friendship. On being ordained he served as curate at Great Witley, Edlesborough and Little Gaddesden. In 1869 he was presented to the living of Little Gaddesden by Earl Brownlow. There he remained until his death 22 years later. He was also private chaplain and librarian to Lord Brownlow. He was on the Board of Management of the Mercers Company. He was Master of the Company in 1890.

His work in the parish of Little Gaddesden followed that of the Rev. David Jenks who had been Rector for 40 years and died aged 84. Lane's work was revolutionary in both church and parish. The Holy Communion was celebrated more frequently, weekday services were held, services became choral, and a choir was built up, with regular weekly practices, annual outings, and dinners. There were carols at Christmas and Epiphany, Advent and Lent services, and Harvest Thanksgiving. He introduced *Hymns Ancient and Modern*, and choristers in surplices. There were adult bible classes, lectures, readings, a glee club, a brass band, men's meetings, clothing and medical clubs, penny banks, mothers' meetings, a village lending library and reading room. He was remembered for his profound reverence for holy things, for his broad sympathies, for his love of art and nature, for his tact, for his sympathy and understanding. He was responsible with Earl Brownlow and Lady Marian Alford for the introduction of the organ, and for the major restoration and rebuilding of the Church.

The Prince of Wales was one of those who wrote a letter of condolence after Lane's death. It was said that His Royal Highness had at one time offered Mr Lane the Vicarage of Sandringham. He also had been offered that of Berkhamsted, St Peter. His first wife whom he had married on 13 July 1871 died in 1883. The reredos was in her memory. He married Adela Talbot on 24 January 1888 and she survived him. She died on 17 March 1936. He died on 2 November 1892 and was buried on Saturday 5 November 1892.

The Rev. Francis Henry Hodgson – Rector 1893-1900. Educated at Eton, and Trinity College, Cambridge, M.A. Curate of Edlesborough, Curate of Hemel Hempstead, Vicar of Abbots Langley 1879-93, Rural Dean of Watford 1884-1893, Rector of Little Gaddesden 20 April 1893 to 1900. He was then presented to the living of Escrick, York by Lord Wenlock.

He was the son of Sir Arthur Hodgson K.C.M.G. of Stratford on Avon, and brother of Edward Dowling Hodgson of Clopton, Warwickshire (who died 6 June 1896). Sir Arthur lectured at Little Gaddesden on historical subjects, Cardinal Wolsey and Queen Elizabeth I.

On 3 June 1896 the Rev. F.H. Hodgson was married in Winchester Cathedral to the Hon. Odeyne de Grey (sister of Mrs Talbot of Little Gaddesden), Lord Walsingham her brother gave her away. On 5 September 1897 (Sunday) the baptism of Avis Odeyne daughter of the Rector and Mrs Hodgson (Elizabeth Odeyne de Grey) took place.

(N.B. The Rector went to Warwickshire for his brother's funeral. Note dates)

The Rev. H.G. Woods – 1900-04. President of Trinity College, Oxford 1887-1900, became Rector in 1900 but left in 1904 as his wife's health was not able to stand the Little Gaddesden climate. He brought many well-known preachers to Little Gaddesden including the Bishops of Oxford (Dr Paget) and Hereford (Dr Perceval). He gave lectures in the Reading Room (John O'Gaddesden's) 'and I allowed 2 card games, Whist and Beggar my Neighbour' 1903. The new Parish Magazine only lasted for two years. The Rector was relieved because he also had to bear the annual deficit. In 1904 the Prime Minister wrote to say he had the King's permission to invite him to be Master of the Temple. In his farewell sermon he said: 1. Weekly communicants should have been much better. 2. There was idle and uncharitable gossip criticism of neighbours and repeating of rumours. 3. Advent, Lent and Ascension day attendances were not as good as they ought to be.

FROM THE REGISTERS

		s.	d.
1675	Received from Mr Cotton for the Town Acre	6.	8
1675	For Whitsun Communion	1.	4
1675	For banding and glazing ye church windows	5.	7
1675	For bread and wine at East	2.	6
1675	Mending churchyard gates and ye bell wheel	5.	10
1675	For washing ye surplice and ye communion cloth four times this year	10.	0
1677	Four new bellropes	12.	6
1677	From Daniel Cotton for his rent for Church acre	7.	0
	For a prayer book	1.	0

1679	For a lock for the north church door and getting it on		4. 8
1680	For the register book of Parchment		10. 0
1680	For the apparator for his dinner and expenses for his board and horse meat		9. 0
1682	For mending ye church communion prayer book		5. 0
1682	For catching 3 foxes		13. 4
1682	Paid for the man for raysing the great bell which was falled down		1. 0
	For a new bellrope and for work on the bell wheels		3. 0
1683	Paid ye ringers for 5 November		5. 0
1684	Considerable work was done on the church roof in this year – ye plummer		3. 5. 9
		carpenter	5. 0
		bricklayer	6. 4
	For new lead and carting old away		2. 0
	For 32 foot of oak boards		5. 0
1686	For 80 foot of oaken boards to mend ye Bellfree and for a new gate in ye north isle		13. 4
	There appears to have been a new floor in the belfry loft		
	Nayles and oyle for ye bell wheeles		1. 6
1688	Paid ye ringers at ye bonfire		4. 8
1718	Or mending ye lock on ye iron trunk at church		3. 0
	Given ye ringers for ye Victory at Blenein		4. 6
1706	Expended at ye parochial procession (i.e. Rogationtide)		14. 0
	Given ye ringers at ye Victory at Ramillies		1. 0
	To Mr Austin of Watford for repair and making good ye church clock		5. 12. 6
1708	For making a surplice paid to Mr How for Holland to make ye surplice		2. 1. 3
	For ye Master of Arts hood for Mr Eddoes by order of ye bishop		10. 0
1711	Paid at Mr Greenwood's the parishioners charges when they want a processioning		1. 3. 2
1713	Paid ye charges of ye triennial preambulation of ye bounds of ye parish		1. 3. 4
1715	Paid ye appartor for a book for ye thanksgiving and for an order to alter the names of ye royal family		2. 0
	Paid for an order to punish immorality		1. 6
1716	Recd. of ye Earl of Bridgewater for one year's annuity for shutting up ye way thro the Red-Deer Park		5. 0
	Pd. ye ringers upon ye birth of ye young prince		5. 0
1721	To Mr Ellis for writing out accounts		2. 0
	Pd. Mr Groom for covering the tower with milled lead at 5 cwt. to the foot as also for oak boards timber locks and workmanshipp		3. 16. 0
1724	Mending ye clock		9. 4
	Mending ye bell frame		13. 6
	New painting the dyall		2. 6
	Pd. Mrs Hickman for beer, bread and cheese and dressing dinner for ye processioning		16. 6
	Mr Edw. Thorn for meat for processioning		10. 6
1724	For mending the pulpit cloth for silk and mending		1. 0
	the hood		3. 0
	given a great bellied woman		1. 0
1728	Pd. the parator for an inquestment and the benefit after Mr Eddows (rector's) death		5. 6
1731	Thos. Groom for a new crown staple into the second bell		10. 0

	Nat. Vyze (clerk) a year's wages	17. 0
	Sam Haws for looking after clock for 1732	10. 2
	Fary's bill for whitewashing ye church	1. 15. 4
	Thos. Groom for building an addition to the gallery	10. 6
1741	40 sheets of parchment for making a register book	3. 3. 0
1745	Bread and wine for mickelmus	8. 2
1746	6 sparrows	1
	24 sparrows	4
	Dec. 25 Chresmus comven	8. 2
1749	Pd. a bricklayer and labourer for church work half a day	1. 3
1752	Charges at beshepis fesetesoteon	18. 10
	Expences at Welen	13. 10
	Cresmis Comvon	8. 2
1753	Ester Comvon	8. 2
	Pd. for an act of palement	1. 6
	For bear for the workmen	1. 0
1754	Pd. for 2 bootens for the surplis	1
1755	Possoning (processioning) for beer at Brockmar	5. 0
	Bread and cheese and booter Brockmar	2. 6
	Jeams bell for beer	14. 0
	Jeams bell for puding and dresin for backen	2. 6
	Jeams Bell for beef, veal and lame	10. 10
1759	Horse hire for 3 churchwardens	6. 0
	Pd. for 11 ells of holland at 4s/3d and ell for a new surplice	2. 6. 9
	For making a surplice/mending the old surplice	10. 6
1760	2 locks for the chest	3. 6
1761	Recd. from ye Duke of Bridgewater for church acre	12. 0
1762	New bell ropes (4)	1. 0. 6
1762	April 2, pd. ye clerk for taking snow out of church	1. 0
1763	Pd. Mr Arnott for drawing ye dyall	10. 0
	Pd. Wm. Hore for painting ye dyall	3. 6
	For a new bible for ye church	1. 1. 0

Constables Accounts

1687	For carrying the hue and cry to Dagnall in the night	4
	do to Ringshall in the night	4
	do do daytime	2
	Pd. to the Goale Treason and House of Correction	5. 5
1688	For carrying 14 gypsies to Ringshall	2
1692	For a Lancashire woman whose husband was taken by the French	1. 0
	For a musket	1. 0. 0
	For 3 new swords from London	2. 2. 0
	Scouring the musketts, powder and ball	2. 0
	To carrying cripples to Dagnall, Ringhall and Nettledine	1. 1. 1
	For searching houses for felons	4. 4
	Constable's wages for the year 1692	15. 0
	For carrying Ann Groom before the Justices and then to the house of correction	3. 0
	Towards nuns bridge repairing	2. 1
1697	Carrying 76 cripples to Ringsole, Hudnall, Nettledine, Aldbury, Dagnall	2. 11. 9

	For carrying our cripple to Witchcraft	1.	0
1693	For searching for vagabonds and aid to assist me	1.	0
	For rebuilding Hertford goal and for bridge money	1. 17.	8
1675	For passing the hue and cry for horses stolen		2
	For Robt. Ivby, Will Alta and Will Edmunds after his commitment to ye guardians	3.	6
	Henry Tedder to carry him to Hertford goal	4.	6
	For passing a hue and cry after a robbery		2
1676	Paid for the parish share for 2 robberies in the hundred	16.	10
1685	For mending the older muskett	2.	6
	For a new muskett	14.	0
	Paid Sam Hall for mending the muskett and cleaning the sword	1.	0
1687	For Thomas Allen alias Goodem who was taken in this town at Thomas Bulmers. Paid for taking him to the goal.	1.	0
	Paid to Matthew Hoare, Thomas Emarton and James Olding for watching one night & one day, Thomas Allen.	4.	6

ROGATIONTIDE PROCESSIONS 'Processioning', 'Beating the Bounds'.

When Humphry Repton was staying at Ashridge preparing his plans for the gardens he witnessed the Rogationtide procession across the Ashridge Estate.

On Friday, 11 June 1813, William Buckingham records in his diary preparing the bread and cheese required for the persons perambulating Ivinghoe parish and Little Gaddesden. Then he went to meet the 'perambulators'. Ringshall was included in this and they went to the *Horns* for refreshment and on to Little Gaddesden to the Park, where they were met by Lord Bridgewater and Repton and went through part of the boundary through the park and round to St Margaret's, Great Gaddesden, Pipers Hill, Nettleden and up the park to the Red Gate. There they gave a barrel of beer to the company. There was another perambulation on the following day. Rogationtide processions were revived in the 1960s and 1970s.

ROMAN REMAINS

Digging to the west of Little Gaddesden church showed that there was a Romano-British settlement of the first two centuries A.D. There was no evidence to prove later occupation in the part excavated. The sherd of blue-grey pottery fragments were deposited in Little Gaddesden C. of E. School. They were identified and dated by Jacquetta Hawkes.

Coins found in the Little Gaddesden area include (found 1967)—
1. Coin of Emperor Commodus dated 186 A.D. (he became Emperor 180 A.D.) and took the title Britannicus in 184 A.D. He was assassinated in 193 A.D. 2. Coin of Carausius 287-93 A.D. (minted in London). 3. Found 1977. 32 'Barbarous Radiates' include coins of the Emperor Claudius II (268-70), Emperor Victorinus (of Cologne) (268-70) and Emperor Tetricus II (273/4)
Roman Road
The Roman Road from Verulamium to Ivinghoe Beacon passes through the village (see *The Viatores, Roman Roads in the S.E. Midlands*. Gollancz 1964). Mr Richard Wyatt Bagshawe one of the 'Viatores' has permitted the following extract to be quoted.

> From Great Gaddesden the road ascended through a cutting to St Margaret's, and after turning slightly north it continued straight for nearly a mile past St Margaret's Farm, and the site of the 12th century St Margaret's convent. This stretch points to Ivinghoe Beacon 5 miles to the North-West. Past the NW end of St Margaret's Lane a low agger is visible in the NE edge of the field running for a ¼ mile as far as a pond in the NNW corner. After this there is no sign for ¾ mile except for a heavy scatter of flint by the SW corner of Hudnall Common which may be the ploughing up of the road metalling. The agger is then visible running for 150 yards across the field between a narrow

spinney which runs N-S, and Hudnall Lane. NW of Hudnall Lane there is no sign across the first field for 300 yards, and then a footpath marks the course for ¼ mile through the fields east south east of the village of Little Gaddesden. The path bears to the north, 300 yards east south east of Bede Court, and there is no further sign for 600 yards, where the line runs across the fields east of the *Bridgewater Arms*.

From the bend at the North end of the village by the former Rectory, now Benhay, the modern Little Gaddesden-Ringshall road takes up the course and marks it for the next ½ mile to just short of Ringshall Lodge, where the road turns west-north-west. It is interesting to note that this stretch of road is shown on the early maps . . . and is aligned direct on Ivinghoe Beacon. Past the turn, after 100 yards the road is marked by the west side of the Ringshall-Berkhamsted road by a short length of the Bucks-Herts boundary, after which the agger is visible for nearly ½ a mile to the north of the present Ringshall-Ivinghoe road. At the SE corner of Dockey Wood the road begins to coincide with the modern road for over a mile, a change being made on the high point SE of Crawley Wood. In the grassy area to the W of the main road just beyond the woods (now a car park) a low agger is visible followed by a hollow way to the NE of Steps Hills.

Hereabouts the Romanised Icknield Way is crossed. As the Roman road continues along the ridge of the Ivinghoe Hills it coincides with a group of parallel banks and ditches. The course is then marked by a footpath to the west of the 700 feet high hill and then forks into 2 branches. It seems probable that the road was not taken any further in a NW direction.

Wards Combe

The site has a long history. This is in an area with Iron Age remains. Evidence has been discovered of early and late Bronze Age habitation. Roman material has been found and two Belgic cremation burials. One Roman cremation burial urn and Romano-British sherds have been found. The site extended from 300 B.C. to 130 A.D. Mr John Wilson called attention to this site.

Gadebridge

This site was occupied from 75 A.D. Mosaic work of 319 A.D. is amongst the earliest in Britain. The bath is second only to Aquae Sulis (Bath) in Britain, and 309 coins were discovered in the excavations, of which the latest was dated 348 A.D.

A Roman mulling-stone, found at Ringshall by Mr Bagshawe is now in the Luton Museum.

SEATS

The seat at Hudnall Corner bus stop is to commemorate the Jubilee of the Women's Institute. Seats on the Green commemorate the Silver Jubilee of the Queen in 1977. The carving is by Leslie Ouseley. There are commemorative seats on the playing field. One seat facing north in the churchyard is in memory of George Stanbridge. The one in the West Ground is in memory of Winifred Dorothea Patterson, July 1970.

THE ROYAL SILVER JUBILEE 1977 – Sunday, 5 June and Monday, 6 June

Arrangements for the Jubilee included— A Thanksgiving Service in the parish church, which was decorated by representatives of 20 organisations from Little Gaddesden. The choir was augmented for the occasion. The lessons were read by Mr Colin Revell (Chairman of the Parish Council) and Mr S.P. Whaley (Dacorum Councillor). The Rector preached. Another service was held on the Festival Day itself. At the Annual Village Sports on 4 June the prizes were crown pieces minted for the Jubilee. On 6 June there was a gymkhana arranged by the Craib family. An Old English Fair was a central attraction. Mr R. Johnson recited poetry, and there was a procession of characters from the history of Little Gaddesden and Ashridge, together with an accompanying band. There was a maypole and Morris dancing, a ladies and gents cricket match, sideshows, terrier racing, a perambulator show. Two hundred and fifty went on a walk to Ashridge College where they were entertained to tea. Refreshments were provided in front of the Village Hall for the over-60s. In the evening there was a country and western barbecue. A supper dance was held and many other items.

Mr Cyril Buzzacott was the indefatigable Chairman of the Festival Committee.

Two seats were placed on the Green suitably made and inscribed. They cost £50. The profit made on the day was £290, and £190 was donated to the Village Hall committee. A souvenir book was produced containing photographs, signatures and general information about the festivities.

The over-60s visited London travelling the route of the royal procession and went to St Paul's Cathedral to see the decorations and the flowers. This took place two days after the royal celebrations.

TREES

Ashridge. The yew trees standing at the south end of the terrace, adjoining the Italian garden are of the 17th century. They may have been placed there in succession to earlier yews of the monastic period.

The 3rd Duke of Bridgewater, the Canal Duke, invited Lancelot (Capability) Brown to advise on the layout of the Park, and a major work was projected. Brown used Holland to help with the work. Between 1759 and 1769 Brown was paid £3,000 for his work. Brown worked here in the 1780s as well. There was an avenue of lime trees planted in the 17th century . . . the origin of the Lime Walk. Humphry Repton advised the 7th Earl. Some of his plans were carried out, but most were modified. The great cedars along Ringshall Drive and elsewhere are of the 18th century. Ashridge had three fine specimen trees (see *Trees of Great Britain and Ireland*, Elwes and Henry). They were the King Beech, the Queen Beech and the King Ash.

The King Beech was blown down in 1891. It was the largest and finest beech in Ashridge. It was said in 1844 to be 114 ft. high with a clear trunk of 75 ft. (Loudon).

The Queen Beech. In 1903 its height was given 135 ft., girth 12 ft. 3 ins. The straight branchless bole was given as 80 ft. Elwes said: 'This is the greatest height of a deciduous tree apart from an elm, in Great Britain'. It was blown down in the gale of 14 November 1928 and the measurements were 72 ft. to the first branch and just over 110 ft. over all. Its quarter girth at 4 ft. 3 ins. from the ground was 3 ft. 6 ins. It was hollow for 15 ft. from its base.

The King Ash. On 1906 it was said to be 125-130 ft. high with a straight stem of 75 ft. and girth 11 ft. 10 ins. It was struck by lightning and completely destroyed on 27 May 1929. Its timber height was 102 ft. and there were 132 rings. Its butt was hollow for 9 ft. the quarter girth was 3 ft. 6 ins. at 4 ft. 3 ins.

Trees had been planted by Queen Victoria (the oak with an inscription dated 1823). The Shah of Persia also planted a tree in 1889. When the Liquidambar walk was planted in 1936 beneath some of the trees the members of the staff who planted them at the ceremony placed information about the year, and the work of the person planting.

The Rev. David Jenks remembers the planting of the trees on the Village Green. He was Rector from 1829-69.

Wild cherries were planted on the Green after the Second World War one to represent each man killed in the war. In 1953 Coronation year, trees were planted in the playing field, together with one seat. The planting took place 1955/6. There were two double cherries, two common beech, two common oak and one mountain ash. A golden foliage tree was planted opposite the Manor House, provided by Canon Rollo Meyer who lived there. A scarlet oak nearby has a plaque commemorating the local men killed in World War Two. A Liquidambar was planted in 1965 by the members of the Women's Institute between the Manor House and Hudnall Corner to commemorate their Golden Jubilee year.

Kingham's Meadow has a fine specimen swamp cypress (*Taxodium distichum*). This is a deciduous tree, unique amongst conifers in that it will grow standing in water, and grows at the edge of ponds with its root in very moist and waterlogged soil. Cherry trees were planted in Little Gaddesden churchyard in the west section in 1964 and later. Wild cherries were planted in 1971 in memory of Charles Miller who was Parochial Church Council Secretary.

VISITORS

1123, Henry I passed through Little Gaddesden after keeping Christmas at Dunstable, on his way to Berkhamsted Castle. He was at Berkhamsted in 1135.

1290, Edward I at Ashridge.

25 Sept. 1295. *Bishop Oliver Sutton* of Lincoln bestowed his blessing, solemnly on William of Woodford the new Abbot of Peterborough. He was at Gatesden when he bestowed the blessing. He had previously been at Ashridge in 1286.

Edward the Black Prince spent time in luxury in Berkhamsted and was also at Ashridge. He died in 1376. Ashridge College was a beneficiary under his will.

John Skelton, poet *c.* 1523.

Leland. He wrote his *Itinerary* and visited Gaddesden during his journeys. He presented his work to King Henry VIII. Henry was at Ashridge and Little Gaddesden at Christmas 1530, and in 1543. The Prince Edward and Princess Mary and Elizabeth stayed at Ashridge in 1543. A Privy Council was held at Ashridge in 1543. In 1553 Princess Elizabeth was here (having been given Ashridge by her brother, King Edward VI in 1551). In 1643 Cromwell's troops under Captain Washington damaged Ashridge and forced their way into the Little Gaddesden church vaults.

Charles II came as a child, and later issued a warrant to preserve the game.

1748 Peter Kalm, Swedish Naturalist. 1823 Princess Victoria. 1887. The Prince and Princess of Wales (future Edward VII). The Princess visited the Bede Houses. 1889, visit of the Shah of Persia. 1897, the Duke of Westminster rented the Ashridge shooting and resided there with his family in December. In 1900, the Dean of Westminster spent time here. King George V and Queen Mary spent time as children at Ashridge and enjoyed playing on the roofs. Lord Kitchener was at Ashridge on the eve of World War One. In the 1930s many political leaders, especially from the Conservative Party were at Ashridge. George VI visited the war time hospital at Ashridge, and Hudnall Farm. On two occasions Prince Philip, Duke of Edinburgh, visited Ashridge Management College.

WAR TIME

Ballam, Sergeant-Major John. He was one of the best-known characters of the 19th century in Little Gaddesden. Born in Ireland he enlisted in the 8th King's Regiment in November 1834. He served in the West Indies and North America and then underwent the hardships of the Crimean campaign, serving in the trenches and at the fall of Sebastopol. He was offered a commission which he declined. He retired from the army with a pension in 1857 after being wounded by a shell splinter at the storming of the Redan. In 1860 he was appointed Sergeant-Major (his current rank) to the Hertfordshire Battalion of the Rifle Volunteers. He held that position for 23 years. In Little Gaddesden he was prominent in the life of the parish where his military bearing and sterling qualities earned him the great respect and affection of the whole community. He was buried 11 March 1893.

The First World War 1914-18. Lord Brownlow had a small hospital at Ashridge. The Coach House was the ward. There was room for 24 patients. There was one officer and three nurses, two trainee nurses, a cook and a housemaid. The Matron lived at Red Lodge.

The Second World War 1939-45. University College and Charing Cross Hospitals were evacuated to Ashridge. Sixteen wards each with 40 beds were erected opposite the main College. There was an operating theatre. These were built in in 1940 just before the arrival of 500 men from Dunkirk. There were two wards in the House itself . . . the Lecture Room (former drawing-room) for women and the Common Room (Brown Lounge) for men. There were 20,000 patients, 12,820 operations and 3,000 births.

Seven hundred bombs of various types were dropped in and about the parish, but little damage was done. One water pipe was cut. On summer evenings in 1944 flights of bombers looked like swarms of gnats as they flew over south.

General de Gaulle resided at Rodinghead after the fall of France.

King George VI paid a very private visit during the war to Ashridge. At the same time he had lunch with his officers at Hudnall Farm in the apple sheds. Only the people living at the Farm were aware of the visit. The 11th Dragoon Guards were billeted here for some time. Very large army camps were established on Ringshall Common in preparation for the invasion of Europe. The largest tanks and guns rumbled through the lanes and fields. Dutch and Polish soldiers encamped near the Monument. The first arrival of evacuees from London was on 1 September 1939. Some of them travelled from London's Gospel Oak Station to Berkhamsted. Their parents were not told of their destination. They arrived at the old Little Gaddesden Village Hall and were soon provided with billets. They attended Little Gaddesden C. of E. School and played a full part in the School Farm projects of pig-keeping, vegetable growing and marketing. The severity of the 1940/1 winter opened their eyes to the beauty of the snow, hedge high in Hudnall and on the road to the *Bridgewater Arms*. Lasting friendships were made. Mrs John Rogers met her future husband. Mr R. Waters also remained and he too later married here. In both cases the earlier background developed into closest ties with Little Gaddesden and the school.

The Home Guard. No. 5 Platoon 7b Company Hertfordshire Home Guard developed from the Local Defence Volunteers who wore arm bands with L.D.V., on them. The Commanding Officer was Major Neville Grey Q.C. who lived at the Red House. This address became the Command Headquarters, and on the first night a guard was immediately set up, with John Oakins and Alec Andrews to guard the Headquarters. They were provided with rations for the night. After midnight every person passing through the village had to be challenged and identified. The guards were changed during the night. Wire was ready for stretching across the road to trap enemy motor cyclists. Major A.G. Wykeham-Musgrave M.C. was in command of the section. Another Headquarters was at the Four Ways area. Later Vicars Bell and Horace Halsey were in command there, and they patrolled the portion of the road towards Hemel Hempstead covered by the area maps, Nobody's Bottom and the fields and woodlands.

The third Headquarters was at Deer Leap in a wooden shed which was formerly a tea house for the swimming pool. The pool was emptied so that water would not reflect and draw the attention of bombers. Jack Mayling was one of the many on duty here. The Section Leader was E.H. Tyler. A fourth Headquarters was at the Ashridge Golf Club where Major Hopkins was at the time platoon commander. Section Leader Richardson was also in command. It was manned by day only. There were 50-60 members of the Home Guard and manoeuvres were a regular part of their work, so that they knew every part of the parish thoroughly. George Wright became a sergeant; J.M. Finn and L. Lane were corporals. One night they watched as a stick of incendiary bombs fell near Well Farm in a stook of standing corn. The stook did not catch light to the surprise of the watchers. The district covered was Little Gaddesden, Nettleden, Hudnall, St Margaret's, Ringshall and Ashridge. In March 1941 Church Farm was ordered to be an observation post, to be manned from one hour before, to half-an-hour after 'Black-out'. No. 5 Platoon responded to many calls that parachutists were dropping. These were mostly escaped barrage balloons or imagination. On the night of 28 August 1940 a warning caused the manning of the Ringshall post and the searching of Ivinghoe and Dagnall Roads. Sixteen high explosive bombs (four unexploded), two oil drums and hundreds of incendiary bombs fell within ¾ mile of the post. Altogether over a hundred high explosives and hundreds of incendiary bombs fell in the platoon area during August and October 1940.

Roll of Honour 1914-1919

Vernon Batchelor	The Hertfordshire Regiment
William Fenn	The Hertfordshire Regiment
George Hoar	The Hertfordshire Regiment
William Mayling	The Hertfordshire Regiment
Arthur Whitman	The Hertfordshire Regiment

Charles Batchelor	The Bedfordshire Regiment
Frederick Purton	The Bedfordshire Regiment
Alfred Mead	The Bedfordshire Regiment
William Cook	The Bedfordshire Regiment
Albert Bierton	The Middlesex Regiment
William Cooper	The Royal Field Artillery
James Dunn	The Machine Gun Corps
Arthur Fowler	The Shropshire Light Infantry
Alfred Garment	The Northamptonshire Regiment
Bertram Gentle	The King's Royal Rifles
Edward Groom	The Royal West Surrey Regiment
Walter Holland	The Rifle Brigade
Alexander Johnson	The Royal Engineers
Frank Johnson	The Royal Berkshire Regiment
Samuel Oakins	The Royal Engineers
William White	The Royal Fusiliers
George Pinnock	H.M.S. Black Prince
Geoffrey Talbot	The Royal Naval Air Service

1939-1945

Henry Gordon	The Gordon Highlanders
Duncan Gray	The Rifle Brigade
Leonard Hing	The Royal Artillery
William Newman	The Royal Air Force
Ian Patterson	The Royal Artillery
Edward Rogers	The Suffolk Regiment

WATER

The well at Ashridge dates from the time of the College, and probably earlier. It is 224 ft. deep. For the top 28 ft. it is bricked. Below that it is cut through solid chalk. When it was cleaned in 1970 the water level above the mud was 25 ft. The water level rose to 38 ft. by April 1971. At 141 ft. there is an arched recess. The well was mentioned in an inquisition of Queen Elizabeth I in 1575. Earlier, in the time of Henry VIII, dogs were used to help to raise the water. By 1681 Thomas Baskerville could write of the horse drawing up continuously two buckets. In 1778 the water was only 18 ft. deep and in 1779 it was 16½ ft. deep. In 1830 Joseph Harrington 'for attending with the two horses to draw water and some carting' received £58 6s. 4d. for the year.

In 1778 there was a severe water shortage. The pond on the hill called Blew Pot was cleaned. Most of the ponds were very dry and water was scarce and very bad. Mr Elton's well was very dry and he sunk it 10 ft. deeper. Several inhabitants sent barrels to fetch water from Water End for family use. The well in Rigg's Lane was very dry. In 1780 the Rectory pond was cleaned. It had not been cleaned for 60 years. It was cleaned again in 1835. In 1870 it was filled in and the road to the stables was made across it. There was a well in Witchcraft in 1828 from which John Henry Buckingham drew water for his *Robin Hood* Beer House.

The Ringshall well was by the former Fountain's Stores. Water was pumped from here. In 1855 it was 250 ft. deep. It was said not to belong to anyone. In 1855 the well at the Home Farm was 235 ft. deep. In 1855 Seymour's well was 202 ft. The Church Farm well was 224 ft. The well at John O Gaddesden's was 217 ft. Ashridge Pumping Station was built at Little Gaddesden at what was the Works Yard behind the Red House. The Reservoir was built at Ringshall Meadows. The mains reached to Ashridge, Hudnall, Little Gaddesden and Ringshall. This work was completed

1856-58. Previously water was carried by bucket from the wells to the houses.

The pump was driven by a steam beam engine which had two horizontal boilers. The high chimney-stack was demolished by blasting in the early 1930s. The boom engine booked for a museum was taken for scrap. The first electric pump was installed in 1930. Extensions have been laid to St Margaret's, Hudnall Fields, Four Ways, Cold Harbour Farm, and part of Frithsden. The well of the pumping station was dug by hand, 6 ft. diameter down to 255 ft. and a bore hole to 317 ft. below the surface, with headings running NW for 50 ft. and SE for 100 ft. Consumption in 1930 was about 20,000 gallons per day.

In 1980 it was between 130,000 and 200,000 gallon per day according to season. Of the other wells, three are known and two have been lost. All are over 200 ft. deep. The known ones are at Ashridge, Home Farm and Ringshall. There was one at Hudnall Farm. Mr Horace Halsey was 'Waterman' for this area for many years and after his retirement he was in continual demand.

Part Five

14. *The Parish organisations*

THE ART CLUB

The club was founded in 1945, and each summer since 1946 has organised a two or three-day Exhibition. The openers of the annual event have included Lady Davidson, Lady Paget, Judge Shepherd, Mr Dorian Williams, Miss Erhart, Miss Emily Hahn, Mrs Wager, Miss M. Ritchie, Brigadier Hindley and N. Shelley. In earlier years the society had a stall at Hemel Hempstead Market.

Members who have had their work exhibited at the Royal Academy have included Mrs I.

Foord-Kelcey, Brian Bennett, Jennifer Andrews and Mrs Hill-Smith. Portraits have been hung in the Royal Portrait Society's Exhibitions including the work of Mr Pring, and in the Royal Institute of Oil Painters, work by Mr Pipkin.

Others have exhibited in the Royal Society of British Artists and the School of Marine Artists (Christopher Greaves).

The Society has had regular instructors in various aspects of their work including Mr Wynn Thomas, Mr Geoffrey Drewitt and Mr Bernard Adams. Talks have included those by Brian Bennett (Misericords); Mr J. Harvey (Modern Ideas of Craft Education); Harry Sheldon (Water Colour); Gordon Beningfield (Wild Life Art); C. Hart (B.B.C. Design); and R. Pook (Screen Arrangements).

Members have many venues, including the homes of members, visits to the Stanhope Art Club, the Grand Union Canal, Woodcock Hill, Peacock's Wood and Broadway Farm. Visits have included one to Winsor & Newton's Harrow Factory.

The Society has exhibited at the Parish Craft Fairs at Little Gaddesden. Members including Miss Dorothea Patterson and G. Webb have held their own exhibitions.

THE ARTHRITIS AND RHEUMATISM GROUP

The local branch was established in the summer of 1972 and the first effort at Witchcraft Hill raised £70. Since then there have been annual Christmas fairs, cheese and wine parties, fork suppers, concerts by the Vauxhall Male Voice Choir, a garden luncheon and coffee mornings. In 1979 the sum of £1,200 was sent to the Council. The autumn Coffee Morning of 1980 raised £100; the Fork Supper £420 and the Christmas Fair £1,000. The November Fair 1981 raised £1,025 and the total for 1981 a record £1,700. Members receive the journal of the society and are kept well informed about the Research Programme made possible by their work and that of other branches.

ASHRIDGE ARTISAN GOLF CLUB

The Gaddesden Golfing Society was founded on 24 June 1946 at the Old Fire Station, now 'Saxons'. The first President was Major J.N. Gray K.C. On his return from H.M. Forces in September Mr John Oakins was temporarily appointed secretary, a position which he continued to hold in 1981.

On 10 May 1950 the present title for the club was adopted. The affiliation fee paid to the Artisan Golfers' Association was £1. In 1980 The Ashridge Artisan Gold Club paid £16 for affiliation.

The trophies and medals include—
The News of the World Medal
The Wellwisher Cup
The Aggregate Cup
The Gray Challenge Cup
The Hock Trophy
The Home Guard Cup
The Smith Bowls
The Napier Trophy
The Captain's Prize
The N.J.R. Trophy
The J. Hughes Pot
A selection of past winners of trophies
1956   Dr White's Cup, J. Oakins and W. Maynard
1956   The Home Guard and Gray Cup, K. Geater
1956   The Greer Cup, J. Oakins
1956   *The News of the World* Medal, S. Oakins.

ASHRIDGE ARTISAN GOLF CLUB
Presidents

1946	Major J.N. Gray K.C.
1951	Major W.H. Greer
1967	Mr G.H. Smith
1969	Mr J.M. Finn
1975	Mr R.J. Simpson

ASHRIDGE ARTISAN GOLF CLUB
Captains

1946-49	F. Liberty "The Gaddesden Golfing Society"
1950	F. Liberty Ashridge Artisan Golf Club
1951	F. Hucklesby
1952-58	W. Maynard
1959	K. Page
1960	L. Potter
1961	L. Nash
1962	L. Potter
1963	K. Geater
1964	G. Peryer
1965	J. Slatter
1966	W. Maynard
1967	T. Kempster
1968	R. Batchelor
1969	G. Walton
1970	J. McAllister
1971	B. Freake
1972	L. Nash
1973	H. Edwards
1974	F. Fantham
1975	G. Thompson
1976	J. Milsom
1977	W. Kempster
1978	K. Geater
1979	A. Oxley
1980	E. Ford
1981	J. Tarrant

Hon. Secretary 1946-81 John Oakins

BEST KEPT VILLAGE

In 1957 Little Gaddesden was third in the western area of Hertfordshire, and received full marks for the Churchyard, the War Memorial, the Inn and the School.

On 2 September 1961, Lord Brocket unveiled the trophy for the Best Kept Village. This meant that for a year a wooden post with a shield was placed on the Green opposite the Alford Cross. There was considerable division of opinion in the village at that time between those who wished and those who did not wish the village to be known with this title. Some feared that it would become a suburban show-place and lose its rural character. Others wanted to keep the honour and to have every part of the village tidy.

In 1968 and 1971 Little Gaddesden was second and in 1975 a Certificate was received for being the most improved village in the year. For this three trees were received. A walnut was planted on the Green and two horse chestnuts on the playing field. In 1979, when again the village was second in its section, three trees were received.

THE DRAMA CLUB

The club was founded in 1947 when a self-appointed committee from the Gaddesden Society decided to replace the annual Home Guard Concert with a variety show, using only local talent. The Committee was V.W. Bell, Vi Hughes, E. Wager, D. Hughes, E. Hollings, C. Owen and later D.K. Thorn and I. Foord-Kelcey, D. Patterson and L. Ouseley joined them. The first production was *Yellow Sands*. Enid Foxall and F. Cocks were soon associated with the new club.

Amongst the Club *Chairmen* have been — V. Bell, V. Hughes, F. Hawley, D. Wray, F. Cocks, G. Bailey, L. Johnston, G. Catchpole and E. Foxall.

Producers have included — D. Wray, E. Foxall, P. Mountfort, H. Pain, C. Keevil, D. Bailey, N. Ryall, K. Magnay, E. Russell and P. Foord-Kelcey.

Productions. Memorable productions have included *Twelfth Night, Macbeth, Much Ado about Nothing, Blithe Spirit, Anastasia, Oliver,* and *1066 and all that.*

Stage Sets. In addition to the producers, the chief work here has been that of Dorothea Patterson. Costumes, closely allied to the sets have been the responsibility of Gwen Johnston. Lighting work has included that of P. Mountfort.

Other Events. 'Gaddesden Gaieties' and the 'Gaddesden Revue' have been occasions for social and dramatic evenings, beginning in 1959. A Surprise Party in 1956 meant that a dinner party was held progressively, course by course at West Pulridge, Nob's Crook, Bannerdown, and Upper Gade. In that year eight lectures were given on Speech, Movement and Mime.

Club Nights and Play Readings began early in the society's history. Mrs Stanes cast the readers for *Dear Octopus* in 1955; Captain Magnay in that year cast *St Joan. Lady Precious Stream* was rehearsed in the Spinney garden. The new storeroom repository was opened in 1973.

Amongst critiques and comments—

1958	*Twelfth Night.* A first rate performance. The comedy scenes were a bit too reverent.
1963	*The Ghost Train.* A very successful play with superb teamwork and back-up.
1964	*Macbeth.* There were more curtain calls than ever. David Wray as Macbeth was very good indeed. Eleanor Hollings as Lady Macbeth was memorable and outstanding. The set designed by D. Wray and made by Gwen Johnston and Diana Ashby was superb.
1966	*1066 and all that.* There were 47 in the cast. An excellent choice; a full house at all four performances. It should have taken two-and-a-half not three hours.
1969	*Blithe Spirit.* Vi Hughes took the same part which she had played here in 1959.
1973	The plays were not as well attended this year.
1974	The bar opened at a show for the first time.
1976	*The Gaddesden Revue.* The programme mentioned no less than 56 names. 'We pride ourselves in being a family club and all the families of the names in the programme co-operated to make the show a success'.
1977	D. Bailey's production of *Ladies in Retirement* was highly praised as were D. Wray's sets.
1979	*Adventure Story.* A stimulating experience with a tremendous group effort. A marathon in running time; new talent was discovered.
1980	*Albert's Bridge* in the round. The plot was obscure to most of us.
1981	*Much Ado About Nothing.* An outstanding production, superb set, costuming and cast. The acting was of a very high standard

THE GADDESDEN SOCIETY

The Gaddesden Society was founded by members of No. 5 Platoon 7b Company Hertfordshire Home Guard in the district of Little Gaddesden, Nettleden, Hudnall, St Margaret's, Ringshall and Ashridge. It made its first appearance at a fête in the Church Meadow in 1945. In the summer issue of the *Diary 1977* the President, Canon Senar set out the objects of the society.

1. To encourage the spirit of voluntary service
2. To promote a sense of community and good fellowship
3. To preserve the natural amenities. The Society has tried to fulfil these objects in the following ways.

Its principal activity has been the monthly meeting from the autumn to the spring on the third Wednesday each month in the Village Hall. First there have been lectures. Amongst these have been many by authorities on different parts of the world.

Sir Vincent Del Tufo on Malaya
Mrs C. Boxer on China
Captain G.H. Ashby on Polynesia and the West Indies
Mr C. Ainley on 'The Bottom of the world'
Dr Bleackley. Thailand
Miss Reasbeck. 'A travel courier'
Dr Pugh. Everest
Mr F. Leek. Tutenkhamun
Mrs Rose. West Africa.

A second group concerned general subjects of interest.

Dr Clive Rouse. Wall Paintings
J. Lunn and G. Davis. Excavations at Verulamium
K. Ritchie and J. Bell. Prisons and Borstals
Dorian Williams. Horse Jumping
Dr Kathleen Kenyon. Excavations in Jerusalem
Peter Goldman. *Which* Magazine
G. Forestier-Walker. Modern Architecture
Sir Victor Goddard. 'Reminiscences'
Mr Owen Williams. Motorway Construction
Mr Bly. Antiques
Mr J.H. Lewis. 'A young man in the city'
Mr D. Rait-Kerr. 'Cricket in the 1860s'
Mr Bell. The Grand Union Canal
Mr Bull. Cheeses
Mr Muddiman. Modern Farming
Dr Shaw. Dialects
Mr Brian Bennett. Art and Misericords
Richard Mabey. 'Back to the Roots'
Richard Morris. British Archaeology
R.F. Carter. Pewter
John Field. Hertfordshire Place-Names
Dr E. Roberts. The Medieval Architect
Mr Withycomb. Waylines
Mr S.P. Taylor. The Ridgeway Path.

Three oustanding lectures on Bird Life have been given by Ludwig Koch, Ernest Janes and Chris Mead.

Local history attracts interest. There have been meetings with such titles as Gaddesden's Village Magazine, Gaddesden Bygones, Village Forum. Canon Senar has lectured on the parish church, the Bridgewater Family, and on the houses and buildings of Little Gaddesden 'Then and now'. At many meetings the first quarter-of-an-hour has been devoted to matters of local interest. A table of exhibits was for a time popular. One of the outstanding events was the 'Treasures Exhibition' when family treasures were on show for a week-end in the Hall. So valuable were the contributions that all night vigils had to be kept.

Debates have played a regular though infrequent part, for example 'That fee-paying schools should be abolished', and 'That the moon should be left alone'. Mr J.H. Lewis proposed this and Captain David Magnay opposed it. The comment 'We cannot claim in this debate to have advanced the cause of science'.

Book Choice was at one time important. Geoffrey Tandy was a member of the B.B.C. Sunday 'Book Choice' team and expert opinions were of a high level. Latterly there has been a table for magazines on which members have placed good quality magazines for others to borrow. Another section contained guide books to historical places and buildings.

Wine and cheese (and soft drinks) are provided at the end of meetings, but only when question time is over. Question time being always one of the most interesting part of meetings.

A record of the houses of Little Gaddesden was proposed and Mr E.A.Janes agreed to take such photographs for a very small sum, these to be preserved in an album in the parish chest.

Hospital visiting service. For many years the Society has arranged a rota of car owners ready to transport relatives to hospitals at visiting times. Mrs Lane and then Miss Cowdell and Miss M. Crawford have organised this service.

Earlier activities included torchlight processions on Guy Fawkes night and balloon races (one balloon being picked up by a yacht near Cherbourg).

The Annual Sports. These have been organised by the Society since its foundation. Mr J. Oakins the. organiser said that a child of 10 at the first sports he organised would be over 46 in 1981. Mr Sherringham was assisting Mr Oakins as early as 1957. Mr Smalley gave the cup for the Village Championship, and a replica. Monty Williams was for many years undisputed winner.

In 1959 Mrs Bradfield was organising pony rides and the Headington Quarry men entertained. In 1969 the sports winners included Lisa Ball, Mark Hollings, Heather Connor, Lucy Davies, Kevin Geater, David Rogers, Robert Hughes, Kate Mead, Andrew Mountfort, Gillian Rafferty, Mandy Revell, Kate Wilson, Roderick Wilson, Ivan Veall and Elaine Gent. Mrs Thorn presented a cup for the Ladies' Championship.

THE GADDESDEN DIARY

The first quarterly *Diary* was published in the spring of 1955. The Editor was Mrs I. Foord-Kelcey. Nine hundred copies were sold in the first year. The early numbers had an owl on the cover perhaps signifying the wisdom of the contributors. Miss D. Patterson designed new covers in 1959, the colours changing for the seasons, and the dove of peace appearing above the tree. The *Diary* was printed until 1967 when costs enforced the change to its present form. Throughout the years Mrs Thorn and formerly Ken Thorn not only printed the *Diary* but also enabled it to be financially stable by obtaining advertisements.

Subsequent editors have been Mrs Rawdon-Smith, Mrs C. Revell and Canon H. Senar. Miss R.A. Griffiths and Mrs F.A. Moody have prepared the work for the printers and Mrs Francis and Mrs Ashby have served on the editorial team.

The Presidential Foreword or the Editor's Preface have made comment on local life. Principals of Ashridge have been welcomed or bidden farewell, as have village policemen. Mr Sherringham's retirement was marked appropriately with a farewell occasion and a Village Presentation of £115. A note of gratitude was given to Mrs Ward on her work and that of her family for so long at the Village Post Office and Shop. Editorials have been written by the Rector on aircraft noise; on the departure of Spencer Block; the work of Mr Thorn and of Miss Cowdell; the question of the names of houses and of locations of places in the parish; whether or not 'Little' ought to be added to the name of the Society to be more accurate. A request to supply money to supplement the feeding of the deer in the harsh winter of 1963 (Miss H. Cowdell raised £40 for this).

Letters to the Editor have never been frequent. Subjects are various and include one from Mrs Ashby suggesting that people could keep a small section of their garden for growing flowers which would be available to church flower decorators; a letter complaining in 1962 about House Agents' Boards spoiling the look of the village; one from Geoffrey Tandy in high indignation that 'Hudnall Common' was becoming used for various lanes and houses whereas 'Hudnall' was both adequate and correct as being ancient; and one from a good old scout who complained that the Trust House company had closed the public bar at the *Bridge*, and that this was anti-social.

Presidents of the Society have been—

1955	Major D. Heenan
1957	V.W. Bell
1961	Captain G.H. Ashby
1965	Dr C.E.A. Goddard
1967	Mr P.W. Haydon
1969	Mr A.J. Williams
1973	Canon H. Senar
1978	Mrs D. Ashby
1980	Mr L.C. Hopkins

Secretaries in recent years have been Mrs Francis and Mrs Wooster
Treasurers: Mr Francis, Mrs Mountfort.

INFANT WELFARE ASSOCIATION

For many years the Child Welfare Clinic has been held in the Village Hall. Mrs V. Purton was the secretary for over twenty-three years and provided the milk throughout that period. In 1959 the District Nurse was Miss Bickford, and later Nurse O'Dwyer. She managed to get the School Canteen to provide meals for the elderly residents on Tuesdays and Fridays. This has brought great benefit to the elderly. In 1965 seven new boys and seven new girls were welcomed.

In 1970 Mrs R. Corby resigned from her work after 19 years of supplying provisions and baby foods for sale. Mrs Sambrook then took on the work. She was succeeded by Mrs Follis in 1973, Mrs Dickson and Mrs Scott now help with the work.

MOTHERS AND TODDLERS

This group was begun in September 1975 with Gill Slade as the foundress. Numbers grew and baby-sitting developed as one result. The club met in the coffee room at the *Bridgewater Arms* on alternate Friday afternoons. A Christmas party was held there. Later the Society had a sale raising £80. The meetings were transferred to the Village Hall on alternate Friday afternoons. The variety of toys and equipment grew, and the Play Group material was also used. Sales became annual events. In 1978 £130 was raised, and almost the same amount in 1979. By 1979 the time of the meeting was changed to Tuesday mornings once a fortnight.

Gill Slade retired in 1979 and was succeeded by Julie Leonhardt, Diana Jones and Yvonne Cheshire.

THE MUSIC CLUB

The club was established in 1946. Chairmen of the Club have included Mr V.W. Bell, Mr J.H. Lewis (13 years), Colonel D. Coult, Dr and Mrs A. Cassell.

Each year for many years there was one concert at Ashridge House, and frequently there were serenades at the Manor House. On several occasions there have been organ concerts in Ashridge Chapel and concerts in Little Gaddesden and Nettleden churches. Most meetings are in the homes of members, and amongst them have been Denison House, Prince's Riding, Nettleden Lodge, John O'Gaddesden's House, Nob's Crook, Bridgewater Lodge, Red Lodge, Kinross, Quinacres, Tanglewood and 6/7 Little Gaddesden.

In 1960, in response to comments on the programmes it was stated 'The club cannot provide popular concerts in the commonly understood sense of the term without violating its avowed principles. Only the best musicians and live performances'.

Mr J.H. Lewis at one moment mentioned the following as artists whom the society had been fortunate to have playing—

Eugene Goossens, Alexander Young, Maria Korchinska, John Clegg and Helen Watts. Earlier Margaret Ritchie and Miss Erhart had given very great pleasure. Anthony Hopkins, President of the Society, has regularly given memorable concerts and lectures to the Club.

The outstanding occasion in recent years was the 1971 concert in honour of Sir Arthur Bliss, Master of the Queen's Music, at Ashridge College, when Sir Arthur himself was present.

Visits by Berkhamsted and Cavendish School music societies have been well attended. The Fayrfax Singers under David Ireson are very popular visitors. Miss Gaynor Lewis has given immense pleasure to the Music Club since she first began on her musical career and sang to the Club in 1957. Regular visits to London are paid by the Club. These have included being present at a performance of Geraint Evans in Donizetti's *Don Pasquale, Les Sylphides* at Covent Garden and *Manon* at the Coliseum.

Mrs Thorn served as Secretary for 10 years and Mr Morris as Treasurer for 13 years.

Amongst the composers whose work has been most popular and well received down the years have been Mozart, Haydn, Bach, Debussy, Ravel, Schumann, Bizet, Grieg, Chopin, Schubert and Brahms. The Chiltern Players introduced members to many 15th and 16th-century composers and the Fayrfax Consort introduced new carols.

One of the characteristic features of the Club seems to have been the ability of the officers speedily to find very satisfactory replacements when artists have at the last moment been unable to be present.

THE OVER-SIXTIES CLUB

Mr S. Batchelor approached the Rector, the Rev. D. Bickerton, to ask if a club could be founded for elderly people. The Rector approached several parishioners, and in the closing months of 1960 the club was founded by a parish church group. Later it was made an 'open' club.

The first Christmas Supper was held on 15 December 1960.

Officers have included—

Presidents: Mrs Wager, Dr C.E.A. Goddard 1970-79, Lady Del Tufo from 1979.

Chairmen: Mrs Wager, The Rev. D. Bickerton, Canon H. Senar (from 1962).

Secretaries: Mrs J.B. Townsend, Mrs R. Hollings, Mr H. Reasbeck, Mrs P. Price.

Treasurers: Mrs Banks, Mrs Bangay, Mr H. Reasbeck, Mrs Nightall.

Monthly meetings take place on the second Wednesday afternoon.

Speakers with slides and equipment have included Mr P.A. Turnbull, Mr D. Lockhart (Himalayas), Mrs Martlew (Keep Fit), Mr E. Janes (Birdlife), Mr W. Brooker (Aerial photography), Mr S. Broughton (Yachting), Mrs V. Bridges (Songs), Mr Quin (Cycling and 1920 Village Life), Mr Heather (English countryside), Mr Glasser, Rev. A.L. Jones (The Welsh Choir), Mrs R. Edwards, Mr L.C. Hopkins (South America and Gibraltar).

Little Gaddesden School regularly entertains the club.

Visits are paid during the summer months to places of interest. These have included London Airport, Bognor, Eastbourne, London, Whipsnade, Southsea (holiday), Clacton, the Thames Valley, Henley, Chequers, Hatfield House and Waddesden Manor, Windsor, Cheltenham and the Cotswolds, Woburn, Bedford, Worcester and Malvern. Mystery Tours are held in the autumn.

Special occasions have been the visit to London and St Paul's Cathedral in the week of the Jubilee and to St Paul's Waldenbury and church, during the week of the Queen Mother's 80th birthday.

Competitions are arranged each month. The Easter Bonnet competition in 1974 received much press coverage.

Visits have been paid to the theatre and the pantomime. Local clubs entertain the Over-60s regularly. The V.P.A. Supper is a highlight of the year. Guests and other clubs are invited to meetings.

Parties are held for birthdays and Christmas. Members' birthdays are remembered monthly. A monthly poem is prepared and read by a member.

Catering is in the hands of a group under Mrs Harvell, and formerly Mrs Kath. Clarke.

The Social Secretary, looking after the entertainment, is Mrs Nightall.

Transport is provided for those who require it. Mrs Owen Williams arranges this.

Outings are arranged by Mrs Sears.

The Jumble Sale. The Jumble Sale in 1963 produced £65. In 1975 it reached £297 and in 1980, £398.

The St Albans Cathedral service. Members attend the annual service arranged for members of clubs such as this one.

Members provide their own entertainment and once a year act as hosts to the helpers. A fascinating 'War Time Memories' afternoon in August 1981, among other reflections, heard of the remarkable experiences of Lady Del Tufo, Mrs Price, Mrs Williams and Mrs Fleckney.

THE PARISH CHURCH 1929-82

In 1929 the Rev. Lumsden Barkway moved into the new Rectory. He was destined to become Bishop of Bedford and then of St Andrews. He is mainly remembered for his spirituality and for the retreats which he conducted. He lived to a great old age.

He was followed by the Rev. Charles E. Wager who was Rector for 19 years. Trained at the College of the Resurrection at Mirfield, and sent to their house in South Africa he lectured on the scriptures. Mrs Wager whom he met in South Africa was daughter of Rector Haviland of Lilley, Luton, Bedfordshire (where he was a predecessor of Canon Senar there). Haviland was said to have been one of the three richest clergymen in the Church of England. Rector Wager was an

LITTLE GADDESDEN CHURCH, HERTFORDSHIRE

Fig. 23   Sketch of Little Gaddesden Church.

excellent cricketer, and also one who studied widely in psychology and psychiatry. After resigning his living in 1953 he moved to Tanglewood on Pulridge Hill.

On St Barnabas Day 11 June 1953 Robert Campbell Paterson was inducted to the Rectory. He had formerly been Overseas Manager to the National Provincial Bank. Having served a curacy at Dunstable he came to Little Gaddesden as his first living. He was meticulous in his care for detail, and a man of great dedication who continued the work of post-war reconstruction of the parish on sound foundations of pastoral care. On this his successor the Rev. David Bickerton began to build. He became a Canon of St Albans probably as recognition of his service as Chairman of the Diocesan Parsonages Board. He initiated the Over-60s Club, and was specially remembered for a large Confirmation Group which he trained. The parishioners were greatly saddened when he moved after two years, for they had very great hopes for their parish under his guidance.

During the 1950s there was extensive work on the fabric of the church and the east end was underpinned, electric light was introduced, and events were held for the purchase of an electric blower for the organ. The churchyard needed an extension, the new area of the west ground was laid out, and the car park area was also obtained. There was an exchange of the Church Acre to enable the churchyard and car park to be acquired. Alterations were made to Little Gaddesden C. of E. School, and the new classroom wing was erected.

In 1956 Dr C.E.A. Goddard, churchwarden, investigated a box at the bank and found it to contain a flagon, so tarnished that it was at first assumed to be pewter. When he cleaned it, it was found to be a fine piece of Carolean silver, 11 in. high, beautifully proportioned and inscribed on its side and underneath in cursive script 'Litle (sic) Gaddesden Church' with the elongated 'S'. The donor is unknown but the date is 1636. 'It is unfortunately too valuable to be kept in church'. In the same year 1956, it was thought that social events should be run by younger parishioners and a committee was appointed consisting of Dorothy Bailey, Janet Cocks, Donald Hawley, Janet Phillips and Joan Naylor.

The Rector sat on the Green annually during these years from 11.00 a.m. to 8.00 p.m., to receive gifts for the church. At a parish party in the winter of 1957 Mrs Stanes' commentary on a mannequin parade was stated to be masterly. In 1958 the Rector sitting on the Green received £248. The Sunday School outing in that year was to Clacton and 45 children and 28 adults went together. A Christmas market was held for church funds, and this raised £159. The new oil heating was used for the first time at Christmas. Rector Paterson moved to Scotland (Duror, Argyll) in 1959. David Hughes after 14 years on the school staff moved to Canada and Mr A.T. Swinscoe joined the staff. At Christmas 1959 the school children presented *That Night* as a Christmas Nativity Play . . . the following year it was to be performed in church.

An open meeting about Church Schools was addressed by the Archdeacon of St Albans and Mr Davison of County Hall.

The Rev. A.H. Strand former Rector of Aldbury officiated in the interregnum in 1961 before the arrival of the Rev. H. Senar.

In 1962 it was decided not to replaster the exterior of the north wall of the church, but to repoint the brickwork and repair the downspouts, gutters and windows on the north side. A flag pole and flag were received. A beech hedge was planted in the west ground. The Rector asked for four additional bells to make a ring of six, when addressing his first Annual Church Meeting in 1962.

The Family Circle met regularly during this year at Denison House.

The cost of stripping the north wall and revealing the old flints was £600 (including the remaining work on the fabric). In 1963 considerable work was required especially on the windows; the west window of the baptistry was in a dangerous condition. Water for the church was laid on into the churchyard. The churchwardens were Dr Goddard and Mr J. Oakins. Mr Charles Miller, Secretary, enlivened the meetings with inimitable reflections, and minutes in Miltonic style.

Visitors in 1963 included the Archbishop of York, Dr Paget, Dean Thicknesse (recently retired) and Bishop Trevor Huddleston.

The interior of the church was redecorated, stained-glass windows were cleaned and the vestry was turned into a chapel.

Harvest gifts were distributed to sick and elderly parishioners each year.

A confirmation took place on Ascension Day and the First Communion was held on Whitsunday followed by a lavish parish breakfast in the School Hall.

At the Parish Gift Day 1963 it was stated that 12½% of the income of the parish church went for works of mercy. The Rev. V.W. Bell was made deacon at Exeter Cathedral.

A Mrs Jay on a visit recalled the painting of the frescoes on the east wall 70 years ago, by a lady on scaffolding in candle light. The 1964 Gift Day total was £364.

On Wednesdays after each Festival, Holy Communion services were held for sick and elderly people. Mr G.E. Catchpole's "Bus" contingent at Christmas 1964 had an average age of 86 and this was 10 years younger than the most elderly lady in the party.

A Lent Course entitled 'No Small Change' was undertaken by 6,000 parishes in Lent 1965.

New shrubberies and beds were laid out in the west ground, and 1,000 daffodils were planted by Waterer's. The church bell was tolled 90 times on the death of Sir Winston Churchill.

A visit to Coventry Cathedral took place on a Sunday morning.

It was decided to hold parish coffee on the first and third Sundays each month. Mrs Senar was responsible for the rota. A Christian Aid meeting was arranged with Miss Essex as speaker.

The Christian Aid Committee— Rector, Chairman; Secretary, Mr P.W. Harris; Treasurer, Mr R. Parkins.

Mr Brandon-Jones, architect to the church in succession to Mr Neal, reported urgent work needed for the roof of the tower. The lead had perished and the timbers were in need of replacement. Under the old lead— 'Harry Wells, Ringshall, Plumber. Look out for money here' 'July 18 1911 H.W.'. The cost was £413, including flagstaff preparation.

Little Gaddesden School attended church service regularly during term, taking part in the service and fulfilling many duties. Parents joined the school at this worship. After service at summer term end, the leavers were presented with a *Book of Common Prayer* by the Managers, the book plate designed by C. Greaves.

In May 1966 as the final stage of the restoration drew near, it was decided to appeal for the cost of building a new Vestry with ancillary accommodation. The response was very speedy and £4,000 was forthcoming, the members of the P.C.C. themselves providing £1,500. In response to an appeal for 20 gifts at £100, 15 were offered within a matter of months.

The progress on the building by Jesse Mead, under the guidance of Mr J. Brandon-Jones was thorough, speedy and efficient, and at Christmas the Vestry was in use for the first time, much voluntary work on the interior having been offered willingly. The former vestry on the south side was made into the chapel. New silver cross and candlesticks made by John Webb were presented, and also chairs. Mr K.A.M. Dickson accepted the Rector's invitation to be Chairman of the Stewardship Committee.

The Right Rev. T. Huddleston, Bishop of Masasi gave a talk on the day of his return to England. In this year (1968) new churchyard gates were erected for the west ground.

After having a pattern of Sunday Services at 8.00 a.m., 9.30 a.m., 11.00 a.m. and 6.30 p.m., these were altered to omit the 11.00 a.m. service on Sundays, apart from festivals, when there was a 9.30 a.m. service.

The new Remembrance Sunday service authorised by the leaders of all Christian churches was used for the first time in 1968.

The Berkhamsted Review (6d. per copy) carried Little Gaddesden news each month, but only a small amount of space was permitted.

At the end of 1968 London Transport featured Little Gaddesden and its church in a large poster for the Underground, offering praise for the new internal decoration of the church and the 'Red Lady' monument. The poster suggested people should also 'POP IN ST PAUL'S' London.

New hassocks were made under the guidance of Mrs John Mead. Series two Holy Communion and evensong were adopted for an experimental four years.

In 1969 Michael, Bishop of St Albans for 18 years, resigned his see.

A new credence ledge for the chapel was made. A reading desk, chalice and ciborium, together with churchwardens' staves were all presented to the church at this time.

The Stewardship Campaign produced very worthy results both in financial commitment and in the use of time and talents. Generous donations were made to the 'needs of others', including those to a leper settlement in Tanzania at Kindwitwi and to the Children's Society. Help was also given later to the work of Bishop Lee in Seoul, the work of the church in Madagascar and a hospital in Malawi.

In 1970 Robert Runcie was appointed Bishop of St Albans.

Many societies visited the church for Quiet Days and Retreats and meetings.

A new cabinet for Hymn Books was made by John Oakins. Comper purple was used for the new Holy Communion robes.

Mutual visits were paid by Little Gaddesden and Mill Hill, John Keble church, at Rogationtide and Harvest. The Rogationtide procession so familar in earlier centuries was held annually in an attenuated form.

Ian Williams walked the whole of the boundaries.

In 1971 Mr P.W. Harris was secretary and Mr L.C. Hopkins treasurer.

The timbers and gutters of the Chapel had perished and required renewal costing £600-£800. J. Brandon-Jones designed a new door for this Chapel.

In 1973 a new *History and Guide* was published by the Rector. Jack Mayling retired as churchyard gardener. Colonel Day was appointed Church Secretary and Mr J. Oakins and Mr G.E. Catchpole were appointed Churchwardens, Dr Goddard having resigned.

Mr Cyril Thorne was succeeded by Mr Jack Peasnall as Chairman of Stewardship. *A Book of Remembrance* was dedicated, and the old standard of the British Legion was replaced by a new one which was dedicated by the Rector.

Mrs Ashby after many years' beautiful work resigned from being in charge of the church flowers.

Mrs Clarke resigned from the brass cleaning on her removal from the Parish.

From 1 June 1975 the Hudnall area was transferred to Little Gaddesden, Her Majesty the Queen signing the Order in Council on 14 May 1975.

Groups to study the Archbishops' Call to the Nation were established.

The Rector gave the information that he knew of the possibility of obtaining bells from a church which no longer used them, and which could be used with others to form a ring of six. An anonymous donor offered to provide a new ring in memory of Margaret Elizabeth Griffiths. This offer was accepted, and the work set in motion.

In 1976 it was decided that the times of services should be each Sunday at 8.00 a.m. and 9.30 a.m. Holy Communion, and 6.30 p.m. Evensong.

In August the 700th anniversary of Rector Robert de Dukingham was kept.

The Rev. V.W. Bell preached at Harvest.

The Dean of St Albans addressed a parish gathering.

In the spring of 1977 a Major Restoration Appeal was launched, with Mr S. Broughton as the Chairman. The Appeal began in March and by 23 May £20,000 had been promised.

On his 90th Birthday, Dr Goddard was presented with a garden chair outside the Vestry, a cuckoo accompanying his words of gratitude.

By August 265 donations and promises totalling £21,500 had been received.

For the Silver Jubilee of Her Majesty the Queen the church was decorated and Festival services were held. Twenty organisations helped with the flowers.

The annual cricket match with the International Students Hostel continued to be very successful.

Early on Easter morning 1978 the Little Gaddesden bells rang for the first time in their new ring of six (plus the priest's bell). The oldest Saint Katherine Bell was the work of John Daniel of Cambridge and London 1450-61.

The ringing chamber was decorated and furnished and the boiler house was restored. The bishop's visit was delayed so that all the work could be completed.

The Mothers and Tinies Group met in church each month. The Choir was in demand for weddings during this year.

A School Appeal was held under the Chairmanship of Mrs Foxall to raise money for an extension for headmaster's and staff rooms and storage to which 77 people gave £1,150. The Series three marriage service was authorised from 1978.

Peter Haydon former Treasurer and Sidesman who had only recently left the parish had passed away.

The Bishop came to a great service of Thanksgiving and for the Dedication of the Vestry and the bells.

Dr Goddard passed away on Easter Day 1979.

In 1979 a Country Craft Fair was held in beautiful weather, with Professor Richard Edwards as Chairman and Mr K.A.M. Dickson as Secretary. This was very successful indeed.

In September 1979 a Reception was given to the Rector and Mrs Senar, on the 40th anniversary of the Rector's ordination as priest.

Red vestments, frontals and hangings in memory of Dr Goddard were presented to the church.

Mr T. Indermaur Jones was Chairman of a group of the fathers from the Mothers and Tinies Group who led the Parish Appeal for the St Albans Abbey Restoration and Renewal. The parish target was £1,000 and this was reached and a large sum was sent. The oak doors of the main porch were replaced by copies of the original ones, in memory of Dr Goddard in 1981. In the same year the organ was completely overhauled, new stops and a complete new pedal board were added. Mr A.W. Banks and Mrs D. Cocks have both served as organists for over 25 years.

A new edition of the parish church *History and Guide*, in an extended form was published at the Parish Rural Living Fair.

The appointment of Bishop Robert Runcie to be Archbishop of Canterbury was announced and Bishop John Taylor was appointed to succeed him.

John Oakins retired after 25 years as Churchwarden. Colonel Day succeeded him. On 13 April Mr Oakins was presented with a carriage clock at a Reception in the Village Hall. Mr C. Osborn-Jones succeeded Colonel Day as P.C.C. secretary.

The heating system was renewed and renovated.

Throughout these years Mr John Brandon-Jones F.S.A. has been the church architect who has made an incalculable contribution to the parish church.

A set of handbells was obtained for the church which were rung at Christmas 1980 by the St Peter's and St Paul's People.

A presentation for Mrs Hill in appreciation of her work caring for the church took place in church.

A group having the title 'Network' met and organised events to call attention to the needs of the church in Tanzania. The sponsoring of Miss Sarah Rogers to visit the Anglican church in Kenya in August 1982 as a representative of the parish is a parish project for that year.

The *Parish News* was published monthly from 1976.

MOTHERS & TINIES GROUP

This group was established in 1975 with the purpose of providing Christian training for mothers and their pre-school tinies. Meetings are held in the church once a month on the third Friday at 2.15 p.m. All present participate in a meeting where up-to-date publications for children and their parents are on display and for loan. After the meeting which has a prayer background, the members go into the church tower where all take their share in bell ringing. This is followed by a procession with musical instruments brought by the tinies. The company proceeds to the Chapel where an illustrated talk is given. After the service, tea follows in the vestry. Sometimes the meeting takes place in the area outside the church when the weather is fine.

SWORD & KEYS SOCIETY

This society was established in 1962 when the new Rector (Rev. H. Senar) inherited a group of Confirmation candidates from his predecessor, Canon Bickerton.

The first officers appointed were—

Chairman, The Rev. H. Senar

Secretary, Sandra Oakins; Treasurer, Jane Pannell. Committee: Miss Taylor, Miss Thomas, John Bailey, Viv Banks, Hilary Catchpole, Alan Hing, Gordon Horrod, Gail Nash, Adrian Parkins and Jane Wiggins.

A sale of work raised £68 towards the cost of a visit to Samford Courtenay, Devon.

The name Sword & Keys was suggested by Sandra Oakins who made a badge for the society. A barbecue included children from the Leighton Buzzard Home of the Church of England Children's Society. This began a connection with that home which has continued. At the barbecue £3 was collected towards a bicycle for the children.

Members arose one Sunday morning very early for a visit to Guildford Cathedral in the the Catchpole bus.

The bicycle for the Children's Home was the object of collections and exercises and on Christmas Day 1962 it was wheeled down Little Gaddesden church for a blessing before being taken across to the home after service. Mrs J.T. Pritchard was the chauffeuse.

Easter 1963 saw the first of many S.K. pilgrimages to St Albans Cathedral for the Annual Youth Pilgrimage.

Visits were made to the Cross Keys Club in Berkhamsted.

The first of many camps in the north Herts. and Cambridge areas took place at Ashwell.

A visit to Coventry Cathedral took place.

In 1964 Miss Taylor was given a dustbin for her new home, and the Club followed this by camping at Grantchester. Ely was visited. An S.P.G. film was hired.

In the late summer of 1964 an artistic phase began. A night visit to Badger Wood scared off the badgers. A swimming gala was held, and a scavenger hunt through the parish. Whipsnade Tree Cathedral was visited. A Missionary Market was held. A visit to S.P.G. House in London was followed by a mass attack on the Parochial Church Council who in fear and terror felt compelled to promise £100 a year for the society.

The club agreed to arrange the chapel flowers in the newly opened South Chapel. After the Christmas Market when £88 was raised it was said that Mrs Dickson has decorated every Christmas tree in the parish with the tree decorations she had made for the sale.

Churchyard maintenance was next on the agenda and this continued throughout the life of the society, a 'Grass Eater' being bought later in 1975 for the churchyard, perhaps in part compensation for those who having rested on the churchyard barrow found it had collapsed beneath them.

In 1965 the last article written by Sandra Oakins appeared in the Gaddesden *Diary*. Her articles were the wittiest contributions the *Diary* has yet received.

The Rev. R.G. Sanders gave a talk on the 'Broken Home', Mrs Ashby spoke on 'Flower Arranging'. A permanent link with S.P.G. was made.

In 1965 Hilary Catchpole became Chairman, Ann Griffiths, Secretary and Jane Pannell, Treasurer. Ian Catchpole, Philip Mountfort and Ann Tandy formed the Committee with the officers. Viv Banks the Vice-Chairman won an exhibition to Somerville College, Oxford. In 1966 Ann Tandy became Chairman and Pat Griffiths, Treasurer.

The Rector talked on Switzerland and Mr A.J. Williams organised country dancing.

Members visited S.P.G. House, held a Jumble Sale (£47) and planned to buy a new silver ciborium for church. A new banner for the society was made and was dedicated in August 1968.

The society constructed an Easter Garden. Fifteen members walked on foot to the St Albans Pilgrimage service and two walked home also. A chess tournament, a hilarious evening of 'Just a minute', a camp to Grantchester and a Tiddley Wink tournament were held by the club. The annual sale raised £68.

1970 – Members took part in the walk across 19 bridges in London for the Rehabilitation of the Disabled. One evening was spent reciting Shakespeare, another with a barbecue, and other events were planned to raise money for a radio for the Leighton Buzzard Home.

The 1971 sale raised £78.

Visits were paid to Ivinghoe church and Ashridge College and Sister Shaw gave a talk. In 1971 the Alford Memorial was cleaned and a scavenger hunt took place.

During 1972, 40 meetings took place, and a visit was paid to *The Gondoliers* in London. Visits were paid to Wiggington Youth Club, and to Samford Courtenay.

In 1973 *The Yeoman of the Guard* at Sadlers Wells proved popular, the Richmond Ice Hockey rink was visited and the sale earned £117. Jon Williams succeeded Ian Catchpole as Chairman, who had served in that office since 1967. Croquet at the Rectory and bowling in the Hemel Hempstead alley, cutting grass in the churchyard and tidying the Alford Monument were combined with studying Series three Holy Communion service. The holiday this year was in Pembrokeshire.

The children from the children's home were entertained.

In 1974 the seniors went to Cornwall and juniors to Dartmoor.

Donations were given to the Children's Home each year and £100 was given in 1975.

Visits each summer were part of the activities and the Lake District and Cornwall were followed by the Yorkshire Dales.

Reading of classics, poetry and prose and visits to the theatre were interspersed with visits to the Children's Home, in 1976 with a gift of £150. The record player previously presented by the club was still in use.

In 1976 the members decided that it would be sensible to resign in order that younger people might take over. A society dedicated to the service of others in a strong body of friends had come to an end.

ST PETER'S AND ST PAUL'S PEOPLE

The name was chosen by the members of this group of young people belonging to the parish church. In many ways they are the successors to the Sword & Keys Society for they have the same object, to be of service.

Founded in 1978, the officers were Kate Mead, Sarah Rogers and Amanda Glenn. The group sponsors the Easter Monday pilgrimage to St Albans each year. They prepare the flowers in the South Chapel, help at baptisms, look after the Easter Garden and the Christmas decorations. They act as hosts for visiting parties such as the Dunstable W.E.A. They organised an evening for learning flower decorating from Mrs P.W. Harris.

They helped at the Craft Fair and Parish Fair, at the Harvest socials and with the International Students Cricket match. They organised a Disco for the Children's Home, with which they are building a strong link. They transport the Christmas gifts to the Home.

They have held a Christmas Party for children. They help organisations such as the Over-60s at their Jumble Sale. They have taken over the handbells and they rang for Christmas midnight, Christmas morning and for the carols in 1980 and 1981.

Other activities have included cleaning gravestones and recording older ones.

Croquet at the Rectory appears to be one of their few recreations.

THE SUNDAY SCHOOL

The Sunday School has been a continuing part of parish life throughout the whole period. One early mention was in 1830 when the Countess of Bridgewater paid George Garrett of the *Bridgewater Arms* £5 4s. for the use of a room for the year, the amount to include 'firing'. This was for the Sunday school children. In her will dated Christmas Eve 1846 Charlotte Catherine Anne, widow of the 7th Earl of Bridgewater bequeathed to each of the two daughters of my late tenant William Horsham fifty pounds for their attention to the Sunday School for females in Little Gaddesden. In 1854 there were 130 children in the Sunday School. After the establishment of Little Gaddesden Church of England School the Sunday School met there. Since the Second World War the school has met on Sunday mornings both in school and in church. In recent years the venue has alternated between the school hall and the church. When meetings are in the Vestry, the children move into church for the second part of the service. Mrs E.E. Clayton has been Superintendent for many years, and in the 1980s has been assisted by Mr John Leonhardt. Outings and picnics are arranged. Visits to the Cathedral especially for the Christingle service take place. The children have regularly given support to the Children's Society and to mission work abroad. They are encouraged to move to the altar for a blessing at Communion time.

THE PARISH COUNCIL

1955-1981

The Councillors elected in 1955 were Miss Jean Moore, V.W. Bell, J.J.Oakins, F. Hing, R.D. Foord-Kelcey, R.T. Hobbs, Mrs F.S. Hughes.

The Parish Clerk was Mr Michael McCaul and he was succeeded by Mr David Williams.

In 1962 negotiations were taking place for the erection of single cottages.

An arrangement was made with the Education Authority to cut the playing field grass more frequently. The road safety notices were erected at the three entrances to the village. Access roads to the Green were under constant discussion, and permission was given for only one more road across the Green.

In 1962 the Parish Council made a grant to the Parochial Church Council of £15 towards the upkeep of the churchyard.

David Williams was elected to the Chairmanship of the Council in 1963. Mrs G. Bailey was elected to succeed Mr J.C. Yewdall as Parish Clerk. Mrs Foxall and Mr P.W. Haydon were appointed Rural District Councillors.

In 1965 much adverse criticism of the methods of the judges at the Best Kept Village Competition was aired.

Litter was a constant problem for the Council. Drainage, old people's dwellings, footpaths and seats were regular matters for the agenda. In 1965 Mr Hurst of Nettleden 'applied to close the footpath in the Potten End-Nettleden area in the interests of agriculture and to give another pathway along the ridge from the Roman Road to the Birdspightle path that runs from Frithsden to the Golden Valley. This was welcomed'.

The care of gates and stiles was regularly discussed. Mr J. Mead's offer of a site on the road to Ringshall for an old people's seat was welcomed. A netball pitch on the Village Hall car park was approved. The Bridgewater site for the bungalows was abandoned and the Bede Houses' site approved.

Miss Jean Moore retired from the Council, and members elected were Mrs V. Hughes, J.J. Oakins, Mrs Veall, A. Sherringham, Mrs Foxall and Mr Haydon. The last two councillors were returned unopposed for the Rural District Council. Mr David Williams was elected Chairman of the Council.

Hudnall Common and the Green were registered as common land, Ringshall and Ivinghoe commons being registered by the National Trust.

In 1968 Mrs Foxall was elected Chairman of the Rural District Council. The marking of footpaths was almost completed. The Bede Houses were demolished, footpaths were checked and the siting of a new Pavilion was discussed.

In 1969 the Bede Court Houses were officially opened by Mrs Foxall in her capacity as Chairman of the R.D.C. The Rector blessed the houses. Mr and Mrs Haydon arranged for a reception in the Village Hall. Tenants began to move in, Miss Wells' house was used as the representative house at the opening. Mrs Ramsay was appointed first Warden

At the 1970 election the following were elected to the Council. Mr P. Haydon, Mrs Hughes, Mr J. Oakins, Mr D. Williams, Canon H. Senar and Mr C. Revell. Mr Williams was elected to the chair. More frequent cutting of the Green was planned and regular cleaning of the Alford fountain was agreed. The nailing of posters to trees was to be discouraged. Mrs A.J. Williams was appointed clerk to succeed Mrs Bailey who had served for eight years.

Red oaks and a walnut tree were planted on the Green.

Allocation of houses, and discussion of waiting lists took up much of the time of the council. Footpaths, bridle ways and the bus service were under constant discussion, and also the need for houses for younger families, including those who marry and are unable to find suitable accommodation in the parish.

In the 1973 elections Mr D. Williams, Mr Haydon and the Rector did not stand for re-election. Mrs Foxall was appointed Chairman, Mr Oakins, Vice-Chairman and Mrs Hughes, Mr Revell, Mr Sherringham, Captain Ashby and Mr Thorne were elected.

Reorganisation under the new Dacorum Council took place in this year. Mr P. Whaley became the Little Gaddesden and Potten End Councillor. A 30 mile-an-hour speed limit was requested by the Council and the Hertfordshire County Council promised to look into this. Hudnall pathways and access were discussed, and the damage by horses to footpaths and the ploughing up of footpaths provoked concern.

Negotiations took place for purchase of land on the Ashridge College side of the Green. The phone box near the post office was re-sited by the Village Hall in this year (1974). Concern was expressed about the felling of trees near the College. The Jean Moore clock was presented to the Village Hall. On the greatly regretted death of Captain Ashby in 1974, Mrs Mountfort was elected in his place. Walking of pathways was agreed. Mrs Williams retired as Clerk in 1975 and Mrs Creed succeeded her. Mr C. Revell was elected Chairman in succession to Mrs Foxall. In that year in the Best Kept Village Competition, this was the 'most improved village in the year' and trees were received — a walnut for the Green and two horse chestnuts for the playing field.

By 1977 the main concerns in addition to the normal business were aircraft noise, the deer, footpaths, stiles and planning. The future of the *Bridgewater Arms* occupied much time. Deer culling was to be stepped up owing to the increase of deer in the previous five years. Bus services continued to cause great public concern, and the Chairman was unceasing in his discussions and meetings about this. The highway authority was agreeable to take over the land at the entrance to Chapel Close and reconstruct the site to avoid accidents. The Council agreed to help the Parochial Church Council by defraying the cost of the felling of the great elms in the churchyard infected by Dutch Elm Disease.

Young people were organised to tidy the village. At the 1978 Annual Parish Assembly reports were given by individual societies about their work. Public discussion arose out of questions concerning the deer, drainage, road names, house numbers and notice boards.

The Jubilee activities' film was shown.

Consideration arose about the demolition of the former pumping station which was in a very poor state and was no longer of use to the water authority. Mrs Creed resigned as Clerk and was succeeded in 1978 by Mr L. Ouseley.

The Parish Council elected in 1979 was Mrs Ashby, Mr Buzzacott, Mr Corby, Mrs Mountfort, Mr

Revell, Mr Sherringham and Mrs Cassell. The death of Mr Spencer Block who for many years had been Chairman of the Parish Council was received with great regret.

Matters discussed included the bus service, the Hudnall Lane access, flooding at Ringshall, footpaths, failure to get a speed restriction, deer, transport, aircraft noise and planning applications, together with development considerations, the closure of Van der Vieren's factory, trees and traffic speed. A subject of great concern was that of mains drainage and the anticipated expense for householders.

Mr Revell resigned as Chairman in 1980 and Mr R.A. Corby was elected in his place.

LITTLE GADDESDEN PRESERVATION SOCIETY

Founded 1960. At the first Annual Meeting the officers included: Chairman, Captain Magnay; Secretary and Treasurer, Captain Ashby; Committee: Dr Bird, Miss Cowdell, Sir Vincent Del Tufo, Mrs Foord-Kelcey, Mr Neil.

The extension of the Green Belt area to include Little Gaddesden and the implications of this caused much interest. Objections to Planning Permission in one case led to an inquiry. Endeavour was made to win the Best Kept Village Competition. Regret was expressed at the felling of trees on Pulridge Hill and many meetings were held about this and re-planting in that area. In 1962 there were 19 applications received for building.

In 1964 it was established that there would be 'no more building in Little Gaddesden except for purposes to benefit the village'. An application to build an estate at Hudnall was resisted. In 1965 the Society approved the new bungalows proposed by the local council, and spent much time discussing the siting of them.

The intentions of the Trust House company about the *Bridgewater Arms* and its future was on the agenda.

In 1966 the Chiltern area was designated an area of outstanding natural beauty and the foundation of the Chiltern Society was noted.

After 1966 the committee decided that 'as the Parish Council vetted planning applications the society no longer feels it should remark on every application'.

The society had the Ringshall Well renovated without any ownership being thereby accepted. The problem of noise from Luton Airport was important in discussions in 1968. In 1969 it was decided to wind up the group and give the balance of funds to plant a tree in the Park, and beeches on Pulridge Hill.

THE RURAL HERITAGE SOCIETY

Founded in 1975 'to protect and enhance the rural heritage and engage in such matters as shall further this aim'.

There is a newsletter published twice a year. This is now sent to members (which in 1975 was stated to include one-third of the houses between the Deer Leap Garage and Pulridge Hill).

A footpath map based on the 6 in. to the mile Ordnance Map was produced for sale in 1978. Concern was expressed at the importance of preserving footpaths and permissive horse tracks. Thus footpath walks have been organised.

Planning applications are projected and include obtaining protective fencing for the trees on the Green.

The society obtained the approval of the Parish Council for the 're-furbishing' of the old milestone near Cromer Close.

The society objected to the demolition of the Waterwork pumping station behind Red House and was present at a public enquiry about this. The society is affiliated to the Chiltern Society.

It is concerned about the absence of speed limits through Little Gaddesden.

In 1979 the Chairman was Mr Peter Mann, the Secretary Mr R.C. Westmacott and the Treasurer Mr S. Broughton. Mr E. Roe became Chairman in 1981.

THE ROYAL BRITISH LEGION

The Little Gaddesden Branch grew naturally out of the Old Comrades Association formed after the First World War when in 1919-20 a committee of S.J. Oakins, W. Johnson and J. Hing began the work. The Little Gaddesden Branch of the Legion was established in 1923 and was the seventh in the whole country.

Presidents have included: Major Wykeham-Musgrave, Colonel P.C. Field, Colonel Ellison, Mr S. Austin (since 1968).

Chairmen: Mr Willows, Mr S. Austin, Colonel R.A. Corby.

Ninety-one men and women from the parish served in the second world war. Twenty-nine members of the parish lost their lives in the two wars. Their names are inscribed on the War Memorial on the Green and on the War Memorial Tablet in the parish church. On Remembrance Sunday there is an annual ceremony at the Memorial on the Green and a service in the parish church. At this service the names of the fallen are read. The Legion Standard is carried on this day, and is presented at the altar by the Colour Party. The old Colour is laid up in the parish church.

The Legion cares for the memorial on the Green. It is modelled on a continental-style wayside memorial. It was cleaned and restored in 1975/6 at a cost of £500.

Standard bearers have included Joe Hing, Colonel Corby, Bob Hobbs and Bill Green. Colonel Corby won the standard bearer's Cadman trophy at the competition in 1959, 1960 and 1961. Joe Hing had been standard bearer for 27 years when he resigned in 1960. Bob Hobbs was standard bearer until 1965 when Bill Green succeeded him. In 1973 Bill Green carried the standard at the Royal Albert Hall Remembrance Service and also at the Windsor ceremony in 1977. Mr G.E. Catchpole and Mr G. Stone have been members of the Colour Party since 1963 and 1968 respectively.

The Poppy Day Collection was organised by Captain R.R. Oakley for 21 years until 1959. He was succeeded by R. Foord-Kelcey in that year. Proceeds increased from £61 15s. in 1965 to £450 in 1980. For many years Colonel Field was in command of the Annual Parade, and later Colonel Corby.

Mr Foord-Kelcey retired as Treasurer and was succeeded by Mr K.A.M. Dickson in 1966. In 1956 Gold Badges for service to the Legion were presented to Captain Oakley, Messrs W. Wells and J. Hing. In 1967 Mr S. Austin was awarded the Gold Badge. He had served for 28 years in the Royal Navy having served in every rank from Boy First Class to Commissioned Gunner. He had served in battleships, cruisers, destroyers and at Roedean when it was H.M.S. Valiant. He served for 20 years as Chairman of the branch, and did much to keep the branch together.

In recent years the Legion has held an annual sale. This has enabled grants to be made at Christmas time. Two hundred and fifty pounds was raised in 1980.

A new standard was dedicated in 1974 and a revised service sheet for the Memorial bearing the Names of the Fallen was drawn up. In 1965 there were 20 on parade and 28 marched in 1978, including Dr C.E.A. Goddard, aged 92 years.

An Annual Dinner is held each year. Gilt brooches and silver-gilt tie pins were presented in 1978 to ladies who had been Poppy Day helpers for between 10 and 20 years. These included Mrs. Foord-Kelcey, Mrs Marks, Mrs Corby, Mrs Owen Williams and Mrs Austin. Mr Foord-Kelcey also received a recognition.

Berkhamsted and Boxmoor Silver Band accompany the Annual Parade and wore their new uniform in 1980.

THE SCOUT GROUP

In the 1920s there was a vigorous Scout Troop. The Scoutmaster was Mr Harry Temple who contributed greatly to the education in craftsmanship of the members. Not only was there a trained bugle band, together with the customary individualist on one bugle, but also there was training in gymnastics.

Meetings were in the Armoury. There were racks of flint-lock pistols, elephant guns, blunderbusses and other precisely kept military equipment. These belonged to the old Volunteers. Mr Temple taught the use of a box camera, and Miss Bridget Talbot taught fret-work. At the sale of the Estate Mr Temple bought the Armoury.

The Wolf Cub Pack

This was formed in 1956 under Mrs Marshall and Mrs Moyse. The first Church Parade took place on St George's Day, and the Group marched from school to the church carrying their standard for the first time.

The Bob-a-Job Week was successful in earning £7 9s. 8d.

A Committee and supporters' club were founded. The Chairman of this was Miss J. Moore with Mr E.J. Wiggins as Secretary and Mr G. Bailey as Treasurer. He continued as Treasurer to the Scout Group until 1980.

In the autumn of 1959 Mrs Marshall was congratulated for keeping the cubs going for four years.

The Scouts

Mr H.A. Rowe began a Scout Troop in September 1959. The opening meeting of the 1st Little Gaddesden Scout Troop was on 7 September 1959 in the Village Hall. There were nine members. Their ambition to obtain their own headquarters was stated. In September 1960 the first seven members were invested. There was a camp in 1961, and the Scouts paraded at the Remembrance Sunday service. A Jumble Sale and a First Aid course were held, and the Bob-a-Job week kept the scouts busy.

In 1962 Mr H.A. Howe was still Scoutmaster and Mrs Parkins and Mr Bailey helped in his work. In that year Mrs F. Mayling and Mr E.J. Wiggins stepped in to help whilst the Cubmistress, Mrs Marshall, was away. In 1963 Mr Wiggins took out a warrant as Group Scoutmaster.

A Committee composed of Miss J. Moore, Mr Rowe, Mr Wiggins, Mr Bailey, Mr Parkins and the Rector (the Rev. H. Senar) decided to build or obtain a scout hut and to site it behind the Village Hall, the necessary permission being obtained. The hut was bought second hand and Mr Colin Mogg voluntarily did the electrical installation. Dr Goddard gave a trek-cart and Mrs Purton of Wood Ash gave a tent. A bazaar was held with Mrs Wiggins doing the catering. Later an 'Exchange and Mart' was held. By the summer of 1964 the hut was in use. It was officially opened on 27 June 1964. In 1964 Mr Rowe arranged a church parade for scouts, cubs and brownies.

In 1965 it is noted that the number of scouts remained steady at seven. Miss Jane Pannell replaced Miss Thomas as assistant to Mr Wiggins.

Paper collection was begun in 1965. In that year Mr Rowe resigned, and Mr Wiggins became Scoutmaster.

Events organised included collecting silver paper and the reinstitution of the Bob-a-Job week. In that year one scout earned his bob by carting manure, another by acting as paper-hanger's labourer.

Group Meetings took place for events such as the National Cub Jubilee. Camps are held regularly and these have taken place in Ireland, at Phasells Wood, Herefordshire, Chirk, Denbigh, Montgomery, the Cotswolds, Dorset, Stoke Poges, Elstree, North Wales, Gilwell Park and Kent.

Miss J. Moore was Chairman of the Committee from 1957 until her death in 1972. New rules concerning scouts and cubs were promulgated in 1967, with a new nomenclature, and a more up-to-date approach to boys and their needs.

The scouts obtained a new flag in 1968 which appears to have been well received at the next camp at Wicklow, Ireland (it was orange and green). In 1976 there were 26 cubs.

Distinctions won by scouts have included the gold Arrow won amongst others by M. Batchelor (the first in Little Gaddesden). A. Gage, K. Revell, K. Geater, A. Batchelor, P. Faulconer, Ian Memory, D. Middlestorm, I. Veall and B. Stinton won the Gold Award at the cub scouts.

In 1980 Mr E.J. Wiggins was awarded the Medal of Merit by the Chief Scout.

One question in the Gaddesden *Diary* from the Scout report with a supplementary question was—

'Why do so many of our scouts come from Dagnall and Studham? Is it because L.G. parents are anxious that their boys should not get dirty?'

THE BROWNIE PACK

A Brownie pack was formed and had its first meeting on 22 November 1955. The Brown Owl was Mrs V. Mountfort and the Tawny Owl was Mrs Marks.

The pack was re-established in 1964 under Mrs Cowley and Mrs Donovan. Later Mrs Rafferty was in charge. The pack met on Wednesday afternoons during the school term in the Scout Hut.

The pack was re-established in 1980 with Mrs Webster as the Brown Owl and Mrs Leonhardt as the Tawny Owl. Meetings: Thursday afternoon during term. After the first year there were 23 members between seven and 10 years. The pack is active in learning new skills and improving old ones. Money has been raised for charitable causes, elderly people have been entertained, nettles have been cleared, book marks made, and the Royal Mews has been visited. Games are played and all have fun.

In the 1930s the Girl Guide Movement was very active in Hertfordshire and a large number of Guide companies had a gathering and rally at Ashridge Park in 1937.

THE SPORTS CLUBS

The Cricket Club

The local cricket club played at Ashridge and was called the Ashridge Cricket Club. It played there for over a century. In 1854 an appeal was made for obtaining money to purchase a cricket bat.

The Rev. C.G. Lane was a distinguished cricketer and Dr Grace stayed at the Rectory with him. Dr Grace when here played cricket at Edlesborough.

1882 was a good year for the cricket club, and in the following years players came from Little Gaddesden, Ringshall, Dagnall and Hudnall.

In June 1893 a new cricket club was founded for these areas. Sides were picked every Saturday evening at 6.00 p.m. on the ground opposite Ashridge. 'We hope to play some matches before long'.

In 1900 Mr George Stanbridge notes in his diary— 'Old Mr Grace was captain of an M.C.C. team at Toddington today, but it was rather poor cricket'.

The club moved from Ashridge to the Little Gaddesden Playing Fields in 1951. The most enjoyable season since the move was 1955, and 'our enlightened Parish Council has bought a suitable mower'.

Commander G. Tandy the umpire was easily recognised by the topee he wore on duty. A Cricket Club dinner held in the School Hall in 1955 was 'the first in a hundred years'. The President in that year was Mr S. Block, the Secretary Michael McCaul, the Treasurer P. Winfield and the Captain T. Jackson.

In 1956 Christopher Bradby was Captain and Keith Geater, Secretary. V.W. Bell was Chairman. Bill Green knocked 42 not out against Great Gaddesden. He and Bradby scored 62 between them in the annual match against the President's XI.

The club had difficult years and became dormant for several years.

It was refounded in 1962 by a committee consisting of Messrs Block, Bill Green, Barrett, Harris and the Rector (the Rev. H. Senar). Alan Bunting was Captain.

In 1966 it was reported that the club was again on a sound basis. Regular nets were held on Friday evenings, and a grant from the National Playing Fields Association was obtained.

In 1970 Mr Block was President, P. Francis Secretary and P. Welling was Captain. E. Tharby was Treasurer and A. Bunting Match Secretary. P. Haydon was President in 1973.

One of the fixtures enjoyed immensely has been that against 'The Rest of the World' . . . the International Students House XI. This match sponsored by the Parish Church Stewardship Committee began in 1967 under the guidance of Mr J.H. Lewis.

With the erection of the new Pavilion in 1974 the club became part of the Sports Club.

In 1975 the club was on the crest of a wave and won 12 out of 13 matches. They were now called 'The Goats'. Six batsmen scored more than 50 runs and two took more than 40 wickets in the season. Alf Pope coached on Wednesday evenings.

Five tons of loam were bought to improve the square. By 1976 there was difficulty getting a team. In 1977 40 different players played and there was never the same team twice. Derek Green made 17 appearances and R. Jones won the John Lewis award two years running. Mr Lewis had now become President.

1978 was a good season and Alistair Shaw won the President's bat. Four-fifths of the officers, like the players, lived in Little Gaddesden.

1979. R. Jones scored a century against Hemel Hempstead. This was one of the best seasons ever. The Hamlet Cup was won by beating Great Gaddesden at home and away. M. Napier was Captain, P. Francis took the most catches, A. Shaw made the fastest 50 runs. Bill Whitman was Clubman of the Year, and R. Jones the star batsman.

1980. R. Jones' average was 61 and he scored 197 one weekend. David Simpson the Secretary had to resign as he left the district. The Hamlet Cup was lost to Great Gaddesden. At the Club dinner R. Jones won all the major awards for batting, bowling, single wicket and the Chairman's award. M. Smith won the fielding. Tribute was paid to the work for the club of Tim Carnegie and D. Simpson.

The Football Club

In early days before the playing fields were available, the footballers had their pitch behind No. 10 Little Gaddesden. Later they played end-ways on opposite Nos. 18/19. They changed in the cow-shed at the *Bridgewater Arms* which belonged to Mr Andrews. The referees changed in the Harness Room at the *Bridgewater Arms*. Mr Stanley (later Sir Stanley) Rouse and destined to be a leading figure in the football world was at one time a referee in the West Herts. League, and endured barracking at some Little Gaddesden home matches.

At one time there had been a football pitch in the Rectory Meadow and Grey Friars. Gatesdene Close stands where the former goalposts stood.

The Football Club was reformed in 1936.

In 1955 after being without a club, a revival took place and the team joined the Third Division of the West Herts. Challenge Cup and the Aspley Junior Charity Competition.

The 1966/7 season was a good one in both Saturday and Sunday sections. By the spring Alan Bunting had already scored 50 goals. The pitch was receiving extra attention and the project of a future pavilion was gaining impetus.

In 1970 in a high standard of football the team did well. Colts met on Saturday mornings from the beginning of the 1970s. In 1972 the pitch was drained. The team was the leading scorer in the Sunday league. The Colts had difficulty in obtaining fixtures. In the 1971/2 season 80 matches were played, and the summer report stated that the Sunday team was the runner-up in Division One of the Berkhamsted League. The President was G. Bunting and the Chairman and Secretary Alfred Sherringham. The Match Secretary was Bill Whitman and the Treasurer C. Revell.

The A.F.C. and C.C. raised £700 between them for the pavilion.

With the establishment of the new pavilion which was opened on 26 May 1975, the new Sports Club was formed. At this time the Football Club was having an excellent season, but their successes for a time began to fade. Careful training began and the new pavilion and its facilities helped greatly. Fifteen were turning up regularly for Tuesday practices in the floodlight. By 1975 R. Bunting had played in 392 games and scored 400 goals, K. Bunting 195 goals from 332 matches.

In 1976 the club had a good season coming fifth in the League, Division One, West Herts., and the Sunday team was third in Division Two. In the following year the club was top of the West Herts. League Division One. Much work was put in on the pitch. Local support was needed. At the end of the season the club was promoted to the Premier League, and was in the semi-final of the Apsley Cup, while the reserves were runners-up in their League.

The annual Married-versus-Singles Cup was presented in 1977 by Robin Corbett, M.P.

In 1978 metal goalposts were acquired.

In 1979 the club was seventh in the Premier Division West Herts. and bottom in the Sunday League. Mr Sherringham was re-elected Chairman. Mr G. Bunting was President and Mr C. Revell Treasurer.

At the annual prize giving some important records were recalled. Richard Bunting had made over 500 appearances. A plaque recorded that George Bunting had given 50 years service to the club, and a G. Bunting Shield was to be awarded to the Clubman of the Year. The death of George Bunting whose work had spanned from before the Second World War was received with expressions of admiration for his devoted service.

The 1979-80 season was described as unspectacular, but it was to be noted that the club was third in the Premier League and the highest position attained was equalled. By Christmas 1980, Bill Whitman had played 500 matches for the club. A tour for Easter 1981 was planned for either Switzerland or Barnsley according to the result of an appeal for funds for the purpose.

Members have been selected for representative honours.

Mini Rugby Club

The mini rugby club began to meet in 1976 when Ross Barrington gathered up to 20 boys aged between six and eleven. By the end of the season a team was evolving and in one competition group the team was a finalist. In the winter of 1977 progress was clear. In the following year the team won its section at St Neots Tournament and won the President's Prize for the most competent side.

In 1979 several trophies were acquired. After four years the club had its most successful season, and Little Gaddesden won the trophy at Northampton and the members of the team took greater pride in the fact that they were photographed with the British Lions party more than anything else about their achievement.

The Tennis Club

This was originally established in 1923 on courts in a meadow near the *Bridgewater Arms*. The club was re-established after the war in 1948 and played on the courts at Marian Lodge until the end of the 1952 season.

In 1957 it was decided to re-establish the club again and approval was given to the preparation of two fenced grass courts at the south-east corner of the playing field. Clifford Owen was the Chairman and Ursula Stanes the Secretary, with Robina Russell as the Treasurer. The Committee included Ann Marks, Sydney Moyse and Clifford Owen. By the autumn of 1957 there were 40 members. The club, like many other tennis clubs suffered as its popularity fell off. From time to time attempts were made, as for example by the Swords & Keys Society, to clean up the weed-ridden courts. With the new pavilion and Sports Club a renewal of life began. Friends lent their courts. Coaching began and Barbara Bean worked wonders especially with 40 children whom she helped. Ashridge College allowed the use of their courts for the juniors to be coached. The Tennis Club continued its efforts to raise money for new courts and £1,500 was raised by the winter of 1977, the purpose being to obtain two hard courts. The construction of the courts began, after some frustration in June 1978. The total cost was to be £4,600, of which the Dacorum Council would make a £2,300 grant. The balance needed was £800. The Sports Club agreed to match £1 with £1 raised by tennis club members. The Parish Council donated £150.

In 1979 the adult tournament was won by Mike Stinton and L. Hepburn. The under 11's was won by Guy Rabbetts and Susan How. By this time there were 55 members.

In 1980 tournaments were held and were won by Nicola Gillespie and Thomas Moriarty in the junior section. The senior section of this class saw Amanda Glenn and David Wooster successful. The Senior Tournament was won by Tessa Faulconer and Nicholas Webster. There were also away matches.

The Pavilion was opened on the Spring Bank Holiday, 26 May 1975. It had been erected during the winter of 1974/5. Funds had been raised by a Public Appeal and by the clubs, especially the Football and Cricket Clubs. At first it had been thought that the Village Hall Committee would be the sponsoring body for the Pavilion but it was later decided to have a Management Committee. This was to be composed of Colin Revell, Bill Whitman, Alfred Sherringham, C. Culverd, R. Wilkinson, R. Jones, D. Faulconer and M. Stinton. Later L. Nash was made the Warden of the Pavilion. The Committee was to be the central organisation concerned with the clubs, raising funds, helping with kit renewals, sharing expenses and generally looking after the clubs and their headquarters. The clubs were to be represented on the central Sports Club. A total of £350 was raised at the opening ceremony. Mrs Foxall was the Chairman of the opening. The Pavilion is now in constant use.

THE VILLAGE PRODUCE ASSOCIATION

The branch was formed on 1 April 1948 with Dr E.M. Rawdon Smith as Chairman. Miss Kathleen Talbot began the V.P.A. Grow More Food Campaign. There were over a thousand branches and she was awarded the M.B.E. for her work.

Chairmen have included—

1952-57	Miss K. Talbot
1958/9 and 1961	Mrs M. Ede
1960	Mr V.W. Bell
1962-64	Mr M. Wright
1965 and 1970	Mr A. Andrews
1966	Mr M. Franklin
1972	Mrs Harvell
1975	Mr M. Wright
1982	Mr W.T.N. Allen

1952-61 Mrs Blair, Treasurer, Mrs Mogg, Secretary.

From 1962 until 1981 with a short break Mrs Sears has been Secretary, firstly with Captain Ashby and later with Mr E. Nightall, Treasurers.

In 1955 Little Gaddesden became affiliated to the National Organisation. At that time it was running a Home Grown Food Supper each year, a weekly market stall at Hemel Hempstead Market (Thursdays) and with the Legion and W.I. an annual Summer Flower Show. The club bought at wholesale rates, manure, fertilisers, lime (six tons were distributed in 1955 at 2s. per cwt.). There were 100 members in that year.

The club participated in the annual digging competition organised for the county, and at Oaklands in 1956 Tom Bunting, George Bunting, Alec Andrews and T. Sears won the shield. Mrs Mountfort and Miss Munden had also been prize-winners in the annual digging.

There was a V.P.A. anthem which had a refrain 'Prime Plump, Porkers'. The Harvest Supper has been an annual event for almost thirty years, the emphasis being on home produced food and drink. Up to 200 people have been catered for at this event. Guests from other branches are invited. Winter and summer shows have been annual events, sometimes in association with other village clubs. There have also been Daffodil Shows, Rose Shows and Chrysanthemum Shows.

The Society & Show Committee have many cups. These include the Kathleen Talbot Rose Bowl, the Duncan Cup, the W.I. Cup, the Bond Cup, the Bunting Cup and the Legion Cup.

There is a shield for the champion of the three villages, Potten End and Dagnall being the other two. This is for the Inter-village Stall.

Visits are made to other clubs, especially those in Henfield, Sussex and at Martlesham, Woodbridge, in Suffolk. Outings have been arranged to gardens such as Waterperry and Wisley, and also to Oaklands, St Albans and to various nurseries. Major outings have included those to Evesham and Hartlebury, Warwick, Spalding, a four-day visit to Holland, week-ends at the annual conference at Caythorpe Court, Kesteven, Lincs. and a visit to Blackpool. Lectures, Addresses, Quiz Competitions and Any Questions are held regularly. Bingo Sessions are organised on a weekly basis.

The first Winter Show was held in 1958, and at the 1980 Show there were 418 entries. The introduction of a Pet Class proved to be very popular especially amongst the children who exhibit regularly in their section at the show.

The Trading Store was held at Benhay, by courtesy of Professor R. Edwards, and finally permanent premises were built adjoining the Village Hall in 1980.

The V.P.A. staged an excellent display of old crafts and implements at the Parish Craft Fair in 1979 and then again in 1980.

Entertainment at Harvest Suppers etc. is various. Amongst events especially enjoyed have been the Cavendish School Band, Mr Johnston's singers, Miss Hodgson's mountain talks, Mr Brighton on plastics in horticulture, Mr Nightall (Treasurer) on chicken and egg production and Mr W. Brooker with magnificent aerial photographs. Early in the life of the club S. Batchelor and T. Sears featured in a B.B.C. Show after the Annual Winter Show, 'Town and Country'.

Throughout the life of the Society the members have been helped greatly by excellent judging. Amongst the judges has been Miss Robinson who has come regularly since as long ago as 1959, and no doubt earlier, and whose comments are invariably listened to with great respect. Gordon Beningfield of Great Gaddesden has also been very helpful. Mr S. Waller, M.B.E. is also a regular judge.

Amongst the many prize winners whose names have appeared have been the Sherringham family, the Bunting family, the Dawson family, Mrs Ashby, Mrs Oakins, Mrs Brooker, the Sears family, Mrs Senar, Mr Brighton, Mrs Harvell, Mrs Johnston, Mr Andrews, Mrs Neil, Mrs Marks, Mrs Allen, Mrs Mogg, Mr Wiggins, Mrs Spencer, the Scott family and Mrs Hughes.

THE WOMEN'S INSTITUTE

The Institute was founded in 1919.

Presidents have included—

1927, Miss Talbot; 1930, Mrs Barkway; 1931, Miss Talbot; 1933, Mrs Bradby; 1936, Mrs Wager; 1939, Mrs Bradby; 1940, Mrs Miller; 1941, Mrs Hughes; 1945, Mrs Wager; 1946, Mrs Hughes; 1949, Mrs Beer; 1954, Mrs Hughes; 1959, Miss Moore; 1960, Mrs Hughes; 1965, Mrs Thorn; 1970, Mrs Mountfort; 1972, Mrs Johnston; 1974, Mrs Bradfield; 1976, Mrs Johnston; 1979, Mrs Hopkins.

The Institute meets monthly in the Village Hall and is deeply concerned about most aspects of community life.

Drama. There has generally been an active drama section, frequently on a light and humorous note. Mrs Mountfort and Mrs Nash have made a positive contribution in this area since as early as 1956. *The Char's Cantata* involving Mrs Mogg, Mrs Sherringham and Mrs Oakins is recalled. The drama group has entertained other societies, and the Over-60s Club and Harvest Supper of the V.P.A. have benefited.

Talks are a very important part of W.I. In 1960 great concern was aroused by a talk on displaced persons by Mrs K. Dickson and the club became associated with this work. Mrs Strand spoke on the 'Howard League for Penal Reform' in that year. David Wray spoke on painting for pleasure and Dr Doney on wild flowers. Miss King talked on Sierra Leone. There was also a talk on

Windsor Castle archives. Sister Shaw spoke on 'Pitfalls of today's young'. Richard Whitmore of the B.B.C. TV talked on his work. Mrs Riess on her visit to Russia, Mrs Thorn on Canada, Mrs Roberts on shoes and Miss Digby on Moorfields Eye Hospital. Mr G. Beningfield addressed the group.

Demonstrations. These range widely. Recently Mrs Brooker demonstrated her work with dried flowers and Mrs Leek with embroidery. Dressmaking has been a regular feature. Care of the feet and keeping fit (Mrs Hopkins organises a regular class) are important examples of W.I. interests. A sponsored-slim resulted in a total loss of 55½ lb, the champion losing 21 lb and the loser 1 lb. Fashion shows have their place regularly.

Practical work.

The association with the Cheshire Home at Ampthill is of long standing.

The obtaining of prescriptions (earlier done privately by Lady Del Tufo) was taken on in 1965. The Good Neighbours Group is always active.

The W.I. has planted trees in different parts of the village. A Liquidambar was planted to commemorate the Golden Jubilee of the W.I. at the Manor House corner. A seat was also placed there as a Golden Jubilee gift. A Jubilee book was prepared concerning Little Gaddesden in 1965. Money has been raised for many good causes including help with Medical Equipment for the West Herts. Hospital.

Members have participated in various forms of county competition especially in the fields of drama and public speaking.

Sales, fairs and coffee mornings are regular features of the club. The annual parties are popular and a special dinner was held at the *Bridgewater Arms* for the Diamond Jubilee.

A friendly link with Toowoomba, Australia produced much interest and fellowship.

Personal Notes In 1963 after 43 years making of cakes for the W.I. Mrs Liberty said she would like to taste someone else's cake at the birthday party. So Mrs Beer made it and Mrs Bradfield iced it.

At the Golden Jubilee dinner in 1970 Mrs Thorn, President, welcomed founder members Mrs Drewitt, Mrs Johnson and Miss Munden.

Mrs Hughes was one of the 9,000 guests at Buckingham Palace for the Golden Jubilee of 1965, for the National Organisation. Members attended the diamond Jubilee festivities at St Paul's, Waldenbury arranged by Lady Bowes-Lyon.

At the Little Gaddesden Diamond Jubilee dinner 53 members and 11 guests enjoyed a splendid occasion at the *Bridgewater Arms.* From 1970 it was arranged that meetings should be on the third Thursday of each month.

The club regularly visits theatres in London. The Choir has been trained by Mrs Thorn. The club produced a Recipe Book in 1980.

THE YOUTH CLUB

The club has had a chequered life, as is customary with Youth Clubs. Mr Sherringham organised it in 1957 and a social was held at the end of its first year. In 1959 £35 was spent to restore the billiard table. Mr W. Green organised a football section. By 1961 there were over a hundred members. After this peak there was a reaction, the club was closed and leadership was needed for its re-opening. In 1967 Mr R. Light became Chairman and with the aid of Gail Nash, Trevor Hing, P. Halsey, G. Horrod, R. McNab, T. Rogers, R. Smith and T. Welling it began again. There were 120 at the Christmas Dance. Donations were made including one for the church vestry, and another towards the Aberfan Disaster Fund. A record player was bought. Mr R. Smith succeeded Mr Light, and then followed Mr L. Green in the leadership.

After a short closure the club was opened again on Tuesday nights from 1974 (February). Games included darts, table games, bar billiards, snooker, music and table games, together with five-a-side football. Deryck Steer became the leader. At the end of 1974 the club purchased a minibus, won a General Knowledge Quiz and was knocked out of the five-a-side competition for the area in the first round. Andrew Smith represented Hertfordshire in the National Association of Youth Clubs week in London where they were entertained by Jimmy Savile there and in Hampshire.

In 1976 a new committee was formed with D. Richardson as leader and later in the year John Rogers became the leader. A Fun Day was organised, new sports equipment was bought, several senior members camped in Holland. On Monday evenings both juniors and seniors began to meet. Stephen Rogers succeeded his brother. Later the senior's section was closed.

At the Youth Club Management Committee in February 1978 it was decided to re-open the senior club. By this time the Hertfordshire County Education Department was giving substantial grants to the club. Mrs Gillespie was the Treasurer, and Mr W.T.N. Allen became the Treasurer when she resigned. Mrs Allen succeeded Mrs Berridge as Secretary. Mr A.J. Williams was the Chairman of the Committee of Management.

Numbers of juniors kept steady, but the seniors were few. The county organiser Mr Terry Pope was the official leader of the club, and many activities were arranged, although not all were carried out. There was ice-skating, a barbecue, a disco, swimming and midnight skating. The club began to develop a stronger basis. A large party of seniors went carolling, and a very successful Blue Peter sale in which parents of members helped took place early in 1981. Hopes were high amongst the Committee of Management for a strong club with considerable equipment and opportunities.

Bibliography

Ashridge Abbey, *The Topographer*, (March 1790)

Ashridge Estate, National Trust brochure, (1972)

Bagshawe, R.W., *'The Viatores'. Roman Roads in the south-east Midlands,* (1964)

Bagshawe, R.W., *Roman Roads*, (1979) (2nd Edition 1982)

Bailey, B.J., *Ashridge Observed*, (1975)

Bayley, J., *History of the Tower*. Volume 2. (1821-25)

Bell, V.W., *Little Gaddesden,* (1949)

Birtchnell, P.C., *History of Berkhamsted,* (1972), and many articles in local journals.

Bishop, G.W., *My Betters*, (1957)

Brewster, J., Funeral Sermon for the 7th Earl of Bridgewater, (1823)

Bryant, Sir Arthur, *Age of Elegance*, (1950)

Buckingham, W., Diaries 1803-1829, (unpublished)

Buckler, J., and J.C., *Architectural Drawings c.* 1800-1820

Burke's Dormant and Extinct Peerages, (1883, reprinted 1978)

Burke's Landed Gentry, (Vol. 1, 1965 ed.; Vol. 2, 1969 ed.; Vol 3, 1972 ed.)

Burke's Peerage, Baronetage and Knightage, (1970 edition)

Butler L., and Given-Wilson, *Medieval Monasteries,* (1978)

Cassey's Directory of Buckinghamshire, (1865)

Chauncy, Sir Henry, *Hertfordshire,* (1826)

Cholmeley, H.P., *John of Gaddesden,* (1912)

Churchill, Sir Winston, *Marlborough, His Life and Times,* (1947)

Clutterbuck, R., *The History and Antiquities of Hertfordshire,* (1815-1827)

Cocks, A.H., *The Church Bells of Buckinghamshire,* (1897)

Colvin, H.M., *British Architects,* (1978)

Cornhill Magazine, The, September 1861

Coult, D., *A Prospect of Ashridge*, (1980)

Cross, F.L., *The Oxford Dictionary of the Christian Church,* (1957), (Later edition by Ollard, Cross and Bond)

Cussans, J.E., *Hertfordshire,* (1874-78)

Dove, A., *The Bellringers' Guide,* (1968)

Dugdale, Sir William, *Monasticon Anglicanum,* (1817)

Dunnett, B.R.K., *Wards Combe,* (1971)

Dunstable Cartulary, The, (Harleian Society), 1885

Egerton Alix, *Milton's Comus*, (1910)

Egerton, F.H., *The Life of Thomas Egerton*, (1801)

Egerton Manuscripts, The, British Library

Ekwall, E., *Dictionary of English Place Names*, (1936)

Ellesmere Chaucer, The, 1911 photocopy of the original manuscript in the Huntington Library, California

Elvin, C.N., *Mottoes*, (1860)

English Place Names Society –
> Volume 2, Buckinghamshire, F. Mawer and F.M. Stenton, (1925)
> Volume 15, Hertfordshire, J.E.B. Gover, (1938)

English Place Names Elements Vols. 14 and 26, A.H. Smith (1956)

Falk, B., *The Bridgewater Millions*, (1942)

Field, J., *Place Names of the Dacorum District*, (1975)

Gaddesden Diaries, (1955-1981)

Girouard, M., *Life in the Country House,* (1978)

Gunnis, R., *British Sculptors 1660-1851,* (1951)

Hadfield, C., *British Canals*, (1959)

Hertfordshire Genealogist, The, (1899)

Hertfordshire Past and Present, Vols. 10 and 11, 1970, 1971

Hertfordshire Session Rolls, (1905)

Hurcomb, W.E., *Life and Diary 1863-1915*, (1926)

James, M.R., *The Glass in Ashridge Chapel*, (1906)

Jenkins, J.G., *Penn,* (1935)

Kelly's Directories of Hertfordshire and Buckinghamshire, (1847-1885)

Knowles, D., *The Religious Orders in England,* 3 Vols., (1948)

Knowles D., and Hadcock, R.N., *Medieval Religious Houses*, (1971)

Langridge, D., *Ashridge Past and Present*, (1960)

Leland, J., *Itinerary in England and Wales*, (1546)

Le Neve, J., *Fasti Ecclesiae Anglicanae*, (1963)

Lewis, S., *Topographical Dictionary of England,* 4 Vols. (1831)

Lincoln Record Society Transactions, Episcopal Registers, Visitations, Wills (1290-1547)

Lipscomb, G., *Buckinghamshire,* 3 Vols., (1847)

Lockhart, J.G., *Memoirs of the Life of Sir Walter Scott*, Vol I, 1850; Vol V, 1900

Lomas S.C., *Alcuin Club Publications*, 1906, 'Visitation of Buckinghamshire 1552'

Lysons, D., and S., *Magna Britannia*, (1804)

Malet, H., *Bridgewater, The Canal Duke 1736-1803*, (1977)

Milton, J., *Comus, a Masque,* (1634)

Morris J., Gen. ed. *Domesday Book, Hertfordshire,* (1976)

Mullineux, F., *The Duke of Bridgewater's Canal*, (1959)

Musson and Craven's Dictionary of Buckinghamshire, (1853)

Natural History of the Ashridge Estate, J.G. Dony, P.D. Hager and K. Williamson, National Trust (*c.* 1977)

Oxford History of England, (15 Volumes, 1937 onwards)

Papal Letters and Registers, Calendar of, Vol. 1. 1198-1304; Vol. 13, 1471-1484 (ed. W.H. Bliss and J.A. Twemlow)

Parish Registers, Little Gaddesden from 1681
> Ivinghoe and Edlesborough, 18th and 19th centuries

Penny N., *Church Monuments*, (1977)

Post Office Directories, Hertfordshire and Buckinghamshire, 1864 onwards

Rackham, B., The Ashridge Chapel Stained Glass (*Journal of British Stained Glass-painters*, Sept. 1928)

Roberts, E., *Totternhoe Stone in Hertfordshire Churches,* (1972)

Robinson, J.M., *An Architectural Dynasty. The Wyatts*, (1980)

Salisbury, Sir Frank, *Portrait and Pageant*, (1944)

Salmon, N., *Hertfordshire*, (1728)

Sanecki, K.N., *Humphry Repton*, (1974)

Sanecki, K.N., *The Gardens at Ashridge*, (1975)

Saturday Magazine, The, 17 March 1838

Searle, Eleanor, *The Calendar and Martyrology of the College of Boni Homines at Ashridge*, (1961)

Senar, H., *A Guide and History of Little Gaddesden Parish Church*, (1980)

Speed, J., *The Theatre of Britain. Buckinghamshire*

Summers, W.H., *The Lollards of the Chiltern Hills*, (1906)

Tanner, *Notitia Monastica* (1744), (reprinted 1787)

Todd, H.J., *The Bonhommes of Ashridge*, (1823)

Victoria County Histories,
   Buckinghamshire, (1905-8)
   Hertfordshire, (1908)

Whybread, G., *History of Berkhamsted Common*, (1934)

Willis, Browne, Visitations of Buckinghamshire 1552, (Alcuin Club Publications, 1906)

Wilson, A.L., *Witches, Thomas Fossan, Sybil Penn* (privately circulated articles, 1981)

Yarwood, D., *The Architecture of England*, (1967)

Yaxley, S., *History of Hemel Hempstead*, (1973)

Index